CRIMINAL JUSTICE IN CHINA

CRIMINAL JUSTICE IN CHINA

A History

KLAUS MÜHLHAHN

HARVARD UNIVERSITY PRESS

Cambridge, Massachusetts, and London, England   2009

Library of Congress Cataloging-in-Publication Data

Mühlhahn, Klaus
Criminal justice in China : a history / Klaus Mühlhahn.
    p.   cm.
Includes bibliographical references and index.
ISBN 978-0-674-03323-8 (alk. paper)
1. Criminal justice, Administration of—China—History.
I. Title.
KNN1572.M84 2009
364.951—dc22   2008047378

CONTENTS

CRIMINAL JUSTICE IN CHINA

INTRODUCTION

ANGER. Disgust. Fear. These words describe the reactions of the majority of Americans and Europeans toward what they hear about criminal justice in China. Their negative impressions are further nurtured by successful and highly influential Hollywood movies such as the 1997 film *Red Corner,* in which Richard Gere plays an innocent American businessman who is incarcerated and maltreated in a Chinese prison. Memoirs of Chinese dissidents and frequent newspaper reports about human rights violations contribute to the dark picture. Though some of the allegations are undoubtedly true, negative reactions do little to help Westerners understand the forces behind criminal justice in China, and they are also not helpful in formulating well-reasoned political responses. Such responses require a comprehensive knowledge of the whole of criminal justice in China: its past and present, the underlying values and theories, its practices and consequences, its capacities and failures, and, last but not least, the human costs and experiences. The complex history of criminal justice in China—what we actually can know as opposed to what we imagine—is the subject of this book. An examination of China's criminal justice system in the past will tell us something about its present and also prepare us for the future by highlighting the major shifts and dynamics that produced and continue to influence the administration of justice in China.

In charting this sensitive, difficult, and partially unknown terrain, a historical approach will aid in understanding the overall role of criminal justice in Chinese social life and its effects on both state and society. Seen as a historical and social phenomenon, criminal justice is revealed as part of the wider culture, shaping and being shaped by it. It says as much about the society that holds trials and sentences offenders as it does about those individuals brought before it. Criminal justice in China reflects fundamental norms, core values, and significant social hierarchies and relationships in modern Chinese society.

Crime, Punishment, and Justice

Justice is, as John Rawls has put it, "the first virtue of social institutions."[1] Institutions, no matter how efficient and well arranged, become weak and dysfunctional if they are perceived as unjust. To achieve its objectives successfully, the administration of justice and dispute settlement must be accepted as authoritative and legitimate, and it must also be seen as fair. Philosophers have distinguished between two ways of creating fair judgments and compensation: *corrective justice* covers that which is due to a person as punishment; *distributive justice* is that which is due by way of benefits and burdens other than punishments.[2] Criminal justice falls within the realm of corrective justice. It aims at producing justice by way of amending a previous injustice. The parties, as perpetrator and sufferer of the same injustice, are the active and passive poles of a single wrong, which the law rectifies and redeems by holding the perpetrator liable to the victim.

Society's response to socially proscribed wrongdoing usually consists in the punishment of the offender. Pronouncing guilt and finding a correct punishment are at the core of criminal justice. Punishment is one of the oldest human institutions; virtually every society in history has imposed some kind of penalty on those who offend against written and unwritten rules.[3] Beyond that, most religions, too, hold that those who offend against god, or the gods, will be punished either in this world or the next. But punishment is of course not the only way to react to crime. Other reactions may include payment of compensation to the victim, expression of formal censure, or attempts at reconciliation. Punishment is distinguished from other responses by the hard treatment it imposes—most commonly, the infliction of some pain or loss on the transgressor. Punishments thus need to be justified exactly, because they involve doing things that are normally considered to be wrong (depriving a person of life, property, or freedom).

To be more than simply an act of tyranny, a punishment has to be associated with ideas of law and justice and therefore has to pursue a useful purpose. Those purposes, explained in theories that expound the link between punishments, offenses, and objectives, ensure that the penal treatment appears to be deserved, just, and meaningful. Justification and legitimization are produced not only through theories and discourses but also through rituals. The infliction of punishment usually involves some kind of ceremony that can be quite elaborate and that lends the action an aura of legitimacy.

A criminal justice system can achieve its goals only so long as there is a belief in its usefulness and effectiveness, and also its legitimacy. Pierre Bourdieu defined the state as an entity that is able to monopolize the legitimate use of physical and symbolic power over a certain territory and over the entirety of the population living in that territory.[4] The criminal justice system is a key element in this context. It is supposed to provide the state with the means to make legitimate use of its physical and symbolic powers—and the emphasis here is on *legitimate*. Legitimacy comes from detailed judicial procedures, from stability-seeking normative doctrines and rules of evidence, from the use of elaborate rituals, and from extensive theoretical reasoning (penal theories).

Within the sphere of corrective justice there are different approaches to the justification of punishment.[5] But there has been—and is—widespread agreement on the criteria for just punishment: first, the offender must have brought the punishment on himself by his own conduct, and second, just punishment must be properly imposed and the quantum of punishment must reflect the seriousness of the offense.

Throughout China's history a number of theories have been articulated to explain and justify the use of punishment. Some Chinese thinkers have in the main ascribed a deterrent purpose to punishment, while others have focused on the aspect of retribution and requital. There are also strong Chinese statements favoring the rehabilitative or reformative purpose of punishment. In all cases, the various philosophies on punishment have fundamentally influenced criminal justice operations and penal practices. Any adequate analysis of criminal justice and legal punishment needs to take into account the normative rationales that structure official conduct, and any serious critique will have to articulate and defend normative arguments of its own.

Criminal Justice in History

Criminal justice can be viewed as a social institution that is tightly enmeshed in the gears of the social world. As a social institution, it entails great functional complexity as well as an immense density of meaning. Understanding criminal justice in China requires knowledge not only of its specific parts and technicalities (such as criminal law or corrections) but also of criminal justice as an institution deeply rooted in politics, society, and culture.[6] This study therefore examines not only how justice is handled in legal procedures but also how it operates in political, social, and cultural terms: embodied in power mechanisms, traditions, value systems, ideas, and social structure. I will describe how criminal justice in China was supposed to operate at various times in the past, and identify the main components of the system as well as the main actors. I will also trace how legal traditions, value systems, theoretical explications, and political interests have affected China's justice system, and look at the mistakes and successes that have occurred over time.

According to the system paradigm, the institution of criminal justice can be viewed as a cluster of social agencies that are all related to imposing just punishments and controlling crime.[7] These agencies fulfill their functions by making a series of decisions, from first reporting crimes to the police to finally releasing offenders from government supervision. There are several essential ingredients or components that a society based on written laws and a legal system needs in order to make criminal justice operational. First, laws must be delineated, including a substantive body of criminal law that contains definitions of criminal behavior. The law must define which behaviors will be subjected to punishment by criminal justice agencies, and also specify what the punishments will be for specific offenses. Second, procedural criminal law must stipulate the way the laws are to be enforced. It must describe how each step in law enforcement is to be carried out, from apprehension to sentencing. There are basically two approaches here: the rules can be activated to emphasize repressing rule violation (a crime-control model) or to contain the system's level of intrusion into citizens' lives (a due-process model). The third necessary element is penal law. It lays down the punitive treatment of those sentenced to a punishment. Any inquiry into the whole of criminal justice in China needs to take into account this three-column structure—criminal law, procedural law, and penal law—which resonates with three elements of the formal criminal justice system: the law specifies the threat of punishment, the judge imposes a sanction for the misdeed, and the state executes the sentence.

Criminal justice is thus a complex and highly differentiated institution that links lawmaking, conviction, sentencing, and the administration of penalties. In examining criminal justice, we are dealing with a multidimensional organization that involves legal practice, theory and discourse, ritual procedure, and a rhetoric of symbols, figures, and images through which the criminal process is represented to its various audiences.

The society's various statements concerning criminal justice, including crime theory, crime statistics, penal theory, visions of social order, newspaper reports, and literary accounts (such as detective stories and movies), together form a *discourse*. This discourse entails legal knowledge and is created by various methods of documentation, narratives of criminality, and conceptions of reform and moral improvement. The penal discourse as implicit knowledge reflects the dominant perspective on the social world. The discourse not only legitimizes criminal justice but also, and more importantly, creates the very social world it intends to describe. The discourse defines truth by producing the social world through narrative and textual structures. New approaches to law and justice have stressed that narrative is a particularly powerful device that plays a pivotal role in the organization of culture and society.[8] A society promotes certain narrative patterns that are able to bind an individual into the culture. It is the interplay and crossover between the individual and the sociocultural-historical discourse that narrative analysis hopes to tackle. Legal stories, as produced by the criminal-justice discourse, tell about horrible crimes, the misled intentions and wrong thoughts of the guilty, and the subsequent possible redemption of the offenders. In this way these stories offer models of the social world and map that world according to categories of right or wrong. As Jerome Bruner has put it, "A narrative models not only a world, but the minds seeking to give it its meaning."[9] Consequently the penal system, in particular, takes part in "making up people" and forming subjectivities, selves, identities, and mental frameworks. It is important to understand that the effects of these subjectivity-creating practices go way beyond the courtrooms or the walls of corrections facilities. The model of the "law-abiding citizen" applies to all members of society.

By modeling the social world, the social mind-set, and cultural images, criminal justice defines and enforces social norms. In court proceedings, conditions of normality are delineated from abnormal, degenerative, harmful, and criminal behavior, which is to be punished. The penal system, too, holds out an image of what is normal and socially accepted. For Michel Foucault, this function has been central to punishing since the late eighteenth century: "The carceral network . . . with its system of insertion, distribution, surveillance, observation, has been the greatest support, in modern society, of the normalizing power."[10]

Studying the history of criminal justice also allows us to understand the way in which a legal institution creates and reflects a society's norms and values through an interactive process that constructs a particular legal sensibility. The criminal justice system participates in, generates, and at the same time mirrors broader social, economic, and political shifts. It allows the state to intervene in social life by enforcing law and order and inflicting sanctioned forms of violence. While criminal justice is a legal process administered by state authorities, it is at the same time necessarily grounded in wider patterns of knowing, feeling, and acting, and it relies on those social links for its legitimacy and smooth operation.

All this, however, is merely one side of the history of criminal justice. A different perspective on criminal justice emerges if we turn to those who are punished. Whatever their misdeeds, seen from their point of view punishment is not about order and discipline but about fear and pain. The purpose of punishment is supposed to be redemption, but in reality it often has the contrary effect. Pain and suffering more often alienate those punished than they effect social redemption and rehabilitation. All forms of punishment mentioned in this book have undeniably had harmful side effects and consequences, a fact that makes criminal justice itself a questionable institution.

Legal documents and treatises tend to leave out important aspects when talking about crime and punishment. Their blindness vis-à-vis the suffering of those punished is stunning. All too often jurists and politicians are interested in abstract principles—which are perhaps important—but it is equally important to take into account the fact that punishments are something very real that have been inflicted on real people in the past and have often traumatized them.

A trauma is a physical or an emotional wound that causes stress and shock. Although often ignored in historiography on China, large-scale social trauma obviously has enormous historical importance. When such a trauma occurs many individuals suffer, but even afterward the trauma continues to disrupt individual and collective memories and thus to have a profound effect on society and its culture. A trauma has the power to call forth witnesses and narratives of the experience. As an event that is both shocking and striking, it demands action and reaction, description and testimony. These testimonies and descriptions allow us to understand and appreciate the experience of those affected, their predicament and their fate. The inclusion of such testimonies of trauma and suffering poses a historiographical challenge, however. Social trauma and social suffering result from what political, economic, and institutional powers do to people, and, reciprocally, from how those forms of power influence people's responses to social problems. Included under the category of social suffering are conditions that simultaneously involve health, welfare, and legal, moral, and religious issues. Such suffering, in prison in particular, is a collective social experience.

Pain and suffering represent only one possible response to punishment. Those sentenced to punishment also often attempt to resist it. A focus on prisoners' experiences thus illuminates the agency of those incarcerated. Rather than being mere passive objects subjected to an overpowering penal regime, prisoners often are able to adapt creatively to prison conditions. They may also be able to influence and change conditions of their confinement. Many accounts demonstrate the extent to which the imprisoned have resisted their jailers' repression and affected carceral policies and approaches. Episodes of collective resistance and individual sabotage prove that under all regimes prisoners have been able to challenge the authorities.

Criminal justice in general is thus less unilateral than reciprocal and interactive. It engages various parties in a process of negotiation that is open-ended and contested. Legality can be challenged effectively even by a small and seemingly helpless group of convicts. No large organization is needed to attack a government's penal policy. Catchy reports, a sensational picture, or an agitating drawing claiming to depict abuse in prison can call into question the legitimacy of a political and legal system.

As recent European studies on the history of criminal justice have pointed out, three insights can be expected from historical research on crime and punishment. First, law enforcement and punishment have to be seen as one part of a complex set of strategies for ordering society and exercising power. This was of course the great theme of Michel Foucault.[11] Despite the valid criticism that has been directed against some of the arguments presented in his work, nobody seriously doubts that there is an intrinsic relationship between punishment, power, and social order. Foucault's approach, which actually is similar to Emile Durkheim's interest in punishment and Erving Goffman's study on asylums and prisons, sees the way that punishments are inflicted as an index of society's symbols, values, and power structures.[12] To Foucault, deciphering the symbolic language of penal practices can yield far-reaching insights about the society in which it was created and about the people it involves.

Second, this historical research can provide scholars and students with access to the values and norms that were officially promoted and propagated in a society at a certain junction in time. There are, above all, those legal norms that are manifested in the law codes. Provisions regarding adultery and marriage in the Chinese law codes of the twentieth century, for instance, reflect far-reaching changes over time in attitudes toward sexual behavior as well as toward the role of women in Chinese society. By necessity, laws reflect the values of those who wrote them—that is, the ruling elites. The law thus can serve as a powerful tool for the ruling elites to enforce their vision of social norms, morality, and practices. From this perspective, the administration of justice is indeed not only a reflection of but also a generator or an enforcer of social and cultural change and, consequently, in a broader sense, of history itself.[13]

Third and finally, the history of criminal justice is closely related to the history of mentalities: especially of attitudes toward violence and death.[14] Conceptions of suffering, cruelty, and death are, as Philippe Ariès tells us, rooted in social experiences; they are built on the fabric of everyday life.[15] Inasmuch as such attitudes toward suffering, violence, and death change over time because of, for instance, secularization or progress in medicine or general changes in social life, we might also expect changes in the way punishments are inflicted. New sensitivities can arise within society and culture that make people more affected than before by witnessing the public suffering of others. Such sensibilities can lead to demands to abolish cruel punishments or to outlaw the use of torture. Unfortunately, such developments can go in the other direction, too. Long-term exposure to war and revolution can make people more insensitive to the suffering of others and prepare the way for an increased use of torture and cruel punishments. Punishments are socially sanctioned forms of violence, and they tell us about the dynamics of social inhibitions regarding violence and death.

Structure and Sources

Three key dimensions provide the general interpretative framework of this study of criminal justice in China from the late years of the Qing dynasty to the end of the Cultural Revolution. The first of these is the dimension of legal discourse. In simple terms, this means what people said and wrote about criminal justice and punishment, the arguments they used to defend or criticize them, and the ways in which they related them to the wider social and political purposes with which they were concerned. The second dimension is that of culture or society, especially of norms and values. Here, the focus will be on narrating the treatment of offenders in court and in prison in order to analyze the values that were supposed to be transmitted. We will also look briefly at how offenders are moved through the criminal justice system from sentencing to punishment. The third dimension of the book's framework is that of experience. Here we will try to penetrate the walls and barriers that criminal justice institutions use to obscure their operations. This dimension will give the past a voice by allowing those who were caught up in the criminal justice system to recount their experiences. In particular, it will make visible the human component of criminal justice in China.

To date there has been no comprehensive history of criminal justice and the penal system in China covering the modern period.[16] To the best of my knowledge, this is the first book published in any Western language that deals broadly with the whole system of criminal justice and tracks its history throughout the entire twentieth century.[17] My goal is to explore an aspect of historical development in China that hitherto has been overlooked. Most histories of modern China touch only marginally on such issues as social control, criminal justice, and public security. Not only do changes in criminal justice tell us a lot about the governments and agencies that initiated them, but they also affect the lives of millions of people.

In methodological terms, this book is distinguished from other studies in that it not only presents an account of the legal and institutional development of criminal justice but also tries to bring to life the experiences of inmates and prisoners. By combining three levels of history (discourse,

society and social institutions, and human experience), I intend to uncover the dynamics that unfold between these levels, and to bring to the
fore the complexity of human institutions and the ambiguity of human
agency in history. I aim to demonstrate how a history of the (punished) self
supplements a social and cultural history of institutions and thereby
adds an important and meaningful dimension to our reconstruction of
the past.

The starting point for this study is the obvious dramatic change that took
place in criminal justice in China over a remarkably short span of time in
the twentieth century. Major transformations in human social organization and values also occurred during this time. The three central chapters
in the book cover three distinct periods, each of which had a different criminal justice system and a correspondingly different penal regime. Chapter 2
examines the Chinese reforms of criminal justice that started in the final
years of the Qing dynasty and continued throughout the Republican era
until the outbreak of the Second World War. These reforms were driven by
two goals: the building of a strong functioning state and the nationalist goal
of ending extraterritoriality, for which Western powers demanded a reformed criminal justice system. Reforms were based on knowledge of Western models, yet elements of China's philosophical and legal tradition also
found their way into the new system. Within only a few years, the physical
punishments stipulated in imperial law disappeared and were replaced by
the almost universal use of monetary fines and imprisonment. At the same
time, new definitions of crime and the criminal process evolved. The Republican era was a time of unparalleled juridical innovation. Scholars and
law specialists drafted numerous new laws and much legislation that pertained to criminal justice. The chapter also considers the cultural and social
repercussions of this development, symbolized in the emergence of a new
genre of writing in which prisoners described their experiences in custody.
In social terms, new definitions of citizenship were developed in the criminal justice system that extended to society at large.

Chapter 3 explores the changes in criminal justice during the war years,
from the late 1930s to the late 1940s. The Second World War and the ensu-
ing civil war in China had a profound effect on criminal justice operations.
Martial law and a general state of emergency led to the suspension of the
regular criminal justice administration. The civilian judiciary was pushed
to the sidelines as it faced rivalry from and intervention by the increasingly

powerful military and the secret service. Military commissions started to sentence and imprison offenders without involvement of the courts. A secretive system emerged of prisons and camps that were used to incarcerate political groups that the government considered harmful but could not try publicly. A politicization and brutalization of criminal justice occurred that eventually damaged the legal system and perverted the legal standards and procedures. Personal experiences of imprisonment, recounted and published in various writings, pamphlets, and articles, became a powerful political force in this period. Texts revealing abuses and miserable conditions in prison camps played an important role in diminishing the reputation and legitimacy of the Nationalist government. Prison narratives from this era also figured prominently in the rise to power of the Chinese Communist Party. Not only were communist inmates able to wrest from their jailers a measure of control over the institutions in which they were kept, but their prison experiences also contributed decisively to the vigor and political consciousness of the revolution.

Chapter 4 explores the establishment of a new and revolutionary regime of criminal justice by the CCP in the time from the 1940s to the beginning of the reform policy in 1978 and 1979. Already in the early 1930s, at a time when the Republican criminal justice system was not even fully developed, the CCP was starting to look for alternative and revolutionary forms of criminal justice. Based on Marxist theories and on Soviet experiences, a new system of criminal justice was developed: new definitions of criminality were generated, new processional formats were tested, and new forms of treatment of offenders were explored. At the center of the socialist system of criminal justice was labor reform. Inmates were supposed the mold themselves into new persons through engaging in hard physical work. As part of the so-called thought reform efforts, convicts were also forced to take part in study and criticism sessions. After 1949 a vast labor-camp system was built that eventually came to detain delinquents who offended against the rules of the new society as well as the political and social leaders of the old social order, such as landlords, religious leaders, officials, and so on. The labor camp was supposed to be a site of transformation, but as an increasing and diverse body of writings, memoirs, and testimonies by former inmates suggested, it became more of a site of suffering and trauma. Like the prison writings of earlier periods, these testimonies were powerful statements that tended to question the legitimacy of socialist criminal justice. They exposed the profound individual and social effects of what they portrayed as endemic injustice within socialist society.

The three main chapters—Chapters 2 through 4, dealing with criminal justice in China from different perspectives from roughly 1900 to 1978—are framed by two concise historical overviews that intend to complement the narrative on both ends of the time span. Chapter 1 surveys criminal justice in imperial China. Imperial Chinese law was one of the world's major legal systems. It stretched back two millennia, and a clear, documented, codified tradition had existed since the seventh century. Imperial law was an integral part of the Chinese empire, which governed a territory and a population that was larger than any polity in ancient or medieval Europe. Much of the law in imperial China was focused on questions pertaining to criminal justice, the fair and impartial administration of criminal justice was a central concern. Criminal justice in imperial China was a complex, advanced, and sophisticated operation, based on principles and procedures vastly different from those in Western law.

The Conclusion offers a brief and compact survey of developments in Chinese criminal justice since 1978. Over the past thirty years China has enacted nearly 400 laws that have laid the foundation for its modern legal system, including criminal justice and penology. Enormous strides have been made in passing laws; in rebuilding shattered institutions, such as the bench, the bar, prisons, and legal education; and in using laws and legal mechanisms to lend some greater predictability to Chinese society, and in particular to the economy. Nonetheless, significant gaps remain with respect to enforcement of enacted laws, the high number of death penalties, miscarriages of justice, and worrisome conditions in jails and prisons.

The overviews in Chapter 1 and the Conclusion mainly rely on research done by other Western and Chinese scholars. Their inclusion here is motivated by two considerations. One, quite practical, is the hope that this book will be of interest to more readers than just China specialists. For the nonspecialist, the brief surveys on preceding and subsequent developments will be useful. The second consideration is the conviction that knowledge of premodern history is in fact crucial for an adequate evaluation of twentieth-century developments. There are significant connections and historical trajectories between the different periods, and also between the past and the present, that would be lost without the contexts of imperial law and present developments. But the differences between the periods are equally significant. In comparing the imperial and modern justice systems, it becomes clear, for instance, how much the state intruded in Chinese society in the twentieth century. Various Chinese governments built up menacing law-enforcement capabilities that were able to extend control significantly and to penetrate society down to the local level in ways that the imperial government was neither able to pursue nor interested in pursuing.

For the period from the 1900s to the 1970s, this study is based on my own extensive empirical research and fieldwork in China, Taiwan, and Hong Kong. For any one topic, I tried to collect many different sources—ranging from government documents and legal texts to memoirs and witness interviews—in order to compare them with each other and thus to try to reach balanced, nuanced insights and conclusions. Given the lack of reliable statistical data or archival material for the time after 1949 in China, this is at the moment the only way to proceed. This also means that some questions will remain unanswered, and that for others we will arrive at only estimates. Nevertheless, I believe this multiple-perspective approach offers trustworthy insights into the general traits of the various criminal justice systems in China, even if some dimensions, such as official numbers, remain elusive. The testimonies of survivors also touch on other, more fundamental issues, such as how to represent and interpret history through the experience of those who have been victimized and traumatized. This problem requires a balance between a more conventional, objective reconstruction of the past and an empathic, subjective response based on the stories of victims and survivors.

This last aspect looms large. The history of criminal justice in China's twentieth century is a history like no other. The story that unfolds on the following pages is dramatic by all accounts. It is full of twists and turns, moral ambivalence and bitter irony. The cruelty and pitilessness that were regularly displayed are staggering. But as the following pages try to make clear, even in the darkest moments there were individuals who tried to uphold humanity and were able to sympathize with those who had lost their freedom and, unfortunately, all too often their life. Their actions give hope.

1

THE RIGHT DEGREE OF PAIN

Imperial China

THE DEVELOPMENT of Chinese criminal justice in modern times has to be set against China's long legal history, which stretches back almost two millennia. Basic notions of justice, of crime and punishment as they were understood and applied in the twentieth century, were formed and informed by the distinct legal tradition in China. It is virtually impossible to understand criminal justice in China's twentieth century without taking into account the ramifications of premodern legal language, practice, and theory. The practice of punishment in twentieth-century China, for instance, always reflected a vision of the past and a sense of how modern practices had evolved over time, even when innovations were intended to depart sharply from imperial practices. This chapter therefore offers a concise overview of the tenets of criminal justice in premodern China that formed the basis for legal developments in the twentieth century.

Imperial Chinese law did not distinguish between criminal law and civil law. It also did not distinguish between private law and public law. Instead, it was a very complex and elaborate set of concrete directives addressed to all echelons of the imperial administration.[1] For this reason, the structure of the law codes closely mirrored the structure of the bureaucracy. The directives stipulated in great detail what kinds of activities were considered harmful to the government, which behaviors were punishable, and precisely what penalties were to be imposed for what infractions. Finding the correct grade of punishment for a recorded transgression of any of the rules set out in the code was one of the main operations in the administration of imperial law; this was the question around which criminal justice was centered.[2] It is for this reason that some observers described Chinese law as a predominantly penal law, since any human act recognized in the law was linked with a punishment.

The administration of justice in imperial China was informed by a set of values and theories that guided its operations. Three established schools of thought exerted a major influence on penal philosophy and conceptions of justice: Confucianism, Legalism, and the cosmological school. Although the various schools offered very different philosophical justifications of punishment, a synthesis was forged during the Han dynasty (206 B.C.–A.D. 220). This synthesis provided the imperial state with a basic rationale for the administration of justice and punishment that continued to influence the way criminal justice operated in imperial China up to the twentieth century.

Chinese Theories of Punishment

Legal punishments have been known and applied in China since antiquity.[3] Very early in Chinese history, rulers and thinkers came to the conclusion that, freed from certain abuses, punishment is an acceptable and in fact indispensable human institution. Yet most thinkers in antiquity also recognized that punishments, in the sense of (legal) penalties attached to the violation of (legal) rules, raise troubling moral questions. Various conflicting arguments were put forth by political thinkers and moral philosophers to address the moral problem of punishment, but none of them won any sort of general acceptance. The debates surrounding these diverse approaches contributed to the formation of a distinct Chinese philosophy on punishment. Its origins, however, go beyond the time when the first philosophers' texts were written. We can trace the tradition back to the remote beginnings of Chinese civilization, when words acquired their different layers of meaning. The very meanings of the terms "punishment" and "crime" in Chinese were fundamental to the development of criminal justice.

The Chinese character for punishment is *xing*. This character represents, as has been noted many times, one of the most important words in legal terminology in China. In the famous etymological dictionary of the Later Han dynasty (25–220), the *Shuowen jiezi* (The Explanation of Graphs) by Xu Shen (120–?), we find the following definition: "*Xing* means to cut a throat [as punishment]. The character consists of the radicals *jing* and *dao*."[4] *Dao* stands for knife. *Jing* functions as a phonetic carrier. As a pictorial this character also symbolizes evenness. In ancient texts, *jing* is sometimes used synonymously with the character for law, *fa*. On this basis, Vandermeersch has argued that the term *xing* denotes a penal treatment that is centered on the physical trimming of a person; it changes, or evens, the human shape and appearance.[5] *Xing* leads to a literal, bodily "remolding" and "reforming" of the convict. In the writings of the Legalists, the meanings of *xing* as punishment and as shape or shaping are de facto interchangeable.[6]

The other important term is "crime"—in Chinese, *zui.* It has an equally complicated but telling etymology. According to the *Shuowen jiezi, zui* means a "transgression of the law." It contains the radical *xin,* which graphically represents the spiritual authority of the head of a clan *(zu).*[7] This seems to suggest that in its earliest meaning the character denoted an offense against the supreme authority of the clan head or patriarch, especially in the form of infringing on sacrificial rituals presented to heaven and to the ancestors. Such an action was seen as a serious breach of the customs or customary law of a clan and was described with the character *zui.* This reading suggests, first, that notions such as crime and punishment originated with concepts of clan and lineage.[8] Second, it points to the term's religious dimensions. Ideas of crime and punishment were first shaped in the context of religious clan rules and ancestor worship, and the idea of punishment in China was tightly related to a notion of crime as a sacrilege against the religious order and a challenge to the religious authority of a clan head. Punishment in early China was a response to infractions of sacred clan order and it consisted of a physical and behavioral "trimming" of the wrongdoer. Only much later would secular rulers come forward and try to use the power of those religious concepts for worldly pursuits.

Centuries later, the ruler's use of punishment became a central apprehension for Confucius. Confucius (550–479 B.C.) lived in a time of crisis and intense philosophical speculation. He witnessed the slow unraveling of the social and cultural fundaments of the existing order. Against this backdrop, it comes to no surprise that one of Confucius's main concerns was the restoration of social peace and justice. He believed the decline of the Zhou dynasty (1122–256 B.C.) was brought about not by military weakness but by a collapse of the people's faith in the Zhou rulers' commitment to morality and justice. A ruler and his government must be dedicated to fairness, impartiality, and moral values if they are to be accepted and supported by the people. The fundamental conviction that social peace is achievable only through moral commitment lies at the center of the Confucian approach to criminal justice.

Confucius advocated governing in accordance with approved social norms (called *li*, or rites) through persuasion and moral example, rather than governing in accordance with positive law and the threat of punishment. In the *Analects (Lunyu)* Confucius is said to have explained to a ruler:

> In administering your government, what need is there for you to kill? Just desire the good yourself, and the common people will be good. By nature the superior is like wind and the inferior is like grass. Let the wind sweep over the grass and it is sure to bend. (*Analects* XII, 19)

> Guide them by edicts, keep them in line with punishments [*xing*], and the common people will stay out of trouble but will have no sense of shame. Guide them by virtue, keep them in line with the rites and they will, besides having a sense of shame, reform themselves. (*Analects* II, 3)

Confucius emphasized the importance of the exemplary behavior of the ruler for the general state of society. *Li* were concrete institutions as well as accepted modes of behavior; they were in effect the sole instruments of a virtuous government. If the *li* were strictly observed throughout the whole of society, no need would arise for the use of penal law and punishments. In this way, *li* were preventive. Confucius believed their internalization by society effectively kept people from committing socially harmful acts. A ruler who grounded his government on *li* would be able to muster the full support of his people.

In contrast, Confucius held that law is punitive, since it comes into action only when a crime has been committed and harm has been done. Penal laws are compulsive, coercive, and therefore indicate a tyrannical mode of government. For Confucius, punishments fail to unleash any positive moral or ethical force. Penalties cannot guide the population to proper behavior and instill positive values; they can only make people fearful. Moreover, their effect on society is purely negative: under the threat of punishment, the population will simply try to elude the rules and deceive the ruler. Confucius was highly critical of any government that rested exclusively on public laws and used their built-in threat of punishment to maintain control over society. Consequently, early Confucians opposed the codification of penal laws.[9]

But Confucius did not completely dismiss punishments.[10] He accepted in principle that there could be extraordinary circumstances in which a ruler has to apply punishments as a last resort for dealing with determined evildoers who cannot be affected by moral instruction. He acknowledged that the only way to induce such persons to observe *li* is through fear of punishment, even though this is a less satisfactory social mechanism. But even here, Confucius stressed that punishments should be used to demonstrate to the offender the nature of his mistake and should let him repent. He said: "Not to mend one's ways when one has erred [*guo er bu gai*] is to err indeed" (*Analects* XV, 30). If the wicked person repents and changes his life, he can be redeemed. In the Confucian conception, then, punishments are appropriate for the correction of the incorrigible. But when an offender has repented and resolved to reform, further punishment is unnecessary.

Confucius demanded that rulers exercise great restraint when using their powers to punish. He said:

> When names are not correct, what is said will not sound reasonable; when what is said does not sound reasonable, affairs will not culminate in success; when affairs do not culminate in success, rites and music will not flourish; when rites and music do not flourish, punishments will not be exactly right [*xingfa bu zhong*], when punishments are not exactly right, the common people will not know where to put hand and foot. (*Analects* XIII, 3)

This passage stresses a central Confucian belief: punishments have to be "exactly right" [*zhong*]. But when can punishments be considered "exactly right"? For Confucians, the answer is that punishments are right if they meticulously fit the crime. Severe crimes deserve severe punishments; less severe crimes must be punished lightly. It is important to note that there is no mention of retaliation and retribution. The concept of "just deserts" or a *jus talionis* was alien to Confucius. Punishments can never be just, they can only be right, for they do not possess a value in themselves. Penalties are meant to defend the moral order of society in an emergency. Transgressions of essential values should entail heavy punishments and, correspondingly, transgressions of less central values should be punished only lightly. For Confucius, the greatest danger lies in a ruler's inclination to use punishments excessively. Then the people are unable to see the link between sanctioned violence (right punishment) and moral values, and the result is chaos and disorder. The notion of the right punishment is actually meant to restrict the ruler's discretion in his use of punishment.

Another restriction on punishment can be found in Confucius's advocacy of the family's sphere of privacy. Although he did not interpret this in a legal sense as a right or entitlement, he clearly underscored the idea that the family should be free from intrusion by law enforcement agencies. In the *Analects* we find the following dialogue:

> The Governor of She said to Confucius, "In our village we have one Straight Body. When his father stole a sheep, the son gave evidence against him. Confucius answered, "In our village those who are straight are quite different. Fathers cover up for their sons, and sons cover up for their fathers. In such behavior is straightness to be found as a matter of course." (*Analects* XIII, 18)

For Confucius, family solidarity had priority over other concerns. The ruler had to accept the unity of the family and should forbear from intruding into the family for matters of law enforcement. A good Confucian family would supervise the behavior of its own members and act on infractions. Punishments should be carried out within the family rather than publicly, and it was the family's duty to bring about repentance and moral improvement in the offender.

Legalism, the second school of thought that influenced conceptions of justice in imperial China, was eminently political; its central concern was the order of the state and society. Like Confucians, Legalist thinkers sought to redress the symptoms of decay and demise in their own time, but the solutions offered by the two schools could not be more different. Confucius wanted to create a stable, peaceful society by way of propriety, moral instruction, education, and the good example set by a benevolent elite. In contrast, the Legalists sought to use a set of written rules, physical force, and a uniform administrative apparatus to impose order on society. According to Legalist theory, the ruler is the center of gravity for all beings. The Legalists spoke of the ruler with "Machiavellian straightforwardness"[11] and elaborated principles for how the ruler could acquire and enhance his power for the sake of order and stability.

The crucial term in Chinese legalism is *fa*. It is usually translated as "law," but as Benjamin Schwartz has pointed out, *fa* also has the meaning of "pattern" or "model."[12] Legalists promoted the public proclamation of written rules for defining standards of behavior, and they called these written rules *fa*. The *fa* provided an exact standard by which the conduct of all subjects could be measured and judged. The standards in written law applied to everyone, irrespective of rank or relationship. According to the Legalists, men act only out of self-interest, and they will play by the rules only so long as the ruler is determined to defend those rules by all means. Therefore stern punishments are indispensable. The ruler has to establish a system of rewards and punishments so that the subjects are rewarded if they stick to the rules and punished when they do not abide by the *fa*.

The Legalist conception of punishment recognized only one purpose of punishment, deterrence. In *The Book of Lord Shang Yang* (d. 338 B.C.) it is stated that "the nature of men is to like titles and emoluments and to dislike punishments and penalties."[13] The same point is repeatedly made by Han Feizi (280–233 B.C.), who defined punishment *(xing)* as the "infliction of death or torture upon culprits."[14] He wrote:

> Heavy punishments are not only for the sole purpose of punishing criminals. The law of the intelligent sovereign, in suppressing rebels, is not disciplining only those who are being suppressed, for to discipline only the suppressed is the same as to discipline dead men only; in penalizing robbers, it is not disciplining only those who are being penalized, for to discipline only the penalized is the same as to discipline convicts only. . . . For the heavily punished are robbers, but the terrified and trembling are good people. Therefore, why should those who want order doubt the efficacy of heavy penalties?[15]

Legalists would frankly admit that the use of heavy punishments preeminently serves the goal of keeping the population in check through fear. It is exactly this fear that keeps the government's subjects from transgressing public laws and ignoring their duties. In this theory, then, punishments are legitimized by the need to protect and defend the existing order. They are not linked to any other value, such as justice. Unlike Confucians, Legalists maintain that punishments need not fit the crime. Instead the ruler should impose draconian punishments even for the slightest wrongdoing: "What I mean by the unification of punishments," wrote Lord Shang, "is that punishments should know no degree or grade, but that from ministers of state and generals down to great officers and ordinary folk, whosoever does not obey the king's commands, violates the edicts of the state, or rebels against the statutes fixed by the ruler, should be guilty of death and should not be pardoned."[16] The Legalist emphasis on deterrence is based on the notion that the behavior of offenders can be altered only by altering the consequences attached to their behavior. By linking certain actions (crimes) to negative sanctions, the people, so goes the assumption, will try to avoid the negative sanctions and consequently refrain from committing crimes.

In general, however, what is often overlooked is that despite their praise of draconian penalties, the Legalists always believed that the use of punishments was a temporary measure. Shang Yang asserted: "When punishments are heavy, the people dare not to transgress, and therefore there will be no punishments [*yi xing zhi xing*]."[17] Punishments are thus used to pursue the ultimate goal of making punishment obsolete. Of course this was a challenge to Confucians, who proposed to use moral behavior to make punishment obsolete. But the Legalists could find agreement with the Confucians in that, as a final consequence, punishments were supposed to wither away.

The concept and practice of punishment in China was also shaped by cosmological and religious traditions, although these are harder to trace and have often been overlooked by legal historians.[18] Many Confucian texts dating from the Warring States period (475 B.C.–221 B.C.) and the Han dynasty, ranging from the *Book of Rites (Liji)* to the *Book of Documents (Shujing)*, bear palpable traces of the cosmological mode of thinking. It is no exaggeration to state that not only the theory but also the practice of punishment in China was profoundly influenced by religious assumptions.[19] During the Han dynasty, vast tables of correspondences were compiled to identify and organize things in the natural and social world that were thought to provide a meaningful context for one's life. One such set of tables, called Tables of Five, compared the Five Phases, or elements (wood, fire, earth, metal, water), the Five Directions (north, east, south, west, and center), the Five Colors (green, red, yellow, white, black), and so forth. Such classifications included body parts, psycho-physical and affective states, styles of government, weather, domestic animals, technological instruments, heavenly bodies, and much more. The Five Punishments, which were known from earliest times, clearly fall into this category, too, thus illustrating the influence of cosmological thinking on basic penal concepts.

The cosmological philosophy emphasized that a reciprocal relationship exists between the cosmos and the human world: the course of human history is influenced by cosmic forces, and the cosmic state is constantly affected by human actions.[20] Between these two domains there is no cause-and-effect relationship but rather a delicate balance guaranteeing order, peace, and harmony.

Just as the Legalists always viewed punishment in its relationship to the state, so the cosmologists were convinced that the execution of punishments was linked to the larger cosmological order.[21] They saw crime as a disturbance of the human order, hence punishment was supposed to redress and rectify the damage done to social harmony. The grade and severity of the punishment depended on the degree to which the order had been thrown out of balance. The cosmologists believed that without an appropriate effort to remedy the social harm caused by a crime, this disturbance of the human order would affect the larger cosmic order of things. Through negative natural phenomena, such as droughts or floods, disturbances of the cosmos would in turn have a negative impact on the human world. In the cosmological approach, social disruptions that were not properly redressed would provoke complex responses by nature. The act of punishment was thus placed in a wider context: it had a meaning that went far beyond society and extended to the cosmos as a whole. Punitive reactions to crime were understood as an indispensable attempt to resurrect the balance within the world and to smooth any temporary perturbations.

Because of the influence of these notions in China, punishments were meted out not only with the intention to correct evil but also to preserve the harmony and balance that transcended the human world. The basic justification for punishment was not simply the offender's guilt but also the need to rectify the social disharmony and the anxiety concerning cosmological backlashes. Consequently, the degree or severity of any punishment had to correlate exactly with the nature or severity of the crime. These ideas clearly imposed restrictions on the ruler. If the punishments were excessive and unjustified, they would cause negative responses in the natural world.

The influence of these schools of thought is manifest in many aspects of punishment in imperial China. Consider for instance those cases when the body of an offender was subjected to punitive treatment even after the offender had died, precisely because punishment was linked to the criminal act and not to the criminal himself.[22] When a crime had occurred, a punishment had to follow in requital. Another example of the influence of cosmological ideas is the tradition of sentencing for capital crimes, and executing death sentences, only in late autumn or winter. It was believed that in winter nature was prepared for death, while in spring, nature's vitality was increasing. In general, a criminal process had to be conducted with consideration given to such seasonal changes in nature. The *Yue ling* (Monthly Commands), from the third century B.C., gives detailed instructions for the activities and rituals the emperor should perform each month.[23] For instance, in the first month of autumn the emperor should instruct his officials to review the laws, repair the jails, fix the hand and foot cuffs; in the second month of autumn the emperor should order his officials to carry out the sentencing; and in the last month of autumn, he should follow through with justice and punishment. The text also describes the exact calamities that will follow from any violation of the prescribed rules. From the Han dynasty onward, death sentences were carried out only at the end of autumn, with explicit referral to the *Yue ling* as the source for this practice.[24]

Chinese penal philosophy after the third century B.C. was marked by a syncretistic merger of different arguments and theories. One of the most interesting theoretical accounts of punishment that tried to combine different Legalist and Confucian arguments (and that actually preceded Han syncretism) was written by Xunzi (300–230 B.C.).[25] In his essay *Rectifying Theses* (Xunzi, Book 18) he developed a comprehensive theory of punishment.[26] Although he was a follower of Confucius, Xunzi explicitly acknowledged the institution of punishment as an important tool of government. He wrote: "If punishment is balanced against an offense, then there is order."[27] He qualified the purpose of punishment with the following words: "As a general rule, the fundamental reason for punishment is the need to prohibit acts of violence, to instill hatred of evil acts, and further to warn men against committing them in the future."[28] The purpose of punishment thus is manifold: legal punishments eliminate the necessity for private revenge or defense, deter criminals, and educate the population. Xunzi's interpretation of penalties as a warning signal to criminals and those with criminal intent bring the deterring and educating effects of punishment to the fore. His argument was aimed at making deterrence morally acceptable by emphasizing its hortative and preventive effect on society. Punishment is capable of communicating values to the people and admonishing them to remember the importance of rules, thus instilling their repugnance against evil deeds. Xunzi calls for punishments to fit or match ("balance," in his words) the crime, so that they are seen as fair and just. When applied correctly and with restraint, the application of punishments will prevent the need for punishments in the future and thus unfold a further positive impact.

Xunzi's explanation of punishment and his attempt to reconcile Legalism with Confucianism was quite influential for penal theories during succeeding dynasties. The Qin dynasty (221–206 B.C.) leaned toward Legalist theory as an effective means for strengthening the state and unifying the empire, but the harshness of Qin methods made the law unpopular, thus reopening the way to Confucian influence. From at least the Han dynasty, a Confucian-oriented officialdom was able to imbue the law with the values of Confucianism and to use law to transmit and reinforce those concerns.[29] The dominant political orthodoxy during the succeeding Han dynasty began to accept law as a system of punishments and infused it with Confucian norms and ideas, such as the variability of punishments according to status and circumstances. The official legal system thus accommodated a Confucianist view that was reluctant to grant law an important position in the state and the more realistic Legalist view that the harsh penal apparatus that had been inherited was useful for dealing with unruly elements of society and enforcing morality. This merger of different approaches during the Han dynasty continued to be underpinned by cosmological assumptions. It was Dong Zhongshu (195–115 B.C.), especially, who integrated Yin-Yang cosmology into a Confucian ethical framework, creating the theoretical foundation of the inchoate imperial state during the Han dynasty and the long-lasting official ideology of the Chinese imperial state. He related punishment to Yin and virtue or morality *(de)* to Yang.[30] Yin was subordinated to Yang, and by analogy, the ruler should in his rule rest mainly on virtue, not on punishment. Punishment should be a helper of morality as Yin is supposed to be the helper to Yang. Dong also combined political and legal principles with the idea of a dynamically correlative cosmos, in which actions on the level of humanity (whether proper or improper) stimulate responses on other levels. He suggested that such responses occur when humanity disrupts the "ethers" *(qi)* of Yin and Yang. The appropriate and correct use of state violence is crucial in this context. In his memorial to the Emperor Wudi in 140 B.C., Dong explained: "When sentences and punishments are not appropriate, evil spirits will arise. With evil spirits accumulating below and hatred and cruelty lingering aloft, a disharmony will prevail between high and low; thus the relation between the Yin and Yang will be distorted and reversed, and unlucky omens will appear."[31]

The values embodied in classical Confucian writings also informed the first comprehensive law codifications, such as the Tang Code (A.D. 624, revised in 653). Since the basic Confucian orthodoxy did not change thereafter in its essentials, similar rules can be found in the codes of all subsequent dynasties until the Qing dynasty (1644–1911). The continuity of the basic orthodoxy incorporated in the imperial law is very well illustrated in the concept of the "ten greatest wrongs" (or ten abominations, *shi e*), which are found in practically identical form in all the codes from the Tang dynasty (618–907) up to the Qing. Placed right at the beginning of each of the codes in the "General Principles" section, the ten greatest wrongs represented the conduct most detested in Confucian thought.[32] In Article 2 of the Qing Code from 1740, these crimes were described as "[those] actions in which the crimes are very serious and the evil is extreme."[33] These crimes also deserved the harshest punishments and could not be pardoned. The list of offenses in this section included rebellion, treason, gross unfilialness (killing one's father), acts that are not in accordance with the Way or *dao* (such as killing three persons in a family, or dismembering a person), lack of respect (stealing sacred objects for the Great Sacrifice or stealing or counterfeiting imperial seals), lack of filial piety, discord (plotting to kill relatives; striking or bringing suit against one's husband or senior relatives), failure to fulfill one's duty (killing a magistrate or an officer), and domestic disorder (this referred to engaging in sexual relations with relatives). The list of the most reprehensible offenses clearly reflected the most important moral judgments of Confucianism. It produced a ranking of legally significant or punishable acts according to the orthodox Confucian value system.

Apart from the "Confucianization" of the law, the ten-abominations section in every law code illustrated another trait of Chinese law. In practice, legal prescriptions served as an enforceable set of rules and as instruments for adjusting conflicting interests in a fair and transparent manner. But at the same time, law in China had an additional function that went way beyond mere law enforcement.[34] The law as a whole functioned as model or ideal to be aimed at. In this view, the threat of punishment was a tool for articulating certain goals to which the ruler and the society should aspire. This explains why the law codes contained articles that were rarely if ever enforced, such as articles on land transactions or some of the rules on family relations in the Qing Code (1740), for example. They were retained "on account of their symbolic value," because they were thought to provide guides to desirable conduct.[35]

In imperial Chinese law, punishment was employed as a "motivational technique."[36] Its main purpose was to deter the populace from engaging in activities that would violate the dominant value system. It was assumed that punishments would produce beneficial social results by steering behavior. The notion of punishment as a deterrent was widespread and relatively undisputed in imperial China. It is found in an oft-quoted statement, "Punishments are used to end punishments; the death penalty is used to frighten men," that is repeated in many legal documents, such as sentences, commentaries, and so on.[37] Emperors and officials frequently warned against any attempts to mitigate punishments, which would risk reducing their deterrent effect. In the twelfth century Emperor Gaozong (1127–1162), for instance, declared, "[If] we act only in a lenient manner, ignoring the law and using precedents [to reduce the penalties], then men will not be fearful. This is no way to use penalties to restrain evildoers."[38] The Kangxi emperor (1654–1722) echoed this stance in his remarks on the exercising of the emperor's penal powers: "Giving life to people and killing people— those are the powers that the emperor has. . . . The Board of Punishments recommended that Hu [a cruel and rapacious official] be dismissed and sent into exile for three years. I ordered instead that he be executed with his family and in his native place so that all the local gentry might learn how I regarded such behavior."[39]

Deterrence was clearly the key purpose of punishment, but in late imperial China some officials recognized that it also had other purposes. For example there was a sense that, for the wronged party, punishment was a form of just retribution. Officials were well aware that the imposition of punishments might appease angry victims of crime. The state itself did not officially pursue the purpose of retribution, but officials conceded that the wronged parties demanded retribution and that they tended to see this as an important function of legal punishment.[40] Another rationale for punishment that was accepted by many officials was the hortative and instructive effect on the population. Penalties, with the obvious exception of the death penalty, were "designed to instruct."[41] In this view punishments were lessons, designed to transmit moral values and inform people when they had failed morally. Implied here is the assumption that the offender can be corrected through public shaming. We will see later that shaming was mentioned frequently in sections on punishment in the law codes. Shame was believed to lead to moral improvement. This process was called "self-renewal" *(zixin)*—a phrase that can be found over and over again in Chinese amnesty documents.[42] In the context of banishment, too, Qing jurisprudence frequently invoked the conception that the punishment of exile was supposed to serve as a route to self-renewal.[43] Some officials placed particular emphasis on this purpose of punishment and also recommended that the system of punishments be changed so that it would better suit this specific function. Su Song (1020–1101), for instance, favored the punishment of exile with added labor, for this penalty, he said, "would suffice to open up the road of self-renewal, to transform evil into good people, and to change the stupid and vulgar through education."[44] This language is strikingly similar to twentieth-century arguments regarding the purpose of punishment. The imposition of some punishments, such as exile and banishment, in particular, was assumed to initiate a process of self-renewal, redemption, and correction in the punished person.

Another important element in the late-imperial approach to punishment was the concept of appropriateness and requital. These concepts found expression in several basic ideas. One was that punishments should be imposed in accordance with the historical situation, the public morale, and the state of society. Therefore, in peaceful times, sparing men from execution and sentencing them to the lighter penalties was appropriate. But in times of disorder and upheaval, the state had to resort to the most severe punishments to defend the social order. Another idea reflecting the need for appropriateness was the requirement that judges equalize or balance the facts (of the criminal offense) and the law.[45] The basic intention was that a judge should look at the consequences of the criminal act and proportion the punishment to match the extent of damage caused by the offender. Geoffrey MacCormack termed this principle "requital," which focuses on the harm done to the victim, the state, or society.[46] The offender must pay for his deeds by enduring punitive, painful treatment. This justification of punishment is closely related to the language of compensation and forfeiture, which can be found in many of the decisions of the Board of Punishments (Xing-bu) in homicide cases.[47] The Board of Punishments served as the highest appellate court in the imperial legal system.

Social defense, understood as the application of penalties not to deter or redress but to protect the order of state and society against further harm, was another argument that can be found in legal sources dealing with the penal system. In several cases the treatment of convicts clearly shows the state's intention to protect the society through the incapacitation of criminals. The use of tattooing, above all, was meant to incapacitate a criminal by a warning society about him. Fettering was another device used to incapacitate criminals and prevent them from committing further crimes.

Again, one has to be mindful of the cosmological worldview underpinning conceptions of the role of punishment in traditional Chinese law. One reason Qing officials attended so carefully to the fine-tuning of punishments was that, on some level, they accepted the notion that proper punishing for offenses helped maintain cosmic harmony. Emperors and officials connected egregious injustice with floods and droughts, "in the sense that [the theory] focuses on the need for a response to an offense that can be described in terms of 'requital' or 'retribution.'"[48] Jonathan Ocko, in his study on capital punishment, has cited frequent expressions by senior officials of the belief that imbalances between strictness and forgiveness would impede "calling forth heavenly harmony," and of the imperial concern that officials' reluctance to impose death sentences would jeopardize cosmic harmony.[49]

Chinese theories of legal punishment thus show a mixture of goals. Chinese officials and thinkers rarely sensed conflicts or even tensions among the various purposes and justifications for punishment. Deterrence, requital, and self-renewal were the main purposes explicated in legal documents and treatises.

Rituals of Deterrence

Legal punishments in imperial China were carefully orchestrated public spectacles of physical suffering. The public production of pain was believed to serve as a clear message, as a lesson to others and to prevent further transgressions by the convicts themselves. To be effective as deterrents and requitals, the punishments had to be obvious, observable, and of appropriate severity.

Since ancient times, Chinese sources have mentioned the system of punishments called the Five Punishments *(wu xing)*.[50] This is a generic term used to designate the major standard punishments *(zheng xing)*. There is, to the best of my knowledge, no fully satisfactory explanation for the repeated use of the number five in the penal system. Most interpretations point to the fact that the number five plays an important role in the ancient Chinese cosmological system, as mentioned above. Since it was believed that the "Five Elements had created the ten thousand things" *(wu xing sheng wan wu)*, the number five came to represent a harmonic order—that is, an order in accordance with basic principles of the cosmic order. Given this, the Five Punishments most likely symbolized an effort to re-institute the harmonic order in human society that had been severely disturbed by a criminal act.[51] The use of the number five thus legitimized the use of penal violence by the ruler; it sanctioned that form of violence by bringing it into accordance with the principles of order and harmony. It is interesting to note that this concept was so powerful that even in Chinese criminal law codes drafted in the twentieth century the number five in the system of main punishments was mostly retained.

Only sketchy information is available concerning the punishments used in ancient China. Ban Gu (A.D. 32–92), a Han Confucian scholar and the author of the *Book of Han (Hanshu)*, asserted that in ancient China rulers used Five Punishments to punish evildoers and deter "those who were villainous." The earliest Five Punishments are described as tattooing *(qing)*, amputation of the nose *(yi)*, amputation of one ear *(yue)*, castration *(gong)*, and decapitation *(fa)*.[52]

For the Zhou dynasty (1122–256 B.C.), the use of Five Punishments is described in the "Punishment of Lü" section *(Lü xing)* of the *Classic of Documents (Shujing)*.[53] This book is one of the earliest and most important legal texts, since it describes the philosophy of punishment in ancient China and the workings of its criminal justice system.[54] The text portrays the criminal justice system as being unified and highly sophisticated, with standard laws, detailed trial procedures, professional judges, and a multitiered system of punishments. The Five Punishments listed in the *Lü xing* were tattooing *(mo)*, amputation of the nose *(yi)*, amputation of one or both legs *(fei)*, castration *(gong)*, and the death penalty *(dapi)*.[55] According to the *Lü xing*, it was the non-Chinese tribe of the Miao who, in the twenty-third century B.C., first created the Five Punishments. The Yellow Emperor learned the "five oppressive punishments" from the Miao, who had abused them, and in fact the correct and cautious application of *wu xing* is one of the main concerns of this text. In general, judges were instructed to pay attention to the issue of intentionality. When a crime was committed intentionally, the offender was to be held fully liable punished severely. However, when a crime was committed unintentionally, the judges were to resort to lighter punishments. It also appears that different legal regulations were applied for members of other clans, so that in Zhou law a distinction was made between members of the ruler's own clan and those of others.

During the Spring and Autumn period (770–475 B.C.) a new punishment of penal servitude was introduced. The rulers started so see convicts as a possible labor force and looked for ways to make use of them. They found it technically possible and economically profitable to deploy convicts for certain tasks, such as construction or transport.[56] Sources from the Spring and Autumn period also contain clues to another important trait of criminal justice in premodern China. The power of punishment was exercised not only by state officials but also by clan and family heads. As matter of fact, the rulers acknowledged and respected this power of the clan heads over the members of the clan.

Legal penalties in early imperial China were, in the words of Brian McKnight, "intense, irreversible and brief."[57] The dual purpose of deterrence and incapacitation was dominant: some of the mutilating punishments made it literally impossible for offenders to commit further violations. During the following centuries, the mutilating forms of punishment gradually disappeared and were eventually abolished. The Five Punishments underwent a considerable transformation. While they retained their character as corporal punishments, they were greatly mitigated: the punishments became less bloody, less intense, and less irreversible. Tattooing and amputation of the nose and feet were abolished by imperial edict under the Han emperor Wendi in 167 B.C.[58] The punishments to which criminals were then sentenced included exile, hard labor, flogging, castration, and death. Castration, the last remaining mutilating punishment, was ended around 220 A.D. By then, all other mutilating corporal punishments had disappeared, replaced by varying forms and degrees of beating, penal servitude, or exile.[59] The Han emperors still retained the death penalty. Senior officials and members of the imperial family who were sentenced to execution were usually allowed to avoid such a scene by committing suicide. After a death penalty was carried out, the criminal's goods, including members of his family, were confiscated by the state. Those persons then became slaves of the state and were assigned menial or domestic tasks in government offices.

From the third to the sixth century, the Five Punishments underwent further changes. In this phase, each was developed into a category that had fixed degrees or scales of the same punishment.[60] For instance, the punishment of flogging was divided into five grades, from ten to fifty strokes. Penal servitude was developed into five grades, lasting from one year to two and a half years. These modifications obliged judges to take into account the severity of the crime and then to impose the corresponding degree of the designated punishment. The mitigation of the mutilating punishments and the implementation of beating and penal labor promised a number of advantages, from the state's point of view. Beatings carried out in public places served not only as physical and painful punishments but also as a deterrent. At the same time, offenders were not disfigured and left physically handicapped, so their reintegration into society was possible. In this sense, beating was a suitable punishment to redeem the offender and thus to promote moral values and social reform. In addition, beatings could be easily adjusted to the severity of the crime.

The Tang dynasty undertook a new codification of all centralized law, completed in 624. This new code embodied what were considered basic, unchanging normative rules and prescribed fixed penalties for defined offenses. The code comprised statutes as a general body of universally applicable administrative law, regulations or codified legislation supplementary to the statutes, and finally ordinances—detailed procedural laws supplementing the statutes and issued by the departments of the central ministries. Under the early Tang this body of codified law was revised every twenty years. The systematic effort to maintain a universally applicable and comprehensive codification of law and administrative practice was essential to the uniform system of administration that the Tang succeeded in establishing throughout its diverse empire. The Tang Code represents a major achievement in Chinese legal history and as such proved remarkably influential not only in China but also in East Asia. The Tang Code was still considered authoritative as late as the fourteenth century and was used as a model by the Ming dynasty (1368–1644). It was also adopted with some modifications by Japan in the early eighth century and later by Korea and Vietnam.

The Five Punishments in the Tang Code, and in fact in all the codes thereafter until the Qing dynasty (1644–1911), were beating with the light stick, beating with the heavy stick, penal servitude, life exile, and death.[61] Each of the punishments was divided into several grades. Some changes were made, however. For instance, flogging was assigned differently, with sticks of different sizes, and exile or banishment was altered as new places for exile, like Xinjiang, were opened up.

The system of legal punishments as laid out in the last of the imperial codifications, the Great Qing Code of 1740, was elaborate and carefully graded.[62] The lightest punishments were beating with light stick (chi) and beating with the heavy stick (zhang). Both were available in five grades (from 10 to 50 blows and from 50 to 100 blows). In practice, the nominal punishments were regularly discounted to from 4 to 20 and 20 to 40 blows.[63] The commentary added that "[beating with the bamboo] makes one feel ashamed."[64]

Penal servitude (tu) was also available in five degrees of duration, ranging from one to three years. To penal servitude the code added various degrees of flogging, as servitude alone was perhaps seen as too light a punishment. The goal of this punishment is paraphrased in the commentary as follows: "Its [purpose] is to enslave and to disgrace the one [who is sentenced to it]."[65] Convicts sentenced to this punishment were sent from the province of their conviction to another province where they would work in an iron- or saltworks for the term specified. They were required to meet daily work quotas. It appears that, after 1725, convicts were increasingly kept in the province of their conviction and put to work on government operations such as postal stations.

The fourth punishment was exile (liu). The commentary notes: "[Even though the offender has committed an offense punishable with death, because of the Emperor's kindness he] cannot bear to inflict the death sentence, [and the offender] is exiled to a distant territory."[66] There were three degrees of regular exile. All lasted for life, but they were differentiated by the distance of the destination from the offender's native place (places of exile could be from 2,000 li [666 miles] to 3,000 li [1,000 miles] away. Flogging was also added to the punishment of exile.

Under the Qing, the punishment of exile was expanded in proportion and in response to the territorial expansion of the empire. Two forms of deportation were added: military life exile (jun or chongjun) and banishment to the frontier (fapei).[67] Military exile meant the criminal was sent into military service at some distant frontier post, military colony, or military farm (bingtun, of which there were many facilitating the opening up of wastelands or newly conquered areas).[68] There were five degrees of military exile, each of which corresponded to a specific distance from the offender's native place (distances ranged from 2,000 *li* to 4,000 *li*). Banishment involved the greatest distances and was reserved for the worst offenders. Those sentenced to *fapei* were sent to Manchuria, Mongolia, or, later, Xinjiang in the northwest. These regions were considerably farther away than the maximum distance stipulated for regular or military exile. Although banishment was the gravest legal punishment other than death, it was not necessarily for life, unlike the other forms of exile. After serving a number of years banished to the frontier, former government officials and sometimes even ordinary exiles were in fact eligible to return home. For this reason banishment was frequently associated with the idea of self-renewal, or *zixin*. Emperor Qianlong (1711–1799) explicitly described banishment as "the path to self-renewal" *(zixin zhi lu)*.[69] Those banished were admonished to "expiate their crimes by putting forth effort."[70] Moral redemption could be achieved through satisfactory performance in completing the assigned tasks, and once redemption was officially recognized, the convict was eligible to be sent home.

As a rule, convicts in all forms of exile had to work. They were often assigned to essential but dangerous tasks that others were reluctant to fulfill. Work fell into four categories: agriculture (land reclamation, work on military farms), manufacturing, defense, and clerical duties. Annual productivity targets were pronounced for each location. Failure to meet these standards brought additional punishment.

The severest penalty was the death penalty *(si)*, which was available in four degrees: strangulation with or without delay and beheading with or without delay. The commentary explained: "In all cases of offenses subject to the death penalty, inside or outside the capital, apart from those [offenses], which require execution without delay, the accused must be imprisoned to await the Autumn Assizes or the Court Assizes."[71] This regulation was intended to delay executions so that central judicial agencies and the emperor would have time to conduct a careful review of all death sentences. The extensive review system is discussed in detail below. Besides these standard forms of death, there was another form of the death penalty: tormented death *(lingchi)*.[72] It was a later imperial addition to the practice of legal punishments that can be traced to the Liao dynasty (916–1129). In this form of execution, the executioner made a number of cuts with a knife upon the victim, with the final cut consisting of cutting off the head. *Lingchi* was reserved as a punishment for treason and a very few other crimes, such as parricide, mutilation of a living person, and witchcraft. In the Qing Code most of these crimes are listed in the second article, under the heading "Ten Abominations."

Except for limited periods of time, imprisonment was not a form of punishment in imperial China.[73] Although every *yamen*, or administrative headquarters, had a jail, these jails were designed to hold the accused only before trial, during trial, and prior to punishment. It should also be mentioned that fines were not a punishment either, although a magistrate could for certain persons, such as women, elderly persons, children, and some others, decide to commute a punishment of beating to a fine. In these cases, fines were monetary redemptions, and were used as a substitute for other punishments.

Besides the standard Five Punishments, there were several supplemental punishments. These punishments were imposed in addition to the standard punishments, when the judge felt that the nature of the crime deserved a harsher-than-normal punishment. For instance, recidivists who had committed the same crime before would be sentenced to a supplemental punishment in addition to the standard punishment. Often, but not always, the imposition of supplemental punishments was stipulated by a statute in the code. Therefore the application of supplemental punishments often rested at the edge of legality.

The cangue (*jia* or *jiahao*) was originally an instrument of confinement used to limit the mobility of an offender without incarcerating him.[74] The rectangular collar, made of heavy blocks of wood, weighed about thirty-two and a half pounds (in 1812 or 1814 the weight was increased to fifty-four and a half pounds). When it was attached, it encircled the neck of the wearer tightly and made it impossible for him to reach his face or head with his hands. Historically it had been used together with other instruments of confinement, such as manacles, fetters, and handcuffs, to prevent convicts from escaping. Under the Qing, however, the cangue was primarily used as punishment. Normally a sentence would include wearing the cangue for a number of days or months in addition to a standard punishment such as beating. During the Qing, wearing the cangue was a common punishment for thieves and adulterous women. To it was attached a placard stating the nature of the wearer's crime. The intention was to warn the public but also to induce a sense of shame and repentance in the one being punished.

Judicial tattooing (*ci zi*), historically one of the Five Punishments, was used as a supplemental punishment under the Qing. It was usually applied to robbers, violators of tombs, criminals deported outside China proper, and captured offenders who had left their place of exile. For a first offense, the name of the crime was tattooed on the right forearm (in Chinese or in Manchu, or sometimes both). Had the offender committed the same crime a second time, then the tattoo was affixed to the left forearm. For the third and fourth offenses, the face of the convict was tattooed. Tattoos could be removed, for example under an imperial amnesty or when the offender had conducted himself very well. In general the function of judicial tattooing was to warn the public of the offender's status and criminal past.

Exposure or display of the head *(xiao shou)* was a supplemental punishment to the death penalty for notorious criminals, especially robbers and rebels. After decapitation or death by slicing, the severed head of the criminal would be hung up in a cage and left for days or weeks at the execution ground or another public spot for everyone to see. Sometimes the head would be paraded through the streets.

All supplemental punishments (except, of course, the exposure of the head) aimed at publicly shaming those who had committed repeated offenses. Through shame, it was believed, the offender would be encouraged to repent, and true repentance would lead to redemption. Public shaming also had the effect of mobilizing the community and isolating the wrongdoer. It was seen as an effective tool for helping to keep habitual criminals from committing the same crimes over and over again.

The implementation of the punishments described above was carefully controlled by the central authorities. A very important aspect of traditional Chinese administration of justice was the complicated set of rules and regulations designed to constrain the administration's authority to punish. In a nutshell, these provisions were meant to demonstrate that the ruler of the Chinese empire did not act arbitrarily in imposing punishments, but that he was genuinely dedicated to the values of justice and fairness. Therefore, when handling criminal justice affairs the emperor strove to display merciful benevolence in the form of his explicit concern for the welfare of those accused, imprisoned, and sentenced. The emperor exercised his powers not only to make criminals suffer but also to eventually cleanse individuals of their crimes and reintegrate them into society. All penal codes contained rules that, under certain conditions, accorded offenders who were genuinely repentant complete or partial exemption from punishment.

As we have seen, the underlying assumption of the penal system was that punishments would achieve their greatest effect when the severity of the penalty corresponded as closely as possible to the seriousness of the crime. In cases of homicide, for instance, the principle of requital was strictly applied: when one person directly caused the death of another, the loss of life by the victim called for the loss of life by the killer in requital. Even if the death of a victim was an unintended accident, the person who caused the death was normally sentenced to the death penalty.[75] If in a fit of madness a junior relative fatally injured a senior relative, Qing law treated the offender as having acted without malice or intent. Nevertheless, because the act had not only injured the victim but also violated basic human relationships, it had to be requited by the execution of the offender. Although Qing officials themselves carefully distinguished requital from retribution by applying well-established standards of motive and intent, they also understood that ordinary people expected injury to be requited with injury and might not forgo private vengeance unless the state's justice in some measure accommodated their expectations.[76]

When the causal link between an offense and the death of a victim was missing (because of lack of evidence), a capital sanction was not to be imposed, however. Instead a lighter punishment was chosen, its severity depending on the nature of the probable link between act and death. A careful investigation of the criminal act was to be undertaken, to ensure that nobody was punished wrongfully. Even though under the principle of requital the life of the killer was to be forfeit, the greatest care was taken in determining not only whether the alleged offender had committed the offense but also whether any mitigating circumstances might justify a reduction of the capital sentence to exile. The criminal process operated on the fundamental principle that criminal intent was to be measured along a finely graded continuum, beginning with malice aforethought and continuing through a diminishing scale based on when the intent was formulated vis-à-vis the commission of the crime.[77] For this reason, an elaborate procedure for hearing cases was established. Its goal was to take maximum care in determining the facts and identifying correct punishments. The imperial criminal justice system went to great lengths to make sure that every offender would receive the exact degree of punishment appropriate for his crime.

Even with crimes that violated core values, such as violence by an inferior against a superior, death sentences were often nominal. While the formal sentence had to "express the full disapproval of the law, . . . a way was found to prevent its actual implementation."[78] The law was concerned not just with finding an adequate requital but also with ensuring that the punishment demanded by the law should not be excessive. Great attention was paid to the problem of guaranteeing that government agencies did not use penal violence in an arbitrary way and thus engage in the miscarriage of justice.

As a particular example of the care taken in handling capital cases, one can point to the complicated procedure for judicial review once a case had reached the Board of Punishments. Most death sentences were not carried out immediately but were delayed until Autumn Assizes *(qiushen)*. This meant that an offender could not be executed until his case was reviewed by the central law agencies in Beijing. At the Autumn Assizes—special judicial sessions held annually in Beijing—officials reviewed such cases and then classified them into several groups. The two most important categories were *qingshi,* cases in which the death sentence was verified, and *huanjue,* cases that were deferred until the Autumn Assizes of the following year because extenuating circumstances had been found. For all *huanjue* cases, the death penalty was postponed for another year.

The list of *qingshi* cases (verified death sentences) was then submitted to the emperor for a final examination. Only after this last and final review were the death sentences carried out. It should be noted that even cases calling for immediate execution were still subject to a final inspection by the emperor. All executions in the Chinese empire required explicit approval by the emperor, a practice that dated back to the Sui dynasty.[79] It is evident that this final scrutiny by the emperor was undertaken with great earnestness. It was considered to be a crucial part of his government.[80] With the advice of his closest ministers, the emperor personally and carefully went back over each of the cases presented to him; as a result, no more than 20 percent of capital sentences were eventually ratified by the emperor.

If the emperor would not ratify a death sentence, criminals sentenced to death might survive several assizes in the *qingshi* category and eventually be placed in the *huanjue* category. In the eighteenth century, for instance, the number of convicts subject to continuing postponements of execution grew continually and became substantial. Around 1812, almost 13,000 convicts had been placed in the *huanjue* category three or more times. Eventually the majority of those whose executions were deferred at three or more

Autumn Assizes received a commutation of their sentence to frontier banishment.[81]

Only in a few cases was the sentence of strangulation or beheading (or death by slicing) carried out immediately. In cases of treason and other offenses that were thought to pose a danger to the state or the dynasty, however, the emperor might be ruthless in ordering executions. Mass executions without proper hearings were carried out for quelling rebellions, for example. If the sovereignty of the emperor was challenged, he had the power to declare a state of emergency, suspend the regular procedures of the criminal justice system, and resort to unrestrained violence against his subjects.[82]

The penal code also had provisions forbidding the imposition of heavy punishments for the very old or the very young. By general principle, the younger or older an individual was, the greater the degree of leniency with which he or she was treated by the law.[83] Obviously the idea behind it was that those who did not possess full strength should be spared from the severity of some of the punishments. The treatment of disabled or mentally ill criminals was similar.[84]

Legal amnesties were another way for the government to demonstrate benevolence and restraint. Through issuing amnesties, the emperor exempted offenders from punishment or granted a reduction in their sentence. Amnesties were granted frequently by the emperor, and this system of "acts of grace" was indeed a striking aspect of Chinese criminal justice.[85] The practice was most marked from the Han to the Song dynasty. While its use flattened in the late imperial period, even then acts of grace continued to be issued on a scale unparalleled in other legal systems of the world. The emperor and his government thus appeared as not only "the originator and enforcer of stern punishments, but also the dispenser of kindness and mercy."[86]

There is ample evidence to demonstrate the concern of the throne and its officials for the value of human life, at least in times of peace and stability. The reasons for this particular concern were manifold. In part it stemmed from the Confucian emphasis on *ren* (benevolence or humanity), which obligated the ruler to take into consideration the welfare of his subjects. Legal commentaries of the Qing period often interpreted *ren* as a humane and merciful approach to criminal and penal matters, seeking to spare life whenever possible, to exercise restraint, and to restrict the use of state violence. But practical considerations certainly played a role too. In 1812, for instance, there were 1,293 districts that, on the lowest level, had daily administrative contact with the population.[87] This means that 1,293 judges had to handle criminal matters arising in a population of 430 million people.[88] Moreover, these officials were responsible not only for criminal matters but also for all other affairs of local government, such as tax collection, public works, and water regulation. The imperial state clearly lacked the resources to administer criminal justice in an intensive manner. The state also was unable to provide adequate security facilities to enforce exile or penal servitude effectively. Amnesties, acts of grace, and reductions in punishments were ways of releasing the pressure on the criminal justice system.

Even after the decision was made to carry out a punishment, a major concern was seeing that corporal punishments were applied uniformly and with precision. The government was alert to the fact that the infliction of punishments might be abusive or arbitrary. To limit abuses and maltreatment, exact and detailed regulations stipulated how the death penalty and other corporal punishments were to be carried out.

The law specifically demanded of all law enforcement officials that legal punishments be applied in "accordance with the law" (*yifa*)—that is, that the correct measure of punishment be inflicted and the correct prescribed method be used.[89] In regard to flogging, for instance, the magistrate had to ensure that the proper number of blows was given and that the beating was administered on the correct part of the body (buttocks and thighs). In fact numerous regulations governed these beatings, including timing, place, and who was to administer them. Beatings were not supposed to be inflicted on sick convicts or when convicts still bore wounds from previous beatings. The law also decreed the use of appropriate and legal instruments and prescribed their dimensions in length, width, and weight. A description of all instruments permissible for use in punishment and torture was found at the beginning of the code.[90]

When a punishment caused a serious injury or the unintended death of an offender, the circumstances of the punishment and the exact cause of death had to be examined by provincial authorities.[91] The Qing Code specified a number of crimes that involved the faulty imposition of criminal punishments. Most important in this respect was Article 413: "Executing a Sentence [in a Way That Is] Not in Accordance with the Rules."[92] According to this paragraph, those responsible for accidental harm and intentional maltreatment had to be tried and punished.

The article made a distinction between punishments that were meted out "not according to the law" *(bu ru fa)* and punishments that were implemented in a completely "illegal" fashion. If inappropriate but legal instruments were used (a heavy bamboo stick instead of a light one, for instance), or if the amount of punishment given to the offender exceeded the stipulated punishment in the sentence, then the law saw this as executing punishment in a way "not according to the law"—a criminal offense. In such a case, the official was sentenced to 100 blows of bamboo and had to pay ten taels for funeral expenses if the victim had died. If the accused had been beaten on parts of the body other than the buttocks and thighs or if an illegal instrument had been used, this was "truly illegal" *(fei fa)* and was punished with 100 blows of bamboo and three years of penal servitude. There were furthermore a number of statutes concerned with the correct implementation of legal punishments, such as Article 396: "Intentionally Incarcerating Law-abiding Persons and Putting Them to the Question" (meaning interrogation under torture) and Article 410: "Exposing Injustices and Misapplication of the Law." While the multitude of regulations may have created legal confusion because in a sense they were competing, they also bespeak the concern of the traditional justice system for correctly and fairly imposing punishments.

When compared with the execution of corporal punishments in early modern Europe, what stands out in the Chinese case is not only the concern that punishments should be inflicted correctly but also the government's reluctance to stage executions in the elaborate way that was common, for instance, in France, Germany, and Great Britain.[93] Michel Foucault opened his book *Discipline and Punish* with a chilling description of the execution of Robert F. Damiens in 1775, a torment that lasted several days and involved burning and using horses to pull the body apart.[94] In China, too, executions were carried out in public execution grounds located in shopping streets and marketplaces.[95] There are a few descriptions of these public executions, and they all indicate that executions in late imperial China were no match for the ferocious events staged in eighteenth-century Europe, where "spectacles of suffering" (Spierenburg) drew huge crowds and were conducted in a carnival-like atmosphere. On the contrary, a Qing dynasty imperial edict demanded that "whenever criminals marked for execution at the Autumn Assizes have been assembled at the execution ground, guards fully sufficient for maintaining good order must be sent there in advance, and crowds of noisy spectators must be prohibited. Moreover the commanding officer of the local garrison is personally to witness the executions."[96] There was no platform or stage on which to present the execution to the masses; preparations, if any, were related to security and to preventing disturbances by a possibly agitated crowd.

The executions themselves were quick, as one Western witness described: "The criminal does not lay his head upon a block to be chopped off by an axe, but is placed kneeling with his hands tied behind him. One assistant holds him in position by the rope with which his hands are tied, another pulls his head forward [seizing his queue for this purpose], and with one stroke of his sword the executioner whips it off."[97] Immediately afterward the executioner and soldiers would leave the execution grounds and the crowd would be disbanded.

In China, the public displays of bloodshed and violence were thus implemented in a simple manner. Any elaborate procedure was avoided. The imperial authorities obviously took no pride in executing subjects, since according to Confucian teaching the mere occurrence of crime and punishments implied a failure of the state and society. It was the emperor's sovereign right and duty to put murderers to death as a deterrent to crime in the population, but the whole arrangement was much plainer than the "gloomy festival of punishment" witnessed in early modern Europe.[98]

Reordering Society: The Management of Crime in Late Imperial China

Since the mid-nineteenth century, Western diplomats have dismissed the administration of law in Qing China as a widely dysfunctional system chiefly distinguished by its arbitrariness and brutality.[99] This judgment has been based in part on comparisons with Western legal standards, which made the Chinese legal system look deficient and inferior. Overall, China was perceived as a backward, semi-civilized country, well below the nations of the West on the great evolutionary timetable. Recently, however, studies based on careful examination of plentiful archival materials have demonstrated that administrators in late imperial China used great care in the formulation and application of laws, and in enforcing the rule of law in a uniform and impartial manner.

In the late imperial period an extensive and elaborate bureaucracy was responsible for the administration of justice.[100] The Board of Punishments was the highest agency responsible. In matters of criminal justice, it served as a buffer between provincial authorities and the emperor. The empire was divided into circuits, which were units of supervision rather than administration. Within these circuits, officials, or intendants *(ancha si),* were charged with overseeing the civil administration. Below these intendants were the actual administrators. These included provincial governors and, on the next lower level, prefects *(fu),* whose positions were divided into several grades according to an area's size and importance. Below the prefects there were district magistrates (*xian* and *zhou,* also called subprefects), in charge of areas corresponding roughly in size to counties. The duties of these magistrates were catholic, for they were supposed to tend to virtually all aspects of the welfare of the people in their area. This was the lowest level of direct imperial rule (though there were some petty officials at levels below the district). Because the members of government working at the formal civil service level were so few, actual administration within the *yamen,* or local administrative headquarters, depended heavily on the clerical staff. Beyond the *yamen* walls control was in the hands of an officially sanctioned but locally staffed sub-bureaucracy.

The magistrate held open court on certain days of the month, when individuals could first bring forth their complaints or questions. All subjects of the emperor were under obligation to report incidents of rebellion, sedition, and treason.[101] Failure to denounce evildoers for these crimes could result in heavy punishments, sometimes even capital punishment. With respect to other offenses there was no duty to inform, although rewards were offered to encourage people to give information. It was the magistrate's duty to investigate all cases reported within the area of his jurisdiction, to apprehend suspects, and to bring them to justice—that is, to investigate and study the facts and decide under what section of the penal code the case should be entered and what punishment would be appropriate for the accused and any other persons concerned. If no section of the code exactly covered the case, the magistrate could resort to analogies and suggest relevant principles as expressed in a comparable case.[102]

For dealing with criminal cases, exact time limits were specified. Each case had to be disposed of within this period. Magistrates faced administrative punishments if they did not comply with the time limits. If a plaint proved to be unfounded, an unjustified accuser was liable to suffer the punishment that would have been meted out to the accused if convicted, and the magistrate himself was subject to administrative sanctions for any errors that he committed in applying the code. In consequence most individuals were very reluctant to become involved in court proceedings, and magistrates themselves were advised, in unofficial handbooks, to be cautious in accepting cases and to counsel parties to try to reconcile their differences without resorting to the court.

Cases were referred upward through a hierarchy of courts roughly corresponding to the state's administrative structure. Although minor punishments, such as various degrees of beating, could be administered locally, all cases requiring punishment more serious than beating with a bamboo stick (such as penal servitude or death) or confinement in the wooden cangue had to be referred to the next superior level in the hierarchy, that of the prefect or provincial governor, for rehearing. This complex procedure was known as "retry and pass on" *(shen quan)*. Depending on the severity of a case, a sentence was reviewed at various levels of the justice administration, reaching from the prefectural level to the provincial judge or overseer to the governor of the provinces, and perhaps all the way to the Board of Punishments and the emperor. At every level, the accused, the witnesses, and the evidence were all reexamined to determine whether the magistrate had conducted an adequate investigation and reached a reasonable sentence. All cases with sentences heavier than penal servitude were automatically forwarded for final scrutiny by the central judicial agencies and ultimately by the emperor himself. The prefect's or provincial governor's decision was final only in cases of penal servitude and in some exile cases.

Apart from capital cases, all cases beyond the competence of lower-level offices (meaning the lower court was unable to dispose of a case for whatever reason) and all cases judged by analogy were also routinely referred to the central judicial authorities. This level was composed of three chief legal bodies (called *sanfa si*): the Board of Punishments, the Court of Revision (Dali Si), and the Censorate (Ducha Yuan). At this highest level, the greatest care was still taken to see that the correct facts had been asserted. In its proceedings the Board of Punishments, together with the other bodies, was constantly alert to the dangers of collusion, deceit, and prevarication and to the risk that the lower tribunals had not been successful in unraveling the truth. After careful reexamination, the board, in cooperation with the other offices, might finally determine cases in which the punishment was exile, but all those in which the sentence was death were to be finally considered by the emperor himself.

Unsatisfied individuals could appeal to higher courts. A slight procedural distinction was made between cases requiring a ruling concerning personal affairs (marriage, property inheritance, and so on) and those involving prosecution for crimes—a difference not quite the same as the Western distinction between "civil" and "criminal." At the provincial level, cases of the "personal" category were referred to the provincial treasurer's office and went no further, whereas those of the "criminal" category went to the provincial judicial commissioner.

The complex justice administration in late imperial China was charged to meticulously enforce the regulations of the law code. In theory, law enforcement agencies and judges had little leeway in meticulously executing the code, although in practice magistrates used discretion in applying the code. The law code embodied the fundamentals of the late imperial system of justice. The comprehensive text of the code articulated all standards and norms and served the administration as the most important basis for its decisions.

The imperial Chinese codes resembled, in the words of William Jones, a "sort of giant grid on which any legally relevant act, such as eating another's melons, including all the ways of varying the basic fact pattern, such as the relationship between trespasser and owner, could be located."[103] The Great Qing Code (Da Qing Lüli) of 1740 was based on that of the Ming. The code had seven divisions and thirty subdivisions.[104] The first division was "Names and General Rules"; the other six divisions corresponded to the six principal departments of government: the civil service, military affairs, ritual affairs, judicial affairs, financial affairs, and public works. The sixth of the seven divisions had the heading "Laws Relating to the Board of Punishments" (xinglü). It contained statutes 254–423, which dealt with the various offenses and their corresponding punishments.

The code contained a total of 436 statutes (lü) and 1,049 substatutes (li). Approximately 30 percent to 40 percent of the statutes were retained unchanged from the Tang Code of 653, which in turn was closely modeled after the lost code of the Sui dynasty from 581. This might seem to suggest that imperial law was static and lacking vitality. However, a different picture emerges if one takes into account the important role of the numerous substatutes, which during the Qing were constantly added and deleted and which actually took priority when in conflict with *lü*. These substatutes were legal formulations that functioned as supplements to the basic *lü* and had their origin in imperial edicts or, more commonly, in individual legal judgments pronounced by the Board of Punishments and then confirmed by imperial endorsement. Apart from these, a vast web of administrative regulations and the use of analogy allowed for appreciable changes of the law as necessary to cope with the changes of society.

Yet while Chinese law was able to adapt to accommodate societal change, the similarities in structure and content across legal codes from the Tang to the Song point to a major trait of law in China. One of its main purposes was to preserve traditional moral values, as well as to maintain the existing social and political order. Over a period of more than a thousand years, the definitions of the severest crimes and the penalties attached to them did not undergo any dramatic change, and this continuity speaks of a literal legal conservatism. A similar attitude is of course embraced by other law codes worldwide, as the law has a tendency to serve as a stabilizing fixture in the midst of a world in constant flux.

In any society, the law is also a tool of the ruling elites that reflects their vision of the ideal social order. In China the law code embodied moral values related to the public order and to social and familial hierarchies. Other values, such as respect for life, leniency, benevolence or humanity, and repentance, were evident in the implementation of the law, but the centerpiece was the overarching hierarchical order—which clearly privileged senior over junior and male over female.[105] Consider, for example, the many articles on fornication in the code.[106] The code's main focus was on heterosexual intercourse outside of marriage, an act that was put under threat of punishment. The basic aim was to control men's access to women through the institution of marriage. It is no mystery why heterosexual acts would have concerned the Qing judiciary (or its predecessors): the defense of the patriarchal hierarchy was part of the larger, venerable project of upholding the familial and social order as means to preserving political order.[107]

Loyalty *(zhong)* to the emperor and the ruling dynasty was another central value that the Qing Code clearly intended to protect.[108] Neo-Confucian thought stressed the connection between the duty to show proper filial respect and the duty of the subject to be loyal. The failure to show loyalty was seen as a fundamental offense against the empire—a failure to perform what was a key duty of every subject. Such a transgression was understood as a crime against the achievements of social order and civilization. Some of the most severe punishments were indeed reserved for presumed acts of rebellion, sedition, or treason. Not only were those who had taken part in a plot put to death by slicing, but their family members, too (the closest male members), were punished by death, penal servitude, or banishment.[109] While under all dynasties these deeds attracted the greatest condemnation, the severity of the punishments was greatly increased under Qing law. The death penalty was extended to a wider class of people and the range of relatives selected for punishment was also greater.[110]

The criminal investigation process in late imperial China was inquisitorial, and the magistrate had the duty to ascertain the truth from the parties involved, witnesses, and the evidence. Testimony by witnesses and forensic examinations were the main components of the magistrate's truth-finding efforts.[111] Once the truth had been ascertained, the magistrate had to identify the relevant rules of the code (*lü* or *li*), apply them to the facts, and determine the correct punishment. His discretion in the process was, in theory, minimal. In practice, however, magistrates exercised a certain amount of discretion and there was debate over case decisions throughout the system.[112] The basic format of this initial process for criminal prosecution, consisting of careful investigation through oral inquisition and the application of law according to a publicly known set of rules, is not too far from the process conducted in early modern Europe at roughly the same time.[113] But there are a few peculiarities that reflect the specifics of the social and cultural world of imperial China.

In China, kinship and social status were essential elements in determining punishments.[114] While the law stipulated exact punishments for specific crimes, many sentences were increased or decreased depending on the status of the persons involved. This flexibility in sentencing was inherent in a social system characterized by differential treatment based social status.

Imperial Chinese law operated on the basis of status categories, and punishments were decided with reference to these categories. The particulars of status shaped how the nature of the crime was conceptualized and thus shaped presumptions about motive, intent, and the like. At the broadest level, this always led to consideration of who was "senior" and who was "junior" as measured by the individuals' positions within family, social-class, and administrative hierarchies. Persons who had to appear before a court were thus not treated alike. To begin with, they were divided into three ranks below the level of emperor: the privileged (officials, ex-officials, and literati), the commoners (ordinary free people), and the unfree (slaves). The criminal justice process also recognized the gradations of the kinship hierarchy.[115] When a criminal case came before the court, the first thing the magistrate ascertained was the precise family relationship (if any) between victim and offender. Other relationships were also considered, such as whether a case was being brought between a free person and an unfree person, or between two officials or an official and a commoner. Under the Qing, an additional legal category was introduced: the magistrate was called upon to consider the ethnic relationships involved, the most important one being that between Manchus and Chinese. Once such relationships had been determined, the magistrate had to descry which rule of the penal code was applicable to the precise (ethnic, social, familial) relationship in which the victim and offender stood.

Certain groups enjoyed legal privileges. Officials, for example, whether active or honorably retired, enjoyed exemptions with regard to government levies and some legal actions; the higher their rank, the more extensive their privileges.[116] Qing law conferred on all officials a procedural privilege that removed them from subjection to the ordinary legal process when they had committed a crime. It also overhauled the system of punishments available for officials and literati. Administrative punishments *(chu fen)* were imposed on officials for breaches of standard operating procedure, such as failures to meet deadlines or quotas (for solving criminal cases or collecting taxes) or concealment of information; only criminal acts, such as corruption, were punished with the legal sanctions. The administrative penalties included demotion in rank, transfer to a less desirable post, and monetary fines.[117]

Article 3 of the Qing Code mentioned the eight privileged classes that enjoyed special treatment.[118] These included officials, literati, members of the imperial family, and imperial subjects who had shown exemplary virtue, such as loyalty or chastity. Members of these groups were entitled to special consideration in the criminal justice system. For instance, they were exempted from torture. In the case that a member of a privileged group was sentenced, the magistrate had to forgo the exact punishments stipulated in the code, which could result in a significant reduction or even defeasance of the punishment. The idea behind this rule was to "forgive" those who had earned merit through their service to the empire. Imperial law explicitly recognized not only social and familial status but also moral status by explicitly rewarding those who had displayed extraordinary virtue.

As a result of these considerations of status, in cases involving injury, for instance, the severity of punishment varied according to the relationship between the parties concerned; an injury inflicted on a person of higher rank or seniority in the kinship hierarchy or official hierarchy carried a harsher penalty than injury to an equal or inferior person (there was no penalty at all if the injury was viewed as a legitimate exercise of discipline). An official who committed a crime was punished less harshly, if at all, than a commoner who committed the same crime. These distinctions, which were made throughout the criminal process, had far-reaching consequences. For any given offense, one person might be punished more heavily than another person, even when their offenses were apparently identical. The criminal justice process did not consider the criminal actions to be identical precisely because in each case the relationship between the offender and the victim was different. In sentencing, the magistrate would generally have to observe the principle that a senior who had committed a crime against a junior was punished less harshly than a junior who had committed a crime against a senior.

The underlying rationale for treating people differently according to their position in their family and society was that the specific form of behavior and social role appropriate to any person was determined by his or her position. Social order required that people adhere to their proper roles and maintain the corresponding relationships. Although unequal, these relationships also carried mutual responsibilities that would reward the subordination of the inferior to the superior. Ideally, the responsibility of superiors for inferiors mitigated the inherent inequalities of the law. In this view, social hierarchy and societal harmony were interrelated and interdependent. The law reflected these considerations and therefore tried to protect what were known as the Five Relationships (ruler-subject, father-son, husband-wife, elder brother–younger brother, elder friend–younger friend), which spelled out the different social roles and the hierarchical relationships between them.

Revisions of the Qing Code during the eighteenth century, however, increasingly emphasized the duty of juniors and diminished the obligation of seniors. This was particularly true in the case of husbands and wives: many of the revisions to the Qing Code effectively weakened the legal position of wives. The Qing's legal system, more than those of its predecessors, drew its legitimacy from the orthodox moral order of the values it embodied and from the consistent and unyielding application of the law.

Another important trait of the justice process in imperial China was the requirement that the accused person must confess his guilt. A confession served two purposes: it was supposed to establish an objective truth, which the magistrate had to uncover in the course of his investigations, and it also demonstrated to officials that the offender had started to understand his crime and was on the way to repenting.

In the criminal process in late imperial China, a confession was ordinarily required before a case could be closed, irrespective of the strength of evidence otherwise available to the magistrate.[119] Until the offender confessed, the magistrate was unable to pronounce a sentence. Since there were strict time limits for each case that the magistrate had to comply with or face administrative penalties, the use of coercion was a practical necessity in all cases in which the offender was not willing to confess and refused to admit guilt. To extract a confession, torture was legally permitted. One must consider the fact that legal punishment and legally authorized torture were described by the same word, *xing*.[120] This linguistic connection demonstrates the connection between torture and punishment in the criminal process. Like other legal punishments, torture was a sanctioned form of state violence.

If deemed necessary, torture was also applied to secondary suspects or witnesses. To elicit facts from recalcitrant parties, the magistrate was allowed to use the following treatments: twisting of ears; slapping or beating; pressing sticks *(jiagun)*, which were applied to the shins, ankles, or fingers; making the accused kneel on an iron chain; and head-squeezing bands. The pressing sticks were frequently used by magistrates: they painfully compressed the fingers, ankles, or shins and often brought on multiple, very painful fractures.[121] Beatings were imposed with small sticks or rods and were given on the soles of feet, the face, or the back.

However, while such treatment was allowed, there were rules in the code designed to prevent the uncontrolled application of legal torture and to keep it within legally defined boundaries. Torture could be used only after enough evidence had been gathered by the investigation. Limits were set on the amount of torture, the instruments that could be used, and the parts of the body that could be affected. As we have seen, members of certain groups (the elderly, the young, the disabled, the sick, pregnant women, and the eight privileged groups) were exempted from torture.

Although the law sanctioned the use of torture in principle, it was sensitive to the problems created by the abuse of power and the miscarriages of justice that could arise. The law also defined limits to this power and threatened to penalize those who transgressed the area of permissible violence. The application of unauthorized instruments and the killing of a prisoner as a result of the misadministration of torture were punishable acts. These regulations not only existed on paper but also were strictly enforced—as numerous examples in case collections prove.[122] Authorized and unauthorized officials were severely penalized for violating the regulations, and the scale of punishment for those offenses was high. There were also practical reasons that law enforcement agents were constantly admonished to exercise restraint when applying torture. Qing officials were well aware that the accused could make false confessions in order to shorten or avoid the torturous treatment. The Qianlong emperor therefore warned his officials that "confessions obtained by *jiagun* and cudgel are not necessarily entirely reliable."[123]

Since confession was also understood as an expression of repentance, a full confession made before the magistrate could lead to complete or partial exemption from punishment. Further, a person who voluntarily confessed to a crime before law enforcement officials became aware of it could be pardoned and go completely unpunished.[124] A full pardon was possible, however, only in cases in which the harmful consequences of the crime could be completely undone. Voluntary confession in homicide or injury cases was therefore not honored with exemption from or reduction of punishment, since the effects of these crimes were irreversible.

While by modern legal standards the court proceedings of imperial China may have been flawed, by virtue of the inherent inequities and the use of torture, an examination of case records reveals that for capital crimes the law was conscientiously and rationally applied in most cases. The elaborate and redundant procedures for adjudicating and sentencing for capital crimes bespeaks a serious concern for justice, a diligent search for truth, and a sincere regard for both victim and offender.

In every discussion of criminal justice procedures during the late imperial period, one has to keep in mind that many offenses were never adjudicated by the formal criminal justice system.[125] Instead, most were dealt with by unofficial mediators within the family, clan, village community, or guild. Local groups dispensed a wide range of punitive sanctions against offenders that included public censure, fines, ostracism, servitude, and corporal punishment, such as beatings.

In premodern Chinese society, the social group on which an individual depended for livelihood and emotional support could exercise enormous pressure for conformity. Such pressure was especially great on the local level—that is, in the neighborhood, the clan, and the family. The law recognized this special function of the local community, clan, and family and tried to integrate it into the system of criminal justice.

One of the most marked phenomena of law in premodern China was that parents were treated with extreme leniency for harm and injury inflicted on a child. In contrast, children were treated with great severity if they did harm to a parent. Under neo-Confucian influence, the concept of filial piety was interpreted as the almost absolute duty of the child to cause no harm or distress to a parent whatsoever. At the same time, filial piety also included the unquestioning obedience and submission of the child to the authority of the father. This paternal authority was formally acknowledged and respected by the law. The law also provided the household head with the means to enforce his authority even against resistance of his kin. In general, a household head was not violating the law by inflicting corporal punishment on an adult child who had ignored his instructions or committed a crime and thus brought shame on the family. In fact, a father was obliged to punish a child who had committed a crime. Even when this punishment was so severe that it caused injuries or the death of the child, the patriarch was not charged with a crime. The law even accepted that a father might intentionally kill a child as a penalty.[126] When a child scolded or injured his own parents, for example, his parents could kill him without fearing criminal charges. The punishments imposed by male household heads on members of their family were approved by society and explicitly authorized by the law.[127] The law also gave the patriarch the right to appeal to the magistrate for imposing punishments on his child on his behalf. In this case, the magistrate acted as agent through which the parental will was carried out.

The preconditions for the father's authority to punish were twofold: the child must have violated his duty of filial piety (that is, disobeyed the father's instructions) and the father must have given instructions with the intention to defend orthodox values and legal norms. The following case illustrates these points.[128] A son had committed theft. Upon learning about his son's crime, the father bound his son up with the help of a neighbor and then struck him with the back of an iron axe. The son screamed and rolled on the ground. The father then severed his son's leg muscles. Shortly thereafter the boy died of his wounds. The Board of Punishments found the father not guilty of murder because the son was a habitual thief and had disobeyed his father's instruction to cease stealing. But other instances in the case collections demonstrate that a father could not kill a child without justification, nor could he use excessive or unreasonable force. Much of Qing appellate practice was concerned with ensuring that hierarchical superiors did not baselessly and capriciously abuse their status power.

Other provisions that acknowledged and strengthened the families' role in controlling deviant behavior and crime were related to confession, accusation, and mutual concealment.[129] The Qing law stipulated that family members were entitled to conceal offenses committed by one of the family.[130] It also barred family members from bringing forth criminal charges against each other or accusing each other before the magistrate (except in cases of physical injury or the wrongful taking of property). If a junior relative put forward accusations against a senior relative, he was penalized even when the accusations proved correct. These legal provisions put the family almost outside the reach of the formal criminal justice apparatus, since they effectively denied the justice agencies the opportunity to detect and punish many crimes committed within the privacy of the family. At the same time, the state made to sure to retain its primacy and control over the family in important issues concerning state security, as illustrated by the law providing that the one time a son could not conceal his father's crime was if the father had committed or was implicated in an act of rebellion. The legal protections granted the family, together with the broad leeway given to male heads of household, clearly demonstrate how the law effectively protected the patriarchic hierarchy within the confines of the household.[131]

There is another dimension to the role of the family in the penal system that deserves our attention. An individual could be influenced to stay within the law by the knowledge that actions would be taken not only against himself but also against his family. During the Song dynasty, for example, a system was introduced under which a sign was nailed on the gate where the family of a criminal lived.[132] Chinese law also allowed collective prosecution, meaning family members and relatives could be punished for offenses committed by another member of the family.[133] The extension of punishment to relatives was frequently imposed for crimes of rebellion or sedition.[134] It was also possible for collective responsibility—and collective punishment—to be extended to neighbors.

It is a significant feature of criminal justice in late imperial China that several extrajudicial and informal institutions, including the family, carried out functions of crime control and the administration of justice. The goals were, on the one hand, to put pressure on members of the community to comply with the norms promoted by the state and, on the other hand, to expedite pretrial mediation and local reconciliation. Both goals, when met, allowed the penal apparatus to function as a last resort.

As our narrative approaches the nineteenth century and the modern period, one has to be mindful of the growing signs of distress and crisis within the imperial criminal justice system. China's rising population and an increasingly commercialized economy not only fueled violent disputes but also created incentives to refine the criminal justice process. Consequently, local magistrates began demonstrating a greater degree of flexibility, relying not only on law but also on local custom and culture.[135] This sort of flexibility was possible in civil cases, which, unlike capital crimes, were not automatically reviewed at higher levels of administration. Local officials could also enlist the assistance of the local community in civil matters. This common form of dispute resolution, in which cases were settled by a process that combined informal community mediation and magisterial opinion, has been dubbed the "third realm" of Qing civil justice.[136] Local magistrates increasingly relied on assistance from the community, neighbors, family, and lineages to resolve disputes. Numerous examples can be cited that indicate an official willingness to respect local customs. Mutually acceptable solutions were more valued than adherence to the letter of the law.

But in the turbulent economic environment of nineteenth-century China, even the best efforts of the most innovative local magistrate were not sufficient to forestall violence when the ethical foundations of society were being shattered. In the nineteenth century, the pauperization of the rural population, unresolved land disputes, and general dissent broke out into the open and triggered large-scale rebellions such as the Taiping Uprising (1851–1864), a Christianity-inspired rebellion that aimed at establishing the

Heavenly Kingdom of Great Peace, or Taiping. The legal system failed to contain many everyday conflicts and became dysfunctional. It also was no longer believed to operate in a fair and impartial fashion, and people decided to take their affairs in their own hands. The rebels favored revenge and lynch-mob justice. And the state responded with mass executions. At the end of the century, a deep crisis was tangible within the imperial justice administration, and calls for reform were growing louder.

Law and Moral Order in Imperial China

The criminal justice system in imperial China was founded on the principal penological theory that to punish was to deter and to renew. Hence two main purposes of criminal justice stand out. On the one hand, the system was built on the belief that an offender could redeem himself by enduring the hardships of legal punishment (with the exception of the death penalty), and that once redemption had been achieved he could be reintegrated into society. On the other hand, the publicly executed physical punishments were clearly intended to deter potential criminals and onlookers—that is, to secure public order and protect society from criminal violence by way of instilling a carefully calibrated fear of punishment.

The punishments carried out in imperial China were largely reversible and relatively bloodless, marked by the intention to carefully refine and graduate the use of state violence. Punishments such as beating, tattooing, the cangue, penal servitude, and exile, which were applied in the late imperial period, were conceived not as much as spectacles of suffering as procedures for inducing in the offender a sense of shame and repentance. This notion was coupled with the belief that an offender might "renew himself." When certain members of the community were not socialized to be good by way of education and moral instruction, then they needed to be instilled with shame and fear to make them refrain from doing evil in the future. This view also implied a recognition that the society had failed in preventing these infractions.

The determination of the right degree of punishment was the central task of criminal justice. Significantly enough, the law code opened with a definition of the Five Punishments and their degrees. To be appropriate, punishments had to fit with the circumstances—the crime that was committed and the harm that was done to society and the state. The imposition of punishments in this system was based on a sophisticated and elaborate criminal justice process laid out in the numerous and complicated provisions of the law code. Every human act that the code recognized was linked with a punishment.[137] The code represented the social world as an interwoven web of punishable actions, and all legally significant behavior was to be translated into an appropriate measure of punishment. The court hearings had to ascertain whether a violation was the result of the offender's fault and determine the underlying degree of intent. The punishments were then calculated and graded in accordance with the degree of that fault.

Many rules of the penal code were designed to enforce behavior deemed by Confucian orthodoxy to be essential for the maintenance and proper functioning of the central family and social relationships. The penal codes were concerned with ensuring that the subjects of the emperor complied with the behavior inherent in the fundamental human roles expressed in the Three Bonds, which included the father-and-son (or, more generally, parent-and-child) and husband-and-wife relationships that structured the family. The dominant philosophy in traditional China was that a society functioned properly only when its members behaved in accordance with their social roles, and that the state had an obligation to enforce the underlying moral prescriptions by punishing those who behaved improperly. There was a fundamental congruence for the Confucians between legal rules and accepted standards of behavior, so that it is difficult to decide where to draw the line between law and morality in imperial China.

The penal codes also reinforced the social divisions and hierarchies in imperial society by treating offenses committed between members of different social classes in a discriminatory fashion. This was most obvious in connection with the actions of unfree persons in relation to their masters and the masters' relatives, as well as in relation to the free population, but there was also discrimination in favor of officials in relation to ordinary people. Finally there was discrimination in favor of the male head of household in relation to younger kin and female kin. It is easy to see criminal justice in imperial China as a system in which social status and moral judgments constitute the basis of the law. The system in China produced a ranking of legally significant or punishable acts according to how morally reprehensible they were and according to the social status of the parties involved.

Through a complex system of reviews, balances, and double checks, the

Board of Punishment and the emperor exercised fairly stringent control over the criminal justice system. The supremacy of civil rule and the law codes protected the individual against misuse and arbitrary abuse by local echelons of the bureaucracy. The clearest indication of the system's concern for justice is seen in its treatment of officials who arbitrarily yielded their power or mistreated innocents. Officials were punished for the wrongful treatment of prisoners or offenders not necessarily because the convicts were seen as having rights, but because the state intended to stop officials from exceeding their proper authority. The decisions and controls of the Board of Punishments were, at a minimum, clearly designed to prevent official malfeasance, and as a result they also in effect protected the innocent from unimpeded government encroachments.

When dealing with the history of criminal justice in late imperial China, and especially with an eye toward twentieth-century developments, one also has to bear in mind the small size and limited capacity of the imperial law enforcement agencies. The formal criminal justice system in imperial China, in terms of the number of officials and the many tasks they had to perform, was simply too small and too thinly spread to administer justice in an intensive manner. It had to rely to a large extent on informal agencies and extrajudicial mechanisms. In policing society, the dynasty relied heavily on local leaders and neighborhood organizations. And due to its relatively small size, the imperial criminal justice apparatus was incapable of holding, processing, and punishing criminals in large numbers.

At the center of this whole system stood the emperor, who directed his complex administration and ruled his vast empire through the interwoven text of the law code. Every subject was expected to fulfill his duties as assigned by the emperor and reflected in the code. All human activity had to be carried on so as to fit into this scheme for directing society. When a subject failed, the code prescribed in detail the action that was to be taken. Consequently, the law took notice of human activity only when it affected the state's or the emperor's interests. Imperial sovereignty also found expression in acts of clemency and efforts at moderation. By offering a reprieve to offenders who had been condemned to death by due process of law, for instance, the sovereign demonstrated that he was, in the end, above the law. While the imperial laws were promulgated to make sure that the interests of the emperor and the state were advanced, the interests of the individuals were also protected against government intrusion and abuse.

When our discussion enters the twentieth century in the following chapter, we will quickly discover how this connection was reversed. The proclaimed intention of twentieth-century governments in China, to recognize the individual and the individual's rights, frequently led to increased government intrusion into spheres and domains that the imperial system had left untouched.

2

THE PRISON REGIME

Republican China

I N T H E F I R S T half of the twentieth century, Chinese governments set out to overhaul and transform the way social control and crime prevention were managed in Chinese society. The significance of these efforts can hardly be overstated. Crossing all political divides during the first fifty years of the twentieth century, the legal reforms initiated in the last years of the Qing were continued by the Republican governments, despite practical obstacles and organizational challenges. As a result, many conflicts, disputes, and crimes came to be handled in ways that differed from the practices of the nineteenth century. For better or for worse, all Chinese citizens, especially those in urban areas, were affected by the unrelenting emergence of a criminal justice state in China.

Two broad themes loom large in the legal reforms. The first is the expansion of the criminal justice apparatus deeper into society. By installing new courts, police forces, and procurators (state or public prosecutors), the state tried to centralize functions that used to be the task of local bodies and bring them under its own direct and unmediated control. The second theme is that of norm setting. Parallel to its vigorous outreach into society, the state used criminal and penal laws to define and enforce a new set of state-sponsored social values. The Chinese criminal justice state increasingly began to rely on legal definitions of values and norms in order to carefully guard and enhance its authority. The overall goal was undisputed: to erect a viable and durable social order flexible enough to accommodate processes of industrialization and commercialization, yet at the same time powerful and binding enough to enable the state to enlist support and mobilize the population in times of crisis.

Although considerable resources were committed to reforming the system, the nature of the state's expansion into society remained limited. The new Republic of China quickly realized that its criminal justice operations depended just as much on local elites as did the Qing's, and in many cases it had little choice but to leave the mediating functions to traditional local bodies. Similarly, in terms of norm setting, the Republic still had to accommodate Qing criminal law and the traditional values that remained in place especially in rural areas.

The strategies and plans in play for reforming criminal justice came into clear focus in the Republican prisons. A new form of state punishment was crystallized in the prisons' high stone walls, watchtowers, iron gates, and cagelike grilles. From the very beginning, Chinese officials and jurists found imprisonment compelling because it promised to pursue both incapacitation and rehabilitation. Consequently the punishment of imprisonment would allow the state to accumulate moral capital and to discipline inmates of the prison. The state could appear benign and authoritarian at the same time. Such considerations led Chinese governments to invest heavily in the establishment and expansion of new prisons.

Just as the legal reforms were ambitious but only partly successful, the Republican prisons never lived up to their promises either. Not only did the prison system fail to carry out its mission of clean punishment and effective rehabilitation, but in the public realm it also quickly degenerated into a cipher for violence and political arbitrariness. Instead of delivering moral capital to the Republican government, the prisons damaged its reputation and its modernization agenda. Beginning in the late 1920s and early 1930s, a flood of books and articles depicted the prison as a place of cruelty, violence, and alienation. The dark and dirty prison cell was drawn as a miniature battlefield where the socially disadvantaged groups of Chinese society united and trained to overthrow the whole Republican system. The prison was originally intended to be the hallmark of the criminal justice state in China: it would carry out punishments humanely, though with firm consequences. Instead, it became a symbol for discontent and revolution.

The Transformation of Criminal Justice in the Republican Period

In the twentieth century the Chinese legal system went through a period of a far-reaching change. Criminal justice, in particular, was a field in which the change was fast and visible. The following sections analyze the shifts in criminal justice within four different frameworks. The legal system, global developments in criminal justice and diplomatic pressure exercised by foreign powers, the sprawl of new social and legal theories, and, finally, the efforts of institution building all worked to reshape the system of Chinese criminal justice.

The development of a new legal system in the first half of the twentieth century was a complicated and daunting task for all the governments involved. Despite obvious difficulties, and hindrances like a lack of financial resources and the existence of only a small legal profession, legal reform was high on the agenda of every government administration in the Republican period. The construction of judicial infrastructure and the training of legal professionals were, together, seen as indispensable prerequisites for a successful overhaul of the Chinese state and society.[1]

The process of legal reform was conducted in three phases. In the last ten years of its rule (1901–1911), the Qing laid the foundations for reform by producing drafts for important new laws. The Beiyang government (1912–1927)—otherwise noted in Nationalist Chinese historiography for having failed to keep China united—contributed considerably to the formation of the new legal system with a very proactive body of legislation based on the revised Qing texts. And before the Second World War, the Guomindang (GMD) government further consolidated and extended the new legal system.

It was under the so-called New Policy *(xinzheng)* after 1900 that an overhaul of the imperial system of criminal justice was finally initiated, after a lengthy period of debate. In 1902 an Office for the Revision of Law (Xiuding Falü Guan) was established. Two officials who had a reputation as specialists in legal matters, Shen Jiaben and Wu Tingfang, were appointed as ministers and codirectors.[2] The office had three main tasks: to study and translate important Western texts on legal thinking and legislation; to evaluate the Chinese legal tradition in comparison with that of the West; and to draft new laws based on a synthesis of Western law and Chinese tradition. A few years later, the Qing government started to overhaul the institutional structure. A Judicial Ministry was created in September 1906 to replace the old Board of Punishment, and with the same edict the Imperial Supreme Court was established.[3]

Shen Jiaben and Wu Tingfang quickly moved forward with an ambitious reform program. Altogether twenty-six translations from foreign countries were published, including one text on penology. An examination of foreign law was conducted by sending study delegations to various countries. Members of these missions not only collected written law and sought discussions with leading legal scholars but also made visits to police offices, procurators, courts, and prisons.[4]

The reformers started to introduce the separation of civil and criminal law.[5] The office drafted separate criminal and civil codes as well as rules of criminal and civil procedure. Reformers also undertook a differentiation within the body of criminal law. Shen argued for a formal division between criminal law, criminal procedural law, and penal law. For Shen, all three branches of criminal law were autonomous and equally important. Therefore, the office drafted a "New Criminal Law of the Great Qing" and a "Draft of a Procedural Law for Criminal Matters of the Great Qing" (Da Qing Xingshi Susonglü Cao'an). The draft of the criminal code, completed in 1908, was based on the Japanese criminal code, which in turn owed its inspiration to the German code. After lengthy discussions, it finally went into effect in 1910.

The execution of sentences and legal punishments was another main area of the reforms. Between 1905 and 1907 several leading officials, including Shen Jiaben, Wu Tingfang, Zhang Zhidong, Liu Kunyi, and others, proposed the abolition of all Five Punishments listed in the old Qing Code, one by one. In 1905 such physical penalties as torture, slow slicing, the public exhibition of heads, the beheading of corpses, and the penalty of tattooing were abolished.[6] In the same year, other physical punishments, like flogging, were replaced with fines. The concept of collective responsibility was also abolished. The newly drafted criminal code limited punishments to three basic forms: fines, imprisonment, and the death penalty. Institutional confinement became the main form of punishment for most offenses. Within a very short period of time the public display of painful punishments disappeared. Punishing offenders now became a task for trained experts, to be practiced in specialized institutions removed from the public eye. The death penalty, too, was no longer to be carried out in public but only in the isolation of a prison.[7] The method of execution was strangulation. Shooting was permissible under the law for the suppression of robbery, insurgency, and brigandage.

A prison law (Da Qing Jianyulü Cao'an) was drafted in the final years of the Qing, starting in 1908. Shen Jiaben wrote: "The state has to be organized with the help of law, this is also true for the prison."[8] This first Chinese prison law had twelve sections and 240 articles. It never came into effect because of the 1911 revolution, but like many other laws drafted in the late Qing period, it served as a basis for later legislation.

After 1911 the Beiyang government inherited the task of legal reform from its predecessor. It was particularly urgent to get on with legal reforms after the demise of the Qing, because law and justice would provide the new republic with a viable organizational and moral basis. Despite many political changes and numerous different administrations, the new judiciary system offered remarkable institutional stability and continuity. There was considerable consistency in administrative structures, institutions, and personnel as well as in basic legal principles and discourses. The need to continue the reforms was widely accepted not only under different conditions but also in difficult and unpredictable political circumstances.

Under the Chinese Republic a new commission was created for carrying out the law reforms. Like its predecessor, the Commission for the Revision of Law Codification was charged with revising the laws.[9] A provisional criminal code was promulgated on March 19, 1912. The new government wanted to be internationally recognized as the legitimate government of China, and the provisional code was a signal to the international community that China intended to proceed with the reforms started under the Qing. This first draft was admitted by the Yuan Shikai government to be defective and imprecise; therefore work on the provisional law was restarted immediately after promulgation. Two revisions were made public in 1915 and 1919 that were supposed to remedy the most obvious shortcomings.

The Beiyang government was also actively pursuing new legislation for the administration of the prisons. The law, titled Prison Regulations of the Republic of China (Zhonghua Minguo Jianyu Guize), went into effect in December 1913. It was based on a draft prison law written during the last years of the Qing dynasty and finished in 1910.[10] The revision of 1913 was completed by Wang Yuanzeng, warden of the Beijing First Prison.[11] It placed all prisons under the control of the Ministry of Justice (Article 1). The law also introduced a new concept: it explicitly recognized the basic rights of prisoners. When dissatisfied with treatment or punishments received in prison, a prisoner could appeal to the office in charge (Article 8). Prisoners who strictly obeyed regulations could be given additional visiting rights, monetary rewards, or additional food. Prisoners who violated regulations would be punished by reprimands, the suspension of privileges for writing and receiving letters, a reduction in food, the suspension of physical exercise, confinement in a dark cell, or the reduction of monetary rewards. The law also stipulated that punishment should end once the prisoner showed satisfactory signs of repentance. Conditional release would be granted to prisoners with sufficient evidence of correction.[12] The law also contained detailed rules and regulations for prison work, instruction, and the recruitment and training of prison personnel. A few years later the administration introduced a unified naming system for all prisons and detention centers.[13]

In 1928 China was nominally unified, although there were large areas that were still controlled by local warlords. Against this backdrop, the new Guomindang government, and above all its leader Chiang Kai-shek, aspired to create a strong state in which law would serve as a powerful tool for completing the Nationalist project of unification and centralization. Hence law and criminal justice remained high on the agenda of the government in Nanjing. In general the Nationalists adopted all major legislation from their predecessors in the Beiyang government, but tried to modify and revise the laws to bring them in line with the new political and constitutional order. A revision of the prison law was adopted in 1928 and remained in effect, with only a few modifications, until 1949.[14] A modified version of the criminal code was made public in 1928, too, passed by the Legislative Yuan, together with new law for criminal procedure. Both had in substance been drafted by the Beiyang government, but the new government in Nanjing believed that they needed to be updated. Intense discussion accompanied further work on these codes in the 1930s. Some officials, members of parliaments, and scholars expressed reservations about the ways in which the new criminal code threatened to subvert the core moral values of Chinese culture— in particular the legal authority of the head of the household.[15] After four years, a new criminal law code was promulgated on January 1, 1935. Revised criminal procedures followed one year later.

The system of punishments in the criminal codes of the Nanjing government, while based on that of the Beiyang government, was much more elaborate. Altogether five main punishments *(zhuxing)* and two accessory punishments *(congxing)* were provided for in the code.[16] The main punishments were the death penalty *(sixing)*, imprisonment for life *(wuqi tuxing)*, imprisonment for a definite period *(youqi tuxing)*, detention with forced labor *(juyi)*,[17] and fines. Detention (up to two months) and imprisonment for a definite period (two months to fifteen years) were to be carried out in a prison. The two accessory punishments were confiscation of property *(moshou)* and deprivation of civil rights *(chiduo gongquan)*. Three of the punishments listed in the code consisted of custody *(ziyou xing)*. Two punishments were property punishments *(caichan xing)*. The death penalty was called life punishment *(shengming xing)*, and deprivation of rights passed for competence punishment *(nengli xing)*.

It is worth considering the nature and logic of these punishments. All punitive actions listed in the Chinese criminal code of 1935 basically involved the suspension of fundamental liberties, from suspension of the liberty to move freely, suspension of the liberty to possess and enjoy assets unconditionally, and suspension of the liberty to participate fully in public affairs to the ultimate and indefinite suspension of the most fundamental liberty—life itself. Punishment had indeed become, in the words of Michel Foucault, an "economy of suspended rights."[18] This was a far-reaching change that affected not only the realm of law but also society and culture: in administering society, the state now exercised power by granting or taking away liberties. Liberty or freedom thus became a valuable asset, and at the same time it could be limited or revoked entirely by state authorities. Apart from liberties, individuals could also be dispossessed of political participation and property if rules or regulations were violated. The state was thus not only setting norms and prescribing behavior but also drawing fault lines between decent citizens, who enjoyed full rights and liberties, and those who played away their legal entitlements. When China set out to establish a constitutional state, the borders and limits of the new social order were drawn at the same time. The state reserved for itself the power to define those lines and thus to decide who had access to and affiliation with the new order. Access to citizenship was treated as a revocable privilege, subject to the discretion of the state.

In 1935 a newly drafted prison law (Jianyufa Cao'an) was circulated. It introduced the so-called Accumulation and Progress System (Leijin Zhi) for inmates sentenced to shorter terms of imprisonment.[19] According to this system prisoners received daily points for their behavior. On the basis of point accumulation, a prisoner would proceed from the lowest level to higher levels and finally become eligible for conditional release or parole. Whereas the 1935 prison law still adhered to "transformation through education" *(jiaohua)* as the basic principle of imprisonment, the education component was interpreted differently. It now entailed less religious or moral instruction than basic intellectual education and vocational training.

After the Second World War, the GMD government reissued several regulations for prisons and detention facilities. In January 1946 a comprehensive Law for the Execution of Prison Punishments (Jianyu Xingxing Fa) was passed, together with the Prison Statutes (Jianyu Tiaoli) that governed more administrative aspects of the prison.[20] Both sets of legislation synthesized several different laws and regulations concerning imprisonment in Republican China, by and large following the principles laid out in earlier legislation. Among the innovations was the nationwide introduction of the Accumulation and Progress System, now called Accumulation and Progress Handling (Leijin Chuyu). This system, along with instruction and vocational training, formed the core of the Chinese prison regime. With the scarcity of resources after World War II, prison administrators also looked for ways to turn the prisons into profitable enterprises. Consequently productive work and prison labor were emphasized as well.

Apart from criminal law codes, other legal regulations also imposed state punishments. In 1928, a Law for the Punishment of Police Offenses of the Republic of China was promulgated. It laid out punishments for a multitude of petty offenses, and included fines and short-term detention in a police detention center. The punishments were to be imposed by the police as administrative sanctions. There was no criminal process conducted.[21] In a similar way, the Emergency Law on Crimes Endangering the Republic (Weihai Minguo Jinji Zhizui Fa) from the 1930s and the Law on Crimes Endangering the State (Weihai Mingguo Zhizui Fa) provided the basis for arrests and detentions without the involvement of the judiciary.[22] The latter laws, in particular, demonstrate that the GMD government increasingly appropriated extrajudicial powers. It was inclined to use the declaration of a state of emergency for suspending regular criminal justice operations.

With respect to the establishment of a new criminal justice system, one certainly has to be mindful of the fact that the institution of new agencies and laws did not automatically end all earlier legal practices. During an extended period of transition in the 1910s and 1920s, old and new laws appear to have coexisted, and both were applied in criminal proceedings. The result was an unresolved and often confusing set of legal practices. The new laws sometimes criminalized formerly noncriminal behavior, such as opium consumption. In fact, drug use represented one of the most bifurcated spheres of behavior in the law. Another source of confusion was the fact that certain traditions of imperial law continued to hold sway. Throughout the Republican period, for example, adultery continued to be prosecuted as an offense against the marital and familial order.[23] Other examples of this may be seen in sentencing: in the 1928 criminal code, heavier punishments were still handed down for crimes against parents or seniors and for the murder of a lineal ascendant relative.[24] In the 1935 code, punishments could still be lessened if an offender offered "admission of guilt" (section 62). But in other cases, as when the Beijing Supreme Court pronounced the decriminalization of "a person who has been seduced," the new principles triumphed over old customs.[25] An important modification regarding adultery was made in the 1935 code: to show its commitment to equal rights for women, the GMD government made adultery punishable for both women and men (section 239).[26]

There was, in short, constant conflict between traditions and new concepts. The legislative bodies were regularly bound up in long and winding debates about individual laws and single provisions. Questions of criminality and punishment constantly exposed growing divisions between the traditional norms dominant in the society and the new legal standards that were to a considerable extent informed by foreign legal traditions. Definitions of some offenses as enacted by the modernizing state departed from prevailing legal customs, for example regarding acts of revenge and feuds, filial behavior, marriage practices, and the authority of the head of the family to impose punishments on younger family members. This predicament often resulted in a lack of mandatory criteria for the interpretation of the laws by police, procurators, and judges.

Overall the development of criminal law and punishment in the Chinese Republic can be characterized by a general and continuous effort to redirect the focus of criminal justice away from the crime and toward the criminal.[27] In imperial China the criminal act itself was the actual object of criminal law, and much effort was devoted to assuring that the punishment fit the crime. In the criminal laws of the Republic more emphasis was placed on the individual perpetrator. Republican law maintained that the punishment should be adapted to the specific condition of the individual criminal. This principle was called the "individualization of punishment."[28]

Recognizing the importance of the specifics of the individual case, all new versions of the criminal code acknowledged individual mitigating circumstances (see, for example, section 62 of the 1919 criminal law and section 59 of the 1935 criminal law). Hence, the criminal codes provided judges with ample scope for exercising discretion in sentencing. The judge was directed, before passing sentence, to consider not only the state of the offender's mind and his motives but also his past conduct, general intelligence, the conditions of his upbringing, and his conduct subsequent to the offense and his arrest.

The aforementioned legal reforms were driven by modern China's overwhelming impulse to join the world on equal terms. As William Kirby has pointed out, a defining characteristic of modern China is not only its rise as a recognized and independent nation-state but also its simultaneous incorporation into global systems.[29] Whether one speaks of intellectual, political, economic, or cultural trends, China's participation on an international level grew considerably over the course of the twentieth century. This is perhaps nowhere more visible than in the field of modern Chinese law. The Chinese Republic's new legal system and its new criminal laws were carefully modeled on German and Japanese prototypes. By adopting international standards, the Chinese hoped to satisfy international requirements for recognition and hence to rid themselves of extraterritorial interference. Western-inspired prison reforms were also a central part of the internal effort to strengthen the Chinese state by deploying foreign models.[30] Given this view, a high priority was placed on the creation of a new criminal justice system.

China had come into contact with Western and Japanese criminal justice in several ways, most directly through the overseas travels of Chinese envoys on diplomatic missions during which studies of law and criminal justice were conducted.[31] These travelers wrote reports about their visits and praised the social benefits and advantages of the criminal justice states they observed. Li Gui, for instance, conveyed the goal of rehabilitation in the familiar Confucian language of self-cultivation. He used the phrase "repenting the crime and reverting to the good" (*huizui qianshan*) to describe the mission of the prisons he observed. Wang Tao described European prisons, which in his view successfully addressed the need to educate the criminal and to provide him with vocational training.

Another way in which new criminal justice practices entered China was through the various foreign trade and missionary settlements. A fast-growing number of merchants, missionaries, diplomats, and specialists were settling in those areas under foreign administration in the treaty ports along the China coast. Increased travel and interactions with outsiders brought new economic opportunities, but also opportunities for conflict between foreigners and their Chinese counterparts.

During the period of the Canton system of trade from the 1750s to the Opium War, when contacts between foreign merchants and the Chinese were carefully controlled, any incident involving the death of a Chinese person at the hands of a foreigner, accidentally or otherwise, produced intense conflict. Qing authorities would cut off trade to force the surrender of the accused for trial, and for their part, foreigners would use a variety of tactics to avoid the prosecution of their nationals in Chinese courts, where they believed there would be little attention paid to determining the actual guilt or innocence of the accused. Westerners claimed the criminal process in China was arbitrary and that the punishments employed were barbaric and unacceptable for Europeans. Descriptions of cruel and bloody mutilating punishments appeared frequently in Western reports and in travel writing.[32] The conflicts became a powerful political issue when Westerners in China, with the support of their respective governments, rejected Chinese jurisdiction in such disputes. Their arguments served to justify demands that China cede its sovereignty in all legal matters concerning foreigners.

Extraterritoriality—the right of foreign consuls in China to retain legal jurisdiction over their own subjects—was established in the treaties resulting from Britain's victories in the Opium War (1839–1842) and the Arrow War (or Second Opium War, 1856–1860). Initially Chinese officials agreed that the "barbarians," who spoke different languages and had different customs, should be allowed to govern themselves in the enclaves granted to them for temporary settlement. For many centuries this strategy toward foreign communities had been applied by the Chinese emperors, with great success.[33] It provided relative stability and at the same time allowed for limited interactions between Chinese and foreign communities. As the nineteenth century wore on, however, Chinese officials were confronted with the fact that this very strategy led not to stability but to a considerable loss of sovereignty and authority. Extraterritoriality in the case of Western merchants and missionaries, who were backed by their governments, had the effect of insulating them from the reach of the Chinese government in terms of both person and property. Missionaries, for instance, could use their extraterritorial privilege to protect communities of Chinese Christians and thereby constantly question and overturn Chinese jurisdiction. The imperial archives contain numerous files concerning conflicts between Chinese and Western merchants, as well. Foreign businesses operating in China could achieve protection from Chinese claims by invoking extraterritoriality.[34] As applied in the foreign-dominated enclaves and the so-called spheres of influence, extraterritoriality became a powerful tool because it made foreign merchants and missionaries—and to some extent their Chinese employees, converts, and hangers-on—immune to Chinese authority.

This development was accompanied by the spread of Western jurisdiction and new Western forms of punishment employed in foreign-dominated trading enclaves along the coast.[35] The Chinese population living in the various concessions and leaseholds found itself completely or partly under foreign jurisdiction. The steady influx of foreign legal thinking and legal practice contributed to the rise of an alternative legal system to which foreigners, Chinese in the foreign-dominated enclaves, and Chinese Christians could resort. Since the justification for this development was the Western assumption that the whole criminal process in China was unjust and corrupt, the very existence of this alternative structure dealt Chinese authority a severe blow.

The granting of extraterritoriality in the treaties of 1840 and 1860 following the Opium Wars caused many scholars and officials in China to undertake a critical examination of the imperial judicial system.[36] They started to use arguments similar to the ones employed by foreign diplomats. For the first time in the field of law, Chinese intellectuals advocated global standards and brought international perspectives to bear on China. They proposed to abolish corporal punishments, to improve conditions of the prisons, and to replace penal servitude with custodial sentences, in order to obtain moral and political equity with foreign powers. A significant turning point was reached when Britain, the United States, and Japan in the trade treaties of 1902 and 1903 offered to abolish extraterritoriality in exchange for legal reforms to be carried out by the Chinese empire. This promise gave China a further strong incentive to undertake reforms in the realm of criminal justice. Not only would this allow a full restitution of Chinese authority, but it would also help to curb conflicts between Chinese and Western citizens in the coastal enclaves.

Both the commitment to reform the legal system and the scope of the reform were clearly related to international pressure and criticism. An explicit recognition of this criticism can be noted in many documents calling for legal reform.[37] Shen Jiaben, for example, proposed in a memorandum dated May 15, 1904: "The criminal law of the Western nations used to be crueler than the Chinese criminal law. Only within the last hundred years Western law became mitigated because of the contribution of Western jurisprudence. . . . Now the rigorous Chinese law is seen by Westerners as being inhumane. . . . Instead of upholding our traditional law and giving the foreigners a pretext, we should study the law of the foreign countries and implement changes."[38] Many Qing officials and reformers held the view that only an end to extraterritoriality could clear the way for reestablishing the authority of the Chinese state and consolidating Chinese society. The adoption of Western legal practices was a condition for the attainment of that goal.

Like its imperial predecessor, the government of the Republic of China viewed the revocation of extraterritoriality and the nullification of the "unequal treaties" as preconditions for gaining full sovereignty. After the May Fourth Movement—student demonstrations on May 4, 1919, in protest against the unfair terms of the Treaty of Versailles—the rising sentiment of nationalism further propelled the government to follow any policy that pursued the establishment of full equality with the West. Chinese officials were fully aware of the West's critical view and wanted to prove, now more than ever, that China in the modern guise of the Republic was able to establish and maintain a penal regime that was civilized, modern, and effective. While the Versailles Conference of 1919 brought no progress on the issue of extraterritoriality, which was so important for China, the whole problem came to renewed public attention on the occasion of the 1921 Washington Conference on Limitation of Armaments in East Asia. The Chinese delegate Wang Chonghui argued in his address that China had striven to bring its judicial system into accordance with that of the Western states. In regard to extraterritoriality, he remarked that this "injury to Chinese sovereignty is regarded as a national humiliation (guo chi) by the Chinese people."[39] The Chinese delegation requested, therefore, that "immediately, or as soon as circumstances will permit, existing limitations upon China's political, jurisdictional and administrative freedom of action are to be removed."[40] But as in the 1902 and 1903 trade treaties mentioned above, China obtained only the vague assurance that the Western powers would relinquish, "either progressively or otherwise," their right of extraterritoriality when they had ascertained the success of judicial and legal reforms carried out in China. For this purpose a commission was sent to China with the task of investigating the conditions of courts, procurators, and prisons and delivering a detailed report that would serve as basis for deciding whether to give up extraterritorial rights in China.[41] Since China strove to end extraterritoriality for political, economic, and social reasons, it had no choice but to adopt global standards, including those for criminal and penal law. When determining concrete steps and laws in its reforms, China had to be aware that all legislation and institutional innovations would later be examined by Western powers.

In 1933 Zhao Chen wrote in the preface to his book on prison science that the conditions in China's prisons had served as a pretext for the Western powers to maintain extraterritoriality.[42] He expressed the hope, therefore, that his book would contribute to Chinese prison reform and that this would soon lead to the end of extraterritoriality. Thus in the mid-1930s the wish to bring an end to extraterritoriality still formed a major incentive for the reform of criminal justice in China.[43]

Apart from Western criticism there was also growing domestic dissatisfaction with the penal practices of the nineteenth century, and this formed another strong impetus for reform. One concern of reformers was the conditions inside the Chinese jails. Officials noted that conditions in the jails were miserable, with many inmates suffering from disease, negligence, or maltreatment.[44] There is also evidence that incarceration increasingly became a "de facto punishment" toward the end of the nineteenth century, especially in difficult cases.[45] Even before the actual introduction of imprisonment as a legal punishment, there was a growing group of inmates who found themselves in institutional confinement. Most of these institutions, however, lacked the equipment and the capacity to deal with long-term inmates.[46]

The prison situation is but one of the many phenomena related to the profound state crisis China was facing at the end of the nineteenth century. Rapid social and economic changes in Chinese society overwhelmed many imperial institutions, including the criminal justice system, and they were no longer able to function properly. Several thinkers recommended placing emphasis on the role of law and justice in administering society. They also criticized the malfunctions and deficiencies of the traditional judiciary. Such criticism was a powerful force in undermining confidence in the existing criminal justice regime. What is important in the context of this study is the way Chinese intellectuals and some officials dealt with this crisis at the turn of the century. The flaws in the Chinese state were seen as originating in the loose relationship between the state and the people, which in turn seriously limited the ability of the state to uphold its sovereignty.

A good example of one holding these views is Liang Qichao, who urged his fellow Chinese to abandon their parochialism and transform themselves into new "citizens."[47] As he explained in his treatise *Xinminshuo* (On the New People), citizens are individuals who have rights *(quanli)*. Liang therefore advocated the establishment of a constitutional monarchy, which would grant certain rights to every citizen. Liang also advocated limiting state power and defining the freedoms, rights, and responsibilities of individual citizens. The need to "preserve the nation" led Liang to an appreciation of the public good. Protecting the public good required state building through law reform, which in turn necessitated the education of the masses in citizenship. Liang stressed the intrinsic connection between legal rights and the power of state: "The power of the state [*guoquan*] is built upon the right [*quanli*] of individuals. . . . That the people [*min*] are strong means that the state is strong. That the people are weak means that the state is weak."[48] Theories like this emphasized that the reform of law and criminal justice and the general political state of China, domestically and in the world, would be directly related.

Globally circulating knowledge and theories were used in China to promote a new vision of political and social order in which power was vested in the nation. In the face of increased foreign aggression, a radical transformation was gradually imagined. Chinese political thinkers started to look upon Western law as an important instrument for strengthening the state, producing a much more engaged connection between ruler and ruled, and establishing an organic, unitary, and stable society. Criminal justice reform was part of an ambitious program to build a strong Chinese state, and in this sense the reforms were also a consequence of more indigenous Chinese concerns.

In general, the whole discussion of law reform displayed a remarkable receptiveness among the Chinese toward techniques and technologies from other parts of the world. Outside pressures and demands coincided with the feeling of a growing internal crisis and a steady readiness to learn from the world. Nevertheless, the impulse to reform the legal system and legal punishments arose from one common notion, namely a perceived weakness of the Chinese state. With the help of new Western-inspired law, the reformers intended to build a strong, organic state that would be able to defend itself both within and outside the nation's borders.

By way of transfer, translation, and travel, Western legal knowledge found its way into the Chinese social science discourse. In the twentieth century China started to appropriate the knowledge and techniques that were circulating worldwide. Specific scientific legal discourses formed the epistemological basis for a new body of knowledge and beliefs in China regarding the purpose and forms of criminal justice. New rationales and norms emerged to underpin the birth of the criminal justice state in China and structure its operation.

In 1906 a Prison Bureau was established within the Ministry of Justice that eventually became the leading promoter of reform in the field of criminal justice. With the support of the ministry, educational institutions throughout China were encouraged to offer courses in law. In 1906, a special course on prisons (*jianyu zhuanxiuke*) was placed on the curriculum at the Capital Law School (Jingshi Falü Xuetang) and later at other universities.[49] From this time onward, prison science and criminology occupied a prominent place not only in legal studies but also in the social sciences. Many theoretical texts were published on a spectrum of related topics, from the philosophy of the custodial sentence to the administrative details of imprisonment. During the 1910s numerous prison schools (*jianyu xuexiao*) were set up in cities throughout China, and penology could also be studied in police training academies and legal administration schools.[50] All these institutions contributed to the rapid dissemination and maturation of this new field of knowledge.

Prison science seemed to offer an innovative, rational, and enlightened way to deal with offenders and criminals who threatened the social order. To many officials and even intellectuals, this new science offered ways to reestablish order and strengthen the authority of the state. In many schools prison science entailed studying the following: elementary jurisprudence, constitutional law, criminal law, law for the organization of the judiciary, prisons, rules of prisons, prison administration, policies of criminal administration, reformatory schools, protection of persons discharged from prisons, method of identification by fingerprint, the police system, social psychology, hygiene, statistics, and prison construction.[51] Thousands of specialists graduated from these schools. Building a new China also became a project of judicial specialists and prison experts. Their task was to establish stable structures of state authority, secure social stability, punish offenders, and prevent society from falling ill and becoming infirm.

The founding father of prison science in China was the Japanese expert Ogawa Shigejirō (1863–1924).[52] From 1908 to 1910 he served as adviser to the Xiuding Falü Guan, or Office for the Revision of Law. During this time he helped draft the new prison law, taught penology at the Capital Law School, and drew up the design for the Capital Model Prison. His influence on Chinese prison theory was profound. In 1905 a Chinese translation was published of what must have been one of the first modern texts on penology in China. This work opened with the following remarks: "The prison is a small society. It can also be called a miniature picture of living society. Therefore, among the hundred affairs between human beings, there is not a single one that has not to do with the prison. If one wants to realize the goal of prison administration, one cannot study the prison alone but must take into account all related affairs."[53] The prison-society analogy lies at the center of Ogawa's prison science. Prison, he said, is not simply an important part of the legal activities of the state. It is more than that—prison *is* society, in the sense that it reflects and mirrors "living society." Ordered prison life and ordered social life are inseparable. The prison resembles a clinical laboratory. Insights into social life derived from the prison laboratory were considered to be applicable to the surrounding "living society." Throughout his book, Ogawa stressed the importance of enforcing rules and upholding discipline in the prison.

This work reconfirmed for Shen Jiaben and other reformers that prison reform was urgently needed in China—that otherwise, social disorder could not be curbed. However, they did not simply copy the theories and suggestions presented by Ogawa, but instead modified his ideas and set slightly different priorities. This becomes evident in a book on the history of the prison in China, published by the official Tu Jingyu in 1909.[54] Tu had been sent to take part in the Seventh International Prison Conference, held in 1905. In the foreword to his book, Tu stressed the necessity of reforming the jails in China along Western lines. Although China had known county jails since the time of the Three Dynasties, Tu said conditions inside them were miserable. He presented a dark picture: he pointed to corrupt and incapable wardens who lacked proper training, inhumane conditions, and insufficient food and clothing, as well as torture. He concluded that China had to learn from the West in order to remedy its own shortcomings. Tu's basic motivation for writing his book was to understand how such inhumane conditions could exist in a country proud of its high level of culture. The issue Tu highlights is not the question of discipline, which interested Ogawa so much, but that of moral capital in the form of the humane treatment of the prisoners.

Shen Jiaben shared these concerns. In a memorandum on prison reform, he urged the government to establish new prisons in China, saying: "Use the prison location to apply the method of instruction [*jie jianyu zhi di, shi jiaohui zhi fang*]."[55] He also said, "The key principle in setting up prisons is not to cause suffering and bring disgrace, but to change the inmates."[56] According to Shen, imprisonment would make possible an inner transformation of those who had damaged the social order. By treating criminals in a benign way, the state could acquire moral capital. Compared with painful corporal punishments, imprisonment would not only be more humane but would also be more effective, since the transformation of criminals would undoubtedly promote social stability and harmony. The prison would be able to release good citizens, who would never again come into conflict with the law and threaten society. These concepts came to influence legislation, as seen in Article 9 of the prison law: "The punished must be induced to respect the dignity of national law and to wholeheartedly value national law. After being released, the former prisoner must be able to lead an ordered life in accordance with the law."[57] Obviously this article of the draft prison law represented a synthesis of Ogawa's stress on discipline and respect for the law and Shen Jiaben's emphasis on the instruction and transformation of the prisoner.

The emphasis on education and moral improvement played a major role in Confucian theory. Confucianism regards, in the words of Benjamin Schwartz, "the sustained inner states (of a person) as of utmost relevance to public behavior."[58] While reformers of the twentieth century obviously didn't share Confucius's distrust of law, they were convinced that human institutions like the state could not be based on laws alone. The Confucian beliefs in teaching proper moral behavior and its positive effects on social stability influenced the Chinese concepts of crime, punishment, and prisons just as much as Western models. In fact, Chinese and Western penal theories came together in their belief in man as perfectible and correctable. This confluence of different strands explains the ease with which Western theories were transmitted and translated into Chinese law and society. In the Chinese prisons, then, the indigenous emphasis on moral instruction melded with exogenous techniques for rehabilitation, discipline, and surveillance.

The career of Wang Yuanzeng offers an example of this blending of philosophies. He was perhaps the first leading prison administrator in Republican China.[59] He served twelve years as head of the Capital Number One Prison (from 1915 to 1927), and he lectured and published widely on the subject of penology. More than 300 prison wardens were trained under him at the training institute of Capital Number One Prison. After receiving six months of training they went on to assume positions in other prisons throughout the country, bringing along not only their experience in the most respected penal institution in China but also detailed knowledge of administrative practices and penal regulations. In 1928 Wang became director of the Prison Bureau in the Ministry of Justice.

In 1924 Wang Yuanzeng published his book *Prison Science*, in which he defined punishment as an intrusion on the legal interests of a person.[60] He argued that such an intrusion was vindicated not so much by the offense of the criminal as by the purpose of punishment. According to Wang, the single purpose of punishment was reformation—the process called *jiaohua*.[61] In Wang Yuanzeng's opinion, three tools should be applied in order to realize the goal of reformation: "Moral instruction and education, together with prison discipline and forced labor are the three important pillars for successfully carrying out penal reformation."[62] Like Wang Yuanzeng, the first generation of penologists clearly built their theories around the notion that *jiaohua* (later also called *ganhua*) was the core function of punitive custody. The concept implied repentance and moral reformation. In prison, the criminal was to be affected *(gandong)* and changed *(bianhua)* by way of education and instruction. The concept of *jiaohua* suggested admonishing the offender in prison, guiding him by providing a model, changing him through persuasion.

Another person highly influential in setting up the new criminal justice system was Zhao Chen (1899–1969), a professor of law. He had studied law in Japan, and after his return to China in 1924 he taught at various Chinese universities, became a judge at the Supreme Court, and eventually joined the Ministry of Justice in 1948.[63] The main tenet of his penal theories was his staunch belief in the educative function of the prison. Hence he vehemently advocated a welfarist-therapeutic approach to criminal justice.

The second chapter of Zhao Chen's best-known book, also titled *Prison Science (Jianyu xue)*, dealt extensively with theoretical aspects of punishment. He began with a definition: punishment, he said, let the penalized suffer by impairing his legal interests *(fayi)*.[64] Punishment should also serve two goals, those of special deterrence and general deterrence. Special deterrence *(tebie yufang)* referred to the offender and the term meant "to correct the error and revert to being good" *(gai guo qian shan;* 258). General deterrence *(yiban yufang)* was aimed not at the offender but at society as a whole and meant "to punish one and deter one hundred" *(cheng yi jing bai;* ibid.). The purpose of punishment was thus twofold: to correct the specific criminal and, as a consequence thereof, to deter other possible offenders in the general public.

As Zhao argues, the only punishment that meets the requirement of this twofold deterrence is imprisonment. The prison is therefore the sole place where this complicated goal has a chance of being achieved. As Zhao Chen expounds: "The state has built prisons for the criminals in the same way it has built hospitals for the sick: the goal of the hospital is to cure the sick, while the goal of the prison is to reform the criminal" (259). He strongly believed in the possibility of transforming an individual in prison. For this reason he also made a strong case for indeterminate terms of imprisonment. The date of release for a prisoner should be set only by the prison authorities, he said, depending on whether or not the convict has shown *gai hui,* or "change and repentance" (259).

In the text he goes on to ponder the effectiveness of punishment. It rests, Zhao asserts, in its mechanical and spiritual components. The mechanical component of punishment comprises its material sanctions, such as taking away life, freedom, or property. The spiritual component involves psychological sanctions and pressures, like inducing unhappiness and repentance. Therefore, deterrence comes from the mechanical component, whereas reformation of the convict results from the spiritual component. Specifically, he wrote that "the execution of punishments must have a deterring factor" and that "the execution of punishments must also have a reformative factor" (261). Zhao laid out a comprehensive penal theory. Punishment should be therapeutic as well as repressive, encouraging the convict to change while at the same time imposing material sanctions.

In the mid-1930s critical voices grew stronger. They started to express skepticism in regard to the achievements of the Chinese criminal justice reforms. Some scholars and jurists were not satisfied with the state of the legal system. They noted that the policy of reform had not succeeded in establishing an effective and functioning system, and more fundamentally, they questioned the overall direction of the reforms.

One of these critics was Sun Xiong.[65] He had spent his entire career in the Chinese prison system and had served as warden in several Jiangsu prisons throughout the 1920s and 1930s. In regard to the purpose of punishment, he also stressed that "the criminal is ordered to be confined to the prison as the sick person is segregated in a hospital in order to prevent him from infecting other people."[66] The aim of custody should be the incapacitation of the convict and the deterrence of potential offenders in society. Sun favored labor as the best tool for rehabilitation. At the center of his penal theory was the "laborization [*laodonghua*] of punishment."[67] He praised the benefits of prison labor for the health of the prisoners, their character formation, and their general skills and qualifications. Increasingly penologists focused on the prison not only as a site for transformation and reform but also as an economic unit. As an economic enterprise, the prison would teach useful skills and could bring about earnings and profits for the nation. Some even suggested that the whole prison sector could be turned into an important buttress of national productivity.[68]

In Sun Xiong's vision, the ideal prison would allow a thorough social ordering and monitoring. He favored a strong welfarist approach: Sun called for concerted intervention in the economy, state support for industry, national health plans, population control, and eugenics. The prison was one of the levers by which the state could exercise control over the citizens for the general public good.

Conjoined with these shifts in attitude toward the reform policies was a reorientation away from Western European and American models. This becomes evident in the writings of yet another influential penologist, Li Jianhua, who taught at Fudan University and Shanghai Law Academy.[69] Li Jianhua said that the new prisons were overcrowded and unhygienic, and, most important, they failed to rehabilitate the convicts, just like the jails in imperial China. He rejected moral and religious instruction as practiced in the Republican prisons as unsuitable and ineffective.[70] He stated that inmates were not provided with work and basic education but instead were forced to be idle and to listen to lofty religious or moral lectures. Li Jianhua listed cases in which prison administrations had been forced to release prisoners because conditions in the prisons were unbearable. His own penal theory was in fact a reaction to the failure of reform as it was perceived by him and others. In general, Li Jianhua and other penologists began to oppose the Beiyang prison rehabilitation programs centered on ethical or religious instruction.[71] Instead, they stressed the importance of intellectual education and labor.

Li Jianhua praised Soviet forms of imprisonment as progressive and effective. He argued that corrective labor *(laodong ganhua)* as practiced in the Soviet Union should serve as a model and inspiration for Chinese prison reforms.[72] Inmates of Soviet prison camps were detained not in single cells but in groups. They lived and worked together and would collectively strive for correction. Li Jianhua stressed that, according to reports from foreign visitors, the prison compounds in the Soviet Union did not even look like prisons but looked more like factories and farming villages. He left no doubt that Soviet penology was superior to Western European and American forms.

For Li Jianhua, punishment was the core of the legal system. He applied an almost legalistic argument when he wrote: "The authority of law is based, is built upon the fundament of punishment. If there was no punishment, the law would be a document of white paper with printed text on it." As many other Chinese penologists had, he went on to explain the purposes of punishment: "Nowadays criminal law applies the principles of reform and education. Today's prisons have nothing in common with the prisons of the past. The prison is an application, not a goal. The basic principles of the prison are to 'correct mistakes and revert to good,' 'to change the heretical and return to the orthodox' and to produce the good citizens [*liangshan gongmin*] needed by the state."[73] For Li Jianhua, crime arose out of socioeconomic inequalities. Lack of proper education as well as destitution and poverty were the roots of criminal behavior. Criminals in that sense represented the result of neglect by the state, for the state had failed to provide them with adequate opportunities for education and work. The prison now had the task of dealing with these social failings and making up for past mistakes. Consequently, Li Jianhua identified two main fields of activity in the prisons—work and training. The prison had to provide inmates with proper work in order to train them in useful trade skills and crafts, and the prison had to provide basic education to raise prisoners' intellectual abilities. Li Jianhua was vehemently opposed to the use of religion in prison, and he was also at least skeptical about the emphasis on traditional moral values. He fell short of demanding that moral instruction be abolished in prison, but he proposed to combine moral and intellectual education.[74] One can see that the center of gravity for prison reform had clearly moved away from the prison as a site of moral instruction and exhortation to the prison as an institution for work and training within a program of coercive education. Important shifts were thus taking place in the field of penology. Religious and moral education receded into the background as basic, intellectual education and labor emerged as key elements of the prison rehabilitation program.

Many if not all Chinese penologists placed an emphasis on a therapeutic approach to crime and the criminal, hence the dominant analogy of the prison as hospital. The prisoner should, these authors argued, be viewed as a sick person in need of therapy and curative care. The prison was seen as a clinic, where the pathological or infirm were to be cured through a process of reeducation. But despite its paternalistic and benevolent tone, the medical metaphor did in fact assert the totalitarian capacity ascribed to state authorities. The reach of the state was pervasive. It included manipulation of the individual's inner world and intervention in the production of the self. Discipline was not to be restricted to extrinsic patterns of behavior but should intrude into the mind of the convict. The prison reforms demonstrate the growing interest of the Chinese state in developing techniques and technologies that would extend its regulatory competence to all aspects of the individual's life. In other words, in the laboratory of the Chinese prison, the new subjectivity of the loyal, good, disciplined citizen was created.

A series of institutional reforms in the first half of the twentieth century was aimed at establishing a new criminal justice system. One of the first items on the agenda of reforms was the separation of civil administration and the judiciary.[75] This was a precondition for the creation of an independent, specialized criminal court system. The new formal court system was created in several stages, starting with an experimental stage in 1906 and moving to its countrywide introduction beginning in 1912. In 1914 there were 46 new-style courts in China. That figure expanded to 72 in 1923 and 136 in 1926.[76]

In the beginning, the new courts were primarily established in the most advanced urban areas, like Beijing, the provincial capitals in the northeastern provinces, and along the Yangzi, as well as on the east coast. In rural areas there were still 1,800 old-style *yamen* courts that continued to handle most criminal cases throughout the 1920s. While the new criminal law was applied there, too, criminal procedures in those courts still more or less followed patterns going back to the time of the Qing.

After 1928 the Nanjing government strove for a considerable increase in the number of new courts on all levels. In 1930 the government laid down a comprehensive plan aimed at replacing all *yamen* courts within ten years.[77] The new courts were divided into civil and criminal benches, and there were three levels of courts: the Supreme Court, the provincial high courts, and the district courts. Each court had a procurator, who was given a monopoly on prosecution in all criminal matters. The criminal trial was now conducted as an oral accusatory process in which, during a hearing, the procurator brought the charges and the defendant was allowed to defend himself by pointing out exonerating or mitigating circumstances. The draft criminal law of 1910 introduced legal representation by lawyers on behalf of both the defendant and the plaintiff.[78] In major Chinese cities, bar associations sprang up quickly after 1910.

The verdict in a criminal trial was supposed to be reached by an independent judge, who would weigh the different arguments and evidence given by the defense lawyer and the procurator and, after careful assessment of all circumstances, decide on the sentence. There is evidence that judges regularly made use of the wide discretion afforded them in the law.[79] While insufficient funding, lack of training, and lack of familiarity with new procedural provisions certainly posed limitations on criminal processes in the first years of the Republic, the foundations were laid for the development of a viable new criminal justice system.

Parallel to the founding of new criminal courts, new-style "model prisons" were established in several provincial capitals. Many of the prisons were newly constructed, following costly architectural designs based on foreign models. Some prisons, however, like the Tianjin prison, evolved from the former "craft learning houses" *(Xiyi Suo)*.[80] In 1903, when certain forms of exile were abolished in favor of custody in a workshop, so-called craft learning houses for convicts were established in some provinces. In these training centers, vagrants, idlers, beggars, unemployed farmers, unskilled workers, and petty criminals were grouped together. The inmates were offered vocational training and assigned manual labor. Craft learning houses existed in Baoding, Tianjin, Fengtian, Shanxi, Anhui, Zhejiang, and Hebei. They had no specific architectural design, often used existing buildings, and could accommodate only a rather small number of prisoners. Confinement in the craft houses was thought to serve as an effective tool for dealing with social problems. The rationale was simply to keep deviants and troublemakers out of mainstream circulation and protect the general population from harm that could otherwise be inflicted by them if they were not imprisoned. Sometimes confinement was used as a preventive measure, as well. People without support or family, such as vagrants, the unemployed, opium smokers, and prostitutes, were confined without ever being sent to a court.

The first "modern" prison built in China was the Hubei Model Prison, constructed in 1907. In Beijing, work on a new prison began in November 1909 but was not formally completed until 1912, after the Xinhai revolution in 1911. The new prison, Capital Number One Prison (formerly Capital Model Prison, later Beijing Number One Prison), was certainly the best-known example of the new Chinese prison. The prison building, which opened on October 10, 1912, had a fan-shaped design that laid out radial wings of cells. The building was equipped with electric lights and alarm bells. Initially there were 156 individual cells and 46 common cells.[81] The whole structure was designed to accommodate 556 prisoners. Several workshops were attached to the wards, and the prison was surrounded by a tall brick wall. To enter the prison one had to go through a large black iron gate. In several other locales, for example, Fengtian, Shandong, Shanxi, and Guangdong, similar new prisons were constructed.

The number of new prisons grew steadily during the Republic.[82] After 1911 the Ministry of Justice laid out a plan for penal reform that called for increased spending on the construction of modern prisons. In the first stage, 60 modern prisons were to be built in provincial capitals and major cities; in the second stage another 240 prisons were to be added, so that every six or seven counties would be served by a modern prison.[83] But the construction of prisons was more costly and the rate of progress slower than anticipated. The total number of new prisons grew to 74 in 1925, but there were still 1,622 old-style prisons. In 1930, 81 new prisons were counted by the government.

In the 1930s renewed hopes and expectations were placed on the prison's role in society. Besides being a site of transformation and rehabilitation, it was also to become a prototype for a complex profit-making, wealth-producing organization. In 1930 the Ministry of Justice adopted an ambitious plan according to which 215 modern prisons were needed in China, thus calling for the building of more than 100 new prisons. Five years later, however, in 1935, only 100 modern prisons were in operation. Two prisons for youth offenders *(shaonian jianyu),* in Shandong and Hubei, had also been set up.

A new wave of reformism from 1935 to 1937 led to ever more grandiose schemes. In 1936 the Ministry of Justice announced plans for constructing forty new prisons, among them six maximum-security prisons in Shanghai, Nanjing, Beiping (Beijing), Hankou, and northwest China that were of an enormous size, with a capacity of 5,000 inmates each.[84] Setting up new prisons obviously followed some pragmatic considerations, but at the same time it became an issue of prestige and authority. The GMD government wanted to show it was able to get rid of old bad practices, awaken China, and bring a new state and society to life. The prisons were seen as a symbol of the nation's progressiveness and a hallmark of modernity.

During the Second Sino-Japanese War, the continuation of criminal justice reforms was severely impeded owing to the Japanese occupation of large parts of China and the destruction caused by the fighting.[85] The Ministry of Justice continued to supervise prisons in areas under control of the Republic. Efforts were also made to improve conditions in the county jails. But in the battle zones in eastern China the prison system was severely damaged. Prisons in or near the regions where fighting took place were often bombed, destroyed, or simply abandoned when inmates escaped or were released.[86] In several instances prisons that held valuable informants or prominent prisoners were relocated to temporary facilities in the hinterland.[87] Facing mounting difficulties trying to operate the new prisons in regions where a state of emergency and martial law had been declared, the Ministry of Justice decided to regulate the release of prisoners in all regions directly affected by the war. In September 1937 legislation was passed that called for recruiting all able-bodied released prisoners into the army. The prisoners were organized into so-called reformation brigades *(ganhua dui)*. As a result, several thousand prisoners fought in the war against Japan until 1945. A few years later a small brochure on prison reform pointed out: "By serving party and country, they redeemed their crimes and renewed themselves."[88]

Almost immediately after the war, a reconstruction of the war-stricken prison system was started. In 1949 a plan was adopted to improve prison conditions and readjust prison policy and administration. While there was no fundamental change in policy as compared with the prewar period, the plan called for better training of the wardens and an expansion of vocational training in the prisons.[89] In 1946 all remaining prisons went back into operation and the rebuilding and renovation of damaged facilities was initiated.[90] Although it proved to be a very costly undertaking, the GMD government succeeded in bringing almost all prisons back into operation by 1948.[91] In 1949, when the GMD government was forced to move to Taiwan, 120 new-style prisons were in operation.

The Chinese Prison Regime

The management of crime, punishment, and criminal justice in Republican China responded not only to political and administrative schemes but also to long-term transformations in Chinese society. As economic relationships and social structures in Chinese society underwent profound changes caused by industrialization and the global marketplace, social conflicts increased and crime patterns changed. The state reacted to these changes by setting up a specific prison regime to address the social problems of a transforming society.

An appropriate starting point for our discussion of this regime is the procedure for the admission of inmates into the prison world. Another significant aspect is the architectural design of the prisons. The spatial organization of the buildings, designed for physical constraint, structured and channeled the inmates' movements through the prison environment. Time management was essential, too. Taking time away from the inmates and organizing it in a new way was an effective tool for coercion and training. Finally, instruction and work were important elements of imprisonment in Republican China.

The social ecology of the prison in the Chinese Republic was in two ways fundamentally linked to the world of urban China. First, the city provided the spatial and social setting for the prisons, since almost all prisons were constructed in urban areas. Second, the population inside the prisons was mainly made up of Chinese urbanites. Indeed, the legal reformers had a clear focus on cities. Costly and expensive institutions like prisons were primarily established in urban settings. The city was the place where authorities deemed it necessary and justified to spend the large part of a constrained budget on prison construction, although authorities certainly hoped that the reforms would radiate outward from the cities into the hinterland.

The preference for cities as prison locales, however, was not so much based on favorable judgments about urban dynamics as on more negative perceptions of urban China as a place of growing tensions and violent conflicts. The Ministry of Justice kept detailed statistics that proved, above all, that the Chinese cities had witnessed rapidly growing crime rates.[92] Accordingly, the number of trials and the number of convictions in the cities grew, as did the size of the prison population as a whole. From 1920 to 1926 the number of inmates in all three new-style prisons in Beijing doubled from 1,112 to 2,478.[93] A further big jump seems to have occurred after the Northern Expedition in 1927 that unified China and brought it under the control of the Nationalist Party. At Capital Number One Prison, the number of inmates almost doubled again within the year from 1925 to 1926.[94]

A 1928 study by a Chinese sociologist, Zhang Jingyu, demonstrated that most prison inmates were young (age 20 to 30) and unemployed or impoverished.[95] Convictions frequently were related to property offenses, such as theft, robbery, and burglary; drug crimes, like opium consumption; and sex-related crimes, like forcible abduction and forced prostitution; as well as to gambling, murder, and injury.[96] In 1916, for example, 53 percent of the inmates in the Capital Number One Prison had been convicted of robbery or burglary. Ten years later, in 1926, 84.55 percent of all male inmates in Beijing prisons had been convicted of economic crimes. Sexual offenses accounted for 2.91 percent of all convictions, while convictions because of violent assaults came to 12.53 percent.[97]

All these data contain clues to the social transformations and dislocations occurring in urban China. This was a society undergoing rapid and tremendous change in its economic life and social structure. On Beijing's streets one could encounter the nouveaux riches side by side with officials and intellectuals, shopkeepers, gangsters, peddlers, and beggars. As Yan Jingyue argued, in this bustling and dynamic city certain adverse conditions beyond individual control could lead people into criminality. Unemployment, poverty, natural calamities, overcrowded households, war, illness, and disappointments stood behind rising tensions, violent crimes, and the outbreak of conflicts. Criminal records indicate, above all, a steep increase in domestic violence and neighborhood conflicts.[98] Families suffered from anxieties about uncertain economic developments, and urban families lived in overcrowded neighborhoods where frustrations and pressures mounted. The disintegration of large clans into smaller nuclear families also deprived many families of the resources and mechanisms to solve internal disputes.

Urban quarters turned into sites of conflict and struggle. With violence becoming an almost normal mode for dealing with disunity, conciliation and civil mediation became ever more difficult. The social and economic tensions lowered tolerance and heightened aggression among urbanites. Moreover, institutions like the community and charitable organizations that in imperial times had served to mediate conflicts and bring relief to the needy either fell apart or operated on only a limited basis. With traditional institutions failing and new welfare institutions not yet fully in place, conditions motivated or forced people to commit crimes.

The Republican state responded to these developments by deploying new institutions to maintain order and stability. Law enforcement agencies played a significant role in the efforts to rein in the social fragmentation.[99] The Republican police force, also known as Bureau of Public Safety (Gong'an ju), underwent an astoundingly fast development. By the 1930s Beijing was divided into twenty-three police districts under which 341 neighborhood police stations were operating. The Beijing regional garrison also set up gendarmerie troops for dealing with large-scale riots. The responsibilities of the police in Republican China went far beyond the usual tasks of crime prevention and enforcement of the law. The police were also supposed to administer and educate, to instruct and influence the people. Chiang Kai-shek called policemen the "teachers of the people."[100] The police ran a large number of detainment places, such as detention houses, confinement rooms, and criminal reform factories. They were also in charge of charitable institutions, such as poorhouses, madhouses, and reform schools, dedicated to the poor and other socially problematic groups. These institutions functioned as a sort of overflow reservoir for urban society. At the same time, their benevolent and caring character added to the state's moral capital and effectively strengthened its position in Chinese society.

During the Republican period, law enforcement became the main tool for upholding stability and order in urban areas. With traditional residential communities and neighborhoods dissolving, urban citizens often had no choice but to appeal to law enforcement agencies for solving conflicts. Many disputes ended up in court. This outcome became so common that one could say within a decade that litigation was a significant part of daily life in urban China.[101]

In the Chinese city of the twentieth century, one of the most fundamental changes was the increasing number of institutions of confinement. These included a whole array of institutions—orphanages, poorhouses, workhouses, houses for the elderly, reformation centers for prostitutes, mental asylums, prisons, and reformation factories—all of which emphasized the need to transform vulnerable categories of people into productive citizens.[102] Confinement and social exclusion, together with individual rehabilitation, were portrayed as the solution to many urgent social problems in urban China: the troublemakers and deviants could be removed, thereby advancing the goals of improving general cleanliness and public health, upholding a swift and friction-free social order, and erecting spatial and social hierarchies. These developments were driven by new and conservative concepts based on social discipline. Michel Foucault described this way of thinking as a "military vision of society; . . . its fundamental reference was not to the state of nature, but to the meticulously subordinated cogs of a machine, not to the primal social contract, but to permanent coercions, not to fundamental rights, but to indefinitely progressive forms of training, not to the general will but to automatic docility."[103]

Officials and administrators of the Chinese Republic subscribed to this conservative vision, which was circulating around the world. The disciplining of a modern citizenry by the power of the party state was propagated as a solution to the political upheaval and social disruption that had accompanied China on the path to modernity. Confinement provided the Republican authorities with a variety of effective techniques for enforcing norms and standards of behavior. Homogeneity and uniformity appeared to them as positive and desirable attributes of a well-functioning social order. In contrast, otherness and dissidence tended to indicate social disturbance and organizational disintegration. The Republican nation-state demanded undivided allegiance and loyalty from its citizens, in particular from those who had already violated the rules and thus harmed the nation.

Many new architectural forms and styles changed the appearance of streets, business districts, and residential areas in the twentieth-century Chinese city. Among the newly designed buildings were the prisons that sprang up in the cities and on their outskirts. In regard to size and design, the prisons could hardly be overlooked. Chinese prison architects were using international designs, customized to fit the specific circumstances in China. Jeremy Bentham's principles for his Panopticon, for example, were widely known and admired by Chinese prison reformers.[104] Since most prisons were being newly constructed, prison planners in China were able to implement these new ideas.

One important principle of prison construction was impermeability. High walls around the prison and large iron gates symbolized the impermeable nature of the modern prison, in which inmates were cut off from the rest of society. Central towers, closed corridors, and armed guards ensured that no prisoner could escape, and access to the prison was strictly controlled. A second principle was transparency. The spatial organization of the world inside the prison was dominated by the principle of visibility, and thus the most popular forms for prison buildings were a radial fan-shaped design, a cruciform design, and the ray-of-light design, which had five or six wings radiating from a central tower. Prisoners were to be supervised by the guards at all times—from a central observation tower, from observation posts throughout the prison, from special heightened positions in the workshops and instruction halls, and from cell-door observation holes as the guards made their rounds of the wards. The inmate became an individual object in a pervasive "economy of observation." There would be no room for hiding from supervision.

Prison architecture also mirrored the hierarchical order of the prison world. The buildings had a clearly visible center and multiple subcenters that provided the spatial structure for ordering, separating, and regulating prison society. With walls, corridors, and gates, the prison authorities were able to regulate and manage the prisoners' space. This space could be reduced by closing doors and shutting off corridors, and enlarged by granting privileges of movement. In some prisons and detention centers inmates had the added confinement of wearing heavy iron chains locked around their feet.[105] Prison authorities' ability to compress or expand the space available to the prisoners provided the staff with an efficient lever for exerting pressure on the individual convicts.

Besides the compression or expansion of space, time could be used to exercise control and inculcate discipline. This happened within the framework of strict daily routines. Prisoners had to rise, wash, eat, work, exercise, and listen to instructions, all at set, scheduled times. Prison life in the Capital Number One Prison, for example, followed fixed timetables that varied in accordance with the season.[106] Schedules also regulated periods when prisoners could go to the latrine: two short spells lasting several minutes each, called *fang feng*, were allowed per day. Moreover, all these actions were to be performed silently by the prisoners.[107]

The prisoners' activities were thoroughly controlled through technologies of supervision such as timetables, training, observation, and examinations. Control could be exercised by breaking prisoners' space and time into ever smaller and more useful segments. This disciplinary control of activity produced, in Foucault's words, "a positive economy; it poses the principle of a theoretically ever-growing use of time: exhaustion rather than use; it is a question of extracting, from time, ever more available moments and, from each moment, ever more useful forces."[108]

The prison regime imposed on convicts a set of routines composed of carefully orchestrated actions. These routines included procedures for admission to the prison, the organization of daily life inside the prison, and certain institutional ceremonies. Taken together these operations were intended to mortify the inmates' sense of self and force them to adhere to the values and norms the Chinese prison officially propagated.

On admission to prison, each convict was put through a set of routine actions.[109] Some were intended to clean the convict. Prisoners were washed on arrival, had their head shaved, and underwent a medical inspection to detect contagious diseases and mental disorders. A second set of measures dealt with the identity of the convict. The status of the inmate was recorded, in particular his occupation, conduct, preferences, and medical history. All the data were put down in the prison's Identity Record Book.[110] His picture and fingerprints were taken, and any identifying characteristics were noted. A third set of measures dealt with the prisoner's personal belongings. All personal property was impounded, to be returned on release, and prisoners were issued gray uniforms. Each uniform had an identification number on the back. Instead of names, these numbers were used to call and identify the prisoners throughout their term in prison.[111]

As Erving Goffman has argued, such admission procedures and rituals have an important effect. The prisoner's nakedness (during washing, medical examination, and dispossession) marks a midpoint between his leaving of his earlier, individual identity and taking on a new role. A transfer between different, mutually incompatible social roles occurs, and the admission process marks this passage by performing a set of rites. These rituals strip the inmate of the attributes stemming from his previous civil roles, which, of course, provided him with his identity in civil life. On admission to the prison the convict suffers a "personal defacement."[112] The dispossession of personal belongings leads to a process of "disculturation," which actually amounts to a "civil death."[113]

The truncation of one's name and the loss of all the other belongings lead to a curtailment of the inmate's self and identity. The prisoner loses his "identity kit," which was tied to his earlier self, and he becomes a part of a social category. The technology of power inside the prison transforms the subject—an individual person with a certain standing and identity in civil society—into an object dressed in a gray uniform with a number on his back. The power of the prison lies in its ability to frame and reproduce the inmate as an object, by stripping him of all attributes and elements that contributed to his subjective self. These techniques fit well with the plans of officials in Republican China to promote the production of good loyal citizens.

The assault on the self of the inmate was not limited to the process of admission to the prison. After admission, the Chinese prisons continued to mortify the self of the inmate through a variety of carefully orchestrated routine operations involving, for example, sanitation, observation, and record keeping. Much effort, for instance, was devoted to maintaining proper hygiene among the prisoners. One of the reports of the Capital Number One Prison stated: "Besides education, sanitation and hygiene are very carefully looked after in this prison."[114] Each cell was inspected daily, its condition recorded by the guard. On the surface, this is just another manifestation of the disciplinary regime in the prison but it had a deeper meaning, too. When they were required to clean the cells or latrines, inmates were forced to expose themselves to direct physical contamination.

Another important part of the daily routine in the Chinese prison was concerned with record keeping and examination. The systematic examination and recording of daily processes in the prison represents an example of formalized bureaucratic rule in a Weberian sense that featured numerous sophisticated methods of recording, cross-checking, and evaluation. It also constituted a violation of the inmate's personal privacy. The prisoner was not able to conceal facts or information about himself. He also had to be aware that discreditable information about him, his convictions, or his past conduct could be made public in the prison, as well as on the outside, at any time. This demonstrated that in the prison, authorities were able to neutralize the boundary between the individual and his environment. These operations were designed to mortify the inmate. The territory of the self was deliberately violated; boundaries between the individual and his surroundings were continuously broken.[115] A community of power was erected by means of such invisible, nonphysical techniques of coercion.

After successfully assaulting the self of the inmate, the prison attempted to reorganize the inmate's identity by offering new role models, sanctioned patterns of behavior, and desirable values. This was achieved through a variety of institutional ceremonies aimed at personal rebuilding and instilling new values. Most important in this respect were, of course, the instructional sessions, which are described in detail in the next section. In addition, other techniques were deployed to help to spread the prison's official values. Such techniques included the propagation and visualization of official values, a privilege system consisting of rewards and punishments, and institutional ceremonies.

Propaganda and the visualization of the official values were undertaken by different means. One method was to post instructional sayings or slogans throughout the prison. Prisoners in the 1920s found themselves "surrounded by the ubiquitous visual symbols and words to be studied and memorized, all representing the values they were expected to embrace."[116] Flags, posters, and other articles were employed. In the 1930s these propaganda efforts were complemented by the use of loudspeakers and broadcast systems in the prisons.[117]

A second and very widespread method was to use moral terms to designate specific areas inside the prison. In the Hubei Number One Prison, China's first new prison located in Wuchang, opened in 1913, each of the cell rows was identified with a Confucian moral term: *dao* (way), *de* (virtue), *qi* (evenness), and *li* (propriety). The Dao and Li rows had twenty single cells each, the De and Qi rows, twelve communal cells.[118] The Suiyuan Number One Prison in Guisui, Inner Mongolia, had four sections called Gai (change), Guo (errors), Qian (shift), and Shan (good). The four characters together formed a sentence meaning "Change evil ways and do good."[119] Inmates were placed in the one of the four sections according to the nature of their crime. Criminals with serious offenses were mostly confined in the Gai section; those to be released soon were usually put in the Shan section. Wards in the Jiangsu Number Two Prison were named Ren (benevolence), Yi (righteousness), Li (propriety), Zhi (wisdom), and Xin (faith).[120] In Beijing the road leading to the main entrance of the Hebei Number One Prison was named Zixinlu: Self-Renewal Road.[121] This naming system within the prisons was more than a mere curiosity. By placing convicts with similar crimes together in certain sections under a common designation, prison staff imposed a classification system on the prison population. Thus the very diverse society of prisoners was regrouped and reorganized according to official categories and the classification system of the prison.

On special occasions in the prison, such as special commemoration days, funerals, amnesties, or paroles, large assemblies lasting up to two hours were held. At such events, a special lecture would be presented by the prison instructor or the prison director.[122] National days, too, were celebrated in the prison. On all national holidays, prisoners were given an extra meal of bread and meat.[123] At special assemblies, selected prisoners would come forward and describe the process of their reformation. They would express their thoughts and feelings and describe in detail their former suffering and the way to reformation after entering the prison. This was designed to move and guide the audience. These ceremonies were called prisoner repentance talks.[124]

Instructional activities were the most important routines aimed at reorganizing the mind of a convict in the Chinese prisons. Instruction was therefore called "the primary essential element" within the whole program of penal confinement.[125] One of the challenges facing prison reformers in the Republican period was the content of prison instruction. During the final years of Qing rule it was undisputed that Confucian teaching should be the backbone of prison instruction. But after the 1911 revolution, a debate erupted among prison reformers about the proper content of instruction in the prison.[126] Some reformers maintained that Confucianism was too esoteric and "lofty" to suit prison education. Other officials and legal scholars held the view that the content of prison education should be widely accepted, easily comprehensible, and entrenched in the social life. Therefore they supported the use of popular religion, especially Buddhism, but to a lesser extent also Daoism and Christian teachings. Others voiced criticism of the use of traditional morality in general. They recommended heightening the patriotic feelings of prisoners or cultivating loyalty toward the governing party by having prisoners read texts by important political leaders or teaching them about important national events. In the end, however, the content of prison instruction was in most cases an eclectic synthesis. The prison appropriated ethical values and symbols identified as belonging to the Chinese traditional culture and being common to the people, thereby joining an assumed core of Chinese culture with the newly introduced concepts of the nation and citizenship.

All prisons had to offer instruction to every prisoner.[127] While it is clear that the quality, length, and intensity of prison instruction were dependent on a variety of local factors, most prison administrators recognized the importance of instruction. Prisons strove to hire qualified instructors and assistants, bought books, set up libraries, and encouraged instructors to edit teaching materials.[128] New media were embraced too: at Capital Number One Prison, educational and newsreel films were occasionally shown during instruction sessions.[129] Prison authorities made considerable efforts to develop an effective and diversified curriculum. The following quote from the official brochure of Capital Number One Prison is a good example for the general emphasis on instruction: "It is universally known, that the cause of committing crime is the lack of moral and intellectual education. As the principle of a modern prison is to make prisoners repent and to make good citizens out of the ignorant, scandalous, and weak, moral and intellectual education is indispensable."[130]

Three forms of moral instruction were applied: collective moral instruction *(jihe jiaohui)*, classification moral instruction (*leibie jiaohui*, which was instruction addressed to particular categories of prisoners), and individual moral instruction *(geren jiaohui)*.[131] Weekly collective instruction was normally given in the instruction hall where all the prisoners assembled. In Capital Number One Prison, the instruction hall was located within the observation tower at the center of the prison building. Prisoners were seated in little wooden stalls built so that they could not see each other and could look solely at the lecture podium. The lecturer, standing on a small platform, could see only the prisoners' heads.[132] Behind the lecturer's platform, portraits of Confucius, Laozi, Mohammed, Christ, and John Howard had been painted on the wall.[133]

The weekly two- to three-hour-long lectures were given either by the prison instructor or by a specially invited religious leader from the outside, such as a famous Buddhist monk, a well-known Christian priest, or a well-respected member of the Salvation Army.[134] The prison welcomed any teaching or religion so long as it offered the prospect of helping to reform the prisoners. In their lectures the instructors used short quotations or phrases from popular moral writings that were written on a blackboard and had to be repeated or memorized by the prisoners. It appears that "famous sayings" and "fine words and deeds" by a wide range of historical role models from both East and West were very popular and formed the core of prison instruction.[135] The prisoners were to be provided with inspiring examples. Texts and quotes used during instruction had to be easy for every prisoner to comprehend, regardless of his previous education.

Classification moral instruction was conducted by the wardens with small classes of prisoners after each meal, in the working room. It was therefore more commonly called workshop instruction or ward instruction. This form of instruction lasted half an hour to an hour. Individual instruction was given in special sessions on a prisoner's entering and leaving the prison. But not all prisons could afford to perform all three types of instruction. It appears that collective assembly instruction and individual instruction were used most widely, and also deemed the most effective.[136]

When the instructor worked with individual prisoners instead of speaking to the whole assembly, he was able take into account individual problems and experiences. Before the first session, the instructor would carefully investigate the prisoner's files. He made himself familiar with the prisoner's personal data and criminal records. With this knowledge in mind, the instructor tried to make a diagnosis in terms of the origins of the prisoner's breaches of the law and decide on a treatment. He then scheduled an individual conversation with the inmate. The instructor was supposed to try to gain the prisoner's trust and sympathy.[137] To lead the prisoner back to a law-abiding lifestyle, he had to confront him with his basic guilt and have him confess his crime again. He attempted to arouse feelings of repentance *(huiyu)* with respect to the convict's past crimes and to turn his attention toward the merits of "reverting to being good."[138] When confronted with intransigent behavior, instructors resorted to sharper tones. They would try to criticize, rebuke, accuse, threaten, and intimidate rebellious inmates. In general, instructors emphasized internal examination and recognition of moral failings. This process was designated moral self-cultivation *(xiushen)*.

A look at the content of prison instruction reveals the official moral universe propagated by the prison authorities. The prison libraries contained both Chinese and Western works, including so-called old and new ideas.[139] Browsing through the books and their titles, an astonishing eclecticism stands out. By the mid-1930s library holdings in the prisons were diverse. Religious tracts stood side by side with Sun Yat-sen's *Three Principles of the People, Aesop's Fables* was followed by Buddhist treatises, a *Short History of National Shame* might be shelved near a popular morality book like *The Sacred Collection of Taishang.*[140] The diversity of the library collections is also corroborated by prisoners' reports. Yang Chih-lin recalls that in a prison in Inner Mongolia the following books were given to prisoners: the *Ledgers of Merit and Demerit of Lord Wenchang* (a popular morality book), the *Daodejing* by Laozi, the Confucian *Four Books* and *Five Classics,* and the *The Three Principles of the People* by Sun Yat-sen.[141] Yang reported that instruction consisted of quotations from those books, repeated over and over again.

If one sorts out the bewildering variety of topics, styles, schools, and philosophies encapsulated in all these books, four fundamental strands can be distinguished. Taken together, they form the scaffolding of the moral world inside the Republican prison. One of the major strands in prison instruction certainly was religion. Christian and Buddhist teachings seem to have been initially dominant, with Buddhism growing ever more important in the 1930s.[142] Several Buddhist *baojuan* (precious rolls) were used by instructors. Most prison instructors also reported using a book titled *A Record of Reformation (Ganhua lu).* The text had been compiled during the early years of the Republic, particularly for use in the prison, and overall it conveyed Buddhist teachings as a way to individual salvation for prisoners. The interest of the prison practitioners was focused on so-called *baoying* (retribution-recompense, or cause-and-effect) theories, according to which all human actions would receive corresponding consequences in response to their moral quality. The aspect of retribution in Buddhism made this religion attractive for prison reformers. Moreover, *baoying* was a concept that was widespread in Chinese popular culture.

The second important strand was popular ethics, which was fed by a variety of diverse sources, all coming out of the popular culture of late imperial China. The most telling indication for the role of this tradition in the prison world is the widespread use of "morality books" *(shanshu)*. The aforementioned *The Sacred Collection of Taishang* or the *Tract of Taishang on Action and Response* dating from the twelfth century were regularly consulted in the prisons.[143] This genre of literature flourished during the Ming-Qing dynasties and was also very popular in the late Qing period. Cynthia Brokaw, who studied the morality books, defines them as "texts that teach people to do good and avoid evil." In the moral cosmos of these books, the principle of retribution looms large—that is, "the faith that heaven and the gods will reward men who do good and punish those who do evil."[144] The ledgers of merit and demerit, a subgenre of the morality books, contain lists of good and bad deeds describing what deed one should do to earn rewards and what deeds one should avoid doing to escape punishment. These tracts and texts all evoke the persistence of a supernatural compensatory justice, remaining intact and untouched by historical change, judicial failings, or political crisis.

Texts stemming from the Confucian tradition also continued to be widely used in prison, and these constituted the third strand of prison education. Apart from extracts from the classics (Confucius, Mengzi, *Xiaojing*) and certain neo-Confucian writings (Zhu Xi), family instructions and short sayings by famous officials were popular among prison instructors. The latter were deemed easier to comprehend and thus more appropriate for use in prisons than original Confucian texts. Prison instructors also often reverted to Zeng Guofan's *Family Letters and Family Instructions*, which was first published in 1879 and in the 1920s and 1930s was available in several popular editions (dated 1905, for instance) as well as in short digests.[145] Zeng's letters and instructions to his family offered guidelines for moral self-cultivation. In essence, as head of the family he urged his family members (especially his younger brothers and his sons) to be obedient, selfless, loyal, dutiful, self-disciplined, and diligent. He appealed to his male family members to withstand the seductions of laziness and leisure and to stay focused on common goals and values.

The fourth strand consisted of guides to civics, patriotism, and political doctrines. After the late 1920s, prisons were required to integrate Sun Yat-sen's *Three Principles of the People* into their curriculum.[146] The 1930s witnessed an increasing emphasis on party doctrines. As early as 1927 Warden Hu Yimin even spoke of a "partification [*danghua*] of education" in the prison. Extracts were used to teach party ideology *(dangyi)*.[147] Nationalist history texts were also found helpful. Under the heading *A Short History of National Humiliation,* decades of defeat and shame at the hands of Western powers were depicted.[148] These and similar books called for national renewal by reminding the prisoners of the crisis all Chinese citizens should be aware of. Finally, the new genre of guides explaining duties and rights of citizens in a constitutional state were very popular among prison instructors. Titles likely to be found in the prison libraries included *Manual for Citizens (Guomin Bidu)* and *Civics (Gongmin Jian,* a translated American textbook).[149]

These four major strands in prison education were mingled together by prison practitioners. With pragmatic syncretism, they combined without the slightest hesitation religious and secular, elite and popular, indigenous and foreign elements. A dense, hybrid moral climate was produced and nourished within the prison walls that was designed to foster a nationalistic and patriotic spirit among prisoners while at the same time offering valuable clues and concrete instructions for how to lead a decent life and become an integrated and respected member in the social fabric of the Chinese civil society.

In the mid-1920s several compilations were published that synthesized the different strands and made them readily available for use in the prisons. The lectures by the leading prison instructor in the Republican period, Shao Zhenji, were well known and regarded as exemplary. Shao was instructor at Jiangsu Number Two Prison in Shanghai. He published his lectures in 1925 under the title *Introduction to Moral Instruction.* This volume eventually became standard reading for moral education in prison during the Beiyang government and afterward under the Nationalist government in the 1930s.[150] The lectures collected in this volume offer vivid glimpses into the nature of prison instruction.

In his lectures Shao instructed prisoners in all aspects of life in Chinese society. He covered a wide spectrum of topics, starting with health and hygiene and ending with an appeal to prisoners to abstain from lust and sin.

He also talked about the relations between husband and wife, the role of female virtue, and the importance of chastity. Shao sternly condemned all sexual liaisons outside of the reproductive purposes of the family. In particular, Shao attacked customs and habits that in his view contributed to moral degeneracy and crime. Among those were, for instance, prostitution, gambling, and alcohol and drug abuse. Referring to Chinese medical treatises and morality books alike, he urged prisoners to adopt healthy lifestyles instead of abandoning themselves to vice. Shao Zhenji taught convicts the five Confucian ethical relationships, with particular emphasis on filial piety and family harmony. He progressed from the ethics of individual conduct to those relevant to the broader society and the state. Further lessons had the titles "Harmony with the Clan and Peace among Neighbors," "Venerate the Old," "Kindness to Youth," and "Charitable Enterprise" (in the latter he praised those who gave aid to the poor and to orphanages). He recommended mutual aid as a prerequisite for social harmony and stability. In general, he urged mutual care among members of society and the sharing of resources, instead of greed and profit seeking.

A dominant theme in Shao's lectures was the nation-building project. He gave talks entitled "Public Hygiene," "Public Morality," and "Public Welfare." He spoke about the duties, responsibilities, and proper demeanor that were required and expected from every single citizen. He promoted beliefs and values in which the "public good" loomed large. Private morality, he said, served the purpose of perfecting one's own character, whereas public morality aimed at the preservation of the social order.[151] Welfare generally played an important role in this concept: preserving public welfare fostered social benefits for the masses and thus advanced state and society. Shao also appealed to the prisoners to consider the fate of the nation and to see the necessity for collective mobilization and change. Lectures in this regard included: "Prisoners Should Not Forget National Shame," "On Revoking Extraterritorial Rights," "The Citizen's Duties," and "Patriotism." He portrayed national humiliation as the defining theme in modern Chinese history. The nation should awaken to its shame and be aware of its crises. The modern citizen, as trained in the Republican prison, should be conscious of the nation's weaknesses and political threats and contribute to a solution to the crises by fulfilling his duties and by loving the "nation like a family."[152]

Finally, Shao emphasized that the impoverished and uneducated prisoners could even have a special mission in China's overall reformation. He explained: "Criminals in a nation are like worms in an organ or a body stopped up and swollen with constipation. With villains and prisoners in droves, how can we attain a strong and flourishing national civilization? Therefore, in intending to seek the reform of the national destiny, we should begin with the self-renewal [*zixin*] of the prisoners."[153] The correction of the most problematic portion of society would determine the fate of the nation. Furthermore, penal reformation is here imagined as a model for the transformation of the minds of all citizens. Wang Yuanzeng, warden at Capital Number One Prison, directly related prison education to the wider goal of spreading patriotism and nationalist ideals. He held the view that education in the prison should teach the prisoner that "the essential duty of the people is patriotism." The teaching of history, for example, should focus on "national humiliation" (*guochi*).[154]

In his lectures Shao Zhenji combined traditional morality with ideas of public or civic morality (*gongde*) within a civic community belonging to a modern nation.[155] His instruction was based on the notion that the moral attitudes of each individual citizen are decisive for maintaining social order and realizing a modernizing society. Self, society, and state formed an intrinsic relationship in this thinking. Prisoners should be taught to judge good from evil and to make the right decision, even in the face of adversity or temptation. Each prisoner should be able to revive his original good nature and thereby to contribute to national salvation.

Singing was an important element of prison instruction, too. Singing was considered to be an effective tool for reaching the minds and hearts of the largely uneducated and often illiterate prison population. The *Hebei Number One Prison Report* from 1935 explained that during collective instruction, prisoners regularly had to sing songs or listen to music because this would "cheer up the depressed."[156] Xue Dubi's songbook *Songs to Exhort the People (Quanmin ge)*, published in 1922, was later assigned for the singing courses in the prison and widely used.[157] The book contained forty-three songs that used popular folk tunes but had new, didactic lyrics written by Xue Dubi. The songs can be grouped into different categories. The first and largest category was patriotic songs. Among this group was the national anthem of the Beiyang government ("Auspicious Clouds") and songs with such titles as "Remember the National Shame," "Use National Products," and "Song to Inspire Patriotism." The second group consisted of songs that contained moral advice and instruction, for example: "Exhort

Knowing a Sense of Shame," "Exhort Knowing Propriety," "Exhort Showing Filial Piety," "Exhort Diligent Study," and "Exhort Diligent and Bitter Toil." The last category of songs provided practical advice for a sound lifestyle, such as the songs "Abstain from Drinking Alcohol," "Abstain from Opium," "Abstain from Whoring," "Pay Attention to Hygiene," "Plant Trees," "Repair Roads," "Song to Exhort Getting Up Early," "Abstain from Greed," "Abstain from Fighting and Cursing," and so on. By establishing and actively spreading a culture of self-examination and self-control, including through song, the prison staff tried to achieve an important goal of imprisonment: instilling self-discipline. Self-control is, in the end, much more effective than surveillance. The latter addresses only the externalities, whereas the first penetrates mind and soul.

A basic education in reading, writing, arithmetic, composition, music, and singing, as well as physical exercise, was offered to juvenile inmates under the age of eighteen. The curriculum followed that of China's new primary schools. Four hours of teaching were given every day.[158] In 1924 a directive of the Beiyang government sought to expand basic education in the new prisons and eventually to include all unskilled prisoners. The Prisoner Education Plan recommended the implementation of a standardized three-year prison education curriculum that would increase the prisoners' basic intellectual skills and knowledge, strengthen their bodies through sports, and foster the moral character of all prisoners, not just the youth.[159] In addition to lessons in writing and reading, basic math skills, and general knowledge (social, political, and geographical), the curriculum contained moral and ethical instruction and lessons in patriotism and the duties of the citizens. The latter topics were touched on in a course titled Citizenry (Gongmin). The ministry ordered that the 1924 Prisoner Education Plan be put into practice, but owing to organizational and financial limitations, it was only partly realized. In the 1930s another attempt was made to enhance education in the prisons. The Hebei Number One Prison reported in 1935 that all inmates under the age of twenty-five took part in the education program.[160] This initiative appears to have been somewhat more successful than earlier ones, as the number of prisoners who received basic education had increased considerably.

In the prisons, the modern Chinese state started to assume the new task of training citizens and setting norms through mass education. Prison education was connected to the much larger national project in the 1930s of mass education. The New Life Movement, for example, intended to train all modern citizens equally to meet minimum requirements of literacy, basic math skills, general knowledge, good health, proper hygiene, morals, and patriotism. New forms of discipline and standardization radiated from the prison laboratory and extended to the society at large. The new prisons were among the first institutions charged with the mission of developing the concept of the decent law-abiding citizen and injecting it into broader policy, curricula, daily admonitions, and detailed instructions.

A rather optimistic attitude seems to have held sway on the part of instructors and reformers in regard to prisoner instruction and its potential. At the core of the instructors' optimism was their belief in the medical metaphor with its strong therapeutic approach, and their confidence in the potential of social engineering.[161] Their position implied that the prison should not so much punish as cure the individual prisoner. The prisoner was seen mainly as an object for therapeutic counseling and social welfare. This was considered to be an important step toward any form of effective social prevention. The dominant approach allowed, even obliged the state to actively transform convicts and delinquents. In regard to this goal the state also had to convey values, guidelines, and helpful, positive advice. After assaulting, overpowering, and disciplining the former self of the inmate, his new identity was inculcated by way of lectures, songs, training and programming, treatment and counseling. The individual's moral, physical, mental, and behavioral qualities became a target for intervention and a priority for effective administration.

The reaffirmation of traditional morality in a state that considered itself revolutionary seems contradictory at first glance. However, the recourse to tradition must be seen in the context of the expansion of the modern state. Tradition does not simply live on within society. Rather, it is recreated and reconstructed within a new system of meaning and reference. Penal reformers were much more interested in the normative, integrating function of tradition than they were in preserving any Confucian values or Buddhist ethics per se. They tried to use the self-disciplining and self-regulating potential of the well-established moral schools. Centuries-old forms of control thus were integrated, redeployed, and refined by the modern state. In this process the prison functioned as a key institution in combining traditional and newly imported "technologies of the self."[162]

Apart from education, labor occupied a prominent place in the Chinese prison regime too. Especially during the 1920s and 1930s, much attention was devoted to prison labor and its goals of counteracting economic causes of crime. On the one hand, labor was a form of discipline that trained fixed sets of movements. On the other, prisoners were expected to learn valuable skills, which would help them find a decent job after their release from prison. In addition, through prison labor, the state could open up a new resource and new revenue. Hence in the Republic's new prisons, the life of the inmates was increasingly centered around work. So important was labor in the new prisons that the prisons gradually developed into large-scale workshops.

The emphasis on prison labor was widespread among prison administrators in Republican China.[163] The goal of prison labor was to make prisons largely self-sufficient. In 1916 Capital Number One Prison reported with pride:

> From the establishment of the Prison to the present time hardly any articles for daily use [are] supplied from the outside and many articles are made by prisoners to supply society. By means of the various trades every prisoner is fostered into diligent habits and converted into a productive person. Therefore the untrained becomes trained and the lazy industrious. All prisoners are transformed into a new and better life which differs from the old one. They are dependent on society and society is dependent on them. Through their trades they are able to earn a livelihood. Society begins to have relations with them and they will be mutually dependent. They can offer their work to society, while in return society will give them means for their livelihood.[164]

According to the official view, labor would serve many positive goals: it facilitated the reformation of the prisoners, and at the same time society at large would benefit from the contribution of prison labor to the national economy. This would by no means constitute an act of exploitation; on the contrary it would restore the bond between the inmate and society, from which the inmate had estranged himself by breaking the law. Therefore, to obtain profit from prison labor was not only acceptable but even important for the goal of reformation.

Most prisons operated workshops on their compounds. In the workshops the prisoners were kept occupied and were trained in basic handicraft skills or, in some cases, the operation of tools or machines. The Capital Number One Prison, for instance, had workshops for lithography, type printing, woodblock printing, type making, typesetting, book binding, sewing, weaving, metal casting, preparing rice, washing, making rattan goods, masonry and carpentry, and agriculture. Almost all of the 556 prisoners were at work every day. Some of the workshops, in fact, were economically very successful. The prison's printed materials were sold out as soon as they were made. There was also a huge demand for prison-made rattan goods.

Beijing Second Prison succeeded in making considerable profits. In 1922 it showed in its books a net profit of $11,000, mostly from the marketing of bricks and rattan and bamboo goods. This prison had 600 prisoners working in sixteen departments. The brick-making department's output was 134,000 bricks a month. Another example is the successful marketing of prison-made carpets, rugs, and cushions at the Zhili First Prison in Tianjin. It reported a net profit of $13,000 in 1922.[165]

With the continuous increase of inmates entering the prison system, administrators found it difficult to provide all prisoners with meaningful work. In the 1930s some inmates had only temporary jobs.[166] The prisons often produced supplies for government offices or the military, and in order to expand their production they had to find other customers or develop new markets, which was becoming more difficult during the economic slowdown in the 1930s. Another means of raising production and enhancing profitability was to contract prison labor to private workshops. But in this case the exploitation of prison labor easily outweighed the intended rehabilitative purpose for the prisoners.[167] While most prisons still in the 1930s did earn money through prison labor and could thus make a contribution to the costs of imprisonment, the highly acclaimed goal of self-sufficiency was increasingly difficult to realize.

When assigning labor to prisoners, supervisors took into consideration a number of factors, such as the age of the prisoner, the nature of the committed crime, the length of the prison sentence, and the social standing, skills, future profession, and physical condition of the inmate. Working hours varied according to the seasons, between ten and twelve hours a day.[168] All convicts were paid for their work, provided, however, they had been diligent and had obeyed the rules. In some cases up to one-third of the income derived from prison labor could be given to the prisoner, to be paid upon his release. Since the pay depended not only on the work of the prisoner but also on his behavior, the work income was used as a financial incentive for good behavior. But in fact only a small percentage of prisoners received any financial rewards.[169]

In the 1940s several prisons started to open so-called cooperatives.[170] In these facilities prisoners could buy cigarettes, beverages, food, and clothes. It was a move to suppress the roaring smuggling and black-market trade that existed in most prisons. Another benefit of the cooperatives, authorities hoped, would be the added work motivation, since with the cooperatives prisoners could actually use their financial rewards to improve their living conditions inside the prison. Some prisons were very creative and issued a special currency.[171] Prisoners were paid for their work in prison with this special prison currency, which they could then redeem for certain goods.

Prison labor served many purposes: it was supposed to teach skills and industrial discipline, and to help cover at least part of the expenses for the prison. Prisoners were to be turned into productive members of society, and they were also expected to pay back their debt to society by being productive not only in the prison but also *for* the prison. For the prisoner, then, labor was a tool of correction, a privilege and a punishment at the same time.

The Violence of Confinement

Seen from the outside, the new Chinese prison appeared to be a milestone of modernity and an embodiment of the state's new capacity to exercise control and solve social problems. Seen from the inside, however, a different picture emerged. The prison accommodated a social world that was first and foremost determined by violence. Not only was the relationship between inmates and staff dominated by this violence, but the interactions among the inmates were also marked by violent behavior.

However, in the history of prisons, the role of the inmate is never limited to that of a passive victim. Actions and reactions of the imprisoned essentially contribute to the success or failure of penal custody. One of the problems for the prisons in the Chinese Republic in fact resulted from the mostly intransigent behavior of the prisoners. The prisons' disciplinary regime could not prevent, and might even have provoked, the very defiance that prisoners in China often demonstrated.

Life inside the prisons was shaped by a variety of factors. The spatially miniature world of the prison housed a rather complex and unique social universe. Social structures and hierarchies and material conditions, as well as physical and bodily states, influenced the experience of imprisonment. Most inmates were constantly struggling for some control over their environment by manipulating the structures within the prison world. They attempted to create for themselves small enclaves of self-affirmation and pockets of resistance.

Records of the experience of imprisonment in China's new prisons are somewhat elusive, but descriptions in the form of fiction, memoirs, and interviews do exist. Beginning in the 1930s, a whole new genre of writing developed in China around the topic of the experience of detention in the Republican prisons.[172] It appears that these reports quickly assumed considerable popularity and public influence in the Republic of China, and after 1949 their role became even more important. Books and memoirs continued to pour out over several decades, until the late 1980s.

Inmates' experiences are retold and narrated in historical documents and witness reports. But beyond their documentary value, some texts describing imprisonment are also highly symbolic representations. They operate within literary narrative traditions and use rhetorical devices and forceful symbols. In short, these texts can contain very powerful images concerning the Republican prison. As a result, the general public's impression of the prisons was possibly molded more by the various textual representations of the prison experience than by official documents. Ironically, the impressive authoritative appearance of the prison belied its vulnerability to the written words of writers and journalists exposing prisoner abuse and desolation. For this discussion, we will start from documented experiences and observations concerning life in the Republican prisons and then follow the trajectory of those experiences through various literary texts. In the process we will see how prison experiences were converted into a powerful symbol for misery and alienation in the Chinese Republic.

Prison society was made up of two parallel coexisting hierarchies. The first hierarchy was formally imposed by the prison staff. It was based on distinctions made among prisoners convicted of various types of criminal offenses, prisoners in various stages of reformation, and various types of political prisoners, such as communists, suspected communists, members of the (communist) Fourth Army, prominent prisoners, and so on. This hierarchy generally functioned to serve and enhance the prison regime. Prisoners learned quickly, however, that it was possible to manipulate the prison regime and maneuver through it in pursuit of their own goals. An alternative social hierarchy emerged that was created by the inmates them-selves. While there were local variants, a strong subculture with its own values and hierarchies seems to have existed in most Republican prisons. This inmate culture was structured on seniority, prison experience, and group affiliation. It also served as a base from which well-organized groups, mostly members of criminal gangs or the Chinese Communist Party, could dominate prison society and defy prison rules and regulations. By sustain-ing and moving within this peculiar inmate culture, certain groups success-fully immunized themselves against the prison regime and its trans-formative power and systematically cultivated intransigent behavior and organized resistance.

Seen from the perspective of a newly arrived prisoner, the social world inside the prison was diverse and heterogeneous. Members of social groups that in civilian life would hardly meet at all now had to live together in small cells. While the composition of prison society changed over time, a fundamental diversity of the prison population remained a common trait. As one concrete example, in the 1930s the communist cadre Wang Ruofei successively shared his cell with inmates from all strata of society. He was confined, in turns, with a peasant, a murderer, a violent Muslim, a leader of a local gang, and a Mongolian herdsman.[173] In the late 1940s the journalist Huang Genghui observed that in a police detention center in Guangzhou, intellectuals, students, teachers, thieves, gangsters, peasants, opium traffick-ers, local ruffians, and soldiers were all represented.[174]

Authorities tried to impose a hierarchy on this diverse society, based on criteria and values the prison officially promoted. Beginning in the 1930s a formal and complex classification system for inmate society was devel-oped.[175] The system was in the beginning called the Progressive Stage Sys-tem (Jiejizhi). Later a revised and modified system was introduced, called the Accumulation and Progress Handling System (Leijin Chuyu).

According to these classification systems, all prisoners had to be sorted into one of four categories.[176] New arrivals were generally put in the fourth category, while prisoners in the first category were considered to be closest to full rehabilitation. The prison director could initiate a conditional re-lease for inmates of the first category at a time of his choosing. The promo-tion of a prisoner to the next higher category depended on his showing good behavior and working diligently. Prisoners were constantly evaluated and graded by members of the prison staff, who used charts and forms to document performance. Among those forms was, for instance, a Thought Record (Sixiang Lu). Poor behavior resulted in worsening treatment, while improvement would lead to promotion to a higher category.

The imposition of this official hierarchy enabled authorities to classify inmates and obviously also gave them a broad range of options for differential treatment. At the same time, the classification system was designed to enforce a social order based on the official value system. Insofar as the prison succeeded in shaking off the prisoner's civilian self, the imposed hierarchy provided a framework for his personal reorganization. The inmates were offered "an opportunity to live up to a model of conduct that is at once ideal and staff sponsored."[177] The system bestowed on them rewards and privileges in exchange for following the concrete, detailed steps—prescribed in the model—that would bring them toward rehabilitation and reform. Inmates would thus be motivated to achieve individual reformation and correction, if only for reasons of self-interest. The system would foster the willingness of the prisoners to cooperate in prison activities and to support the overall mission of the prison. However, the existence of a peculiar inmate-created culture limited the effect of the staff-sponsored hierarchy.

The inmates in Republican prisons called each other *nanyou* (friends in difficulties).[178] The term in itself points to the tendency toward fraternization among inmates. The prisoners saw each other less as guilty perpetrators who had committed crimes than as people finding themselves in difficult circumstances. Inmates, especially if they shared a similar social background, easily found a common language and sympathized with each other. Words like *nanyou* also indicate the development of a prison argot, a specialized vocabulary and idiom shared by all inmates. Such tendencies often led to the forming of cliques, which were an important phenomenon in Chinese prison society.

Nearly all prisoners' accounts provide ample evidence of cliques in the prisons. Social cliques in general were formed on the basis of membership in criminal gangs, secret societies, sworn brotherhoods, protective militias, native-place associations, and political parties.[179] Cliques in prison frequently were extensions of such organizations in civilian society. The multitude of such organizations in Chinese society explains the frequency of reports on cliques in the Chinese prisons. The leader of a prison clique was commonly called the "cage head" *(longtou)*, and he had considerable power in the prison.[180] Inmates tried to remain on good terms with the cage head. Mostly he commanded a group of trustees. The close-knit solidarity of such a group, the members' readiness to resort to violence as well as their ability to obtain desired goods from the outside, presented them with an enormous advantage over regular unorganized prisoners.

Life in prison was dominated by frequent violent conflicts. Most conflicts were associated with rivalries between different cliques. The largest number of such infractions reported by Capital Number One Prison included "quarrelling," "concealing," and "violent actions."[181] There were almost daily fights between rival groups and cliques. Further indication of the rivalries is found in memoirs by CCP members. When members of the Chinese Communist Party arrived in a prison, one of their first concerted actions was to fight not against the prison authorities but against local cage heads.[182] Since cage heads and their cliques dominated inmate society, the CCP groups in prison took on this enemy first.

The social milieu of the inmates in a Republican prison was centered on seniority, affiliation with prison gangs, or both. This of course formed a powerful social order of the prisoners' making. In everyday prison life, loyalty to cage heads and solidarity with other "friends in difficulties" served to pull inmates through and help them maneuver smoothly through the prison world. Such practical values easily superseded the relevance of the ideal model officially propagated by the prison. The social and cultural formations initiated by the prisoners were as likely to divide the prison population as to bring them together, owing to the rivalries that formed between gangs and along social and political rifts.

In the prisoners' subculture, thoughts and habits prevailed that were quite incompatible with the official value system of the prison staff. This at least partly explains the high rate of recidivism among released prisoners.[183] The prison subculture insulated the inmates and compounded the already difficult task of rehabilitation and reform. One of the reasons for the troublesome tendency toward recidivism—which would bring the Republican prisons to the brink of failure—lay in the insufficient material conditions of prison life.

Building a new system of criminal justice was a daunting task. It called for the establishment of many new institutions, such as a police force, new courts, procurators, and, of course, detention facilities. All were complex and costly apparatuses that could operate well only with sufficient funding.

The Chinese Republic, however, was not able to finance these institutions adequately.[184] While the police force or the courts may not have functioned fully because of insufficient funding, the results for the prisons were more severe, and living conditions inside the prisons became extremely difficult. Living space, the food supply, and sanitation all deteriorated because of dwindling financial contributions for the prisons. As a result, material deprivation and physical suffering became a common part of the prison experience.

The power to shape the prisoner's space and exert control over his material conditions gave the prison staff significant leverage. Almost all recollections describe how inmates strove to adapt to or overcome the limitations set on their living conditions. Under the Republic, the prison population grew constantly. The number of newly opened prisons always lagged behind the fast-growing number of inmates. A Chinese sociologist, Li Jianhua, remarked: "The prisons, which were designed for a limited number of inmates, had in fact accepted unlimited numbers of prisoners."[185] It was not uncommon for a prison to keep more than double the number of prisoners it was originally designed for.[186] As a result the prisons were severely overcrowded, and this placed lasting physical pressures on the inmates, who were literally pressed against each other. It also led to a deterioration in prison hygiene as well as reduced food rations.

Despite their grand ambitions and modernist vision, the prisons frequently failed to have even the most basic utilities. The cells in most Republican prisons were not heated. Even in Mongolia, where the temperatures in winter were below freezing most of the time, there were no stoves, and prisoners had to sleep on unheated brick beds. Since the prison administration did not provide warm clothing, prisoners were "often more dead than alive from cold."[187]

Malnutrition and outright hunger were also widespread. Memoirs and reports by former inmates, as well as official documents, confirm this finding. The insufficient supply of nutritious food was in part caused by bad management, corruption, and embezzlement. But the reduction of food rations to amounts below the minimum standards was also used as a punishment for infractions.

Wang Ruowang spent three years in Caohejing, a prison for juvenile offenders in the suburbs of Shanghai.[188] According to his recollections, the biggest problem for inmates was unclean or spoiled food. The prison diet consisted mainly of two items: rice and vegetables. The rice that was given to the prisoners was often not edible (Wang recalled that on one occasion the rice had been burned in a warehouse fire; on another occasion it had gone bad or been contaminated by kerosene during shipment). Vegetables were added in only very small amounts. The author describes the situation with the following words: "Losing your freedom was of course hard to take, but getting food that wasn't even fit for pigs or dogs made it worse. The call 'Time to eat' hardly inspired our appetite here. We ate only because we had to, because we knew we'd be finished if we didn't. So all we could do was force ourselves to swallow the garbage they fed us."[189]

Almost all reports by former inmates mention unclean and rotten food as one of most repulsive experiences of life in the Republican prisons. Yang Chih-lin's report on nutrition in a model prison in Inner Monogolia is strikingly similar to the descriptions given by Wang Ruowang. Yang writes: "The prisoners were given only two meals a day. This consisted of millet adulterated with sand and fouled with mouse dirt and whatnot. We often had to eat up the leavings of the previous day, or three, four, ten, or even twenty days before. There were no vegetables to speak of. We craved salt, and finger-size pickled vegetables were a rare treat."[190]

To cite one last example: Mao Cheng's experience in the spring of 1929 fully corroborates the witness reports just mentioned. At the local district prison in Suzhou, prisoners had two meals a day. Rations were very small, consisting of twelve to fourteen ounces of rice, vegetables, and a thin watery soup.[191] This is roughly a third less than the amount that was officially supposed to be given to the inmates.[192] Mao Cheng also recounts that the rice had mostly gone bad and the vegetables were often rotten. But, he continues, inmates were so hungry that they treated even spoiled food as if it were a treasure and ate it very slowly. To eat slowly or to treat bad food as if it were something precious was also a way for prisoners to subvert the prison regime.

These descriptions offer glimpses of daily life in prison that rarely appear in official reports. But there are some hints in official documentation that strongly confirm the descriptions by former inmates. In 1921, for example, the Ministry of Justice enacted a decree that stated: "According to a recent investigation by officials of this ministry it has been found out that prisoners in the Zhili Number One Prison did not receive any food for several days and that the food rations in general were insufficient."[193] The investigation mentioned in the decree was undertaken in reaction to an increase in the death rate at the Zhili Number One Prison.

As mentioned, a reduction in the amount of food given to prisoners was not only a by-product of bad management but was also employed as a punishment. Article 82 of the prison regulations from 1913 lists all punishments for prisoners who violate the regulations in the prisons. The "reduction of food by one-fifth to three-fifths of the amount supplied for the regular meal" is mentioned as one of six permitted forms of punishment for inmates.[194] Given the already low standard for normal food rations, this punishment often inflicted nothing less than starvation.

Insufficient food was a fundamental problem for the Chinese prison administration, brought about by the lack of funding and by embezzlement. But whatever the concrete cause of the situation, overall the lack of food appears to have been a more or less dominant characteristic of life in Chinese prisons in the Republican period. These conditions produced a particular form of violence to which the inmates were constantly exposed. Permanent hunger weakened and tormented the body of the prisoner. The violence of causing hunger thus took a heavy physical toll. But hunger also has to be seen within a wider context. Food assumes enormous importance in prison: for the staff it provides a powerful lever for punishing and rewarding inmates; for many prisoners it conditions their life in custody and, in many respects, is symbolic of the prison experience. There is a complex relationship between food and imprisonment. Findings indicate that in prison, where control is taken away as the prisoner and his body become subject to external forces, food is experienced as part of the disciplinary machinery but also as a potentially powerful source of pleasure, resistance, and rebellion.

To be forced to eat food that is either unclean or has gone bad has another important dimension. Besides the fact that it can cause disease and malnutrition, it also has to be viewed as a form of physical contamination, presumably the most severe form. But other forms of contamination were also frequently experienced by the inmates. Those contaminations are mentioned over and over again in memoirs and reports; they represented a constant and severe source of humiliation and distress.

The most obvious type of contaminative exposure was related to the prisoner's bodily evacuations. In China's model prisons as well as in the county jails, inmates were allowed to go to the latrine at only two times specified each day (called *fang feng*). During the rest of the day and during the night inmates had to use a night stool that was placed in a corner of each cell.[195] Especially during summer, the stink of excrement would permeate the whole cell. The prisoners had to sleep and eat near their own excrement. As Mao Cheng described it, "All kind of evil smells arose so that we weren't able to breathe; it was even dirtier than in a pig pen."[196] Sidney Gamble, who saw the night slops during one of his visits, assumed that the toilets "in summer must give off an almost unbearable odor."[197] Yang Chih-lin noted: "In Summer, life in the cells became still more intolerable. The night stool placed in a corner of each cell was left 'til filled to capacity and the stink of it permeated the whole place."[198] Even in the late 1940s the night stools were still used. The journalist Huang Genghui took special notice of the fact that he was forced to use a night stool and had to sleep near his excrement when he was detained by police in 1948.[199]

Other contaminative experiences resulted from vermin. While the modern prisons boasted that they were clean and hygienic, accounts by the prisoners offer a different picture. In the modern model prisons, as well as in the old-style county jails, bedbugs and fleas frequently tormented the prisoners.[200] Contamination could also result from unwanted contact with staff or other inmates. As was mentioned above, upon admission convicts were thoroughly examined. This included physical, rectal, and genital examinations (in order to detect diseases) as well as pawing or fingering of their on-person possessions. This frisking was called *soushen*.[201] Searches of the inmate's body and his sleeping quarters were also conducted on a regular basis.[202]

Another typical source of contamination in prison resided in forced contact with other inmates. Prison authorities sometimes tried to mix prisoners of different ages and social, religious, or political groups. This was obviously designed to impede fraternization among prisoners. However, it could also lead an inmate to feel that he was being contaminated by contact with undesirable fellow inmates. For example, in retaliation for his political activities in prison, the local communist leader Wang Ruofei was reportedly locked in a cell with an inmate who had syphilis. Thereafter, a Chinese Muslim and a leading local criminal were put in his cell with him, in order to punish him and to overcome his resistance. This policy of forcing an inmate into close contact with (as he sees them) undesirable inmates from different, disrespected corners of society is described by the witnessing writer as "extremely wicked measures."[203] Since prisoners normally cannot control with whom they are confined in a small cell, this gives the staff the opportunity to put pressure on certain inmates by mixing them with alien or hostile cellmates.

Erving Goffman has argued that contaminative exposures of a physical or social kind should neither be ignored nor underestimated with respect to the effects they exercise over inmates.[204] In fact, physical contamination has a very strong impact on the inmate. This explains why contamination is so frequently mentioned in reports of former prisoners. Contaminative exposures force the prisoner to experience an invasion of the boundaries that the individual normally places between himself and his environment. Outside of prison, a person can hold himself—his body, his thoughts, his possessions, his acts—clear of contact with alien and dirty things. In the Chinese prisons these personal buffer zones were constantly violated and attacked.

When discussing experiences in the prisons, disease and death are highly significant issues. In general, death rates were comparatively high in the Republican prisons.[205] The underlying causes were mostly the endemic problems of providing adequate food, hygiene, and medicine for prisoners.[206] At times epidemics wiped out large proportions of a prison's population. Approximately one-fifth of the prisoners in Zhili Number One Prison in Tianjin, altogether 234 persons, died during the twelve months of 1921. It was reported that an average of 18 prisoners died of the disease each month. In the following year another 109 prisoners passed away, an average of 9 prisoners each month.[207] The inmates were plagued by ailments like stomach nodule, intestinal inflammation, and blood poisoning. Other frequent diseases included diphtheria, venereal diseases, and beriberi. In the winter of 1931–32, cold and wet weather lead to the outbreak of an epidemic in a Mongolian prison.

While the legal punishment of incarceration was supposed to be humane, it took a heavy physical toll. This clearly demonstrates that imprisonment itself is a form of violence, though the violence inflicted through imprisonment was different from the violence of the imperial Five Punishments. Imprisonment is violence exercised through a reduction or suspension of elementary goods like food, space, and leisure time. By withholding goods for subsistence or restricting liberties and capabilities, violence can be inflicted without ever directly hitting the body of the convict.[208] This could be described as a "violence of decay," and it is a form of violence that can be exercised anonymously. Since the suffering body is hidden from the perpetrator as well as from public, it facilitates a general indifference toward pain and death in prison. But violence also occurred in the prisons in its most overt and direct forms, namely as torture and execution.

Officially, torture did not exist in Republican prisons. Alongside all physical forms of punishment, torture was legally abolished as part of a criminal investigation. Nonetheless, numerous memoirs mention that prisoners were tortured in the Chinese Republic. Apparently there were two situations under which the authorities regularly resorted to physical maltreatment. First, serious infractions of the prison order, such as prison breaks or attacks on officers, were punished with violent assaults on all prisoners involved. Beatings of rebellious inmates were frequently reported.[209] Second, prisoners were frequently tortured during interrogations, especially in detention facilities run by police or the secret service. Torture was applied with the goal of forcing prisoners to cooperate with the police or secret service by giving them information about other suspects still at large. The use of torture during such questioning seems to have been common. Political prisoners, more than any other group, were threatened with torture, because they were seen as most likely to be able to provide valuable information about the whereabouts of their comrades.

The Hong Kong journalist Huang Genghui described how he was tortured in a police detention center in Guangzhou in 1948. During his interrogation and subsequent torture he was completely blindfolded with a towel that was wrapped around his head. The officers who conducted the interrogation asked him if he was a member of the CCP. He denied it. Thereafter the officers silently lead him to another room, where his fingers were tightly squeezed with small bamboo rods. He wrote: "Such a pain cannot be described with words and language. I clenched my teeth and endured [the pain], I could not help but quietly moan and scream, though."[210] From Huang's description, one gets the impression that torture was a routine procedure in this facility, applied to all new arrivals: each step of Huang's torture was carried out without discussion or consideration. Rather, a sequence of routine measures was carried out by a group of silent, experienced professionals.[211]

The different techniques of torture used in Republican prisons can be traced back to investigations conducted by magistrates in imperial China.

However, such practices, which were fully sanctioned in traditional China, were now in conflict with the new laws. For that reason, torture was most commonly used in facilities that were outside of the control of the judiciary.

The prison was not only the place where prisoners were deprived of their freedom but also the site where the death penalty was enforced. The Ministry of Justice provided detailed instructions for the execution of prisoners. The death penalty was to be carried out in a "simple and expeditious" way in order to minimize the suffering of the subject. A "simple mechanical" mode was prescribed, to achieve a mechanical and clinical execution. The gallows were the preferred mode of execution. In the 1930s the death penalty was also often carried out by shooting. Machines, with their scientific precision, replaced the human executioner, so that the punishment would be swift and painless. Even the use of chloroform was discussed. The aim of the death penalty was no longer to inflict pain; it was the clean disposal of a human life unworthy of continuation.[212]

Reports by former inmates about violence, physical maltreatment, and, above all, torture and executions were well known and circulated widely in the 1930s. Newspaper reports about cruel treatments and the torture of prisoners aroused the concern of liberals and intellectuals nationwide. In reaction to the growing number of reported cases, Song Qingling, along with Cai Yuanpei, Lin Yutang, and other writers and intellectuals initiated the establishment of the China League for the Protection of Civil Rights (Zhongguo Minquan Baozhang Tongmeng) in 1932. Among the three major missions of the league, the first was "to work for the release of political prisoners and for the abolishment of torture and other cruel treatments."[213]

It may never be known how many inmates died or were tortured in the Republican prisons. The prisons, and even more so the detention facilities in the Chinese Republic, certainly were places where violence or the threat of violence was pervasive and dominant. With occasional or recurring outbreaks of violence, the rehabilitative mission of imprisonment was seriously compromised. As a result, instead of being rehabilitated in prison, inmates were more likely to be victimized and traumatized. By any account, the use of torture and the death penalty clearly demonstrates that ideas of incapacitation and retaliation still wielded enormous influence on the Republican criminal justice system. Reformation and rehabilitation were to be offered to most offenders, but there was always a strong belief that the incorrigibles need to be rigorously incapacitated.

The disciplinary regime, the pervasive surveillance, and the violent assaults on the prisoner's body and self were conditions to which the inmates had to adapt—and prisoners had different ways of meeting this challenge. Apart from efforts at collective subversive action or resistance, they followed different lines of adaptation at different phases. A closer look reveals that inmates in fact could choose among different strategies in their response to life in prison.

First of all, it is essential to note that breaches of discipline and prisoner resistance were frequent occurrences in the Republican prisons. In 1913, Capital Number One Prison reported the following forms of deviant behavior by prisoners: "resisting orders," "idleness of work," "damaging materials," "stealing food," "talking," "fighting," and "plans to escape."[214] These and similar infractions demonstrate the degree to which prisoners were able to disturb the prison machinery. There are also several cases in which prisoners organized themselves and staged hunger strikes and boycotts in order to improve living conditions in prison. It appears that a part of the prison population responded to the pressures in the prison with passive resistance, disobedience, and sabotage.

Another way prisoners could partly regain control over their situation in this community of power was by influencing prison guards or wardens. Guards were the lowest and at the same time weakest point in the prison staff's chain of command. They represented the most natural target for prisoners. Moreover, guards often came from the same social and economic environment as the prisoners.[215] They received only superficial training and were, above all, poorly paid. They were strictly controlled by the prison administration, and in case of mistakes or offenses like corruption or embezzlement, they faced legal punishments that easily could turn them into prisoners as well.[216] Because of their daily interactions, fraternization in different degrees between staff and inmates did occur frequently. While the Republican prison as an institution very much relied on strict separation between staff and inmates, in practice this line was often blurred.

Guards could be influenced by prisoners through a variety of means.[217] Prisoners could offer them money or other valuable items as well as try to appeal to their sympathy, or—most promising—they could combine both approaches. Prisoners, especially those with good ties to outside groups, such as members of the CCP or of secret societies, could also threaten or intimidate guards, who were vulnerable as soon as they left the prison. Through these methods guards could be induced to buy important things for the prisoners, mostly cigarettes, alcohol, food, warm clothes, and medicine, and also to smuggle in drugs. Another valuable resource in an isolated community like the prison was information. Guards were asked to obtain information about other prisoners, administrative affairs related to the prison, the food supply, and criminal processes and hearings. Newspapers were in great demand. The relatively well organized communists also often wanted guards to deliver messages to fellow prisoners or to local communist cells outside the prison. Collaborating with guards in general made it possible for prisoners to gradually neutralize the prison's impermeability and break the isolation that normally resulted from confinement. The impressive prison walls in fact had loopholes.

In many cases, prisoners even developed bonds with the guards.[218] Recalcitrant inmates could make the warden's life much more difficult, just as the warden could create many problems for the prisoners. Under these circumstances of mutual dependence, regular involvement and strong ties between staff and prisoners could easily develop. Familiar relationships between wardens or guards and inmates of course threatened to undermine the structure of authority and social distance in the prisons. Aside from being a disciplinary problem, such relationships also point to a more fundamental dilemma in rehabilitative incarceration. The ill-paid and ill-trained prison staff faced a contradictory task. On the one hand, the staff had to discipline inmates and force them into obedience, while on the other hand, the wardens were supposed to maintain humane standards and to realize the rehabilitative goals of the prison.[219] The contradictory elements of rehabilitation and retribution broke into the open in the course of daily work. The staff had to ease the tension between these clashing goals and find practical solutions to this fundamental dilemma, which in turn provided inmates with a lever for subverting the overall mission of the prison.

After their release from prison, some ex-prisoners published reports about their experiences. Their writings had different layers and purposes. The prisoners wrote to document and report, but many further intended to restore their sense of self and the world. The prison as an imaginative site provided the setting in which they could reclaim a certain "truth" from the prison regime. In many writings, the prison was made into a symbol for injustice and degeneration. Resistance against the prison regime thus acquired a deeper meaning: beyond purposes of self-protection and defense, resistance could be portrayed as serving a historic purpose and also as encapsulating a cathartic heroism, purifying the hero and thus serving as a moral model reaching far beyond the prison experience. However, the prison writings were always ambiguous, an approximation of the truth, open to interpretation, manipulation, and appropriation.

There are several hidden agendas in extant prison writing that require careful consideration. Three different themes can be distinguished. The dominant theme in the writing of communist authors almost always is the vindication of strategies for the Chinese Revolution. The prison is portrayed as a site for forming a broad alliance of the disadvantaged and exploited. The second broad theme in many writings is self-assertion in the face of pressures present in a total institution. Finally, a third theme is the prison as a symbol for the ambivalence in the political order of Republican China.

Communists or suspected members of the CCP were a distinct group in prison. While their actual number was much smaller than, for instance, that of criminal offenders, most authors of prison writings belonged to this group. Almost all of the writings by Chinese communists started from a common notion: they liked to compare their prison experience with that of school. Not every writer was as explicit and outspoken as Mao Cheng and Liu Zhao. Mao wrote: "They [communist prisoners] were not afraid to turn the prison into their school."[220] Liu Zhao called his prison stint a "University for Revolution."[221] In general, these writers stressed how essential their prison experience was for the Chinese Revolution.[222]

The portrayal of prison as a school or training ground for revolution included several distinct aspects. First, from the prison regime conclusions were drawn about the nature of the GMD regime as a whole. A heroic figure of unabashed resistance, Wang Ruofei, explained to his fearful comrades: "First of all, we must know what this prison is. The old society itself is mankind's big prison, but this prison is only an epitome of the old society. We prisoners can clearly visualize the true colours of the existing society through the dark rule in this prison."[223] The writers emphasized that the prison represents fe   atures of the state and society in a condensed form. Not only could imprisoned communists learn about the true nature of the Chinese Republic, but they would also be able to detect its weaknesses and internal contradictions.[224] Since the prison world and the larger social world were connected by the political system, firsthand knowledge of the Republican enemy would help the party offer resistance in prison and stage revolution on the outside.

A second aspect of the school metaphor was related to the recruitment of CCP supporters among the prisoners. The prison provided an ideal testing ground for the party's techniques of persuasion and conversion. This effort can also be seen as an attempt to conduct a counterconversion to rival the official mission of the Republican prison. Yang Chih-lin describes an ideal political conversion process. A young Mongol herdsman with the name San Mao, who was convicted for collaborating with bandits, was taught reading and writing skills in prison by party member Wang Ruofei. In the process he was also given political instruction. The author explains: "In the course of his studies he had become more and more class-conscious."[225] In the dark and filthy prison cells the disadvantaged, impoverished, exploited, humiliated sectors of Chinese society were assembled.[226] All of them had committed crimes like robbery, assault, or murder. Yet CCP members in prison argued that the injustices of the old society had forced them to commit these crimes. Even if they were serious criminals like gang leaders or murderers, in all instances CCP members asserted that the offenders had no individual guilt. Instead, blame was put on the social order, feudal customs, or economic conditions. All inmates were therefore fully acceptable as fellow fighters and potential party members.

Finally, the prison experience could be used to teach techniques of resistance and struggle. There are many heroic depictions of inmates who resisted assaults, engaged in struggle, endured physical abuse, withstood psychological pressures and interrogations. Writers recount over and over again how they audaciously put forth their demands and fought their attackers both physically and with words. Many memoirs emphasize this point, some in very telling ways. Their descriptions all indicate that CCP members in prison tried to immunize themselves against pressures and strengthen their resistance by forming tight-knit party cells.[227] The party cells in prison resembled a family more than a political group. Many writings assert that genuine affection and love bound the members together—that party members treated each other with care and love "sprung from the love of a class-brother."[228]

To achieve such a high degree of group coherence and identification, a variety of measures was adopted. Party members in prison were encouraged to keep up with their political study and ideological work. CCP cells were always on guard against renegades or apostates who could threaten their struggle.[229] Nobody outside the ranks of the party was to be trusted in prison. Equally important, inmates learned to subordinate themselves to the greater interest of the collective. It was asserted that the individual was unable to survive in prison, that only the collective would prevail. In short, CCP members formed strong moral and political communities in the prisons. To maintain internal coherence, these groups willingly limited outside contacts, distrusted outsiders, demanded subordination of the members to the common cause, and closed themselves off against ideological influences of any kind. Having maneuvered through prison and maintained their solidarity in that hostile environment, these groups shared a powerful faith in the possibility of radical social transformation.

Intellectuals and writers who were not integrated into the close and well-organized structure of the CCP give us a very different picture of their imprisonment experience. Lacking the warmth of a political confraternity, they found themselves in solitude. Although prison life was filled with many scheduled activities and appointments, many inmates nevertheless experienced long stretches of forced inactivity. New arrivals, especially, felt forlorn for long periods of time. Huang Genghui captured the silent loneliness in prison with the following words: "Being silent, I spoke very little. Every time I had a dream in the night, I threw on clothes and rose. The prison was filled with hush, only the guards carrying guns patrolled to and fro, it was chilling and awe inspiring. Sometimes, when I saw pieces of the moonlight or heard the rain dropping down, it became unbearable and I felt unlimited sadness."[230]

Huang Genghui expressed what prison inmates often feel, namely that during their prison term they are "exiled from living."[231] A similar point is made by Xiao Jun when he has his protagonist say about his stretch in prison: "I eat. I sleep. I wear out the floor, my shoes, and my allotted span of youth and life."[232] There is a prevailing sense in the accounts of imprisonment that time spent in prison is fundamentally wasted and senseless. It goes without saying that such feelings negate all efforts aimed at rehabilitation and reformation.

It has been said elsewhere, too, that incarceration wastes the time of inmates, that "it destroys time, empties time."[233] The emptiness of time leads to the emptying of the prisoner's self; as Huang's depiction quoted above indicates, one loses the ability even to speak. The weight and the pressures of the prison regime push the prisoners out of their personal existence and destroy their ability to articulate. Prisoners are thus forced to seek life's essence and meaning elsewhere. A common response among Chinese prisoners in their memoirs and autobiographies was to cling to the written word. Not all prisoners, of course, could resort to writing; it goes without saying that only a tiny fraction of intellectuals or highly educated prisoners could seek to preserve their sense of self through writing.[234] But those who could, wrote to achieve self-expression and self-affirmation. They also intended to put their oppositional work against the official texts and thus seek empowerment. Some high-ranking, well-educated members of the CCP sought to write theoretical or historical treatises on a broad range of topics. Others continued to defend the very positions and opinions that got them into prison.

Du Zhongyuan, for instance, was a patriotic businessman and activist in the national product movement. He was thrown into Jiangsu Number Two Prison in 1935 because he attacked Jiang Jieshi's policy of appeasement toward Japan. In prison he composed several essays defending his position.[235] He described how he desperately tried to obtain political news in prison in order to keep up with recent developments. He also wrote about the true meaning of nationalism and about the spirit of sacrifice. Clearly the author carefully designed his texts to display a heroic posture.

This is in fact a common feature of many of the prison texts discussed here. Efforts at self-affirmation are combined with a heroic attitude. The heroism is centered on the notion of a single individual voice desperately trying to make itself heard within the massive silent presence of the prison. By withstanding the pressures of silence the hero elevates and even purifies himself. The author is shown to prevail in a hostile environment and, despite all suffering, to have held to his true convictions. Being a victim of political arbitrariness, the inmate-author appears all the more authentic and trustworthy in his intentions, and thus his beliefs and convictions are purified.

Writing about the prison experience produced texts that gained their authors a reputation as moral leaders and that were intended to have a lasting influence on how people understood moral leadership and political responsibility. The heroic images of living persons, based on experience and authenticity, acquired a compelling authority. Unlike the anonymous heroes favored by the secret service or the military, these models of self-affirmation were individuals with names and personal histories.[236] Such notions and symbols of heroic individualism impaired not only the prison's public image but also its mission.

For some prisoners, the prison experience was the starting point for their alienation from the Chinese Republic. Luo Longji, a well-known political scientist and activist for human rights, published an article in 1930 in the Shanghai monthly *Xinyue* (Crescent Moon) that was titled "The Outrageous Event of My Arrest."[237] The first part of the article contains a detailed description of his arrest in 1930 and his interrogation during detention. The experience of his arrest left him deeply shattered and frightened. Although he was released after several hours of questioning, he maintained that he had experienced a form of imprisonment. He wrote: "My arrest is actually a very small matter, in the end I wasn't thrown into prison. But do I need to be innocently killed before my case counts? I sacrificed six hours of my freedom, is this nothing? It is a small topic with a great meaning. And therefore, I demand from the leaders of our party state to investigate the police stations all over the country and determine how many innocent people are still detained."[238] In the second part of the article he went on to sharply attack the government. He reproached the state that would arbitrarily imprison or assassinate its critics. Critical voices were, he wrote, lacking legal guarantees and were pushed around by anonymous forces in the form of faceless, violent state agents and police officers. The next two parts contain a rather scathing judgment about the legal reforms in Republican China. He wrote: "Human rights and the rule of law represent in the eyes of the 'GMD comrades' nothing but reactionary thinking" (14). The punch line comes in the last paragraph. He reminded the GMD government of the fate of the Bastille in revolutionary France, which had merely "planted the seeds of revolution." He continued: "Interrogation, arrest, detention, imprisonment, punishment, assassination all are indicators of political chaos. These are stupid methods of stupid people" (17).

Luo Longji was a well-respected liberal with initially strong ties to the Republican state. Nonetheless his deep disillusionment and disappointment can hardly be ignored. His whole article is written in a sharp, accusatory tone that expressed his serious concern, indignation, and outright anger. His reaction mirrors the growth of political activism coming out of experiences of detention and imprisonment. A new consciousness had emerged, with a heightened understanding of the citizen as an autonomous individual with rights, freedoms, and legal entitlements.[239] Luo Longji, too, demanded the acknowledgement and protection of certain securities and guarantees by the Republican state. However, this very notion of inalienable rights and its implied concept of freedom led Luo Longji to distance himself further and further from the Republican state and its modern authoritarian project. The Republican prison increasingly became a breeding ground for discontent and public criticism.

The Prison and the Modern Project in China

In the first half of the twentieth century, when the new Chinese criminal justice system was created, China wanted this system to be essentially modernist and progressive. The new system of punishment and criminal justice was conceived as an intrinsic part of the modern project in China and thus was understood as an important key to a broader overhaul of society. A framework of problems, concepts, and styles of argument that had emerged in Europe at the end of the nineteenth century was carefully examined by Chinese authorities in the course of shaping their own criminal justice state. It was a global and interdisciplinary framework shaped by the concourse of medical psychology, criminal anthropology, statistical data acquisition, social reform, and prison discipline.[240] This theoretical framework was transmitted to China by a score of Chinese legal experts and prison practitioners in an active process of translation and transfer.

In Republican China, then, this framework provided the coordinates for the establishment and diffusion of penal-therapeutic institutions of confinement. The main ideas behind this modernist system were an unshakable faith in instrumental reason, a prevailing vision of a pervasive technocratic state, and a strong commitment to social engineering. Leading officials increasingly agreed on this new approach to imprisonment, influenced by the demand for the reformation of criminals. The principle of reform was championed by Chinese proponents of the modern school of criminal law, which was designed to replace the traditional policy based on deterrence and uniform retribution. Uniform retributive punishment was seen as a remnant of premodern traditional practices, which were irrational, emotional, and without social benefit.

However, foreign models and discourses were never blindly imitated but were adopted in a creative process. In law, court actions came to be guided by a modern code that was first copied from Germany (via Japan), then altered to better fit Chinese realities, resulting in a legal code that represented a remarkable blend of continental European and Chinese legal culture.[241] With respect to the discourse on crime and punishment in Republican China, it is evident that knowledge, techniques, and practices from other parts of the world were combined with indigenous knowledge, techniques, and practices in a flexible and creative process of negotiation and interaction that resulted in hybrid social and cultural forms. In prisons, too, Western methods of time management, spatial control, and visual supervision were linked with instruction centered on Buddhist and Confucian teachings, designed to initiate moral correction and reform in prison inmates.[242] The Republican prison was an institution characterized by a remarkable hybridity, an outcome of this melding of elements from different social and cultural origins. In this the prison mirrored the blurred political culture of the Chinese Republic, which oscillated between the continuation of indigenous traditions and the adoption of exogenous technologies, between authoritarian models and liberal approaches, between cosmopolitanism and chauvinist nationalism, between a leader cult and the promise of democracy.[243]

The policy of reform and correction shaped the Chinese prison. The proper management of crime and the criminal required individualized, corrective measures adapted to the specific case or the particular problem. In Chinese penology and criminology, crime was a social and moral problem that was presented in the form of individual acts. The maladjusted delinquent was the problem, and reformative, correctional treatment was the solution. Accordingly, correctional intervention by the authorities took the form of penal-therapeutic treatment, combining punitive measures with education and instruction. Imprisonment enabled the authorities to gain an enormous degree of power over the inmate. Confined to a small room, without help or support from third persons, the inmate was in fact dependent on prison authorities for every aspect of daily life. Confinement also allowed the authorities to subject the inmate to constant monitoring and supervision through the prison staff. The ultimate goal was to construe criminals as a population of degenerate, deficient types in order to justify disciplinary control and then establish systems of administration and instruction.

This approach to penology framed the penal-welfare institutions that developed during Republican China. At the same time, the prison also became a place where the new social relationship between the individual and state authority emerged. The state tried to transform, educate, train, regulate, and advise its citizens in different ways and on many topics. In prison, the authorities defined detailed norms and standards for personal hygiene, work attitude, political convictions, discipline and obedience, duties and entitlements, and ethical conduct. In the prison, the Chinese nation-state structured a new system of representation and set new terms for individualized self-representation. Modern Chinese subjectivity (individuality, consciousness, conduct), like a docile body, was defined by these new power relationships in which it was constrained and which became most visible in the Chinese prison. Together, these projects of the modern prison formed a powerful social technology of control and persuasion that could be used in other institutions, too, such as the school or the factory. Moreover, this technology also promised to be an effective tool in administering the complex urban society as a whole.

By refraining from draconian measures and adopting a penal-welfare policy, the state under the Chinese Republic expanded into society and intervened in sectors that the imperial state had left untouched. The Republican state took over more and more responsibilities and raised ever greater claims for the need to monitor and standardize the life of its citizens. Under the rhetoric of benign rehabilitation, the state extended its reach to manage not only crime but also the inner self of its citizens through programs of training and instruction. An essential part of the modern project in Republican China was the establishment of mechanisms and technologies that would give the state more efficient control over its citizens on a minute level.

Reports of former inmates describe the many psychological and physical pressures that went along with "confinement as coercive education."[244] The Republican prison certainly did not fail to fully deploy these disciplinary techniques. And there is no point in denying the considerable achievements made by the Republican body politic in establishing several model institutions for carrying out rehabilitative and disciplinary custody. Yet the deficits and weaknesses of the system cannot be overlooked. The Guomindang government set up new-style Chinese courts and judicial regulations, prisons, and judicial personnel in the major cities, where they were visible to metropolitan authorities. These coexisted with the largely unchanged justice system in rural inland areas, with the result that the Republican era was characterized by two coexisting modes of judicial administration, old and new, depending on location. But even the new-style Chinese prison was flawed by conditions of hunger, overcrowding, conflict, and violence. Underworld cliques and criminal groups clashed over dominance of the prison society. While in prison, inmates remained enmeshed in the gears of criminality. Victimization and traumatization were far more often the result of imprisonment than was rehabilitation. The violent side of the Republican prison was partly the result of a still widespread understanding of punishment as a form of incapacitation or retaliation, in part due to limitations resulting from the problems of institution building in Republican China in general.[245] The seesawing of the budget of the Republican state left the prison system financially fragile. Corruption and embezzlement worsened the situation.

While the penal system gave the government an effective tool for maintaining social control, its obvious malfunctions and flaws undermined the credibility of Republican criminal justice. The belief that the Republican government was committed to upholding justice, or able to uphold it, faded away quickly. The whole legal scaffolding of the Republic became vulnerable to powerful narratives that, as we have seen, identified the Republican prisons with the same injustices for which the Bastille in absolutist France was well known.

3

TRIALS OF TERROR

War and Revolution

ROM the mid-1930s to the end of the 1940s China was ravaged by war and revolution, which caused great destruction and enormous losses of life. In the history of criminal justice in China, this phase, too, was marked by disruption and displacement. The legal reforms of the Nanjing years came to a complete standstill: the central government, in exile in Chongqing, was no longer interested in or capable of drafting ambitious new criminal justice legislation. In the territories in eastern China, which were stricken by intense fighting or had come under foreign occupation, the new courts were dissolved and the new prisons destroyed. On a deeper level, too, shifts were taking place that would irrevocably shape criminal justice in China far beyond the period of violent upheaval. It would take several decades, eventually, to undo those changes and to return to the earlier civilian developments of the Nanjing era.

As historians recently have argued, the experience of war deeply influences the political, cultural, and social relationships in a society.[1] Legally, morally, and practically, the Republican state in China and its political adversaries found themselves fundamentally dependent on their ability to use violence. Until 1949, the very real presence of continuous hostilities and civil strife determined the relationships among various political factions and between each of those factions and its citizens. What Carl Schmitt once called the state's "monstrous power" to exercise the power of life and death over human beings began to fundamentally shape Chinese political culture and to affect legal practices on all sides.[2] The emerging divide between opposing political forces led to a growing polarization and politicization of society, which severely affected and in fact radicalized criminal justice operations.

The narrative of criminal justice during this phase therefore has to be divided into discussions of two different approaches and philosophies. On the one hand were the areas under Nationalist control. There we observe what could best be described as a criminal justice system in a state of emergency. Its growing anxiety from being under constant threat and pressure caused the Guomindang government to suspend the existing civilian criminal justice system and replace it with a system dominated by political and military bodies charged with responding to oppositional and hostile forces. And on the other hand were the areas under Communist Party control, where criminal justice was from the beginning understood as a powerful instrument of class struggle. There, too, the main concern was to dispose of the various real or perceived enemies. From a historical perspective, the commonalities between the two different approaches are striking, despite the fact that they claimed to rest on fundamentally different political philosophies. In both camps, the military and intelligence organizations laid claim to a monopoly over legal affairs, allegedly for security concerns. They argued that the war situation did not leave room for lengthy, complicated legal procedures, and that the need for security arising out of confrontations with unrelenting enemies both within and on the outside dictated the need for abridged and accelerated trials. Ideas of justice and fairness receded into the background, as the notion of being caught in a struggle for survival began to hold sway. Expedient systems of justice evolved that were crooked, unreliable, and open to political intervention.

Criminal Justice in a State of Emergency:
The Nationalist Areas

The new courts and prisons in Republican China were all part of the judicial system: they were under the supervision of the Ministry of Justice, and they detained convicts who had been sentenced by a court in a regular criminal process, conducted in compliance with the laws. Especially in the late 1930s and 1940s, however, the GMD government created a bewildering variety of institutions of confinement that did not belong to the formal criminal justice system and were never controlled by the judiciary. These institutions included detention centers run by the police, military prisons under military command, reformatory "self-investigation institutes" operated by the military or the military police, and, finally, internment camps and secret prisons run by the military or the secret service. As demonstrated in this enumeration alone, the military, the police, and the secret services vigorously began to intervene in the realm of social control and repression. Moreover, punishments carried out outside the judiciary became much more important in the late 1930s, so that by the 1940s more offenders were perhaps detained or punished in those facilities than in the new civilian prisons.[3] This tendency began to corrupt the legal system in the sense that the people's sense of justice was offended and the whole system of social control was gradually undermined.

The extensive system of secret prisons, lockups, and prison camps that was built during the war years by the GMD government has evaded scrutiny until now. It is evident that those in the highest echelons of the government and the party were fully aware of its existence. However, because the full extent of this secretive universe is not yet publicly known, many facts, numbers, and details about it remain elusive. But some of these hidden institutions have been described by former prisoners and other witnesses, and some scattered archival information is available.

Despite the emphasis on reform and education in many Republican penological statements, a comprehensive network of nonrehabilitative institutions of confinement came into being in the Republic of China. Basically there were three organizations involved in this development: the regular police, the intelligence services, and the military. The police ran detention centers that were attached to the courts and held prisoners who were awaiting trial. Such detention centers were set up in many areas, and they stood under the authority of the judiciary. Sometimes prisoners were kept in them for very long stretches. Neither work nor instruction was provided.

The secret services also operated their own secret network of jails and detention centers. Some of the most infamous prisons were under their control. These included, for instance, the Nanjing Special Prison (Nanjing Tezhong Zhaodaisuo), Yiyang Prison, and the Southeastern Prison at Jian'an in Fujian.[4] The military intelligence service Juntong alone operated approximately twenty special prisons and detention centers in all major metropolitan areas.[5] Imprisonments in these institutions were carried out without sentencing or the possibility of challenging the imprisonment in a court. The emergency laws that were enacted in the 1930s for protecting state security (discussed in Chapter 2) provided the legal basis for the arrests. These secret institutions of confinement were not controlled by the civilian branch of the government.

The secret confinement sites run by the intelligence community were above all charged with questioning. Numerous reports provide evidence that torture was frequently applied to extract information or to physically punish detainees.[6] At these sites physical suffering replaced any other punitive purpose. In the 1940s the number of cases in which physical punishment was reported increased sharply.

At the same time, a parallel system of military justice arose, with its own codes, military police, courts, and prisons.[7] Time and again military agencies and courts encroached on the civil judiciary, sweeping up many civilian offenders during the process. The system of military punishment primarily sought to induce terror and discipline. Besides imprisonment and torture, executions were part of the array of military punishments. Firing squads were allowed to carry out summary executions ordered by military bodies. These executions mostly were related to the suppression of banditry or rebellion. The legal basis for this was the law titled Regulations for the Suppression of Banditry, which dated back to 1914. The law allowed executions to be carried out "on the spot."[8]

The prevalence and persistence of these practices also point to continuities between late-imperial and Republican patterns of state violence. Even while new technologies of confinement and reeducation spread out, more traditional forms of torture and physical punishment lingered on.

The 1930s witnessed the growth of political forces that were hostile to the Republican system. Foremost among these forces was the Communist Party, which intended to overthrow the GMD government. During the first years of the Nanjing decade (1928–1937), the GMD government relied on existing legal mechanisms (police, the military, prisons) for dealing with communist forces. But the fast-growing wave of opposition and dissidence prompted the administration to look for other institutions that could deal with the special group of communist political prisoners by offering specifically tailored treatment. Basically, two institutions were created: the so-called self-investigation institutes and internment camps. Before the outbreak of the Second World War, the focus was on self-investigation institutes; during World War II internment camps became increasingly prevalent—and virulent.

The first self-investigation institutes *(Fanxing yuan)* were opened in 1928.[9] Three years later, there were seventeen self-investigation institutes in fifteen provinces.[10] In the early years these reformatories played a major role in conjunction with the GMD purges carried out by special courts established following the breakup of the First United Front in 1927. (The First United Front, formed in 1923, was an alliance of the Guomindang and the Chinese Communist Party aimed at ending warlordism in China. Communists were absorbed into the GMD. When the First United Front broke up, the GMD purged the communists from its ranks.) The institutes, in particular, were intended to detain communists who had been active in the GMD. The detainees were to engage in self-examination and cleanse themselves of communist influences that might still hold sway over their thinking. Later, the institutes were used for holding all kinds of political dissidents, in particular members of the CCP or its sympathizers.

The mission of the self-investigation institutes was to enable prisoners to become aware of their errors and crimes, gain a basic education, and acquire vocational training. Prisoners needed to be prodded to "repent mistakes and renew themselves," and to achieve this, political indoctrination and "military training" were emphasized.[11] Military training referred to the imposition of rigorous discipline. Prisoners had to sit with a straight back, and good posture was demanded at all times; orderliness and cleanliness were the responsibility of each prisoner and were strictly enforced. Political indoctrination was carried out in the form of lectures and study sessions focusing on party ideology and political science. In the self-investigation institutes, the moral instruction so common in regular prisons was completely replaced by teachings exclusively related to the state party. The aim was a profound "partification" *(danghua)* of prison education, a policy that of course reflects similar efforts in the education sector in general.[12] The authorities also pushed for prisoner self-administration. They appointed group leaders who were responsible for maintaining discipline and carrying out prison education. This was a novelty in Chinese prison administration. For the first time, prisoners were used to control prisoners in order to enhance and intensify discipline.

The self-investigation institutes were mostly under the control of the military or the military police. Suspected communists were arrested and sent to the reformatories without court hearings. In the mid-1930s the government deliberately created a mechanism that allowed for bypassing the criminal justice system when dealing with political offenders. In many respects the self-investigation institutes anticipated the development of the internment camps, which had a similar mission and were based on similar premises.

The Sino-Japanese War, the internal conflict with the Chinese Communist Party, and growing and widespread dissatisfaction and disillusionment with GMD rule created a deep sense of crisis within and outside of the Republican government. In the tense and polarizing situation during the war, Republican authorities increasingly considered civilian laws as no longer valid.[13] On the contrary they thought that, facing enemies on all fronts, the Republican state had to reserve for itself the capacity to take extraordinary measures to "save the nation."

During the war years, from 1938 to 1949, the GMD government started to open up a number of internment camps for holding alleged political enemies and members of oppositional groups. The main targets were communists, CCP sympathizers, combatants in the communist armed forces, liberal intellectuals, outspoken critics of the government, representatives of so-called middle parties, and GMD secret service members who required punishment for disciplinary reasons. The camps themselves were run under different names and by different political bodies. Altogether four organizations established internment camps in Republican China: the secret services Juntong and Zhongtong, the Sanmin Zhuyi Youth Corps (Sanmin Zhuyi Qingnian Tuan), and the military. The official titles of institutions run by Sanmin Zhuyi Youth Corps often included the phrase "Brigade for teaching and guiding" *(xundao dui)*. In general, the militarist, right-wing faction of the GMD government seems to have been mainly in charge of the camps. As a rule, the existence and locations of these camps were kept secret. Official and published documents made no reference to the camps, and even within the civilian government only few party leaders knew about them.

The system of internment camps was diverse, as the following examples demonstrate. In 1940 Chiang Kai-shek approved the establishment of the Northwestern Youth Labor Camp.[14] More than three hundred high school and college students were detained there. The prisoners were organized in three battalions *(dadui)*. Twice a week they had to attend political study and indoctrination meetings. The camp was steadily expanded, taking in growing numbers of youth activists and students. In 1944 it was reorganized as the Northwestern Branch of the Youth Corps Training Center. While the camp initially had been under the control of local military training units, by then it had been transferred to the authority of the Three Principles Youth Corps.

In 1941 another camp was established in Shangrao, Jiangxi Province; in 1942 it was officially named Southeastern Branch of the Central Wartime Youth Brigade for Teaching and Guiding.[15] In March 1941, the GMD government brought in approximately 600 captured fighters from the communist New Fourth Army, including more than eighty members of the CCP, as well as students and intellectuals. The GMD set up a large-scale prison camp, along with branches in Maojialing, Qifengyan (where high officials were imprisoned), Zhoutian (for hard labor), and Licun (where the Guomindang used soft tactics such as persuasion and indoctrination to win over its prisoners). The prison camps were surrounded by high walls and wire fences, densely ringed by lookout posts and stern guards. An outer guard circle was set up within 30 *li* (15 km) of the camps.

When the Japanese army captured Shangrao in June 1942, that camp was moved to Fujian Province. More than 1,000 prisoners were detained in Fujian. Prisoners there were forced to perform physical labor and to participate in study sessions. The reading mainly consisted of *Three Principles of the People* by Sun Yat-sen and other important party documents. The Fujian camp was eventually dissolved in October 1945. Similar camps run by the Youth Corps were located in Laohekou (Henan), Enshi (Hubei), Yexian (Henan), Hengyang (Hunan), Luoyang (Shanxi), and Lanzhou (Gansu).

Chongqing was the site of perhaps the most infamous internment center in Republican China. The camp was a system of several different internment sites. One, called Bai Mansion (Bai Gongguan)—said to have been the home of Tang poet Bai Juyi—was selected by Dai Li in 1939 as the site for a new "special detention center."[16] In 1941 the Sino-American Cooperation Organization (SACO) was set up in the immediate vicinity under a secret agreement with the United States. American advisers were stationed there to train secret agents and spies. The prison camp itself was under the control of Dai Li's military secret service (the Juntong) and was located in the former Zhazidong coal mine in Chongqing. Prisoners were transferred there in larger numbers from 1943 onward. The compound eventually was surrounded by several guard posts and high-voltage wire. The camp had eighteen barracks, in which more than 300 prisoners were kept. Former inmates reported the frequent use of torture in interrogations, and regular executions. On November 27, 1949, as the People's Liberation Army advanced to Chongqing, almost eighty remaining prisoners were executed. There were also several smaller camps in the vicinity.

Because there is little archival and official information on the camps, it is not possible to produce a complete list of all the camps. No figures are available for the total number of prisoners they held, nor are there reliable estimates for the number of inmates who died. The general purpose of the camps seems relatively clear, though. They were operated by military agencies for the internment of captured enemy combatants. The secret services used their camps as sites for conducting interrogations and investigations as well as for punishing delinquent agents. High-profile prisoners who were thought to possess valuable information were detained in those sites. The camps run by the Three Principles Youth Corps focused on holding civilian supporters and sympathizers of the CCP, above all high school students. In an attempt to deal with the spreading turmoil within its own organization and growing criticism of its rule, the GMD made systematic use of internment camps to try to quell political resistance and tighten internal discipline.

The GMD never officially designated the camps as internment or concentration camps. Instead euphemisms were used. But political opponents and critics of the Guomindang government applied the term "concentration camp" very early on in order to criticize the government and expose what they saw as the true nature of GMD rule. This could easily be dismissed as politically motivated propaganda were it not for the foreign allies who also described the camps as concentration camps. In 1941 an American report mentioned a dozen "concentration camps" set up by the secret police.[17] In September 1945, Philip D. Sprouse, U.S. consul in Kunmin, prepared a memorandum about the "Concentration Camp System in China" and sent it to Washington. He specifically discussed the secret service prison near Chongqing and throughout the report referred to that prison as a concentration camp "where Chinese youth are sent when the Kuomintang [Guomindang] authorities believe that such individuals can be 'persuaded' to correct their thinking and return to a role in society which does not entail opposition to the Kuomintang."[18]

Perhaps more important, in their internal communications Dai Li and the leading Juntong officers frankly referred to these institutions as concentration camps. In the official *nianpu* (chronological biography) of Dai Li, compiled in 1966 by his comrades, Dai Li is quoted by saying: "It is correct, we had concentration camps [*bu cuo, shi you jizhongying*]; but I think that in times of war every state has organized similar institutions, detaining political prisoners of war as well as enemies and spies who do harm to national security."[19] This statement not only provides evidence that in the 1940 the camps were internally designated as concentration camps but it also shows that even as late as the 1960s the Juntong did not hesitate to use the term "concentration camp" for these institutions. It also proves the close involvement of the Juntong leadership in building and maintaining the camp system.

Within the ranks of the Juntong, one camp in particular was regarded as a model institution, one that would play a powerful role in safeguarding the GMD regime from the threats and insecurities of the war years. In the eyes of Dai Li and other leaders this facility was the most important internment camp, and they determined that it should ultimately inspire the creation of a large camp system throughout China. This was the Xifeng camp, and its history provides us with a closer look at the nature of the GMD government during the war.

In September 1938 a group of about 200 prisoners arrived at a small village in the foothills of Nanwangshan Mountain, fifty miles north of Guiyang in Guizhou Province. The group had made a long journey. Originally detained in Nanjing Special Prison, the prisoners had made a complicated odyssey through Dai Li's ramified labyrinth of secret prisons. They were first moved from Nanjing to Wuhan, shortly thereafter were taken to Yiyang in Hunan, and from there they were eventually transported to this remote spot, located five miles south of the small town of Xifeng, seat of the magistrate of Xifeng County. The relocations had been necessary because of encroaching Japanese troops in the summer of 1937. This was the first group of prisoners to be held in the Xifeng area. The prisoners were placed in a farmhouse and were ordered to construct a number of barracks. Because of this, the prisoners and guards called it the "new prison" *(xinjian)*. Its official administrative name was Xifeng Special Branch of the Military Commission at the Republican Government (Guomin Zhengfu Junshi Weiyuanhui Xifeng Xingyuan).[20]

The site of the camp appears to have been very carefully chosen. Xifeng was well behind the front lines of the war with Japan. A secluded place, it was surrounded by hills and mountains and was thus neither easily located nor accidentally sighted. Despite its remoteness, however, it was not far from Guiyang. Transportation was relatively convenient: Xifeng was directly connected to the wartime capital Chongqing by a highway going from Guizhou to Chongqing.[21]

The history of the Xifeng camp can be divided into two periods correlating to the terms of the two directors who were in charge of the camp. The first period runs from the founding of the camp in 1938 until the decommissioning of its first director, He Zizhen, in 1941. During the four years of He's term, conditions in the camp were marked by a high degree of violence, harsh living conditions, executions, assaults on prisoners, and a very high mortality rate. Prisoners were locked up all day. They were given neither work nor instruction. During this time conditions in Xifeng were not much different from conditions in other secret detention sites run by the secret services. Government-instilled hatred of the enemy prisoners, neglect, or simple sadism led to frequent abuses and brutalities.

In March 1941 Dai Li sent to Xifeng a young, ambitious, and capable Juntong officer by the name of Zhou Yanghao, who served as director until the camp was disbanded in July 1946. Zhou Yanghao was one of the few members of the Juntong who had received a college-level education. He had attended the Shanghai Law Academy (Shanghai Faxueyuan) for judicial training, at a time when Chinese criminologists and penologists increasingly looked on the Soviet Union as a model for a successful criminal justice system. In the mid-1930s two leading judicial experts in Shanghai, Sun Xiong and Li Jianhua (of Fudan University and Shanghai Law Academy, respectively), praised Soviet forms of imprisonment as progressive and effective. In a nutshell, they argued that the Soviet Union's use of labor for reform and correction (laodong ganhua) should serve as a model and an inspiration for Chinese penal reforms.[22] They explained that inmates of Soviet prison camps were detained not in single cells but in communal groups, in which they lived and worked together and collectively strove for their correction. Li Jianhua stressed that, according to reports from foreign visitors, the camps in the Soviet Union did not even look like prisons but looked more like factories and farming villages. At the same time, there was also close military cooperation between China and the Third Reich, a relationship that officially lasted until 1936. Officers from the GMD army as well as from the intelligence community frequently traveled to Germany.[23] There was also a group of around fifty military advisers that worked very closely with the GMD leadership, and in particular with the military command.[24] The Chinese intelligence services published a magazine called *Future (Qiantu)*, which featured a series of enthusiastic articles about the Third Reich.[25] Concentration camps and the idea of "protective custody" *(Schutzhaft)* were specifically mentioned as efficient means to incapacitate potential evildoers and pacify society. Thus, for building and enlarging the Xifeng prison camp, two globally circulating models served as inspiration: the model of corrective labor in Soviet Russia and the practice of concentrating political opponents in camps in Nazi Germany were merged and came to influence the policies in Xifeng.

Zhou Yanghao came to Xifeng with a mission—to turn the camp into a showcase prison camp that would be capable of not only detaining but also transforming and reeducating inmates.[26] After his arrival he quickly ordered a complete revamping of prison administration *(yuzheng gexin)*. This laid the foundation for a rapid and systematic expansion of camp facilities. Xifeng Camp grew quickly. It eventually became a vast, well-organized camp complex holding hundreds of prisoners.

The whole camp extended over a large area with hills, lakes, and trees. There were altogether eight barracks for prisoners. Each barrack was divided into three or four rooms, each of which accommodated a group of inmates. The barrack names were key Confucian terms, such as Zhong (loyalty), Xiao (filial piety), Ren (humanity), Yi (righteousness), He (harmony), and so on. The camp also had workshops, buildings for the guards, a large assembly hall that could hold 1,000 persons, a study room with a library, a sports field, a ball court, a shop called a "cooperative," and a vegetable garden.[27]

Under Zhou Yanghao a wide range of functions and duties were assigned to the camp, its organization became quite elaborate, and consequently the camp needed a more efficient administration. At the top of the administrative apparatus was the director. The director was assisted by a secretarial bureau, which was responsible for the day-to-day supervision of all administrative affairs. The administrative structure was furthermore divided into several teams *(zu)*, including a secretarial team (for record keeping), a guard team *(jingwei zu)*, the general affairs team *(zongwu zu)*, and the production team *(shengchan zu)*. Finally, there was also a bureau for educational affairs *(jiaowu suo)*. The education bureau had departments for training, text editing, and library administration. The editing department published two magazines and several booklets.[28]

The number of prisoners in Xifeng constantly fluctuated and cannot be asserted with certainty. On average several hundred inmates were held in Xifeng Camp.[29] Across the board, they were suspected or accused of being political enemies, spies, or traitors *(Hanjian)*. In some cases whole families were detained in Xifeng. No detainee was accused of committing a criminal offense, and thus none was ever indicted in a public court. Many were detained simply because they had been rounded up in a campaign or implicated by denunciation, or because they were victims of revenge and personal hostility.[30]

Society and life in Xifeng Camp were fundamentally shaped by the formal hierarchy imposed by the camp regime. Prisoners were ranked and treated according to their status in this hierarchy. The official classification system determined not only the distribution of valuable goods but also the degree of violence and hardship that inmates had to suffer. An affiliation with a certain group or category determined whether an inmate had to engage in prison labor, whether he had to participate in instruction and education, and whether he was allowed certain privileges, like communication and visits.

At the top of the official camp hierarchy was the large group of so-called comrades *(tongzhi)*, comprising about 70 percent of all prisoners.[31] Juntong agents used to call themselves *tongzhi*. The Juntong agents detained in Xifeng had committed breaches of discipline and duty, or had tried to desert from service.[32] The existence of secret service personnel among the prisoners might seem surprising at the first glance. Dai Li, however, understood very well that the efficiency and power of any secret service rested on its ability to maintain internal discipline and to make sure that orders are carried out. Therefore, every member of the secret service was expected to show unconditional obedience, absolute loyalty, and total dedication. To ensure compliance with these rules, an internal surveillance system was established that extended tight control over all branches and levels of the Juntong. When the integrity of the Juntong bureau's discipline was flouted, it was understood as an infraction against the bureau's *jiagui* (household rules) or *jiafa* (household law). The violators were punished not in public courts but by the secret service's internal disciplinary system. Three forms of punishment were applied: reprimand, confinement, and shooting. Many in the Juntong bureau's backbone of cadres and agents had been confined or reprimanded at least once. In 1941, out of several hundred deaths within the ranks of the Juntong, more than thirty were executions ordered by Dai Li.[33]

Another group of prisoners came from the ranks of the Communist Party. (Because they were not Juntong agents, they were called "noncomrades," or *fei tongzhi*, in the prisoners' idiom—despite their membership in the CCP.) Students and leftist intellectuals also made up a large portion of this segment of the prison population. In addition, there were some persons who were labeled *Hanjian* (Han traitors): they were accused of collaboration with Japanese occupation authorities. In the official hierarchy, these groups occupied a lower position than the former Juntong agents. They had to work harder and they received less food.

A third small and very special category was the group of prominent prisoners who were kept separately from the majority in the camp. Several important prisoners stand out in particular. Yang Hucheng was one: he had been among the initiators of the Xi'an Incident of December 1936, when Chiang Kai-shek was suddenly arrested by army generals in Xi'an. The generals wanted to force him to make peace with the CCP so that the Second United Front could be formed against the increasing threat posed by Japan. Yang was captured by the Juntong after his return from overseas travel a year after the events in Xi'an. The Juntong held him for almost twelve years. From October 1938 until 1946 Yang Hucheng and his family were detained in a small, dark, damp and cold cave close to Xifeng Camp.[34] Another prominent prisoner, Ma Yinchu, was a highly respected professor of economics who sympathized with the Communist Party. He had publicly criticized Chiang Kai-shek and accused the "Four Great Families" *(si da jiashu)* of embezzling from the state treasury. Ma Yinchu was arrested by secret service agents on December 6, 1940, and two days later he was deported to Xifeng Camp, where he was kept in a house near the cave of Yang Hucheng. In August 1941 Ma Yinchu was transferred to Shangrao Camp. In 1942 he was allowed to return home.[35] Prominent prisoners were treated slightly better than the average prisoner in Xifeng Camp. Their detainment was called "protective custody."

Camp life was shaped by strict security. Guards were posted at all entrances and windows. In the barracks, jailors were on duty twenty-four

hours a day to watch and listen to the detainees. After dawn, persons moving about inside the compound needed to know a general password, and
for access to certain buildings a second building-specific password was required. On a hill northeast of the camp was a base camp for a detachment
of sentries. Two lookout stations were erected there, and at night two additional guards kept watch from two hillocks nearby. From those points situated well above the compound, the guards could easily overlook the whole
camp, including neighboring areas, and take notice of every movement.
The sentries, guards, and jailors on duty were themselves constantly controlled. Regular checks, knocking signals, and calls were used to ensure
that they remained vigilant. Because security and control inside and outside the compound was kept very tight, no major rebellions or breakouts
occurred.[36]

For security reasons, harsh restrictions on inmate communication were
enforced. Unlike in other prisons in Republican China, camp authorities at
Xifeng did not allow prisoners to maintain any kind of contact with the
outside world. Family visits were forbidden, too. Even internal communications had to pass through the hands of guards. Because the secret service
sometimes made collective arrests (*liansuo daibu*, literally "chain arrests"),
in some cases not only the suspect but also his family members were detained in the camp. A prisoner's spouse could be imprisoned in Xifeng
along with her husband, or a father and his son might both be detained in
the camp for a long time, but they would not know of each other because
communication among prisoners was effectively cut off. There are cases in
which family members were executed in the camp or died from disease and
the surviving family member in the camp never learned about their fate.[37]

In Xifeng Camp a comprehensive reporting and information system in
regard to the prisoners was set up. Each room had a room leader (*shizhang*),
who had to oversee all actions and conversations of the other prisoners.
When any problems arose, the room leader was held fully liable. To avoid
punishment and gain rewards for meritorious service, the room leaders
often fabricated stories and lied to camp authorities. To spy on certain prisoners, either in the course of a long-term investigation or after the failure
of an inquisition by torture, authorities often sent special prisoners to live
with certain inmates, with the mission of uncovering hidden or secret information. Camp authorities also questioned prisoners individually to
avoid fraternization among inmates and to undo their efforts to shield each

other. During interrogations the staff encouraged inmates to expose each other. The staff also offered rewards for information on other inmates: in every room a report box *(baogao xiang)* was installed in which report slips could be dropped. Thus a comprehensive denunciation system was established. This had an immense influence on the prisoners: even Juntong members were kept in constant fear, because nobody could feel safe from denunciation. Released inmates who revealed secrets of Xifeng Camp or who were incriminated by denunciators could be arrested again. Such unfortunate prisoners were called "people entering the palace a second time" *(er jin gong)*.[38]

Under camp director Zhou Yanghao, the leadership began to systematically implement a policy of thought reform *(sixiang ganhua)* and production *(shengchan)*. These two elements were the buttresses of Zhou Yanghao's prison camp reforms. Emphasis was now placed on prison work and study sessions. The camp's character changed. It gained a new name and was thereafter called a "university" *(daxue)*. Prisoners were designated as "convalescents" *(xiuyangren)*, and their cells were called "classrooms" *(zhai)*.

Through the marketing of products made by prisoners, the camp determined not only to offer meaningful work to inmates but also to become self-sufficient. Self-sufficiency was a priority assigned to Zhou Yanghao by Dai Li himself during one of his three visits to the camp.[39] Therefore it was on top of Zhou Yanghao's agenda. A production team was formed that had two departments, for manufacturing and for transport and marketing. The manufacturing department included a printing office for typesetting and document printing. There also was a sewing department, where prisoners produced textiles for the camp. The department also accepted outside orders for garments, in particular from the local Juntong training unit. In addition, the camp operated a carving department, a woodwork department, a mud work department, and a department for straw sandal production.[40]

The camp also started to manage a cooperative *(hezuoshe)*, where prisoners could buy cigarettes, food, clothes, and even alcoholic beverages. (Similar cooperatives also existed in the prisons run by legal agencies.) For use at the cooperative, Xifeng Camp issued a special currency.[41] Prisoners were paid with this currency when they surpassed their production quotas, and they could redeem the currency for certain goods at the store.

Ideological or political thought reform was conducted by the education department *(jiaowu suo)*. The overall mission was to strengthen control over the prisoners by transforming their political attitudes and beliefs. The desired ideas and ideologies were instilled in prisoners through reading guides and explanatory notes, academic lectures, collective instruction, individual talks, propaganda in literature and art, and so on.

The content of the thought reform was twofold: on the one hand, it consisted of GMD party ideology and anticommunist teachings, and on the other, it contained traditional Chinese moral teachings. Apart from texts by Sun Yat-sen, prisoners had to study Chiang's *China's Destiny,* Zhou Fohai's *The Theoretical System of the Three People's Principles,* Tao Xisheng's *A History of Chinese Political Ideas,* and various anticommunist writings by Dai Jitao. At the same time, traditional works, like *Four Dynasties Study Classics (Si chao xue dian)* and Zeng Guofan's Complete Works *(Zeng wen zheng gong quanji)* were also used as instructional materials.

To measure the change in prisoners' thoughts and attitudes, camp administrators required them to present individual talks and write self-cultivation reports *(xiuyang baogao)* and encouragement reports *(jiangli baogao),* and they conducted examinations of inmates' diaries and notes and the like. The administration also set up an award system for ideological reform: monetary awards were given to prisoners who displayed progress in their thought reform.[42]

Xifeng Camp had a reading room in which newspapers, magazines, and books were available. The library was open to all prisoners. The camp even published two journals, *Yang Zheng Zhou Bao (Cultivate Rectitude Weekly)* and *Fu Huo Yue Kan (Revive Monthly).* Each year on April 4, the commemoration day for the founding of the Juntong's predecessor, the Lixing She (Vigorous Action Society), camp authorities held special literary and art events and presented performances created and rehearsed by the prisoners. Sports and physical exercises were also deployed to instill discipline and military order in the camp. For example, prisoners played on a "cultivate rectitude basketball team" *(Yang zheng lanqiu dui)* organized by camp authorities.

Despite the effort to build a model camp, living conditions for prisoners in Xifeng remained difficult most of the time. The food supply was insufficient, and hygiene and sanitation were poor. Many inmates fell sick and did not receive proper care or treatment. Violence inflicted by the staff was common. In fact, life in the camp was shaped by a constant, high degree of terror and insecurity. Because the existence of the camp was a state secret, it was outside of the reach of law. Contacts with civilian society were prohibited. There were no rules or regulations that would protect inmates, and no chance or hope for judicial review.

Violence inflicted on prisoners by the staff came in three forms: rape, torture, and execution.[43] There are many reports about members of the Juntong harassing and raping female prisoners in Xifeng. Torture was equally widespread. One of the tasks of the camp was to extract information from prisoners, and torture was routinely applied for that end.[44] Many abhorrent cruelties were inflicted. The different methods of torture had peculiar names pointing to the existence of, in the apt words of Frederic Wakeman, a well-established "insider's jargon (the esoterics of cruelty)."[45] Torture methods included "delivering fire and water in order to attack" (*shui huo jiao gong*—that is, scalding with boiled water and burning with a hot iron); "ducking into water of hot pepper" *(quan la shu shui);* and electrical shocks.

Executions were carried out on order from the Juntong central command. Three photos had to be taken of each convict before, during, and after the execution. The photos were sent to the Juntong central department, together with a report, to provide evidence of the death of the prisoner.[46] The cruelties committed in Xifeng Camp terrified even some of the local Juntong troops. Shen Zui, who at time was instructor of the Juntong training class in Xifeng, wrote many entries in his diary relating to the slaughter and inhumane treatment of prisoners. For instance, he wrote: "This human hell makes everybody feel dizzy, this place is really too frightening" and "What I hear makes me feel limitlessly sympathetic and lets my heart feel timid."[47]

While the formal distinctions among different types of prisoners worked well to serve the camp administration, some groups, mostly communists, succeeded in organizing resistance and defending themselves. The available reports indicate that inmates tried to manipulate the camp regime in order to maneuver through the difficulties of camp life. A second, alternative prisoner hierarchy emerged that was based on seniority, experience in underground work, and party affiliation. This subculture supported defiant behavior and outright resistance, as prisoners sought to improve living conditions and even arrange actual breakouts from the camp. Most of the resistance apparently involved a core group of members of the Chinese Communist Party.

Members of the CCP in Xifeng set up a secret organization that organized intransigent behavior and tried to challenge the camp regime. During the initial years of the camp (1938 to 1941) the prisoners' extremely dreadful and violent circumstances did not allow party members to communicate with each other or to forge any form of organization. But in the summer of 1941, with the arrival of Zhou Yanghao as director, the situation changed. The new, less rigid prison regime opened up possibilities for communication, and thus cooperation among prisoners became possible. At the same time, CCP members like Luo Shiwen, Che Yaoxian, and Xu Xiaoxuan, who were experienced in underground struggle, arrived at Xifeng. Their knowledge of underground work and secret organization enabled them to organize the small number of communists in Xifeng. Together with fellow prisoner Han Zidong, who was in Xifeng for a long time, the Secret Cell of the CCP in Prison was founded. This cell was led by its secretary, Luo Shiwen, and it eventually absorbed all members of and even sympathizers with the CCP who were detained in Xifeng Camp. The cell developed its own hierarchy based on party rank and experience.

The cell adopted the following guidelines: "First, to unite prisoners, in order to demand improvements of prison conditions. Once the situation is ripe, strive for release from prison. Second is to strive for the right of reading books and newspapers. Third is firmly struggling against traitors, apostates, and unreliable elements. Fourth, as soon as possible, to establish communication with outside world, let the party know conditions in prison and coordinate rescue mission or breakout."[48]

The collective resistance put up by the group succeeded in realizing three general improvements in their incarceration: Between 6:00 A.M. and 7:00 P.M. doors of the barracks remained open. Guards were admonished not to hit or scold convicts. And the authorities promised to give out more and better food. This became the first victory of the CCP's secret cell in the prison.

Some members of the communist cell successfully strove for important positions in the camp society.[49] Han Zidong and Zhou Kezheng took over the editorship of the camp periodical *Revive Monthly*. Che Yaoxian was appointed keeper of the reading room. Afterward the cell used these positions to introduce reading material like *The Analysis of Chinese Social Classes, New Democracy,* and *The Philosophy of the Masses.* Information and propaganda for the cell was successfully spread throughout the camp in these materials. According to reports and recollections, the secret cell still had plans for a collective breakout, but because the situation seemed not suited, that plan was never carried out. Instead members were urged "to use every opportunity to run off individually, do not miss a single opportunity."[50]

The prison experience turned out to be quite significant for the future development of the CCP, and Xifeng was not a single case. Most of the secret prison camps had as their main purpose the reeducation of communists, and many CCP members went through a stint in one of the camps. Prison camp became a formative experience for Chinese communism. Just as the communists were able to change the prison regime in their favor, imprisonment also shaped the character of the CCP. During their incarceration, CCP members made significant progress rebuilding their organization, studying theory, and above all indoctrinating new recruits. Internment in prison camps such as Xifeng provided the perfect training ground for mastering the techniques of underground struggle. The experience reinforced the Leninist values of secrecy, centralization, obedience, and discipline. Prison writings reflect how the experience in the repressive political environment of the war years solidified the CCP's commitment to Leninist revolutionary strategy.

The case of Xifeng Camp offers us glimpses of the nature of the GMD camp system as a whole. First, the prison camps were intended to absorb political and social groups that the GMD government considered dangerous or harmful but could not or did not want prosecute through the formal judiciary system. The prisoners in the camps never faced a trial and were not sentenced. They were arrested and then disappeared. Their release was uncertain. By establishing a mechanism with which to silently remove dissidents, critics, and opponents from the public, the GMD government obviously hoped to consolidate its rule. The second function of the camps was related to the maintenance of internal discipline. To deal with breaches of internal discipline or defection, the secret services needed their own secret institutions, which would give them flexibility in the punishment of delinquent members. In short, selected civilian and noncivilian groups were concentrated in the prison camps solely for the safety and disciplinary concerns of a one-party state.[51] In establishing such camps for its political enemies, the GMD had learned directly from foreign models such as the Soviet Union and Nazi Germany, but it also relied on assistance from war allies like the United States, especially at the secret training facility in Bai Gonguan (Bai Mansion), in what was known as Happy Valley.[52]

In a very characteristic way, then, the GMD camps mirrored the vague and ambiguous political culture in China in the 1930s and '40s. The "Confucian tone" of the Chinese concentration camps is remarkable. Not only were Confucian terms used as names for the barracks but also Confucian examination-degree ranks were used for the prisoners, and Confucian texts were included in programs for education and thought reform. The term "university" in the camp's nomenclature is significant, as well, for its emphasis on study. One could say that there was a carefully arranged Confucianization of the detainment policy in Xifeng and the other prison camps.

In the theory and practice of imprisonment in the camps, *sixiang ganhua* (thought reformation) served as a main purpose of internment. The camps were to be capable of transforming the thinking of inmates (without being subject to legal restrictions) and instilling in them a hybrid mixture of GMD party ideology and Confucianism. In achieving this goal, camp authorities demonstrated a remarkable blend of indigenous Confucian tactics of persuasion and exogenous technologies of compulsion and violence. This aspect of the camps resonated with similar efforts in the general population, in the course of the New Life Movement and in school curricula. The ongoing importance in the camps of methods of moral cultivation rooted in late-imperial practices of Confucian education challenges the assumption that indigenous approaches to discipline and coercion were necessarily displaced by radical new institutions and thus became irrelevant.[53]

Differentiating the multiple strands of cultivation, brutality, and discipline that emerged in Nationalist China enables us to see the tensions that existed within and across criminal justice institutions. Mapping the disparities and contradictions among diverse techniques of compulsion, coercive education, and indigenous modes of cultivation is also essential for understanding how state power was constituted and reproduced in GMD China. During wartime, the varied modes of discipline, brutality, and cultivation that coexisted under party rule sent mixed messages about government intentions. Coercive reeducation in the camps stressed externalized discipline, homogenization, routinization, and absolute loyalty to the leader. Coercive reeducation was always also juxtaposed with traditional forms of physical violence and Confucian-style moral cultivation.

Criminal Justice in Revolution: The Communist Areas

The establishment of a new and revolutionary regime of criminal justice was high on the political agenda of the Chinese Communist Party. From the CCP's point of view, the Republican prison merely served the demand of a capitalist economy for a disciplined and obedient workforce. With all its strengths and weaknesses, the Republican prison appeared to the CCP as the workbench of the semifeudal and semicapitalist Chinese society that it wanted to overthrow. The whole criminal justice system, from the new courts to the new prisons, was conceived as an instrument of the ruling class for the suppression and exploitation of the Chinese masses.[54] As a weapon of the class enemies, the Republican prison had not only fundamentally failed to produce justice but had also in fact extended the injustices of capitalism. For the CCP, the system of criminal justice established in the Chinese Republic possessed a clear-cut "class character." For this reason, every effort to overthrow the Chinese Republic invariably also implied an attack against the criminal justice system in general and the Republican prisons in particular. Since the ultimate goal of revolution was the creation of a new and just society, the Republican prison, as a source of continuous bourgeois capitalist exploitation, had to be replaced. In the early 1930s, at a time when the Republican prison system was not even fully developed, the CCP was already looking for alternative forms of punishment. Based on Marxist theories and Soviet experiences, a new system of criminal justice was tested in the revolutionary base areas established by the CCP: new definitions of criminality were developed, new procedural formats were applied, and new treatments for offenders were explored.

The new penal regime was based on the ideas of reeducation, thought reform, and the benefits of hard physical labor. Confinement was regarded not as a form of legal punishment but as an opportunity for an offender to correct himself and to become a new person. The transformation of faulty individuals into useful members of society was an essential part of the overall mission of the CCP, which was to change Chinese society and create a new kind of man. The new criminal justice system would not only produce true justice but would also help achieve this far-reaching mission. By remodeling the lifestyle and thinking of POWs, criminals, bandits, gangsters, drug addicts, prostitutes, and counterrevolutionaries and turning them into enthusiastic members of socialist society, the entrenchment of communism in Chinese society would be deepened.

The system of criminal justice as it emerged in the Communist Party base areas was grounded on certain theoretical premises about the role and nature of law, the purpose of punishment, and definitions of criminality. This emerging system was distinct and complex. It took international ideas of Marxist and communist provenance and combined them with Chinese ideas and local revolutionary practices. The development of criminal justice in revolutionary China was therefore fundamentally shaped by two historical trajectories.

The first was the rise of the Soviet Union, the first socialist state that was carefully observed and studied by Chinese communists. This is not to say that China strictly followed the Soviet model, nor that all aspects of the Soviet system were well known at all times. But certain broad approaches and basic concepts, such as the role of labor, the deployment of the collective for reeducation, the functionalist approach to law, and the integration of penal labor in the country's overall economic development were learned from the Soviet example, even if these elements were later partly modified in China. The criminal justice system in socialist China was clearly influenced by the Soviet Union in design and outlook, for it shared the basic principles and designs of state socialism. Just as judicial officials in Republican China studied continental European and Anglo-Saxon law, so Chinese Marxists were interested in learning what early socialist thinkers in Europe had to say about law and punishment, and they also systematically investigated Soviet experiences and experiments in the 1920s and 1930s.

The second historical influence on criminal justice in revolutionary China was the concrete local history of the Chinese Revolution itself, which shaped the experiences of the CCP leaders and also their thinking about law and justice. The Chinese Revolution spanned a period of several decades. During this prolonged phase of struggle and resistance, practices, experiences, and convictions slowly emerged that formed the very foundations of what would become the new socialist order. The revolutionary period was in many ways a principal formative stage for Chinese socialism. Chinese socialism, therefore, while influenced by the transnational communist movement, was also created by its long experience of bitter fighting and violence. There was, in other words, a constant tension between the global current of communism and the local particularities of socialism in the context of the Chinese Revolution.

State socialism is not an ahistorical, unitary phenomenon, and many differences existed between the USSR, China, and the smaller socialist countries in Eastern Europe. Yet despite those differences, all the socialist countries shared a basic political design. Their political systems were dominated by a dictatorship of the people (the proletariat), as represented by the

Communist Party. The party monopolized the state agencies, the administration, and also the judiciary. In this design, law did play a specific role, but ultimately a subordinate one. While socialist law was to be developed during the transitional period of the dictatorship of the people, in the longer term it was assumed that it would wither away along with all other state institutions.[55] Law was to fulfill merely a limited, temporary function in socialism. Socialist law, in the period of transition to stateless communism, was characterized by the radical replacement of political and legal institutions of bourgeois society, as well as by informality, flexibility, and the explicit dominance of political objectives. In the realm of criminal justice, there was a dominant, instrumental conception of law as being parental, educational, and pragmatic in order to serve the needs of the political order. The concept of punishment in this design was specific, too. It rested on one central element: the transformative power of labor. This idea originated in the European labor movement, and from there it traveled throughout the socialist world and finally reached China.[56]

In the European labor movement in the nineteenth century, labor was viewed as an essential, historical given. The German union leader and socialist Wilhelm Liebknecht, for instance, explained in 1875 in a speech at a party congress in Gotha: "Labor is the activity of manhood. It is through labor that man becomes man. Worker means man—a man who acts as man." He added that the labor party was essentially the "party of true fighters for culture, a party of people struggling for culture and manhood."[57] Such a view tended to valorize unskilled physical labor and to put it on equal terms with other activities like administration, the arts, and skilled crafts. Labor was not to be thought of as inferior. In the theoretical thinking of the early socialist leaders, labor attained an almost mythical status. Every form of physical labor was viewed as a pure expression of human culture. Only a person who engaged in manual or physical work had worth and was a true human being. It also implied, as Liebknecht said, that the "mere consumer or not-worker is not a true human being." He called them "parasites of humanity." The second of the "ten commandments of the worker," adopted by the party congress in 1875, stated: "Do not tolerate idleness next to you."[58]

Similar ideas dominate a small piece written by Friedrich Engels one year later, in 1876, titled "Anteil der Arbeit an der Menschwerdung des Affen" (The Share of Labor in the Development from Ape to Man).[59] Engels's essay was included in the official volume of Marx and Engels's selected works and published throughout the socialist world. It easily was the most widely read and influential single article on the topic of labor. Like Liebknecht, Engels described labor "as [the] first prerequisite of all human life . . . that actually made man."[60] Engels outlined how labor actually formed the hands of early man, how the need to coordinate the hands' action in order to fashion and use tools actually formed the human brain, and how in the process of cooperation in labor, language was developed, giving another boost to the brain. Thus labor was at the core of the process of civilization: the real propelling force for human progress was no longer the scholar or the ruler but the worker.[61] The primacy of physical labor in this process was established as an orthodox principle of human development. Throughout the world of state socialism, such ideas provided the theoretical underpinnings for paleontological exhibitions showing human development from ape-man to man; for an entire array of ritual practices linking communist cadres to physical labor, to make sure they remained a part of the laboring classes; and for such wholesome institutions as labor camps, which were designed to transform counterrevolutionary beasts into men.[62]

For Engels, human evolution demonstrated the primary role of labor in every achievement in human history. Labor engendered a continuous refinement or amelioration in man that in the end brought man into modern civilization. Thus the single most important factor distinguishing man from animal, culture from nature, civilization from primitivism was labor. From this view, it was only a small step to the argument that labor should be the very first method used to reeducate and correct offenders and wrongdoers. First of all, criminals as well as political offenders could be defined as persons unwilling or unable to perform the labor required of them. They were often treated as parasites and idlers living off of the labor of others. Social and political status was linked with entitlements and rights that were contingent on being a member of the group of workers. Only those who worked deserved to be treated as a human and have rights—or, to be more precise, one's basic entitlements all depended on work. Second, if labor had transformed ape into man, it certainly could be expected to transform an idle person or exploiter into a productive member of society. These ideas were popular and widespread among Chinese communists. They frequently cited the following quotation from Marx: "Physical labor is the best disinfectant for preventing social viruses."[63]

Labor and work thus attained a peculiar meaning in the discourse of socialists and Marxists. It should not be confused with the concept of work prevalent in the Republican prisons in China, or elsewhere in bourgeois, capitalist societies. Labor in Marxist discourse is not valuable because it creates wealth or conveys discipline or industrial skills, but because it has a transformative quality in itself. For Marx and Engels, labor was far more than the indispensable and inevitable hard work necessary to make one's living; it was above all a civilizing process that elevated one to a higher stage of civilization. Regardless of the kind of work that was performed, labor as a wholesome activity refined, ameliorated, and elevated the body and mind of the subject. Therefore, throughout the world of state socialism, labor became a specific tool for reforming and reeducating class enemies. Indeed, prisoners in socialist China's labor camps were meticulously taught Engels's ideas of labor and development as part of their reeducation. On many occasions Chinese leaders evoked Marx and Engels's notions of labor for justifying the legal punishment of reform through labor. Labor was interpreted by Chinese communists as an appraisable and beneficial activity that would change and transform both the subjective and the objective world of the citizens of the Chinese socialist state.

Notions of physical labor were of course present in traditional Chinese thought. In traditional China, labor was valued as part of a larger concept of social order in which each group had to fulfill its duties according to its origins, place in society, and education. The Confucian philosopher Mengzi had stated that "some toil with the minds, others toil with their physical strength."[64] It is clear, however, that while for Confucian thinkers physical labor was a necessity, they did not commonly hold it in high esteem and some even considered it beneath the educated man. In contrast, the word used for labor in modern Chinese is *laodong*—a neologism that was first introduced in the nineteenth century from the Japanese.[65] It has two components: *lao,* "to exert oneself" or "to wear oneself out," and *dong,* "to move." The lexeme thus means hard physical work resulting in concrete movements or physical changes. Labor is a quality in itself that allows humans to transform their physical environment. The modern Chinese use of the term *laodong* suggests not only that labor is seen as a valuable activity in itself but also that this very activity is the basis for social movement or progress. Thinkers of the May Fourth Movement as well as GMD administrations had already recast physical labor as a requirement for industrialization, but only the Chinese communists actively promoted a positive, if not mythical, enhancement of labor. On the first Labor Day celebrations of the People's Republic of China, on May 1, 1950, Liu Shaoqi delivered an address that was reprinted in all major newspapers in China. After saluting the world's working class, he explained: "It is because the world of man and even man himself are the creation of labor. Labor is the foundation on which human society exists and develops. Workers are the creators of civilization. Therefore, labor must command the highest respect in the world; workers must command the highest respect in the world."[66]

Labor in Chinese communism was above all understood as a cultivating activity for transforming the mind-set of those who were engaged in it. This was an aspect of labor that loomed large in Mao's thinking. From very early on Mao Zedong stressed in his writings the close connection between practice and knowledge. For Mao, the truth could be discovered, verified, and developed only through practice. Practice was, in Mao's view, able to transform both the objective world and—and this is his original contribution—the practicer's subjective worldview or knowledge about the world. Consequently, labor was not only an activity for producing and changing the world of objects; it also changed the laboring person by developing his subjective knowledge and consciousness. Practice, knowledge, and reality were variables in a complex function and stood together in a dynamic relationship.[67]

Mao concluded, therefore, that changing the world meant changing oneself—which, by the way, was a familiar idea from neo-Confucianism. Revolution had to be accompanied by the change of the subjective world—that is, the realm of knowledge, thinking, and worldview. A revolution can be fully realized only if all opponents and hostile forces have been transformed, too. At first they have to be compelled to change; later they can be allowed to change themselves. The goal is that "all mankind voluntarily and consciously changes itself and the world." Transforming the self of the opponents is therefore a prerequisite for the realization of the final stage of communism. That transformation cannot be achieved through education (knowing) alone, precisely because of the relationship between theory and practice. Changing one's consciousness cannot be realized through theory alone but needs to be realized through practice—namely, physical labor. Thus, years later Mao concluded, "The working class remoulds the whole of society in class struggle and in the struggle against nature, and at the same time remodels itself."[68]

The notion of labor was a key concept that emerged out of the global spread of socialist theory. There was a broad transfer of knowledge within the socialist movement worldwide, through the exchange of principles, practices, and technologies among communist parties in various nations. This cross-socialist transfer included the appropriation of legal practices and new methods of administering justice. Most important in this respect were the developments in the Soviet Union.

The Soviet Union was the first country in the world to develop a specific socialist form of criminal justice that was based on Marx and Engels's notions of justice, crime, and punishment as well as the value of production and labor. The criminal justice system of the Soviet Union underwent tremendous change over the course of time. But despite frequent changes of names and administrations, there were principles and policies that were consistently adhered to. After the October Revolution, labor camps appeared alongside traditional forms of incarceration, namely prisons and detention facilities. In the summer of 1918, Lenin ordered that "all suspicious persons are to be incarcerated in a concentration camp outside the city limits."[69] The new camps were to become the primary channel for enforcing state punishments in the Soviet Union, and their number grew quickly. By November 1921, there were 122 camps for the incarceration of "special" people—that is, enemies of the new order.[70] The camps were above all supposed to help consolidate the victory of the Revolution and eliminate resistance against the new regime. Enemies of the Bolsheviks were to be isolated from the rest of the population. By placing offenders under custody and forcing them to perform work, their dissident spirit would be broken. Creating special sites for dealing with political enemies and oppositional groups introduced an important legal dualism into the Soviet criminal justice system. Class enemies were to be treated differently than criminals.

On October 16, 1924, a corrective-labor code was issued to regulate "general places of incarceration," such as prisons, labor colonies, transit points, and so forth. The official goal of labor prisons, camps, or colonies was the reeducation of offenders through work. Lenin had written in 1917: "The basic cause of social excess [and a crime is a form of social excess] is the exploitation of the masses [by the capitalists]. The removal of this cause will lead to the withering away of excesses."[71] Viewing the state as an instrument used by one class to exploit another, he added that crimes would disappear with the withering away of the state. Specifically, Lenin believed that crime would diminish and eventually cease once communism had replaced capitalism. Because the environment drove people to crime, there was no individual guilt, only social guilt—the exploitation of workers by capitalists.

Prison labor or forced labor would serve as the main tool for the correction of the exploiters and class enemies. The Sixth Soviet Congress, in October 1918, discussed the idea of labor as a form of correction, and from 1918 onward, forced labor was used as the principal means of reforming delinquents.[72] Prisoners' pay was to conform to trade union rates for comparable work. Inmates received one third of their salary, and the remainder went to the administration.

But contrary to the assumption that crime would be reduced under socialism, the Soviet Union saw a growing number of trials and a substantial increase in the prison population, which was difficult to explain. The high number of detention facilities also created a great financial burden for the already constrained state budget. During the 1920s, the government sought to reduce the number of prisoners being held, but the effort produced no results. On the contrary, the collectivization of farming led to a sudden and unexpected sharp increase in the number of inmates.

In the late 1920s another reform became necessary to systematize and unify the camp system and enlarge its capacity.[73] One incentive for the additional reform was the need to reduce the cost for the government. Beginning in 1929, the camps were included in the Soviet state's Five-Year Plan. Prison labor was to be used in the lumber industry and for huge construction projects, such as digging canals and building roads. In the context of the reform efforts, a Statute on Corrective Labor Camps was made public in 1930. For the first time in Soviet legislation the term "corrective-labor camp" *(ispravitel'no-trudovoi lager')* was applied in the text of a law. It referred to all internment camps under the control of the security police. In July 1934 a unified administrative branch within the state security organization was created for all prisons, detention centers, and corrective-labor camps. It was referred to as GULAG, the Russian acronym for Glavno Upravlenie Lagerei (Chief Administration of Corrective Labor Camps).[74] The agency oversaw and controlled a complex network of institutions and facilities in which inmates performed forced labor with the goal of correction. While corrective labor was initially used only for class enemies, by the mid-1930s it was extended to all convicts.

The whole system finally grew into an essential buttress of the political and social order in the Soviet Union, and it existed in this form at least until the mid-1950s.[75] Numerous corrective-labor camps were established in northern Russia and Siberia, especially during the First Five-Year Plan, from 1928 to 1932, when millions of well-to-do peasants were driven from their farms under the collectivization program. The Stalinist purges of 1936 to 1938 brought additional millions into the camps.[76] The Soviet occupation of eastern Poland in 1939 and the absorption of the Baltic States in 1940 led to the incarceration of large numbers of non-Soviet citizens. Following the outbreak of war with Germany in 1941, the camps also received Axis prisoners of war and Soviet nationals accused of collaboration with the enemy. After the death of Joseph Stalin in 1953, many prisoners were released and the number of camps was drastically reduced.

In the Soviet view, imprisonment in a corrective-labor camp was not a punishment meted out to the criminal but a means of reforming the prisoner and providing him or her with a second chance. The length of the sentence, therefore, depended not on the severity of the crime but on the correction of the individual prisoner. As soon as a prisoner showed signs of being reformed, he or she was to be released. Assuming that petty offenders would be reformed after five years, the government set a five-year maximum sentence for all small offenses.

The government also facilitated experiments to learn how best to use labor in prison to achieve both an effective correction of the prisoner and a profitable enterprise. Most influential in this respect were the experiments undertaken by Anton S. Makarenko in his penal colonies for juvenile offenders in the 1930s. More than anybody else who was working in the Soviet penal system, Makarenko conceptualized and theorized about his experiences in several publications that circulated widely.[77] Because his writings allow us to understand the official theoretical underpinnings of the corrective-labor institutions in the Soviet Union, his work deserves our full attention, especially in light of later developments in China. Makarenko's work and theories were intensively studied in China. As a pedagogist and educator, Makarenko influenced the labor reform system in China more than any other legal expert or political thinker.[78] In 1954 a selection of his writings was published in Chinese under the title *On Communist Education*. Two years later, in 1956, a second edition of this book was published. Apart from that, several films were shown in China that introduced Makarenko's life and work to the Chinese audience. Because of his experience in working with juvenile offenders, his work received considerable attention by the founding practitioners of the labor reform system in China.

In the 1920s Makarenko ran the Gorky Colony, a rehabilitation settlement for children who were made homeless by the Russian Revolution and were roaming throughout the countryside in criminal gangs. In 1931 he was appointed head of the Dzerzhinsky Commune, a penal institution for young offenders. Both institutions were organized along military patterns: inmates were grouped in brigades and troops. Uniforms were handed out. Newcomers were called "pupils," and they had to strive to become full "communards." Like the early socialists, Makarenko regarded work as basic to intellectual and moral development; he believed all delinquents should be assigned tasks requiring labor and should be given positions of responsibility in order to learn the limitations of their individual rights and privileges. In the Gorky Colony agricultural work dominated, but in the Dzerzhinsky Commune industrial work was performed. Makarenko spoke of labor as an almost mystical process—one of beauty, satisfaction, and fulfillment. He used descriptions like "the symphony of labor" and compared a railway factory to a "fairy-tale castle."[79]

Thus, his first principle for a socialist upbringing was: "Place the maximum possible demands on a person and treat him with the maximum possible respect."[80] Such demands consisted of production goals, administrative tasks, and responsibilities. In the Gorky Colony and the Dzerzhinsky Commune, the communities were run by a general assembly of inmates. Inmates were involved in all administrative affairs and were given access to important positions. Makarenko stressed that without concrete and heavy demands, any education of delinquents would be impossible. He also ascribed the greatest importance to the collective. Therefore another of Makarenko's principles was "education in and by a group—a *kollektiv*."[81] The overarching goal of his social experiments was to set up strong groups that shared a certain code of behavior. He expected that members would impose their norms of behavior on newcomers. Rewards and punishments would thus represent the approval and disapproval of the group. When the group norms were accepted and internalized by group members, a general friendly pressure to conform to those norms would develop, the authority of which rested with the *kollektiv* and would not be questioned or resisted. Collectivism thus meant that each member would act in accordance with norms of the *kollektiv*. Makarenko considered the "friendly pressure" of the collective to be a new Soviet style of discipline. He saw discipline not as a result of extrinsic training and surveillance (as practiced in the capitalist prison), but as coming from broad educational influences exercised by the collective. He wrote: "Discipline is a product of the sum total of the educative efforts, including the teaching process, the process of political education, the process of character shaping, the process of collision—of facing and settling conflicts in the collective, the process of friendship and trust, and the whole educational process in its entirety, counting also on such processes as physical education, physical development and so on."[82]

Unlike a few educators in the Soviet Union, Makarenko did not reject the concept of punishment. In fact, he tried to develop a Soviet form of punishment. He saw the goal of punishment as "settling and eliminating a conflict."[83] He held the view that old-style punishments created new conflicts by causing suffering and by letting bystanders watching the spectacle of suffering. In his commune, punishment was not to produce moral or physical suffering: "What then is the meaning of punishment? Knowing that the collective condemns your action. The culprit must not feel crushed by the punishment, but it will make him think over his mistake, and ponder on his estrangement, however slight, from the collective."[84] Makarenko also asserted that punishment was effective only if it was carried out and supported by collective pressure. The main goal should be to isolate the offender from the collective so that the pressure of the collectivity could bear on the offender.

These remarks point to a form of discipline widely overlooked by most scholars, who tend to be influenced by the Foucauldian approach. For Foucault, discipline in the modern age was individualized and individualizing. Yet here we see discipline produced within and through the collective that also is presented as progressive and modern. It opens up a historical trajectory reaching back to the forms of discipline enforced in monasteries and other tight-knit groups. Their alternative strand of discipline and social organization would eventually reemerge in state socialism.

To summarize, changes in the Soviet criminal justice system followed broader shifts in politics, state, and society in the Soviet Union. Collectivization, mounting economic pressures, the needs of the war economy, and the requirements of political repression provided the stimuli for the changes. In the first years, imprisonment in labor camps was used to isolate real or suspected enemies. Thereafter, a more systematic approach to imprisonment was developed. Two elements can be identified as the major features of state punishment in the Soviet Union: first, the emphasis on the correction and reeducation of offenders, and second, because crime was officially seen as a result of parasitism and laziness, the belief that labor should serve as the main tool of correction.[85] The following methods were applied to organize and encourage labor in the camps: long working days, high production goals, collectivism, competition between groups, the granting of food rations and other privileges depending on the scope of the work done by inmates.[86]

The whole internment system increasingly took over important social and economic functions in Soviet society. It gradually evolved into a pervasive control mechanism that was used to deal with a broad range of social, political, and economic issues. Once they were incorporated into the state's Five-Year Plans, the camps were organized on a massive, industrial scale and used as dumping grounds for entire classes of people excised from society because they had no place in the new Soviet Union (such as the kulaks, or wealthy peasant farmers). Prisoners were deployed as disposable laborers on projects to reclaim wasteland and extract natural resources in inhospitable places. The result, in the end, was a huge loss of life with little actual attention paid to rehabilitation. Revolution, economic need, and terror were the driving forces. For this reason, the historian Andrzej Kaminski likened the Soviet camps to modern-day institutions of slavery.[87] The rise and expansion of the internment system, created its own dynamic. To meet its growing expenses, the system demanded an ever greater number of inmates. The GULAG thus became, as Alexandr Solzhenitsyn described it, the slowly growing "cancer" of Soviet society.[88]

The criminal justice system established in the Soviet Union was deliberately offered as a model to other socialist countries, with "labor reform" or "corrective labor" as its central element. This exact model was not mandatory in all its legal or organizational details, but it represented a baseline from which other socialist countries could start. The consensus within the leadership of the Chinese Communist Party, up until approximately 1958, was that the experiences of the Soviet Union represented a basis for the establishment of socialism in China. The Soviet model offered specific examples and blueprints for the organization of the state, economic development, the modernization of the armed forces and the establishment of political structures.[89] The Soviet criminal justice system, in general, was also seen by the party scholars as the best and most valid way to deal with criminality in China. However, despite agreement concerning the fundamental validity of the Soviet model, it was never imitated blindly and uncritically. During both the phase of the revolution in China and the phase of socialist construction, common sense dictated that all ideas and institutions borrowed from the Soviet Union had to be compatible with the reality in China. Where they were not, modifications of the model were to be carried out.

Since 1926 Mao Zedong had argued that the fate of the revolution depended on its success in rural China.[90] In September of the same year, Mao declared the question of rural society to be "the central question of the national revolution."[91] The masses in the countryside could be mobilized only if the party was able to respond to their needs and demands and the values of rural society. For this, the party needed to adopt a flexible, pragmatic approach, and the question of how to produce and manage justice in rural China was crucial.

Because the revolution was based on the notion that the old society was unjust, neglectful, and exploitative, the Communist Party aspired to transform the social order and also, inevitably, its justice system. To this end, the legal status of whole social groups needed to be changed. Some groups in rural China saw their rights drastically limited while others enjoyed an elevation of their legal status. New definitions of criminal behavior were also put forth. Resistance against the change brought by the revolution quickly was declared by the new power holders to be one of the most severe crimes. After the revolutionary transformations, orderly conditions needed to be established. A revolutionary legal system was to be put in place that would create real justice.

Before the People's Republic of China came into being, the Communist Party had instituted revolutionary laws and courts in the areas under its control. Many features of the criminal justice system in the PRC in fact have their roots in the early years of the revolution. In the various base areas, the CCP had the chance to refine its strategies under the conditions of an actual rural society and to adapt to the social reality of the Chinese countryside. Answers to basic questions could be tested: How to win popular acceptance and approval of revolutionary innovations, how to make use of popular hatred and resentments to further the goals of the CCP, how to resolve existing and newly arising rural conflicts, how to accommodate popular conceptions of justice.

The base areas functioned as a laboratory of sorts for the regime of punishment and criminal justice that was later established for the whole of China. Primary were the early experiments in criminal justice made by Communist Party authorities in the Hailufeng Soviet (1927 to 1928); these were followed by similar experiments made in the Jiangxi Soviet (1929 to 1934). The first efforts at establishing a revolutionary justice system were all ad hoc in nature. In contrast, more systematic and carefully prepared steps were taken in the so-called liberated areas that were founded in North China after the Long March in 1934 and 1935.

In the counties of Haifeng and Lufeng, ninety miles away from Hong Kong, the first communist government in Chinese history was proclaimed on November 1, 1927. A congress formed by workers, peasants, and soldiers elected the new government.[92] Almost all members belonged to the peasant alliance headed by Peng Pai (1896–1929), who had been active in both counties since 1922 and had lead the struggle of the peasants against landlords and the provincial administration. The new Hailufeng Soviet government ruled over a territory of 30,000 square kilometers. Half a million people lived in this area. There were 850 villages, almost every inhabitant of which worked in farming. Several months later, GMD troops stormed the area and put an abrupt end this early communist government.

During the several months between the proclamation of the Hailufeng Soviet and its end, a revolutionary justice system spontaneously emerged. The ideas and practices of justice that were forged in this period later proved to be very influential. Communist authorities made a fundamental distinction between "regular crime" and "crimes against the revolution" or "counterrevolutionary crimes." The crime of counterrevolution was treated as a more severe offense than any regular criminal act. Regular criminal acts, such as theft, would often receive light punishments or even pardons.[93] The peasant alliance sought to side with the masses of poor peasants against the small group of landlords, who were branded as evildoers who had exploited the masses for centuries. In his "Report on an Investigation of the Peasant Movement in Hunan,"[94] written in 1927, Mao Zedong praised how the peasants took action against rich landlords. The revolutionary punishments imposed by the peasants on the elites of rural Hunan society included "auditing the accounts" (to expose embezzlement and other wrongdoing), "imposing fines" (for irregularities), "levying contributions" (for the relief of the poor), "minor protests" (to denounce a local bully or bad landowner), "major demonstrations" (including slaughtering the local bully's or bad landowner's pigs or consuming his grain), "parades through the villages in tall hats" (for public humiliation), "imprisonment in the county jail," "banishment," and "shooting" (reserved for the worst offenders). These punitive measures were intended to assault the elite class of landlords and local gentry. They were designed, in Mao's words, to "really create terror in the countryside," and they succeeded.[95] Eliminating "feudal injustice" as imposed by the old social order demanded not only that the landlords be removed from their premises and lose their wealth and power, but also that they pay for their previous lifestyle. Physical punishment during the revolution aimed not at correcting the offender; instead it almost exclusively pursued the purpose of retribution and retaliation. To fully realize its mobilizing power, physical punishment also had to be staged as a public spectacle. The more onlookers the spectacle could attract, the more widely could the message of revolution be spread. Through accusation trials and public punishments, the peasants could be emotionally worked up, mobilized, and directed to turn their anger against the landlords. Peng Pai and his followers took pains to directly involve the local population. A speaker would read the crimes of an accused landlord aloud to the people in the crowd, who in turn would express their opinion by shouting and yelling. The final sentence would be passed immediately by simple popular vote, with the punishment carried out on the spot.

The whole process was intended as a form of "democratic terror." It was a form of terrorizing that was exercised in the name of class justice, legitimized by the masses, and therefore regarded as democratic. The treatment of the convicts was indeed humiliating, bloody, and cruel. During such mass trials—as these spectacles later came to be called—the accused were humiliated, beaten, and forced to wear hats. Many accused landlords received a death sentence, which was carried out by beheading. Their heads were placed on poles and displayed at the marketplace (a supplementary punishment that was practiced in imperial China). There are also reports about ritual cannibalism. In traditional China, to eat the organs of one's enemy was to take full revenge for his misdeeds. Bloody spectacles of revenge were an efficient way to assemble the peasants, brand political targets, and transmit a clear political message.

Peng Pai represents within CCP history the tradition of rural peasant communism. His supporters were landless seasonal workers, vagabonds, bandits, soldiers, smugglers, and prostitutes. Their notion of punishment was quite simple: to punish meant to take revenge for previous defeats. In the course of the Chinese Revolution this was only a temporary, chaotic, and bloody phase, after which more orderly and systematic policies were applied. Yet Peng Pai introduced some innovations that proved to be quite durable in Chinese communism: his focus on counterrevolutionary crimes as distinguished from other crimes, organized rallies, mass trials, direct participation by the masses, and public humiliation of class enemies belonged to a tradition of revolutionary punishments that were resurrected time and again when class struggle was called for.

Mao Zedong developed his fundamental strategy for revolution in the Jiangxi Soviet. At the same time, he also oversaw the development of new penal practices. The timing of these developments was highly symbolic. Having repulsed the third campaign of the GMD military in September, the CCP leadership felt strong enough by November to proclaim itself the government of the newly constituted Chinese Soviet Central Republic. Mao Zedong was named the governmental leader. Befitting its new government status, the leadership announced a range of new laws on land and labor. The central authorities also abolished all corporal punishments, which seem to have been still widely used in rural areas. All inhumane treatments of prisoners were strictly forbidden. This was proclaimed by Mao Zedong to be a "great historical reform."[96]

The authorities also started to formalize the soviet's internal security structure.[97] To this end, two new ministries and a new bureau came into existence, offering the promise of a more formal approach to policing and justice after years of ad hoc populism. These new ministries were the Ministry of Judgments and the Ministry of Internal Affairs, while the new bureau was called the Political Protection Bureau. By far the most important of these three agencies was the Political Protection Bureau, for it was charged with the task of protecting political security. Nevertheless, together these three institutions would be in charge of all the base camp's prisons, civil police, and political and security matters. Generally speaking, it was the Ministry of Judgments that would run the prison sector. It effectively replaced the Committees for the Elimination of Counterrevolution that had been running detention prior to this. Not only were their prisons brutal and unhealthy places but they also lacked any sense of order. Indeed, they were so disorganized that they failed even to separate convicted criminals from those who awaited trial. The problems encountered in the detention sector only added to the new government's feeling that the committees had outlived their usefulness once order in the CCP base areas had been established. The decision to institute a more formal penal sector under the Ministry of Judgments can be seen as part of the process of paring down the power of the committees and developing a more orderly governmental structure.

On February 19, 1932, the Central People's Committee backed a report by Liang Botai recommending the establishment of a formal system of institutes of labor persuasion *(Laodong ganhua yuan)* to be run by the Ministry of Judgments (Caipan Bu).[98] This decision stripped the suppression committees of some of their power and also placed a more demanding task on the prison authorities themselves. From this time onward, detention and penal incarceration would be separated. Watch-houses would hold short-term convicts and unconvicted prisoners while institutes of labor persuasion, or prisons, would hold convicted felons who had been sentenced to periods of five years or more penal labor.

In relation to the detention sector there were, in fact, four separate forms of detention in operation in Chinese Soviet areas after this. Detention could differ depending on whether one was deemed a political prisoner or a common criminal, whether one was arrested in a newly established base camp or in an older one, and, later, whether one's case was to go before a revolutionary court or an ordinary one. The different types of detention reflected the administrative divisions within the newly established government. In the main, political prisoners would go to centers run by the Political Protection Bureau, common criminals would be held by the Ministry of Judgments, and newly established base camps would use detention centers still run by the Committees for the Elimination of Counterrevolution. After 1936, and principally in Shanbei, the office for those awaiting trial under the revolutionary courts would also run centers for those awaiting trial.[99]

While detention centers operated under a variety of departments, the prison sector was entirely the responsibility of the Ministry of Judgments. This was the case even in those places where it appeared otherwise, such as prisons run by the provincial and county-level revolutionary courts. They were still regarded as ministry-run because the courts were in fact judicial wings of the ministry.[100] In some revolutionary base areas, such as the E-Yu-Wan (Hubei-Henan-Anhui and Chuan-shan Sichuan and Shanxi) base camps, the term "prison" rather than "institute" was used but the function and operation of both facilities were identical. Both were organized on the basis of the "Temporary Regulations on the Institutes of Labor Persuasion," which was issued on August 10, 1932. In that document it is stated that each institute would have one head, one deputy, a number of section heads, and a complement of ordinary workers. The deputy head of the institute and the section heads were to form the prison management committee, and the institute head was to chair this committee. Section heads would be in charge of education and production; in women's prisons special female inspectors would be brought in to ensure the institutes were run in an orderly fashion.[101]

While the role of these institutions was stated as rehabilitative, conditions within the prisons suggest otherwise. Sanitary conditions were so poor that many inmates died; communist guards, drawn from among the local peasants, were said to treat prisoners more like slaves than inmates; and "beatings, cursing, discrimination, corruption and exploitation were common occurrences."[102] Even apart from these clear breaches of the rules it is doubtful that the prison sector was able to live up to its promises. For financial and human-resource reasons, the new government found it hard even to provide twenty-four-hour supervision over the prisoners. This resulted in a system that relied on having prisoner-informers among the inmates to keep other prisoners in check and extract information from them about the enemy.[103]

Prisons were established in each of the revolutionary base camps, but most were in the central area, which had seven. These institutions were, in theory at least, the forerunners of the reform-through-labor system that dominated post-1949 penal development, for they were said to combine political and ideological education with labor. In 1933 Mao Zedong stated: "In the soviet area when dealing with criminals we realize the idea of corrective labor. We apply communist spirit and work discipline in order to educate the prisoner and to transform the nature of the criminal."[104] Recently Chinese penologists have suggested that in fact the prisons were the forerunners of contemporary penal reform.[105] However, despite this claim there is little evidence that the rhetoric of labor as reformative was present at this stage. Labor in these early institutes was undertaken solely to repay a social debt and ensure that prisoners were not a burden on the soviet.[106] The labor assigned in these prisons consisted of construction work and some food and clothing production, and any prisoners sentenced to longer than five years had to work while wearing manacles.

The Long March in 1934 and 1935 brought the CCP from Jiangxi to North China, where a new base was erected at Yan'an. During the following long years at Yan'an, Mao finally emerged as the core leader of the CCP, as a result of his ability to articulate basic political doctrines in powerful speeches and written discourses. In the context of these broader developments, the CCP also came up with the first relatively consistent and comprehensive approach to the administration of criminal justice. Two aspects of the CCP's approach stand out: the promotion of thought reform *(sixiang gaizao)* as a channel for transmitting new values to offenders, and the introduction of labor brigades in the penal system.[107]

Thought reform was at the center of the rectification campaign carried out at Mao's behest from 1942 to 1944.[108] The campaign was in part a reaction to the change of party membership that occurred in Yan'an. Many of the new members were young, came from urban areas, and were well educated. Among the roughly 800,000 members, differing conceptions were floating around concerning the mission of the CCP and the strategies for revolution and socialism in general. Mao felt that it was time to strengthen and unify the party's political mind-set. A "coherent-discourse community" was to be created that would be strongly rooted in a clearly defined value system. What was a loose gathering of activists would be transformed into a rigorous community of like-minded party members who had internalized the party's norms and values and would follow the same code of behavior. For this purpose, party cadres were called on to form study groups in which carefully selected texts were read and discussed collectively (altogether eighteen mandatory texts were collected in a small volume called *Rectification Documents*). At these discussion meetings participants were encouraged to bring forward their own experiences and feelings. This form of study was not so much centered on memorizing certain doctrines as on engaging in an open-ended process of self-examination. Participants were asked to write "thought examinations." Mao is reported to have noted: "Get everybody to write their thought examinations and write [them] three times, five times, again and again. . . . Tell everyone to spill out every single thing they have harbored that is not so good for the Party."[109] Study, self-examination, and thought examination were expected to lead to a revelation of "wrong" thoughts, evil ambitions, and bad feelings. Particularly through confession, cadres were supposed to rectify and reform their thinking. Party members with wrong thinking would be discovered, and would confess and start to reform themselves.

The initiators of this campaign not only counted on voluntarism but also deployed a set of coercive measures to keep the campaign going. They conducted interrogations and mass rallies that terrified members of the party. At public meetings in front of large crowds, young volunteers were forced to confess to being spies and to name others.[110] Violence and torture were often used to extract confessions. This coercion was accompanied by the expansion and strengthening of the party's security apparatus.[111] Intelligence work and an internal surveillance network were used to monitor party members who were in the process of rectification. Interrogations and arrests were made by CCP detectives and security agents with the goal of uncovering hostile GMD agents, traitors, and Trotskyites. Some alleged "enemies" were executed after mass trials, without any actual court hearings.

Several elements of the rectification campaign lasted far beyond the actual Yan'an period: for example, the security and police apparatus that were established and deployed as coercive measures, and the emphasis on public trials, public confessions, and coercive reeducation to further the instilling of new values. The most important and lasting effect of the rectification campaign, however, was that Mao and the party greatly enlarged the number of people directly or indirectly involved in repression, including torture.

The rectification campaign in Yan'an was, of course, designed for Communist Party members, to indoctrinate new members and create a cohesive single group. What does internal party discipline have to do with criminal justice? The nexus is to be found in the philosophy and social practices of thought reform that evolved out of the Yan'an experience. After 1949, not only was thought reform widely practiced throughout Chinese society (far beyond the party) with the goal of regime consolidation—for instance in schools, universities, government agencies, work teams, communes, and prisons—but it also became a deeply rooted tenet of Chinese socialism. Everybody was supposed to examine himself constantly. Creating a new man and a new society required continuous psychological and ideological purification. Through this process, everyone would be able to shed the remnants of the old, evil society that impeded the building of the new, socialist one. As we will see, this general philosophy left deep marks on penal principles and criminology.

The emphasis of penal treatment was clearly shifted toward its reformative function: education was to be primary and punishment secondary, as prisoners needed to be "renewed" *(zixin)* if they were to become disciplined and useful members of a communist society. Thought reform by way of confession and political study became an integral part of the penal treatment for offenders. In line with this new policy, all sentenced criminals had to spend time in an institution of confinement, where they would have the opportunity to reform themselves through labor and study; true repentance would lead to early release, while the sentence of an obstinate prisoner could be increased.

After 1941, a number of communist-controlled border areas and administrative areas established prisons or instruction teams to reeducate convicted felons, although reports on their management show that new penal policies were not fully implemented until 1944 and 1945, and that sanitary conditions and prisoners' health continued to be neglected in many places.[112] In the liberated (communist) areas, a bewildering multiplicity of institutions were responsible for penal custody, including: (1) detention centers (for suspects awaiting trial or sentencing); (2) "handicraft learning centers for self-renewal," which overwhelmingly kept so-called Han-traitors *(hanjian)* or collaborators; (3) "surveillance brigades" *(guanzhi dui)* for the reeducation and investigation of former GMD cadres and officials, mostly set up in the cities and under the control of public security organs; (4) penal instruction teams *(xunyu dui)* for the detainment and training of traitors and GMD agents; and (5) prisons *(jianyu)*, which held offenders who had committed more serious crimes, including war criminals, Han-traitors, GMD secret agents and assassins, leaders of reactionary organizations, criminal landlords, and bandits, as well as petty criminals, such as swindlers, gangsters, thieves, and habitual criminals.[113]

The multitude of penal institutions and designations demonstrates that no unified system was yet in place. Pragmatic considerations dominated the penal policy of the CCP in the years of revolution. In response to military instability, organizational problems, and scarce resources, the local CCP in Shandong, for instance, abandoned the idea of using prisons to confine convicts much earlier than the Yan'an authorities did, instead quickly moving toward a system of mobile labor teams and camps dispersed throughout the countryside that displayed many of the hallmarks of the post-1949 Laogai, or reform-through-labor system.[114] Local authorities continued to follow a penal philosophy of reformation *(ganhua),* but shifted the site where reformation should take place from the prison to the labor camp. As confinement in prison seemed to generate a whole series of problems that judicial authorities were unable to solve—such as problems with the food supply and prison administration—the use of prisoners in labor teams in the countryside offered an alternative. In Rongchang, Shandong Province, for example, local authorities decided to deploy prisoners as workers on a farm, to reclaim wasteland. "Penal instruction teams" for prisoners were set up throughout the district: landlords or GMD party or government officials who could not be safely detained in their villages were to be reformed through labor on these teams. Teams were established at the county level, under the control of judicial departments. A team was made up of eleven or twelve prisoners; this was called a "small team." Three teams, in turn, formed a squad. Each team selected a leader, someone with a positive attitude toward work who was also ideologically reliable.

The organization of instruction teams was later actively promoted by the provincial authorities, who recommended in the spring of 1946 that small groups of prisoners be sent to work in the villages, under the supervision of the local militia. These teams were required to build small prison cells for themselves and to achieve economic self-sufficiency through their labor. From the beginning, however, the teams were burdened by such problems as inefficient teaching methods, a lack of properly trained cadres, and inefficient work assignments. In 1947 it was suggested that prisoners be concentrated in large facilities, as large camps were seen as better able to increase productivity and improve education. As an alternative, the establishment of penal education institutions was proposed. With a sudden growth in the number of prisoners after Japan's surrender in 1945 at the end of World War II, the penal instruction teams gradually developed into labor camps, where the production movement was designed to remedy the shortage of supplies and promote economic self-sufficiency. Thereafter, large labor camps that held up to 2,000 prisoners became common.

Yet in urban areas, the prisons were still in operation. The hundreds of costly prison buildings that had been erected with so much enthusiasm by Republican administrations were, at least for the time being, very useful to the new rulers. Of course, when the CCP moved in and took over a city and its prisons, the prison administration was changed. One of the first measures the new authorities would take would be to sort out the prison population.[115] CCP cadres distinguished between inmates incarcerated for their participation in revolutionary activities and criminals who had done harm and damage to the people. The criminals were kept in custody, while those in the former group were released from prison. The wardens were also carefully examined. Those in the higher echelons of the prison staff were removed from their posts, but those who belonged to the group of technicians, doctors, or accountants who worked in the prison could remain on the job. The next step was the creation of a new prison administration and a new prison regime. Stress was placed on "education" and the organizational "integration of productive labor with education" in carrying out the prison term. The architectural designs of the existing prison buildings were well suited to this endeavor, since labor and reform were already integral elements of imprisonment in Republican China. The experience at Harbin Prison illustrates the transfer of prison authority and its consequences very well. It also offers a glance at the evolving penal program of the CCP.

In 1946 Harbin Prison came under control of the CCP.[116] It was one of the first prisons in urban China to fall into the hands of the communists. Soon after the takeover of Harbin Prison, CCP leaders decided to remake the prison into a model institution for the new penal system that was emerging in the liberated areas. This was a very ambitious endeavor. In late 1949 at the First National Conference on Public Security, Zhu De called Harbin Prison a "model prison" *(mofan jianyu)* of the new government.[117] At the time of the communist takeover, the prison housed 1,800 inmates, who were guarded by 90 wardens. The new prison director, Wang Huai'an, intended to build Harbin Prison into a showcase for the efficacy of communist concepts of punishment and incarceration. The new prison administration overturned all existing regulations governing the prison and introduced new rules, step by step. Many new comprehensive regulations were issued governing prison discipline, prison work, sanitary conditions, visits and communications, rewards and punishments, operation of the sick yard, and so on. The prison administration went to great lengths to exert its influence on inmate society. To obstruct the emergence of leaders and tyrants within prison society, inmates were organized into "prisoner self-administration committees." These committees had many responsibilities. They were supposed to help the wardens uphold prison discipline, and they were also responsible for organizing everyday life in the cells, maintaining prison hygiene, and conducting study sessions. Another field of activity for the committees was the organization of work competitions, designed to energize inmates and encourage them to give their best effort in carrying out prison work.

As part of the project of creating a model institution featuring a new form of penal treatment, Harbin Prison administrators paid particular attention to cultural and ideological education. The prison staff took great pains to develop new textbooks and curricula for use in the prison. One popular text used for prison education was *The Historical Development of Society,* which introduced Engels's concept of labor as a determinant of human development.[118] In 1948 the prison published *Cultural Lessons for Convicts,* which contained several chapters that could each be used for a lecture or a discussion group. Chapters had the following headings: "To Serve the People," "The Great Chinese Communist Party," "Attack Chiang Kai-shek, Liberate all of China," "Rules for Abiding by the Law," "How to Write a Plan for Reform," and "A Letter from the Family of a Prisoner." Ideological education also included the reading of newspapers and attendance at regular meetings during which current events and political issues were discussed. Finally, the prison administration organized an amateur theater group made up of prisoners. The group wrote plays and performed them on special occasions. Some of the plays that were staged featured political themes and reportage, including such works as: *Atrocities of the American Armed Forces, Chiang Kai-shek: The Great Skipper,* and *Chiang Kai-shek Must Die.* Others raised issues related to the official mission of the prison, such as *The Road to a New Life, Recollections of a Criminal, Prison Letters,* and *It Is Good to Know Characters.* The prison also published a journal called *Prisoner's Life Weekly.* All these efforts were aimed at establishing an exemplary institution that would successfully transform political and social deviants into productive members of a socialist community.

Harbin Prison was famous, above all, for its success in making a considerable economic contribution to the revolution. The prison had four factories: a steel mill, a printing shop, a weaving mill, and a plant that made products from hog bristles. All of the factories produced goods for the People's Liberation Army. The steel mill, for instance, produced ammunition and weapons. The weaving mill delivered uniforms, and hog-bristle brushes were also made for the military. The printing shop turned out landownership certificates to be used for the land reform. Harbin Prison became self-sufficient within one year (in 1947), and a year later it was generating profits that were transferred to the people's government. In 1948 the prison started to draw up labor brigades and send them to work on farms or in mining pits. Organizing the prisoner transports and maintaining control over the detachments proved to be very difficult. Therefore, that same year the Harbin court proposed to the Dongbei People's Government that a unified system of labor reform sites be set up outside the cities and closer to mines, factories, and farms. These labor-reform detachments *(laogai dui)* would receive only convicts who had been sentenced to shorter terms and whose crimes were not considered to be severe.

While Harbin Prison was not a labor camp, it developed many features of the later labor camp system. The organization of inmate society in the prison; the emphasis on self-administration, thought reform, and political study; and the insistence on an economic contribution that prisoners owed to both the party and the state—all of these factors would eventually become hallmarks of the Laogai. Harbin Prison thus became a model institution and demonstrated that, given the right organization, the prison could be turned into a catalyst for the revolutionary transformation of Chinese society.

The Brutalization of Criminal Justice

The 1930s and 1940s saw tremendous shifts taking place in the Chinese criminal justice system. On a most fundamental level, the Republican system under the Guomindang government was challenged by the rise and spread of an alternative system of revolutionary criminal justice being formed by the Chinese Communist Party. Yet while the systems in areas under CCP or GMD rule were based on different theories and regulations, it is striking that similar developments on both sides pushed the respective criminal justice systems in comparable directions.

In the GMD-ruled areas there arose a large network of prisons outside the criminal justice system. The targets were political offenders—a category that was broadly defined. It included political opponents and rivals as well as social competitors, such as leaders of local society. The GMD intended to suppress criticism and remove all groups from society that could pose a threat to the government. The dramatically shifting modes of criminal justice contributed to the increased dominance of security concerns and political anxiety. All pervasive, fears of losing power began to shape penal practices and institutions in ways that were on one level rational and justi-

fied, but that too often were underpinned by darker sensibilities and a desire to exclude dissenting voices.

One shortcoming of the whole GMD system of criminal justice was its
increasing susceptibility to politically motivated intervention. A political
judiciary thus gradually developed to make use of the existing penal system
for political goals. The government's aim was to have unlimited power, un-
trammeled by legal rules and regulations. The GMD under Chiang Kai-
shek tried to push the powers of law enforcement in directions not seen in
the early decades of the twentieth century, when a strong belief in the rule
of law had widespread support.

In the areas controlled by the CCP, a new form of revolutionary criminal
justice started to hold sway. Its multiple origins can be traced to Marxist-
Leninist theory, the Russian Revolution, and legal developments during the
late Qing and the Republican periods, as well as to early Chinese penal philosophy. On the basis of their familiarity with European and Russian socialist theories and indigenous legal traditions, and their concrete experiences
from the Chinese Revolution, leaders and thinkers in the Chinese Communist Party generated a distinctive penal philosophy that became one of the
hallmarks of Chinese socialism. The CCP's criminal justice policies also
evolved, however, in response to war and GMD repression, military instability, and local constraints and problems: direct borrowings from penal
ideas and practices from the Soviet Union began to appear only in the late
1940s. As one gets closer to the CCP's revolutionary victory, one can increasingly discern the key tenets and structures of the system that was coming into being. In the revolutionary system, fighting against enemies was a
main concern. Show trials and mass rallies, where certain targeted culprits
were forced to confess their misdeeds, were powerful and efficient vehicles
for educating the masses and instilling discipline. The CCP regime, not unlike the Bolsheviks', was an example of a "theatricalized state," in which
public drama and criminal justice were merged to extend the powers of the
regime in its struggle against perceived enemies.[119]

This approach can in fact be traced back to the late 1920s and early 1930s,
when an extensive if underdeveloped and underfunded system of dramatic
revolutionary justice was formed. At the beginning, the judgments were often summary and bloody. A more ordered approach to penal incarceration
first appeared in Jiangxi, where prisons were renamed "institutes of labor
persuasion." In Yan'an these institutes incorporated techniques of thought

reform into the reeducation program. It was out of the Yan'an experience that the later ethos of reform through labor first emerged in embryonic form. It was also in Yan'an that productive work was first cited as having an educative effect on prisoners' ideology.[120] Indeed it became one of the key goals of the system to organize prisoners into productive labor groups, so that the material wealth of society would be increased and, at the same time, the prisoners would be reformed. Through labor, prisoners would take on a work ethic and learn techniques of production. After 1941 a systematized form of incarceration emerged in which the justice department held common criminals and the security forces controlled political criminals. When the communists entered the cities in 1948 the system began to expand and develop one of its earliest "innovations," namely, the labor camp. At that point the various prison authorities from the liberated areas entered the cities and were faced with increasing numbers of people to detain, and city prisons were already overcrowded. Consequently, a number of area-level justice units decided to move prisoners to the countryside where they could develop farms and mines that would be productive in terms of both material goods and a new prisoner consciousness.

More and more, in GMD and CCP areas alike, criminal justice was reduced to the question of penal treatment. The process or trial component of criminal justice was oversimplified and diminished beyond recognition. Sentences for the accused were determined within hours, by either administrative decree or public pronouncement. The ruling parties were no longer interested in finding or even defining criminal guilt and instead allowed suspicion and denunciations to take the place of material evidence. The criminal prosecution process degenerated into public accusations or was skipped altogether. As criminal justice administration was veering toward becoming an instrument of power and politics, the idea of justice seemed to lose any significance. A part of this transformation was the pervasive brutalization was that was taking place. Small villages and big towns alike were subjected to swift raids by the secret services or party members; within hours, perceived enemies were tried and executed—in not small numbers. These brutal tactics of course terrified people, which was most likely the reason the GMD and CCP used them in the first place.

A further commonality seems important: as the Italian antifascist Carlo Rosselli first pointed out, it was a feature of mid-twentieth-century ideological states that they rather readily blurred the boundary between internal and external enemies, and thus redrew the legal lines within their own societies between those deemed loyal and those regarded, in practice or potentially, as beyond the pale.[121] In both the GMD and the CCP this same binarism started to hold sway. In this respect, they differed sharply from their nineteenth-century predecessors, including the Qing, for whom disloyalty and treachery were two separate concepts. Thus a political and legal system evolved that made systematic the distinctions between friend and enemy.[122]

The division between friend and enemy framed law in China in a basic sense from the mid-1930s onward, so that all policies operated almost entirely according to this binary divide. The system created fundamental differences in legal status and legal rights for political prisoners and drew a formal distinction between regular crime and political crime. Criminal justice matters were determined or overridden by the perceived need to police the distinction between friend and foe. This ultimately political question of loyalty versus betrayal surpassed all other concerns, severely impairing the operation of criminal justice in China for several decades.

4

REFORM THROUGH LABOR

The Communist State

BUILDING on experiments made in its base areas during the revolution, after 1949 the Chinese Communist Party introduced a new nationwide system of criminal justice for the People's Republic of China. It is quite difficult to draw its contours as a unitary system, since the criminal justice apparatus was repeatedly reshuffled and reshaped in the wake of political changes and internal party disputes. Criminal justice under Chinese socialism also was hardly an independent administrative system but was integrated into a network of social control and political mobilization. Enmeshed in larger bureaucratic circuits, the institutional boundaries of criminal justice began to blur. Criminal justice agencies began to pursue goals far beyond crime control or conflict resolution per se. At the same time, informal institutions that actually were not part of the legal system started to take on functions that used to fall under the authority of the judiciary, such as criminal investigation, adjudication, and sentencing. In short, the criminal justice system in the PRC was for a long time very much in flux, and it became mixed up with many other government agencies and political organizations.

Under the new system, most legal punishments were carried out in the form of labor reeducation or labor reform. In camps and brigades set up for "reform through labor" (Laogai), criminal offenders were to be transformed into productive citizens. From the beginning, reform through labor was supposed to play a central part not only in criminal justice but also in the whole project of building socialism in China. Labor camps quickly grew into a major institutional component of the socialist state and were tightly woven into the network of social control. Additional institutions were created to support the reform program and the far-reaching goals associated with this new form of justice.

In the beginning the criminal justice system reported many cases of successful reeducation. The last emperor, Pu Yi, was one of the showcase examples widely touted in Chinese state propaganda. Apart from his well-known case, there were also numerous Guomindang generals and functionaries, as well as Japanese war criminals, who came forward and described their reeducation in writing or in interviews. Not only were many in China won over by these published reports, but so were many observers in the West, who praised the idea of turning prisons into schools for reform. Quite a few said they expected crime and punishment to disappear in China altogether.

But after the end of the Cultural Revolution, reports and publications began to come out that no longer praised successful reeducations, but instead told of the physical deprivation and psychological trauma that inmates suffered in China's labor camps. Witness reports, which could not be easily dismissed as anticommunist propaganda, profoundly shattered the public's confidence in the Laogai, in both China and the West. Their texts conveyed the concrete reality of Laogai as experienced by witnesses and survivors. Through these texts, individuals with stories, feelings, and memories become visible in the Chinese criminal justice system, and a more nuanced and complicated picture emerges.

The Criminal Justice System after 1949

The communist victory in 1949 brought to power a peasant party that had learned its techniques in the countryside but had adopted Marxist-Leninist ideology and believed in class struggle and the possibility of rapid industrial development. Its extensive experience in running the revolutionary base areas and waging war had created in the CCP deeply ingrained operational habits and proclivities. After 1949, the center of gravity for CCP policy had to shift from the countryside to the city, but Mao Zedong insisted that the revolutionary vision forged in the rural struggle would continue to guide the party. This, of course, included the party's approach to criminal justice and punishment. The criminal justice system was to play a powerful role in enforcing social transformation and educating Chinese citizens. It was widely believed that it could make a significant contribution to the socialist transformation of Chinese society.

The situation in urban China, however, differed greatly from that of the rural regions. The social structure in urban areas was more diverse and the economy much more internationalized. Furthermore, in urban China the GMD government had created many government agencies and institutions that had taken over important functions in city administration and the urban economy. When war and revolution caused serious economic disruption, the cities suffered far more. In 1949, many Chinese cities were in fact in social and economic chaos. Growing unemployment, spreading poverty, short supplies of basic goods, and a sharp rise in criminality and violent conflicts shattered urban life.[1] Creating a viable system for the administration of justice in urban China was an urgent matter.

While the CCP leadership wanted to build on its revolutionary experience, no grand blueprint was actually in place for how to administer justice in a complex urban setting. Very soon, seemingly irreconcilable internal differences came to the surface. Two distinct concepts were in play: one was to establish a Soviet-style legal system with a professional, hierarchical, and largely independent judiciary, and the other was to build a decentralized, revolutionary system that was based on strict party control, the participation of the masses, and the involvement of local units and nonprofessional personnel. Neither concept could generate any agreement. As a result, the party was almost constantly switching back and forth between implementing bureaucratic and campaign modes of law enforcement in the first decades of CCP rule.

The development of law in the PRC until 1978 can be divided into three phases.[2] The first phase, from 1949 to 1953, witnessed the dismantling of the GMD judicial system, the purge of judicial personnel left behind from the GMD system, and the use of criminal law as an effective tool for consolidating the new state. In the second phase, from 1954 to 1957, considerable efforts were made to establish an orderly and comprehensive judicial system that would bear many resemblances to the judiciary in the Soviet Union. Emphasis was placed on professionalization of the judicial apparatus. The third phase, from 1958 to 1978, saw a complete reversal of the developments of the preceding phase. The judicial system was dismantled and at times even ceased to operate.

In the first phase following the military victory of the CCP, the party faced a serious challenge: how to consolidate its rule and maintain enough control to enforce compliance with central directives. Overall, its tasks were to smash the old order, to remove residual personnel, and to produce structures to support the overarching goal of socialist transformation. It would take a dual approach to meet those ends. The party would construct a reliable judiciary apparatus to provide authority and stability, and at the same time it would make carefully calculated use of flexible extrajudicial mechanisms to coerce the populace into compliance.

In September 1949, on the eve of the founding of the PRC, the Chinese Political Consultative Conference adopted three documents, the Common Program of the People's Political Consultative Council, the Organic Law of the Central People's Government, and the Organic Law of the Political Consultative Conference. During the period from 1949 to 1953, the Common Program provided the fundamental framework for the legal developments in the PRC, while the two Organic Law documents outlined the formal structure of the future Chinese government. Article 17 of the Common Program formally abolished all laws and legal institutions of Nationalist China.[3] The judicial order that had been so high on the agenda of all administrations in the Chinese Republic came to an abrupt end. However, while the CCP's new laws suggested that the new state sought to distance itself from all legal traditions, the breakup was not as complete as it first appeared.

Having done away with the Republic's laws root and branch, the new state delayed in supplying substitutes. As early as 1950 discussions were begun about the drafting of various laws, such as the "basic law," an outline of the penal code, organizational regulations for the people's courts, general regulations for judicial procedure, law on the reform of criminals, and company law, but no concrete results were made public. Instead of producing more comprehensive legal codes, the state started to issue numerous single decrees, orders, resolutions, and regulations, each of which dealt with a specific issue. Many of the statutes made public in this period demonstrated that the state was first and foremost concerned about the suppression and elimination of political forces and groups deemed unreliable or dangerous to the new order.

The Common Program of the People's Political Consultative Council (Article 7) had already stressed in 1949 the necessity to suppress opponents and punish counterrevolutionaries.[4] Hence, among the earliest legislative measures adopted were the Statutes of [the] State Administrative Council and the People's Supreme Courts Concerning the Suppression of Counter-revolutionary Activities, dated July 21, 1950, and the twenty-one articles of the Statute on Punishment for Counterrevolutionary Activity, dated February 20, 1951.[5] The latter's purpose was "the suppression of counterrevolutionary activities and the strengthening of the democratic dictatorship of the people" (Article 1). In later years, a large number of Chinese citizens were sentenced for counterrevolutionary crimes based on the 1951 statutes, and until late in the 1970s the 1951 statute was the closest legal text the PRC had to a criminal code.[6]

The term "counterrevolution" was defined as "any activity that aims at overthrowing or undermining the democratic dictatorship of the people and the socialist system and therefore puts the PRC in harm's way."[7] The 1951 statutes included a comprehensive list of concrete offenses, all related to security issues.[8] There was a high degree of severity in the punishments specified. For nearly all offenses (95 percent) listed in the statute, the applicable punishments were the death penalty, life imprisonment, or determinate imprisonment.[9] Retroactivity and the principle of analogy granted the adjudicating institution a great deal of discretion. This was in fact a general feature of criminal legislation produced during this period. Instead of applying fixed, limited punishments, the judicial authorities had ample discretion in meting out punishments, depending on the special circumstances of each case.

Another law that imposed punishments for certain activities was the Land Reform Law of June 30, 1950. Resistance against land reform was punished with imprisonment or the death penalty. Many landowners in the countryside were tried under this law and sentenced to death or long terms of imprisonment. Furthermore, a series of regulations and statutes imposed sanctions for such economic crimes as smuggling or tax evasion, disturbance of railways, and illegal lumbering.[10] While many civil laws were also produced quickly within this period, such as the Marriage Law and the Trade Union Law, some of the most frequent crimes, including theft, robbery, and rape, were not covered by any laws made public during this period of time.[11]

Under the Common Program a unified, nationwide system of "people's courts" *(Renmin fayuan)*, procuracy, and public security agencies was organized. On the basis of experiences in the various soviets and base areas, a three-level, two-trial system was set up.[12] The three levels were county courts, provincial courts, and the Supreme People's Court. The county courts were courts of first instance; the provincial courts served as courts of second instance, or courts of appeal. As a rule, a judgment could be appealed in a trial at a court of second instance, the decision of which would be final. The police (public security) and the prosecutorial segment of the system (the procuracy) had the task of prosecuting crimes and bringing indictments against malefactors. The procuracy was also charged with reviewing police actions of arrest and prosecution. Criminal processes at this time were usually conducted in secret, although several major cases were carried out in public mass trials before numerous onlookers.

Several factors impeded the operation of the courts in the period under discussion.[13] Well-trained judges and other judicial staff were not available in sufficient numbers, resulting in long backlogs of cases in the courts. There were also many instances of incompetence, bribery, graft, and miscarriage of justice. Many judges were holdovers from the Nationalist government and were deemed unreliable and disloyal to the new state. The central authorities considered the judiciary's conservative formalism, dubious worldview, and reluctance to mete out harsh sentences to enemies of the state to be serious problems. It was only after the so-called Judicial Reform Movement that lasted from August 1952 to April 1953, during which many judicial holdovers from the Republic were purged, that courts were put into regular operation.[14] At least 80 percent of the judicial personnel were removed from their posts in the course of this movement. Apart from removing Nationalist holdovers, the movement's goals included ending judicial maladministration and eradicating such bourgeois legal values as the importance of a separate judiciary, independent from politics and political authority. An equally important goal was the quick informal disposal of the many cases that had accumulated since 1949. In the course of the Judicial Reform Movement almost all judicial personnel were subject to public examination at what were called struggle or accusation meetings. They were expected to undergo "criticism and self-criticism" and to publicly renounce their previous errors. By means of disciplining and spreading fear, the movement and the party established a firm grip on the judiciary apparatus.

From 1950 onward, many delinquents were convicted not in the people's courts but by people's tribunals *(Renmin fating)* or military courts. People's tribunals existed alongside the people's courts, but they were ad hoc in nature and lasted only through the duration of a given campaign.[15] In the early years of the PRC, they actually represented one of the most important levers by which the new government wielded state power.[16] The tribunals were first introduced in the context of the Land Reform Movement in 1950. The tribunals operated under a set of regulations that was made public on July 20, 1950, as the Organic Regulations of People's Tribunals. The tribunals were formed by people's governments at the provincial level or above and were dissolved upon completion of their tasks. Their main task was "the employment of judicial procedure for the punishment of local despots, bandits, special agents, counter-revolutionaries, and criminals who violate the laws and orders pertaining to agrarian reform."[17] The tribunals were allowed to make arrests, detain suspects, and pass sentences extending from imprisonment to the death penalty.[18] Those selected to serve on the tribunals mostly came from local party organizations. Thereafter, many were appointed to positions in the regular courts on the grounds that they had received judicial training through their work in the tribunals. The mass tribunals can be traced back to the period of revolutionary struggle, where they played a significant role in fighting against the enemies of the CCP.

People's tribunals used such devices as mass trials and accusation meetings to dispense justice. Three formats were widely used for the tribunals: accusation meetings *(kongsu hui)*, "big meetings to announce the sentence" *(xuanpan dahui)*, and mass trials *(gongshen)*.[19] Each form could involve up to tens of thousands of people. They were organized to best mobilize the populace, educate through negative example, and deter through public punishment. Bypassing the formal court system, people's tribunals, in cooperation with public security and party organizations, often carried out massive purges. Between 1950 and 1953, in nationwide campaigns and movements, several social groups were singled out and isolated from the rest of society: landlords (the Land Reform Campaign, 1950 to 1952), counterrevolutionaries (the Campaign to Suppress Counterrevolutionaries, 1950 to 1951), corrupt bureaucrats (the Three-Anti's Campaign [anticorruption, antiwaste, antibureaucracy], 1952), capitalists and private entrepreneurs (the Five-Anti's Campaign [antibribery, anti–tax evasion, antifraud, anti–theft of state property, anti–leakage of state economic secrets], 1952), and the educational sector and intellectuals more generally (the Thought Reform Campaign, 1951 and 1952). While the campaigns differed in scope and intensity, they all saw the deployment of tribunals as a major vehicle for dealing with target groups. Campaigns ware also carried out in the second half of the 1950s. The *Sufan* Campaign ("Cleaning out the Counterrevolutionaries") was launched in 1955, followed by and partly overlapping with the Anti-Rightist Campaign in 1957–58 and the "Little Leap" in 1960. These campaigns were smaller and were mainly conducted in factories, residential units, and government agencies.

The following example describes the course of an accusation meeting held during the Campaign to Suppress Counterrevolutionaries (Zhenfan Yudong). The Beijing Municipal People's Government held a huge public meeting for the accusation of counterrevolutionaries on May 20, 1951. Addressing the aroused crowd, Luo Ruiqing, minister of public security, suggested that some 220 among the 500 or so accused persons be sentenced to death. He was followed by Mayor Peng Zhen, who wrapped up the process by saying:

> People's Representatives! Comrades! We have all heard the report given by Minister Luo and the accusations of the aggrieved parties. What shall we do to these vicious and truculent despots, bandits, traitors, and special service agents? What shall we do to this pack of wild animals? ("Shoot them to death!" the people at the meeting shouted.) Right, they should be shot. If they were not to be shot, there would be no justice. . . . We shall exterminate all these despots, bandits, traitors, and special service agents. We shall shoot as many of them as can be found. (Loud applause and loud shouts of slogans: "We support the people's government! We support Mayor Peng.") The other day, the Public Security Bureau transferred the results of its investigation to the Municipal Consultation Committee for discussion. Today those results were further discussed by all of you. You have expressed your unanimous opinion on that matter. After the meeting, we shall hand over the cases to the Military Court of the Municipal Military Control Committee to be convicted. Tomorrow, conviction; day after tomorrow, execution. (Loud applause and loud shouts.)
>
> The present accused only represent a part of the counter-revolutionaries. There is still a group being kept in jail. Moreover, there are not a few who are concealing themselves in Peking. All the people of the municipality should rise and cooperate with the public security organs to liquidate and exterminate them (loud applause).[20]

Carefully arranged and organized, the mass trials and accusatory meetings followed clear and meticulously prearranged patterns. Dramatic devices such as staging, props, working scripts, agitators, and climactic moments were used to efficiently engage the emotions of the audience—to stir up resentment against the targeted groups and mobilize the audience to support the regime. Mass trials and accusation meetings were held in every urban area, as they were in most villages. Through the organization of such events, the government tried to rally popular support behind the regime, extend the coercive formal and informal instruments of the revolutionary state, and vertically integrate and enhance the rule of the bureaucracy.[21] Significant personal and financial resources were set aside for the campaigns, indicating that they were a high priority for the regime.

In the course of the movements in the early 1950s, according to official (and probably incomplete) statistics, an estimated 4 million arrests were made by the police, the army, or party organs without any real involvement of the regular courts.[22] Hundreds of thousands of "class enemies" or "enemies of the people," perhaps a fourth of all persons arrested, were sentenced to death and executed.[23] In mass trials, the death penalty was carried out immediately or the next day.[24] Most executions were public. The convicts were forced to kneel and were then shot from behind with a single bullet. These public displays of excessive violence had a profound impact on society. They showed unequivocally what the "class struggle" ultimately entailed. In its campaigns against opponents, real or suspected, the Chinese Communist Party proved itself ready to employ violence and terror against its own nationals, and, if necessary, to substantially alter or pass over key provisions of its own fragile socialist law.

Still, the scope of arrests and executions and the willingness of local cadres to participate in the movement seemed to have caught the leadership by surprise. The longer that campaigns like the Land Reform Movement and the Campaign to Suppress Counterrevolutionaries lasted and the more blood was spilled on the execution grounds, the more urgent grew the appeals to local units from the central party to exercise restraint.[25] The campaigns were apparently used by many local individuals and groups (cadres, militia) to settle old scores with neighbors and to decide long-term local conflicts in their favor.

The accusation meetings, mass trials, and mass campaigns were meant to complement and augment the formal criminal justice system in a significant way.[26] Their main purpose was to engage the populace and stimulate active participation. The people were to be "stirred up" *(fadong qunzhong)* and invited to play a vicarious part in the policy imposed by the state, thus collectively reaffirming its popular legitimacy. The close and direct participation of the masses in this process was carefully rehearsed. Those who served as material witnesses were not only exhaustively instructed as to what to say and when, but they were also carefully chosen for the degree to which they would attract the sympathies of the audience. The organizers liked to involve as witnesses and accusers the very old, the very young, and women, all of whom were likely to arouse sympathy when they testified in front of the people and spoke about their grievances.

The numerous trials and campaigns drew in people from all sectors of society, mobilizing the rank-and-file cadres and rallying them behind the government-sponsored objectives.[27] It was incumbent on the central state to win over the leading local and municipal cadres on whom it relied to implement its directives. The campaigns and tribunals thus played a very important role in the imposition and enforcement of norms set by the government, for they provided the central state with a forceful set of ideological and moral incentives with which to elicit compliance and responsiveness from low-level cadres and officials as well as from the broader population. While the judicial system continued to serve as the organizational core of the sanctioning process, mass trials and campaigns functioned as flexible and informal mechanisms for the effective, direct, and rapid transmission of sociopolitical norms and the mustering of broad popular support for those norms and their enforcement.

The Campaign to Suppress Counterrevolutionaries not only established a more structured form for the tribunals and mass trials but also, with official encouragement, enabled them to become more powerful. By the time the campaign ended in 1953, China had 170,000 resident or work-unit security committees with an activist base numbering more than 2 million people.[28] These activists formed a support force for the numerically weak public security units, solving a problem that had plagued that ministry since the time of liberation. Operating under the leadership of the local public security agencies, work units, villages, and towns, their combined strength allowed them to stretch across all facets of social life and to protect the social order right down to the street and work-unit level. Because of their reach, they were also able to help the police monitor any suspected or minor counterrevolutionaries within their own work and living spaces.

The first phase in the development of criminal justice under the PRC was thus characterized by the drafting and promulgation of legal regulations and statutes that imposed punishments for activities the new state deemed dangerous and therefore sought to suppress. The approach to law in this period was therefore instrumental: above all, law was but one of the techniques available for securing and consolidating the new political system. Paralleling the establishment of a rudimentary judiciary, informal extrajudicial mechanisms and techniques were simultaneously developed and deployed to extend the reach and power of the central state. Rule by law and by merciless terror were the two faces of the new order. Together these measures pushed the power of law and the enforcement of social norms in directions not seen in the periods before the revolution. In its continuing assault on the structure of feudal-capitalist authority, the revolutionary leadership thus was able to score an enormous success. Most dissidents and opponents of the party's policy initiatives were eliminated within the first years. Given these developments, the leadership had to shift its attention away from its preoccupation with the counterrevolution if it was to maintain credibility and ensure its continued existence.

After destroying the old order, the CCP leadership faced the delicate and complex task of initiating the promised socialist transformation of Chinese society. Without a certain core of positive public laws, without professional legal personnel, and without state institutions holding forth the promise of regularity and predictability, this goal seemed unreachable. Having decided in the early 1950s to adopt the Soviet economic model, the CCP leaders also seemed to be willing to emulate a Soviet-style legal system. The second phase in the development of criminal justice in the PRC therefore saw efforts to establish a more comprehensive system for the administration of civil and criminal justice. At the same time, the deployment of mass trials and tribunals was notably reduced. The government promulgated a constitution, founded the Ministry of Justice, published several organizational laws, and created a professionalized system of criminal justice. All of these efforts point to the goal of establishing an orderly system for the administration of justice. The ambitious implementation of a judicial system underscored the new order's need for legitimacy.

The organization of the judiciary was regulated in detail in the Law of the PRC for the Organization of People's Courts, which was promulgated a week after the first formal PRC constitution, on September 20, 1954.[29] The courts were given the following tasks: adjudication of criminal cases and punishment of criminals; adjudication of civil disputes and resolving civil conflicts; through adjudicative processes, education of the litigants and the general masses in regard to the norms of the new state. The last responsibility proved to be very significant. Public trials were often held not only for sentencing an offender but also for educating and instructing the public. A basic function of court hearings in the PRC, therefore, was the fundamental remaking of the people's political thinking as well as the inculcation of norms and values.[30] For this reason the mass trial—seen as the most educative form of public trial—was still frequently employed, even outside of specific campaigns. To fulfill the educative function, a carefully crafted spectacle before the masses was still considered the most effective. Such an approach to law and court hearings might be dubbed "paternalistic jurisprudence."

Other specific laws governed the responsibilities and duties of the procuracies and the public security agencies (including the police).[31] On paper, these laws provided legal protection for the people, acknowledged the need for and the value of due process, and limited powers of the police to make arrests and enforce detentions. The law also stated that the courts should be independent in administering justice (Article 78 of the 1954 constitution).

The function of criminal procedure was fourfold: to investigate, to accuse, to defend, and to adjudicate. In the period from 1954 to 1957 all of these functions were vested in four autonomous and separately constituted agencies: the agencies of preliminary investigation and inquiry, namely the Bureaus for Public Security; the office of the procurator; the people's assessor (representing the masses); and the regular criminal courts.[32] The criminal process was conducted in a distinct and particular way that differed from criminal processes conducted in Republican China. The pretrial investigation was essential in evaluating the evidence and determining the crime of the defendant.[33] A requirement of full pretrial discovery of all evidence had the effect of purging all elements of surprise from the trial process. Because the judges had unimpeded access to all the pretrial investigative materials in a case, they were not at the mercy of the counsels in their efforts to seek out critical evidence.

The Chinese inquisitorial system was viewed not as a duel between opposing counsels but as a tripartite search for the objective truth, and not merely the legal truth. All the major participants in the process—the judges as well as the prosecution and the people's assessor—were expected to cooperate in the search. Moreover, because of the special situation of the defendant, who usually had no counsel of any sort in a criminal trial in China, the obligation was on the judges and the prosecution to bring out both the incriminating and the exonerating features of the case.[34] The defendant's role was confined to seeking either an acquittal or a mitigation of punishment. What this meant in practice was that the principal actors in the criminal process—the judges, the prosecutor, and the people's assessor—were supposed to work to defend the rights and legal interests of the defendant. While this system certainly had flaws and tended to disadvantage the defendant, Jerome Cohen concluded that "later public trials were often authentic attempts at determining the degree of the defendant's guilt and the appropriate punishment."[35]

During the period under discussion, the leadership frequently emphasized the importance of law for the development of socialist society.[36] In many speeches and public statements the leadership expressed its appreciation of the judiciary's work. President Liu Shaoqi, who was one of the strongest defenders of the legal system, declared at the Eighth National Congress of the CCP, in September 1956, that the period of revolutionary struggle was past and the aim of the struggle was to be turned to the safeguarding of successful development. Therefore, he stressed, the establishment of a "complete legal system" was an "absolute necessity."[37] The head of the People's Supreme Court, Dong Biwu, admonished party cadres against interfering in the judicial process.[38] The new governmental arrangements emphasized hierarchical, organizational control of judicial decision making. The courts were supposed to operate on the basis of national legal standards, and their potential mistakes were to be corrected exclusively by higher echelons of the judiciary. The establishment of judicial institutions would provide the new state with stability, protection, and regularization. Uniformity, centralization, and professionalization were expected to move state and society beyond the chaos and violence of the years immediately following the Chinese Revolution. At the same time, the existence of a viable, valid court system was supposed to limit or impede mass campaigns.[39]

In the decade following the promulgation of the 1954 constitution, more than eleven hundred laws and decrees were enacted to supplement the statutes that had provided a loose framework for the administration of justice in the consolidation period from 1949 to 1956.[40] Given this very active legislature, it is all the more notable that the drafting of comprehensive legal codes for such areas as criminal law, civil law, and procedural law appeared difficult and delayed. In October 1954 legislative work on a draft for a criminal law code was officially started. By June 1957, twenty-two drafts had been written but none was near completion.[41] The work on the criminal code, the civil code, and the code of criminal procedure was interrupted several times by internal disputes over fundamental characteristics and of course by the political movements that shattered Chinese society. It was not until 1979 that the complete codes and organizational laws describing the fundamental nature of the criminal justice system passed through the national legislature. For thirty years no coherent, comprehensive law codes existed to regulate the criminal justice system in the People's Republic. Basic rules and procedures for punishment were all provided in numerous single laws and ordinances, and were made and applied only on an interim basis. The impasse that emerged in the mid-1950s clearly demonstrates that the push toward erecting a socialist legal system was not supported unanimously within the central leadership. The legal system became contended territory.

A good example for how the system operated without a comprehensive legal code may be found in an administrative decree called the Security Administration Punishment Act (SAPA), dating from October 22, 1957. The SAPA imposed sanctions for a long and quite detailed list of minor delinquent behaviors and misdemeanors. It was not, however, enforced through formal criminal procedures but through the government's administrative powers. Article 2 of the SAPA provides that "whoever disturbs social order, endangers public safety, infringes upon a citizen's rights of the person or encroaches upon public or private property" shall be punished in accordance with the SAPA "if such an act is not serious enough for criminal punishment" and if a "security administration punishment should be imposed."[42] Penalties under the regulations include: a warning; a maximum fine of 5,000 yuan (625 U.S. dollars); and an administrative detention of not more than fifteen days. The public security entities (and not the courts) had the exclusive responsibility for imposing these penalties.

In the various law texts and regulations, both the criminality of and the punishment for a particular act always depended on whether the "circumstances" of the act were "serious" or "minor." All the laws, however, failed to provide a clear definition of either minor crimes or serious crimes, even though the distinction between them pervaded the legislation. Although judicial interpretations and unpublished regulations helped to clarify the regulations and other laws that imposed punishments and were thus hailed as an "indispensable" source for understanding Chinese law, the broad and indeterminate language found in the interpretations resulted in a wide scope of discretion in their application.[43]

Given the lack of a comprehensive and codified system of criminal law, judicial interpretation and case collections played an important role in the Chinese criminal justice system. They indicated how to correctly understand the meaning of the law and how to describe the concrete standard of sentencing within the statutory punishments. They also served to draw the line for guilt and for when the law required giving a heavier punishment because of "serious circumstances" or "especially serious circumstances."[44]

The substantive body of criminal law emerging in this phase was thus characterized by a multiplicity of single pieces of legislation, a highly provisional approach to their application, and relatively indefinite measures of punishment.[45] In general, these features granted the judges a high degree of discretion with respect to the interpretation of the legal texts and the sentencing process. Judicial-precedence decisions accordingly played an important role. Nonetheless, comprehensive codifications were initiated by the mid-1950s and China seemed to be following a path toward a Soviet-style legal system. The laws that did exist, even if they were flawed by inconsistencies and deficiencies, provided the grounds for a reduction of the postrevolutionary violence and insecurity. The gradually evolving judiciary started to put legal limitations and supervisory controls on police and military actions. Yet to many in China, these developments were not coming quickly enough. In May and June 1957, when Mao called for the country to "let a hundred flowers bloom, let a hundred schools contend," harsh criticism of the legal system was articulated. Some legal scholars accused the party of a "nihilist standpoint towards law," of manipulating the legal system, of making arbitrary arrests, and of violations of legality.[46] Mao apparently was caught by surprise. His response to the crisis was the decision to cease the legal buildup.

During the third and longest phase of the three periods under discussion here, from 1958 to 1978, the PRC undertook a complete reversal of the legal stabilization and regularization that had marked the second phase. The broad discontent expressed by intellectuals in the course of the Hundred Flowers Campaign as well as later intraparty criticism aimed at Mao's Great

Leap Forward prompted a faction within the party leadership around Mao Zedong to abandon the party's commitment to maintaining a comprehensive legal system. Mao sensed that doubts about his vision for a socialist society and his charismatic leadership were spreading in Chinese society and even within the party.

Clinging to his ideals, Mao Zedong came to the conclusion that the new bureaucratic institutional-administrative structure that had come into existence was resisting the necessary continuation of the revolution. He became increasingly convinced that the existence of a complex system for the administration of justice and society had led to the persistence of bourgeois values within the socialist society and even within party ranks (as evidenced by elitism, arrogance, abuse of authority), had limited the power of the party by binding it to complex bureaucratic procedures, and had impeded its ability to perpetuate the revolutionary project by initiating quick changes and its own thorough transformation.[47] Mao maintained that laws, ordinances, and regulations all were products of a certain stage in the overall social, economic, and political development, and that they had to be superseded by new regulations as China entered a new stage of development and faced new challenges. According to this position, legal principles and doctrines possessed no universal or even long-term validity. In short, Mao's goal of continuing the revolution proved to be incompatible with upholding a set of fixed principles or institutionalized procedures, for the exigencies of the movement were in constant flux. From 1957 and 1958 onward, Mao promoted the necessity of a nationwide rectification *(zhengfeng)* campaign that would address the nonparty masses and would be relatively free of organizational and legal restrictions. The rectification campaign was finally implemented as the Great Proletarian Cultural Revolution. For him, the unmaking of the judicial apparatus was an inevitable step toward reigniting revolutionary fervor.

During the second phase, the emerging judiciary had already been hampered by the political movements that had occasionally swept the country.[48] Beginning in 1958, then, law in China became increasingly "less formal, less professional and ever more responsive to political shifts."[49] The Anti-Rightist Movement of 1957–58 that followed the Hundred Flowers policy led not only to the prosecution of those who had ushered in criticisms of the party, but also to the arrest of many prominent judicial experts and professors.[50] Measures were adopted that fell short of an outright suspension of the whole judiciary apparatus but succeeded in severely obstructing its authority and capacity. The legal codification work and the operation of the judiciary were almost halted in the late 1950s and from 1966 to 1976 were completely inert (no laws were passed). Directives were simply issued in the name of a combination of central organs (in fact often simply by Mao himself), for the Ministry of Justice was abolished in 1959.[51] The courts became almost invisible, although the court system was retained in the structure of the government as it was laid out in the 1975 constitution.[52] The defendant's need for defense counsel or a so-called people's lawyer was rejected during and after the Great Leap Forward.[53]

The most serious blow to the formal legal structure came during the Cultural Revolution. Because the Cultural Revolution was supposed to reinvigorate class struggle, these years witnessed the reemergence of the revolutionary criminal justice approach. In 1967 Mao instructed the Red Guards to "smash Gongjianfa (police, procuracy and courts)."[54] The procuracy was dissolved and its functions and powers were transferred to the Public Security Ministry. Finally, law schools were closed and any judicial was training stopped. On February 14, 1967, the *People's Daily* carried an editorial that called for the complete destruction of the bourgeois legal order so that proletarian law could be established. The editorial had a very telling title: "In Praise of Lawlessness." In light of the suspension of the judicial process, other forums would be used for the adjudication of offenders: minor crimes, for example, would be dealt with by semiofficial organizations such as work units and communes.

For political crimes—the prosecution of real or assumed dissidents and disloyal party members—"case examination groups" were set up on all levels and in all branches of the party and government structure between 1966 and 1979.[55] The CCP had always maintained its own internal disciplinary channel for party members, separate from the criminal and administrative punishment process for nonparty members. Thus the courts and other agencies never had to deal with corrupt party officials, unless the CCP wanted to publicize the event. The task of the case examination groups was to gather evidence against suspects by examining documents and interrogating the apprehended individuals. Arrested suspects were forced to submit to prolonged questioning in one of the secret prisons. The case group would also determine the sentence after conviction. It was apparently customary for the case groups to hand over convicts directly to the labor camps and prisons.[56] Most offenders were sentenced to some form of labor reeducation. The central case examination group, headed by Kang Sheng, handled the cases of approximately 1,250 leading government and party officials; in all, more than 2 million cadres were prosecuted and punished by case examination groups.

While minor criminals were dealt with in their work units and communes and political dissidents were handled by the case examination units, those accused of more severe crimes were disposed of by way of military tribunals and mass trials. The revived institution of the mass trial once again became the main forum for prosecuting major crimes.[57] By recalling the revolutionary fervor of earlier mass trials and inciting popular anger anew, the public condemnation and punishment of "enemies of the people" once again became expressions of popular will. The death penalty was frequently called for and carried out on the spot. The trials' ritualized spectacles of condemnation and mass execution, often staged in urban centers, were final terrifying pageants of revolutionary power, and they had, of course, a profound effect on popular consciousness. The violent elimination of these "enemies" conveyed the unequivocal message that the class struggle promoted by the Cultural Revolution ultimately entailed the spread of physical brutality and bare violence.

Behind these policies of the Cultural Revolution was the thoughtful and well-planned effort to restate and augment the political supervision of the criminal justice process. The priority of party policy over the law was openly asserted, as the following quotation from a 1958 book on the legal system demonstrates:

> The law is enacted on the basis of party policy; it is policy made concrete and articulate. Thus it cannot be denied that to do things in accordance with law is to implement party policy. Nonetheless, it must be realized that party policy is the soul of the law; it is only by interpreting the law on the basis of party policy that one can truly understand the spiritual essence of law and apply it correctly. Thus in applying law, one cannot but take party policy as the basis.[58]

The party stressed that it needed to control and supervise the adjudication process in order to maintain true justice, which would be achieved only when the political party line was guiding the sentencing process. Party supervision would also guarantee that the legal system was used as an instrument in the fight against the counterrevolution. After 1958 Mao Zedong and Luo Ruiqing repeatedly stressed that the counterrevolutionaries, while their ranks were reduced, still represented a grave threat. One of the most important tasks assigned to the criminal justice system was to stage the struggle against the counterrevolution.[59] In the 1975 version of the constitution, courts were given responsibility not only for the people's congresses but also for the local revolutionary committees that in the Cultural Revolution served as the local people's governments.[60] All staff members of a court, from the president to any judicial worker, were appointed by the governmental revolutionary committee of the same level.[61] The party's leadership in the court was "absolute" and therefore extended to the adjudication of every individual case. The overall goal was to strengthen party control over the whole system of justice administration.

The CCP leadership declared that public security and the justice system should fully implement the "mass line" and called on public security and judicial organs to accept party supervision. Legal and public security workers were sent to the countryside or to the factories for indoctrination and to participate in production, and at the same time, ideas of "judicial independence and legal mysticism" were explicitly challenged.[62] Judicial procedures were greatly abridged and simplified, and justice was to be carried out quickly and on the spot.

Legal workers formed so-called joint workgroups, composed of public security officers, a procurator, and a judge. When crimes were reported, the workgroups would leave the office and, in close cooperation with local organizations such as work units, neighborhood committees, party cells, and the like, dispose of the cases on the spot.[63] The suspect's conviction and sentence were pronounced by the workgroup; the court then was left the task of reviewing the conviction and fixing the precise punishment. The whole process was conducted in close coordination and debate with the mass audience in attendance. The sentence was proclaimed and the delinquent was expected to show repentance, admit his crime, and accept the punishment in front of the people, too. In general, this informal approach was intended to speed up the processing of criminal cases.

In this system, the administration of justice was viewed as an eminently political affair. Because crime and deviant behavior had a class character, according to the party, political factors were inevitably involved when a person committed a crime. There was no room for impartiality; on the contrary, to deal with offenses of all sorts, a clear political stance was considered crucial. This approach required the weighing of several aspects of a case, such as the class status of the offender, the presence or absence of criminal intent, whether or not the crime had a political dimension to it, and, finally, the nature and extent of the social and political damage caused by the offense.[64]

The emphasis on political factors inherent in crime and punishment, as well as the CCP's domination of adjudication, led to a de facto abandonment of the Soviet-inspired constitutional model of formal judicial procedure, which culminated in public trials before impartial judges who heard evidence and legal arguments presented by defense counsel as well as the prosecution. After 1958, the criminal justice process was to be freed from judicial and administrative restraints, to strengthen the party's control over adjudication and to enable the public security force to respond directly and swiftly to criminality and deviant behavior.

Of course not everybody within the party leadership supported the suspension of the judiciary. During the retrenchment policy following the Great Leap Forward, efforts were made to revitalize and strengthen the judicial apparatus again. Liu Shaoqi said in a speech to the Central Public Security, Procuratorial, and Judicial Group in 1962:

> The legal system of the proletariat is the people's democratic legal system or the socialist legal system. A legal system does not necessarily mean dictatorship. There must be a legal system among the people. Government functionaries and the masses must act within the bonds of public rules and regulations.
>
> It is right for the court to judge cases independently, and this is prescribed by the Constitution. No party committee or government department should interfere with the court in this respect.[65]

Because of efforts by Liu Shaoqi and others, the rudimentary structure of the court system was preserved, even if it could operate in only a very narrow, limited way. Liu Shaoqi's remarks, however, got him into trouble later. His words were used against him in the Cultural Revolution to demonstrate his revisionist political stance and to fabricate a case for purging him. Red Guards denounced Liu Shaoqi and others as "capitalist roaders" because they supported the bourgeois concepts of equal justice and defense counsel and resisted the party leadership in matters of legal work.

Many Western observers saw the dismantling of the Soviet-style legal system in the PRC as the beginning of a despotic regime. Luo Ruoqing indeed left no doubt that the implementation of the Great Leap policy in legal and public security areas signaled a renewed effort to arouse class struggle and step up the fight against counterrevolutionaries and the "five elements" (landlords, rich peasants, counterrevolutionaries, "bad elements," and rightists).[66] Yet an alternative justice system was put in place and was in operation for almost two decades, until the late 1970s. The system of workgroups featured simplified procedures that were easily intelligible to the vast group of poorly educated Chinese peasants living in rural areas. Most of the time the legal workgroups successfully resolved local conflicts, property disputes, and petty crimes.

The informal workgroup system did have a theoretical foundation. It was based on the values and ideals of egalitarianism (maintaining a relatively "flat" hierarchy in the criminal justice process), decentralism (that is, having a functionally indiscriminate division of labor in the criminal justice system), participatory justice (integrating trials with mass debate), and a preference for conciliation and mediation over sanctioning criminals. In this system, many if not most conflicts succeeded in reaching a pretrial resolution and conciliation. Only after repeated attempts at informal persuasion and administrative sanctions would an offender reach the stage of formal criminal sentencing. Nearly a majority of smaller criminal offenses were settled out of court. The importance of mediation and informal conflict resolution is one of the hallmarks of justice in socialist China; it therefore deserves a closer look.

After 1957 the legal process in socialist China increasingly relied on the use of nonprofessional bodies, chiefly the primary work units, rural communes, and residence units, to sanction deviants and handle disputes in an informal and flexible way.[67] During the first decades of the People's Republic of China, the Communist Party effectively managed grassroots communities throughout China by using neighborhood committees and other basic units (work units and the like) as bridges between the government and society. Thus the structure of authority in the PRC came to rely on not law, nor even a hierarchical apparatus of coercion, but on the "compartmentalization of society into consensually responsive groups."[68] Neighborhood committees had three important functions. First, they served as governmental institutions in carrying out government directives and collecting information from local societies. Second, they served local communities by representing the common interests of residents and by helping to mediate neighborhood disputes and maintain social order. And third, neighborhood committees also played an important role in law enforcement. They were charged with bringing to light any member's deviation from accepted norms for thinking and behavior.[69] The committees were supposed to have a stake in controlling the actions of their members because they had a say in determining punishments for deviant behavior.

The decentralized, campaign-based approach to law enforcement scored enormous success in eliminating opposition, but its biggest disadvantage was the difficulty of controlling it from the center.[70] Whereas it was possible to effectively target and purge certain groups and to create an atmosphere of fear and terror, it proved difficult to limit and halt a campaign once it was started. Local agencies often stood outside the communication lines, were difficult to supervise, and, because of the power granted to them, tended to defend their autonomy.

The development of the legal system as described was underpinned by rather distinct and even unique ideas and theories about class struggle, law, and justice. It was in particular the "older generations of leaders" who laid down the theoretical foundation, principles, and basic structures for criminal justice in socialist China.[71] Among them, of course, Mao's guidelines were the most crucial, yet they were never uncontroversial or unchallenged. The question of how to deal with deviants (enemies, counterrevolutionaries, and criminals) was a central concern for him. But even given the political and ideological dominance of Mao Zedong, other members of the leadership put forth ideas about crime and punishment that differed slightly from those of Mao. Apart from the leadership, there was also a professional body of experts and specialists who contributed their theories with regard to the new forms of punishment. The discourses on criminology, penology, and the so-called Laogai science *(laogai xue)* or legal Laogai science *(laogai faxue)* are of particular significance in this respect.

Mao Zedong's thinking about crime and punishment has to be set against his general worldview and his understanding of human history. To begin with, Mao's conception of the historical process stressed the momentum resulting from contradictions that are inherent in human history.[72] The dialectical tensions between opposite poles are what forcefully propel history forward. The contradictions are permanent in nature, they will never cease to exist, and, consequently, the objective real world is subject to constant change. Permanently existing contradictions and a world in constant flux confront man with the fundamental challenge of a never-ending struggle. Mao does not seem to have harbored much hope for a peaceful final state of communism. Reading his writings, one gets the sense that he believed that there would never be an end to contradiction in history, and that therefore the fighting would never stop.

Struggle was thus for Mao a basic condition of history and all human existence, and revolution was an essential manifestation of that struggle. Revolution is a struggle between classes, a form of struggle that materialized after history entered the modern age. The idea that the privileged classes could be overthrown by the disadvantaged classes through struggle was thus in full accordance with the laws of historical progress. This idea naturally entailed the mobilization of the oppressed.

While these arguments may not transcend mainstream Marxist theory, Mao made a genuine innovative contribution with his concept of the "mass line."[73] The notion of class struggle led Mao to the importance of the masses and the mass movement, and to what was later labeled the mass line. That term is more than merely a different word for revolution, or a technical device for mobilization. The concept of the mass line has several crucial implications for understanding Mao's conceptions of crime and punishment. The masses are, in Mao's view, the overwhelming majority in society. In human history they have always been members of the lower classes and have been suppressed and exploited. The mass line represents precisely the interests of this disadvantaged and underprivileged majority. In other words, the mass line articulates the masses' claim to equality or fairness. Equality or fairness, in this view, is not a formally reached fair distribution among individuals with equal rights; it is redirecting the sum total of their socioeconomic entitlements to large, historically disadvantaged segments of society. Following Aristotle, this concept may be dubbed "distributive justice" *(justitia distributiva)*; its actual outcome or goal is the distribution of resources. During the revolutionary years, Mao fully developed the idea of the masses and the mass line in his efforts to mobilize the groups willing to commit themselves to the revolutionary project, draw them into the political process, take into account their interests and rely on them for the implementation of policies. Through overthrowing the oppressors and removing them from influence and power—in other words, through struggle and violence—the socioeconomic interests of the oppressed would be reinstated. To Mao, mass movements were the most effective means to secure socioeconomic interests.

Revolutionary distributive justice vindicated the violation of existing laws, because the laws of the old order served only to protect the oppressors and further entrench the injustice. Mao noted that in 1926 the peasants in Hunan had adopted violent measures in attacking local bullies and oppressive landowners. He strongly approved those measures and praised them as higher revolutionary justice, saying that such methods were justified because the bullies and landowners were guilty of severe crimes and cruelties themselves. All punishments are justified when they are a retribution for former crimes. Mao explained:

> The peasants are clear-sighted. Who is bad and who is not, who is the worst and who is not quite so vicious, who deserves severe punishment and who deserves to be let off lightly—the peasants keep clear accounts, and very seldom has the punishment exceeded the crime. . . . A revolution is not like inviting people to a dinner, or writing an essay, or painting a picture, or doing embroidery; it cannot be so refined, so leisurely and gentle, so "benign, upright, courteous and complaisant." A revolution is an uprising, an act of violence whereby one class overthrows the power of another. A rural revolution is a revolution in which the peasantry overthrows the power of the feudal landlord class. If the peasants do not use extremely great force, they cannot possibly overthrow the deeply rooted power of the landlords, which has lasted for thousands of years. The rural areas must experience a great, fervent revolutionary upsurge, which alone can rouse the peasant masses in the thousands and ten thousands to form this great force. . . . To put it bluntly, it was necessary to bring about a brief reign of terror in a very rural area; otherwise we could never suppress the activities of the counterrevolutionaries in the countryside or overthrow the authority of the gentry. To right a wrong, it is necessary to exceed the proper limits; the wrong cannot be righted without doing so.[74]

As can be seen from the above quotation, punitive actions against members of the traditional elite were an integral part of the revolutionary enterprise. Through punishing evil landlords and other elites, the wrongs of the old society would be corrected. Revolutionary justice, in Mao's thinking, inevitably encompassed exceeding the limits in order to right the wrongs of the old order; retribution and retaliation were necessary to achieve fairness. Revolutionary punishments as described and approved by Mao had to be (1) imposed under direct participation of the masses and (2) related to the crimes committed by the landlords, since they were intended to unmake and rectify previous unjust conditions. The punishments carried out by the revolutionary masses were an expression of public indignation over previous crimes and injustices. In general, if applied with skill, public punishments were a powerful tool. They could be used to suppress and eliminate opponents. At the same time, when staged as public theater, the drama of a trial could be used to rally popular sentiment behind the party's course and direct indignation toward targeted opponents. Mao made no effort to hide his notion that this could take on the form of terror. Terror was not only acceptable as a necessary evil but was also, in fact, indispensable for the revolutionary project.

Mao held the view that politics should never be isolated from the necessity of struggle, the apriority of the human condition.[75] In the 1950s Mao came to a second surprising conclusion: that contradictions exist even under socialism, and that this fact in turn accounts for the necessity of continued struggle. Mao Zedong systematically developed and elaborated this theory in several long speeches, talks, and articles. From 1949 onward, it appears that at the crossroads of important political developments Mao always felt compelled to speak out on matters of crime and punishment.

In his well-known speech "On the People's Democratic Dictatorship," given in commemoration of the twenty-eighth anniversary of the Chinese Communist Party on June 30, 1949, Mao Zedong talked about the emerging political and social order in the new China.[76] An important issue in Mao's talk was deviant behavior. What forms of deviant behavior could be tolerated under socialism, and how should a socialist society react to delinquency? Since these were fundamental questions that were being asked at the dawn of a new order, a longer citation from Mao's speech seems justified:

> "You are dictatorial." My dear sirs, you are right, that is just what we are. All the experience the Chinese people have accumulated through several decades teaches us to enforce the people's democratic dictatorship that is to deprive the reactionaries of the right to speak and let the people alone have that right.
>
> Who are the people? At the present stage, they are the working class, the

peasantry, the urban petty bourgeoisie and the national bourgeoisie. These classes, led by the working class and the Communist Party, unite to form their own state and elect their own government; they enforce their dictatorship over the running dogs of imperialism—the landlord class and bureaucratic bourgeoisie, as well as the representatives of those classes, the Kuomintang reactionaries and their accomplices—suppress them, allow them only to behave themselves and not be unruly in word or deed. If they speak or act in an unruly way, they will be promptly stopped and punished. Democracy is practised within the ranks of the people, who enjoy the rights of freedom of speech, assembly, association and so on. The right to vote belongs only to the people, not to the reactionaries. The combination of these two aspects, democracy for the people and dictatorship over the reactionaries, is the people's dictatorship. . . .

The state apparatus, including the army, the police and the courts, is the instrument by which one class oppresses another. It is an instrument of the oppression of antagonistic classes; it is violence, not "benevolence." . . .

The state protects the people. Only when the people have such a state can they educate and remould themselves on a country-wide scale by democratic methods and, with everyone taking part, shake off the influence of domestic and foreign reactionaries . . ., rid themselves of the bad habits and ideas acquired in the old society, not allow themselves to be led astray by the reactionaries, and continue to advance—to advance towards a socialist and communist society.

Here, the method we employ is democratic, the method of persuasion, not of compulsion. When anyone among the people breaks the law, he too should be punished, imprisoned or even sentenced to death; but this is a matter of a few individual cases, and it differs in principle from the dictatorship exercised over the reactionaries as a class.

As for the members of the reactionary classes and individual reactionaries, so long as they do not rebel, sabotage or create trouble after their political power has been overthrown, land and work will be given to them as well in order to allow them to live and remould themselves through labor into new people. If they are not willing to work, the people's state will compel them to work. Propaganda and educational work will be done among them too and will be done, moreover, with as much care and thoroughness as among the captured army officers in the past.[77]

The speech introduced several crucial and far-reaching concepts. Law as a tool, the systematic distinction between the people and the enemies of the people, the need of the people to reform themselves, the justification of bare violence against enemies, the use of mitigation and persuasion for members of the people (although individual cases might demand severe punishments or even the death penalty)—all these were concepts that fundamentally came to shape the criminal justice system in socialist China.

In his speech titled "On Ten Major Relationships" (April 25, 1956), in which he delivered a critique of the Soviet model, Mao also touched upon the relationship between the revolution and the counterrevolution. He started by saying that revolution and counterrevolution are antipodes. Furthermore, he predicted the continued existence of the revolution-counterrevolution contradiction in socialist society. Though this kind of contradiction was labeled antagonistic, it was changeable. In other words, the negative side (counterrevolution) could be converted to the positive side (revolution) if the social conditions and the policy were right. Mao said: "Thanks to the great strength of the people and to the correct policy we have adopted toward counterrevolutionaries, which allows them to transform themselves into new people through labor, quite a few of them have switched to no longer opposing the revolution. They take part in agricultural labor and industrial work, and some of them are quite enthusiastic and have done beneficial work." Mao stressed here that counterrevolutionaries were imprisoned so that they could transform themselves through labor, so that "rubbish can be turned into something useful."[78]

However, while in general the emphasis of the party was on reeducation, in some circumstances the counterrevolutionaries had to be killed, Mao said, because they "were deeply hated by the masses and owed the masses heavy blood-debts."[79] The application of nonrehabilitative sanctions is thus explained or justified by popular resentment and "blood-debts" *(xie zhai)*, an expression that occurs frequently in Mao's speeches and writing. The concept of blood-debt was used in arguing that popular indignation legitimized the party's actions in seeking retribution and retaliation against its worst enemies. Mao also cautioned that counterrevolutionaries still existed in China, so that further campaigns would be necessary in the future. The socialist state had to be vigilant and could not afford to renounce the use of severe punishments: "We cannot promulgate [a policy] of no executions at all; we still cannot abolish the death penalty. Suppose there is a counterrevolutionary who has killed people or blown up a factory, what would you say, should that person be executed or not? Certainly such a person must be executed."[80]

Almost a year later, on February 27, 1957, Mao Zedong gave a talk that later was regarded in China as a "principal statement on law."[81] The title was "On Correctly Handling Contradictions among the People." In this speech, arguments made previously were taken up again, and carried on and refined. Mao's central argument was again that contradictions continued to exist under socialism. At the outset he drew a distinction between "contradictions between the enemy and us" and "contradictions among the people." According to Mao, these two types of contradictions that were existent in China were completely different in nature.

In the current stage of socialism, Mao said, all classes, strata, and social groups that approved of, supported, and participated in the endeavor to construct socialism fell under the rubric of the people, while all social forces and social groups that resisted the socialist revolution and were hostile to or undermined the construction of socialism were the people's enemies. The contradictions between the enemy and the people (or "us") were antagonistic. As for contradictions among the people, those among the laboring people are nonantagonistic in nature, while those between the exploited classes and the exploiting classes had, apart from a nonantagonistic aspect, an antagonistic aspect as well.[82]

Mao's category of the "enemies of the people" was vague and flexible because the boundary between enemies and the people was not absolute. Mao took pains not to set up clear-cut rules and strict laws because he was convinced that, under certain circumstances, friends could turn into foes (as happened later when even party members were accused of being rightists) and vice versa (although this was far more infrequent).[83] In general it seems that, for Mao Zedong, a person's intentions and actions determined whether he or she belonged to the people's enemies or not, although class background certainly counted too. Especially from the late 1950s on, class status was principally hereditary, so that the children of a landlord were considered to belong to the landlord class. A member of the people could only turn into an enemy of the people if he committed a serious crime. Such persons were called "bad elements" *(huai fenzi),* and they included murderers, robbers, prostitutes, and habitual thieves.

With respect to the so-called rightists, who had committed political offenses, the situation was more complex. In October 1957 Mao made the following comments:

> In the past, [the rightists] were part of the people, now I think only one-third of these people belong to the people and two-thirds of them belong to the

counterrevolutionaries. . . . In form the rightists still belong to the people, but in reality they are enemies [of the people]. Let us announce publicly that they are enemies and that the contradiction between them and us is a contradiction between the enemy and ourselves, because they oppose socialism, oppose the leadership of the Communist Party, and oppose the dictatorship of the proletariat. . . . They are poisonous weeds.[84]

The remarks were made at a time when the movement against "bourgeois rightists" was in full swing. The depth of fury and exasperation Mao felt about the course of the Hundred Flowers Campaign can be heard in the tone of his statement. By designating two-thirds of the rightists as "enemies of the people," he approved of subjecting them to the same coercive measures as enemies of the people. Consequently, like bad elements, rightists were "to be sent to labor education and reform."[85]

Apart from bad elements and rightists, Mao specifically also mentioned landlords, rich peasants, and counterrevolutionaries (GMD officials) as being enemies of the people. These groups were of course formed on the basis of class origin. Later the whole category of enemies of the people would be abbreviated as *di-fu-fan-huai-you* (shorthand for the five elements: landlords, rich peasants, counterrevolutionaries, bad elements, rightists). One has to be mindful of the fact that being labeled as an enemy had grave consequences for the person concerned. Over its enemies the socialist state wielded the power of the people's democratic dictatorship. The dictatorial methods used against enemies of the people included suspending their political rights and forcing them "to take part in labor and to reform themselves through labor in order to become new people."[86] "Reform through Labor," or Laogai, appears to be primarily a punishment for the enemies of the people. Contradictions among the people could, as Mao stressed, be solved in a very different way, but for the people's enemies the primary method was noncoercive and consisted of "education and persuasion."

Mao's position seems contradictory: on the one hand, he conveyed the message that socialist China was about to transcend the stage at which full-scale class struggle was still necessary. On the other hand, he maintained that enemies still existed and that the struggle would have to be continued permanently, if on a smaller scale.[87] Campaigns and mass movements, criticism and study were the proper methods for carrying on the struggle under socialism, in order to resolve contradictions. At different occasions Mao gave varying estimates of the numbers of enemies in Chinese society. The proportion ranged from 3 percent to 5 percent of the population, a number that was later employed in the requirement that every unit had to turn in between 3 and 5 percent of it membership base for being counterrevolutionaries.[88]

The outcome of the Hundred Flowers Campaign, however, marked a turning point in Mao's thinking, and he became convinced that a more radical approach was needed. It also prompted Mao to reconsider the nature of the contradictions under socialism. He now believed that bourgeois values and bourgeois consciousness persisted in China and that therefore one could not rule out the possibility of a successful counterrevolution. As Benjamin Schwartz has so aptly characterized Mao's view: "The survival of socialism (and attainment of communism) was not assured by the socialization of property. Only the internalization of a socialist (and communist) ethos could assure ultimate victory."[89]

After 1957 Mao started to call for "protracted and fierce class struggle."[90] Classes, however, were no longer to be defined on the basis of their relationship to the means of production in the socialist period, since collectivization of the means of production had already been carried out. After 1958 Mao increasingly favored political attitude, which could be defined on the basis of behavior and consciousness rather than on objective socioeconomic factors, as a criterion of class. It was on this basis that Mao could refer to those who obstructed his policy as a "bureaucratic class." Seen from a purely Marxist view, a remarkable oxymoron came into existence: classes were formed not as much on the basis of a socioeconomic categorization as on the basis of beliefs or worldviews. One has to be mindful, however, that Mao always started from the assumption that for some, a transformation in thinking was possible. While socioeconomic class criteria conventionally constituted an unchangeable classification, one's worldview was alterable. As Mao put it, "Man can be reformed! [*Ren shi keyi gaizao de*]."[91] Such a transformation could be initiated by way of political and ideological instruction.

Mao had a clear, functionalistic understanding of law. To him, law constituted a tool, not an end in itself. State punishments therefore were supposed to serve a political purpose. Penal laws, in Mao's view, were a tool for intervening swiftly when the social and political order appeared to be violated. Apart from a more conventional definition of criminality (as the intentional commission of an act deemed socially harmful or dangerous), the concept of crime developed by Mao had in fact a much wider scope and included politically motivated deviant behavior and attitudes, which he viewed as equally harmful criminal acts.

The opposition structure that was targeted changed somewhat over time. At first it consisted of political opponents who posed a credible threat to the new regime; then it was seen more abstractly in terms of the bourgeois-landlord social class; and finally the targets were residual elements of that class, variously defined. As Lowell Dittmer has pointed out: "The fact that this progressive redefinition of the opposition coincided with successful efforts to incorporate opponents within the community implied that [the] conflict gradually lost its in-group/out-group clarity and became interne-cine."[92]

Mao's ideas featured an understanding of administering justice as a distributive and retributive act, one that tapped into mass solidarity and the participation of the masses in all economic, political, and legal decisions affecting their lives.[93] He was opposed to the deployment of expert specialists in organizations he considered bureaucratic, such as the judiciary. He clearly emphasized an informal, localized model of social control, with revolutionary consciousness and party leadership as the guiding principles. Mao therefore favored mass participation and decentralization in the criminal justice system, too. He believed mass mobilization and campaigns under party leadership could be used to strengthen coherence among the people and thereby bring about accelerated social and political change.

Mao Zedong's ideas about reform through labor provided an authoritative theoretical framework for the future development of Laogai. All other members of the leadership agreed on the basic idea of Laogai as the fundamental form of punishment in socialist China. There is no indication that the principle of Laogai caused any internal disputes. But Mao's remarks pertaining to Laogai were rather sporadic, and many points remained unclear. In filling the voids in Mao's ideas rather than putting forth ideas of their own, other members of the leadership could exert considerable influence on the development of Laogai too. Mao's long-time heir apparent and second in command in the CCP, Liu Shaoqi, frequently made statements regarding Laogai. While on the surface he agreed to the overall line, the arrangements of his arguments hint at a different set of priorities.

One major issue that was left unclear by Mao pertained to the relationship between labor and reeducation. In early 1956 Liu Shaoqi issued the following slogan in an instruction to Luo Ruiqing: "The policy of the Laogai work is: Reform first, production second."[94] This slogan was frequently included in handbooks, instructions, and decrees to the local Public Security Bureau units that were in charge of the labor camps. It was supposed to direct the unit to place emphasis on the reeducation of the prisoners. The camps were to be organized in a way that would foster the reform of the inmates as opposed to being focused on maximum production and profit.

In his report at the Eighth National Congress of the CCP in September 1956, Liu Shaoqi also talked about the principles underlying the penal system. He said:

> In dealing with counterrevolutionaries and other criminals, we have all along followed the policy of combining punishment with leniency. All who make honest confession, repent their crimes and perform meritorious services receive lenient treatment. As everyone knows, this policy has achieved great results. . . . The Party Central Committee holds that, with the exception of a handful of criminals who have to be condemned to death in response to public indignation at their atrocious crimes, no offenders should be given the death penalty, and while serving their terms of imprisonment, they should be accorded absolutely humane treatment. All cases involving the death penalty should be decided upon or sanctioned by the Supreme People's Court.[95]

In his speech Liu Shaoqi voiced strong approval for the development and deployment of the penal system in China since 1949, including the several movements for the suppression of counterrevolutionaries, and yet he used strikingly different terminology than Mao Zedong and stated different priorities. In September 1956 Liu Shaoqi propagated Laogai (without using the word, though) as a lenient form of treatment, not as a means of exercising the people's dictatorship. Consequently he also proposed to abolish the death penalty, while Mao, on the contrary, had argued only a few months before, in April that same year, that such a move would be opposed by the masses and premature. Liu Shaoqi's statements regarding Laogai indicate a consistent understanding of Laogai as a socialist form of rehabilitative custody. He stressed the leniency and humanity of this penal regime. Rehabilitation and reeducation represented the primary purpose of this punishment, whereas labor and work were ascribed only a secondary role.

Liu Shaoqi's utterances on Laogai and his lenient stance increasingly brought him into conflict with Mao Zedong. Especially after the start of the Cultural Revolution, Liu's ideas about socialist law and socialist criminal justice were openly criticized. The criticism included allegations that Liu had denied the need for the Great Leap in political and legal work, had advocated the theory of the extinction of class struggle, and had demanded that a comprehensive legal system be set up.[96]

Labor reform and labor reeducation formed the basis of the penal system in socialist China. It was called a "Chinese-style" penal system, or a prison system with "Chinese characteristics."[97] The system was regarded by theorists as a localized, Chinese form of stationary punishment that was based on the thoughts of Marx, Lenin, and Mao Zedong and that took full account of the economic, social, and political particularities of Chinese society. The basic principles of criminal justice were devised by the leadership. The task of elaborating these principles and making them into operational rules and regulations was left to officials and specialists.

One of the first and most influential prison practitioners who delved into theoretical foundations of Laogai was the former director of Harbin prison, Wang Huai'an. In a speech addressing faculty of the law department at Beijing University in March 1950, Wang, who had just been appointed chief of staff at the Ministry of Justice, gave a comprehensive account of the theoretical premises of China's penal policy. He started by explaining that the prison is an instrument of the state. "With the emergence of the state, the prison came into existence, too. And when all classes will be destroyed in the future, the state will also wither away and there will be no prison anymore."[98]

Wang went on to explain that in socialist society the prison is an instrument of the Chinese people (as opposed to being an instrument of the feudal, imperial, or bureaucratic forces that ruled China before liberation):

> Our prison is the instrument of the people's democratic dictatorship. It represents and protects the interest of the people; it is used to punish the elements that do harm to the interest of the people. The prison is still an instrument of the ruling classes, but the classes that rule and are ruled are totally different. In former times, reactionary rulers used [the prison] as an instrument to suppress the people, today the people use [the prison] as an instrument to protect themselves. . . . The old prison was an instrument used by the reactionary classes to protect themselves and to rule the people; our prison is used by the people to protect themselves and therefore it is an instrument of the democratic dictatorship of the people.[99]

Wang subsequently discussed whether there was a difference between locking up a thief in a Republican prison or in a socialist prison. The difference, he explained, lay in the fact that the Republican prison detained thieves for the interest of the exploiting classes. Under socialism, however, it is in particular the exploiters of the working class, those who refuse to perform labor and thus harm the people, who will be punished: "Our standpoint is to fight against [a lifestyle of] 'being fed without working' and to struggle against social parasites. We demand that everybody labors, that everybody has work that is useful to the people."[100] He also maintained that another difference between the Republic's prisons and socialist prisons could be found in the purpose of imprisonment. The Republican prison had the function of suppression. Slogans such as "reformation" (ganhua) were used only to deceive the population; in reality, he said, concentration camps such as the Shangrao concentration camp were built by the "fascist regime of Chiang Kai-shek."[101] Wang even took pains to ridicule the textbooks that had been used in Republican prisons that were filled with moral sayings and religious instructions.

In contrast, Wang said, the socialist prison had two functions: punishment through repression and transformation through education. Wang especially spoke out against opinions that described the prison exclusively as a "school" or a "factory." He stressed that the prison should always be able to resort to violence when dealing with "severe counterrevolutionaries."[102] He went on to criticize the many prisons in the liberated areas that had been very successful in reeducating criminals but had not done enough to exercise "the dictatorship over hostile forces." As if he wanted to make himself very clear, Wang again and again pointed out: "The prison . . . is an organ of punishment and coercion; under the democratic dictatorship of the people, we must strengthen and develop its function of control and coercion."[103] It is quite telling that in 1950 there was the stock assertion that imprisonment had to have a repressive violent function.

Wang went on to deal with the subject of prison administration. He advocated the introduction of a classification system (fenbie zhi), according to which different categories of prisoners would receive different forms of treatment in different institutions. He suggested dividing the prison system into three branches: detention centers (kanshousuo), labor reform brigades (laodong gaizao dui), and prisons (jianyu).[104] The detention centers would keep offenders until they received a sentence. Unless they were convicted of severe crimes, normally all sentenced convicts would then be transferred to Laogai detachments, the labor reform brigades. Laogai convicts would be organized "on a larger scale in Laogai detachments." The brigades would be located where there was a demand for labor in mining, farming, and road and canal construction. Implicit in Wang's remarks was the notion that prisoners actually had to be deported from the cities to the countryside, where demand for labor was greatest. All along, Wang stressed that Laogai brigades would contribute to the national economy and solve the problem of overcrowding in the urban prisons.

Wang was very blunt about the function of the prison. The prison would subdue the most dangerous and harmful criminals. Rather than reform or reeducation, incapacitation was mentioned as the main purpose of incarceration in the prison. He recommended that each province should open one or two high-security prisons with "high walls, iron grills, severe controls, and armed guards."[105] Convicts in the prisons would also work and receive reeducation, but the emphasis clearly was on control and repression.

Finally Wang talked about the core concept of Laogai: how to reform convicts. According to the experiences with labor reform in the liberated areas, Laogai was able to efficiently reform "parasites and members of the underworld." Specifically, Laogai facilities had been shown to be able to (1) change the thoughts and habits of the convicts and nurture a labor perspective, a labor habit, and an independent work attitude; (2) teach convicts technical skills; and (3) increase the workload of inmates so that the prison became self-sufficient and the burden on the people was reduced. Laogai, in his words, made "parasites, consumers, and criminals of the exploiting classes . . . change completely. Collective life, marching, singing, labor production, oily faces, physical exercise make [the prisoners] stronger. By personally engaging in laboring, they learn how hard labor is and that it was wrong that in previous times they belittled [people who labor]. For this kind of people, unless they are going through forced labor, their reeducation is difficult."[106]

In the Laogai camps inmates supervised and taught other inmates. This, Wang said, had proven to be the quickest way to convey technical skills. For the following reasons, he asserted, inmates were motivated to fully and enthusiastically engage in labor: those who participated in labor received better and more food; inmates derived health benefits from physical labor;

during labor inmates enjoyed freedom to move; after years in prison, inmates like to learn handcrafts; and those inmates who worked diligently could be released before fulfilling their prison term. These factors, in combination with competitions, rewards, and awards, were intended to ensure that the convicts saw labor as a way to improve their personal abilities and overall situation, and to make them understand the meaning and importance of labor.

Physical labor was to be accompanied by thought education, or ideological education *(sixiang jiaoyu)*. The staff offered three forms of education: labor education, ideological education, and cultural education. Labor education referred to the teaching of technical skills. Ideological education was conducted in the form of political classes in which prisoners were taught to distinguish between the old and the new society, to understand the difference between committing crimes in the old society and committing crimes in the new society, and finally to realize the harmful effect of their criminal acts on the people. Cultural education was identical with the primary education offered in schools; in particular, the focus was on teaching basic literacy.

It appears that Wang's whole speech was carefully prepared for his audience. The former prison director was speaking in front of professors and students of law, many of whom were holdovers from the Republic and had been educated in Republican penology. His talk must have sent a chill through the room. He argued against Republican penology and the Republican prison, ridiculing its efforts aimed at reformation. He made it unmistakably clear that a new era had begun. At the same time, he stressed that even when prison administrators talked about labor reform and labor re-education, none should forget that imprisonment always is, and should be, an instrument of violence and coercion. Of course, he acknowledged, the successful reform of criminals was important too. He urged his audience to believe in the possibility of true reform. The success or failure of reform was dependent on the correct organization and combination of labor and education. Finally, he did not miss pointing out the significance of Laogai. In economic, political, and social terms, Laogai would evolve into an essential tool for the revolutionary transformation of Chinese society.

Elements of the penal theory advocated by Wang Huai'an surface in many theoretical discussions of Laogai. Another legal specialist, Liu Enqi, described the socialist state's response to crime as "a combination of repression and leniency."[107] Laogai, he maintained, achieved this combination of leniency and repression by realizing three equally important goals: first, the enforcement of punitive custody; second, the implementation of political-ideological education; and third, the organization of labor and production. He also stressed that Laogai was a weapon of the dictatorship of the proletariat in its struggle against all the forces hostile to the social-ism. In *Lectures on the General Principles of Criminal Law in the PRC,* trans-lated and published in 1957 by the U.S. Department of Commerce, we find similar arguments:

> As we know, punishment is nothing but a coercive means of the state. It has in itself no "purpose." The so-called purpose of punishment is in reality the purpose of the People's Court in applying punishment to criminals. . . . To be stated separately, the purpose of punishment is: (1) To punish and reform criminals so that they will not commit offenses again; (2) To serve a warn-ing to unstable elements in society through the application of punishments to criminals so that [they] will not commit offenses; (3) To educate the citi-zenry and to inspire them to struggle with criminals through the application of punishments to the latter.[108]

Similar arguments and theoretical positions were repeatedly put forth by Minister of Public Security Luo Ruiqing. In 1959, on the occasion of the tenth anniversary of the founding of the PRC, Luo delivered a keynote ad-dress that gave an overview of ten years of the party's legal and public secu-rity work.[109] At the center of the speech was the struggle between revolution and counterrevolution. Though the revolution had achieved many victo-ries, he said, the counterrevolution still posed a danger that should not be overlooked. Luo Ruiqing's preoccupation with the struggle between revo-lution and counterrevolution clearly shows that protecting the socialist or-der was regarded as a major function of the criminal justice system. Luo praised the leniency of the penal policy adopted in China: death sentences would only rarely be executed; as a general rule, offenders would instead be given the opportunity to renew themselves. He emphasized that the spirit of reeducation and reform would permeate and inform the whole criminal justice system in socialist China: "In dealing with counterrevolutionaries and other criminals we adopted the policy of reform through labor, not only to get rid of the conditions that allowed the counterrevolution to do harm, but, more important, to eradicate all class and ideological causes for the occurrence of counterrevolution and crime, so that a counterrevolu-tionary, after completion of his term, cannot fall back to the road of criminality."[110] Here we can clearly grasp the social and political significance of Laogai. Laogai would suppress old feudal influences and other harmful forces that threatened stability and order in socialism. It was seen as an exceedingly important policy that would determine the fate of socialism in China. Therefore, its success was understood as a prerequisite for the attainment of communism.

In 1975 identical arguments were still being made.[111] That year a legal official from Guangzhou explained the Laogai system with the following words:

> The purpose of reform through labor is to make a criminal educate himself so that he becomes a laborer who can live by his own work. This means that we carry out the revenge of the proletariat on the reactionary class. We do not wipe out reactionary elements physically but send them to a place where they can use physical labor to reform themselves. In the course of imprisonment they also receive ideological education. By means of this they are reformed into a new type of man, who can feed himself by his own work. Because these reactionaries did not take part in physical labor before and refused to work, they are ideologically reformed through education so they are able to stand on the side of socialism. They are able to become a man of a new type.[112]

The conception of punishment as outlined above is inexorably intertwined with a distinct understanding of crime. Both crime and punishment in socialist China were explained as historical remnants of class society and therefore considered to be transitional phenomena.[113] It was stressed that, according Marxist theory, the historical basis for crime was the rule and oppression of one class by another class. Crime was regarded by Marx and Engels as a way to express resistance and protest against the existing social order. Under the conditions of a feudal or capitalist society, even normal or petty criminality was the result of "unconscious protest" against the inequalities and injustices of the existing social order. Under socialism the ruling classes changed. Yet even after the victory of revolution, crime was the manifestation of an ongoing class struggle resulting from still-existing influences:

> Because classes, class struggle, and the possibility of capitalist restoration still exist, during the stage of transition there is a need for the socialist state to use the declaration of crime in its struggle against behavior that seriously endangers the interests of the state and the people. . . . As long as the political view-

point and ideological consciousness of the exploiting class have not been thoroughly transformed, it will be impossible to consider the exploiting class to have already been eliminated.[114]

The conception of crime as a consciously or unconsciously rebellious act against the social order has far-reaching consequences: all crime is thus politicized; every criminal act becomes a genuine political matter. This in turn means that crime under socialism always has a political meaning. Legal scholar Cao Zidan explained: "Resistance of the remnant elements of the overthrown reactionary classes is not only the direct cause of the emergence of counterrevolutionary crimes, but it is also the most important source of all criminal acts."[115] In this view, all crime principally resulted from the bourgeois thinking and politics that still permeated social life, from the influence of habits acquired in the old society, and from a deeply rooted (and wrong) ideological consciousness. The mere occurrence of criminal behavior showed that old social and ideological influences persisted and were still active. These residual elements were to be deposed under the dictatorship of the proletariat and forced to change.

Looking through the theoretical treatises and statements, one can see that beneath the officially propagated goal of labor reform, there was always a widespread sense that imprisonment was a punishment and a tool of coercion and therefore should have a repressive and violent character. However, the very important if not central role of labor in socialist penology was underpinned by Marxist philosophy and proletarian romanticism, which made labor the essential attribute and basic requirement of every member of socialist society.

Based on the ideas and theories articulated by the leadership and scores of pundits, the Chinese criminal justice system during the Mao period provided a complex system of punishments for dealing with malefactors. As we have seen, apart from the criminal justice agencies several other institutions and organizations had the power to enunciate sanctions. There were in fact three tiers of sanctions—informal, administrative, and criminal—which, depending on the severity of the offense, differed in regard to strictness and harshness. Accordingly, three echelons of administration oversaw the sanctioning process: the basic work or residential units, the Public Security Bureaus, and the courts. This three-tiered punishment system, which was set up in the early 1950s, retained its basic structure and nominal divisions until the late 1970s, although over time central responsibility shifted somewhat from the courts to the basic units and the Public Security Bureaus. In the 1960s and 1970s, in terms of the number of cases handled, the core of the system rested on informal or administrative sanctions. Only if those sanctions were deemed inadequate to the nature of a crime were the courts and the criminal justice system activated.

Sentencing in socialist China was governed by several distinct principles and the consideration of several criteria. In view of the absence of a comprehensive criminal code listing all criminal acts and corresponding punishments, those involved in the adjudicating and sentencing process had to weigh several factors in determining an appropriate sanction. In the sentencing process, legal workgroups were supposed to consider the following criteria: first, voluntary surrender, confession, and post-crime attitudes such as attempts at reparation or signs of repentance; these factors could lead to lenient treatment and in consequence much lighter punishments. Second, individual factors regarding the offender, such as class background and political attitude, were to be taken into account. In general, being labeled as one of the five elements deemed hostile to socialism (landlord, rich peasant, counterrevolutionary, "bad element," and rightist) meant that the offender received the most severe punishments available.[116] Third, the nature of the crime and the harm done to society were weighed in determining the measure of punishment. Theft of public property was more heavily punished than theft of private property, for example. At all stages in the process of law enforcement and sentencing, emphasis was placed on the involvement of the masses and the basic work and residential units. Public meetings were organized at which participants could express their views on the crime or the suspect. By soliciting the opinion of local groups, the social damage of the crime was assessed. Fourth, party guidelines were to be implemented. Punishments were to be set so as to safeguard and protect the public order against infractions.

The following informal sanctions could be imposed by local units (such as work units, residential committees, or meditation committees):[117]

1. Private criticism education through a member of the local unit, usually a party cadre.
2. Private warning by a functionary or an official.
3. Criticism in front of a small group, such as a work unit, study group, or residential block unit.

4. Criticism in front of a larger group, such as the work collective or the residential district committee.

5. Censure as a harsher degree of criticism, involving oral or written statements of self denunciation, self-examination, and repentance.

6. Discussion session to make the offender see reason. Participants try to exert pressure by shouting accusations and vituperation.

7. Struggle session *(douzheng)*. Offender is subjected to public humiliation, such as by wearing a "bad element hat," and physical intimidation (hitting and kicking).[118]

When the circumstances of an illegal act were so minor that the act was not deemed a crime, or when the circumstances of an individual's crime were so minor that the crime did not merit criminal punishment, the person could still be subject to administrative sanctions. The most prevalent administrative sanctions were governed by the 1957 Decision of the State Council Regarding the Question of Re-Education through Labor (the 1957 Laojiao Decision)[119] and the Security Administration Punishment Act (SAPA) of October 22, 1957. Both laws seem to have been passed with the Anti-Rightist Movement and resistance to cooperativization and collectivization during the Great Leap Forward in mind. According to the legislation, the following sanctions could be imposed by the Public Security Bureaus:

1. Warning, modest fine (up to 30 yuan), and short period of detention (up to fifteen days). The sanctions were described in SAPA and were mostly imposed for misdemeanors.

2. Work under surveillance. The offender was permitted to remain in society, but was subjected to a long, indeterminate period of indoctrination, prescribed labor, and surveillance by police and local units. Release from the punishment depended on success in reforming the offender.

3. "Labor reeducation" (*laodong jiaoyang*, or abridged Laojiao). A sanction imposed on people whose acts were not serious enough to warrant criminal punishment but were, nonetheless, too serious to be handled with any other of the above administrative punishments. Under the 1957 Laojiao Decision, an individual could be subject to Laojiao for an indefinite time, but in 1962 a

ministerial decree ostensibly tried to refine the system by confining the period to one to three years, with a one-year extension "whenever it is necessary."[120]

The third punishment was severe for an administrative sanction imposed through a simple administrative decision without court hearings. As we will see, millions of people were detained under this regulation. It is hard to exaggerate the importance of this law, and it therefore deserves a closer look.

According to the 1957 Laojiao Decision, the purpose of Laojiao was: "to reform into self-supporting new persons those persons who are able to work but insist on leading an idle life, violate law and discipline, or do not engage in honest pursuits"; and "to further maintain public order, thus facilitating socialist construction."[121] The sanctions could be imposed on the following four categories of individuals: (1) "Those who do not engage in honest pursuits, involve themselves in hooliganism, commit larceny, fraud or other acts for which they are not criminally liable, or violate public security rules and refuse to mend their ways despite repeated admonition"; (2) "counterrevolutionaries and anti-socialist reactionaries who commit minor crimes and are not criminally liable and who have been given sanctions of expulsion by government organs, organizations, enterprises, or schools, and as a result have difficulty in making a living"; (3) "employees of government organs, organizations, enterprises, and schools, who are able-bodied but have refused to work for a long period, violated discipline, or jeopardized public order, and have been given sanctions of expulsion, and as a result have difficulty in making a living"; (4) "those who refuse to accept the work assigned to them or the arrangement made for their employment or who decline to take part in manual labor and production despite persuasion, keep behaving disruptively on purpose, obstruct public officials from performing their duties, and refuse to mend their ways despite repeated admonition."[122] The categories listed in the law are broad, indeterminate, and vague. The repeated references to "work refusal" and "difficulty in making a living" reveal that the intention behind this law was to discipline a population that had lost enthusiasm for socialism and started to show intransigent behavior.

Various bodies were able to apply for the imposition of Laojiao. These included "civil affairs and public security departments or the government organ, organization, enterprise, school or other units to which the person belongs; or his or her parents or guardians."[123] The decisions for Laojiao had to be approved by the "People's Committees of provinces, autonomous regions, and municipalities directly under the Central Government or by organs authorized by these People's Committees."[124]

Although it actually did not belong to the official list of administrative sanctions, the practice of "sheltering for examination" *(Shoushen)* should be mentioned in this context. *Shoushen* was designed to allow police to detain and investigate suspected illegal migrants and suspected criminals who had no known status or confirmed residence.[125] It was originally conceived in 1961. According to a report by the Ministry of Public Security published in the same year, the rural population had spontaneously moved into the cities looking for food, shelter, and jobs. The three years from 1959 to 1961 had seen severe famines in the countryside that had forced the rural population to look for ways to survive. Migration was one option chosen by many. The 1961 adoption of *Shoushen* extended police powers in order to deal with this issue. The policy allowed for the detainment of suspected persons for an unlimited time. Throughout the 1960s and 1970s it was mainly used a means to arrest migrants who were moving into urban centers and send them back to their native places.[126]

The public security apparatus in socialist China was not only charged with executive powers but also held considerable adjudicative powers that were not controlled and checked by the judiciary. The punishments meted out ranged from small fines to indeterminate long-term imprisonment. Public Security thus maintained its own system of social control that operated in tandem with the criminal justice system. It also ran a well-established system of administrative detention whereby real or suspected offenders were incarcerated in detention centers or labor reform camps. The responsibilities of the Public Security Bureaus were broad, open-ended, and widely uncontrolled and unchecked by any other government agency. Clearly the indefiniteness and vagueness of the directives concerning police powers opened up frightening possibilities for abuse.

Criminal punishments, which were handed down by the courts, included five types of main punishments *(zhuxing)* and three types of supplementary punishments *(fujia xing)*. The main punishments were:

1. Surveillance. (This punishment resembled the administrative punishment of "work under surveillance." It could be applied for periods from three months up to three years, and extensions were

possible. The punishment of surveillance was recorded in the criminal register and was deemed severe because it was imposed by a court for the commission of a crime. It was frequently used against "historical counterrevolutionaries," that is, persons who had not committed specific crimes under the new government but had been involved in activities before 1949 that were now considered criminal activities. For example, high-ranking GMD government officials or landlords were typical targets. If they did not publicly renounce their previous actions, services, or life-styles, they were put under surveillance. Persons under surveillance had to report to local Public Security Bureaus on a regular basis, engage in productive work, and accept supervision by local units and finally to report all criminal offenses that they learned about or witnessed themselves.)

2. Detention for one month to six months. (This short-term punishment was applied for a variety of common crimes.)

3. Fixed-term imprisonment, six months to twenty years; carried out mostly as reform through labor (Laogai), sometimes as confinement in a prison. (Depending on the behavior of the prisoner during labor reform, the prison term could be extended or reduced.)

4. Life imprisonment, carried out as labor reform.

5.1. Death penalty, with a two-year period of delay. (The death penalty was officially seen as a last resort. In general, if a death sentence was reached by a local court, the case had to be reported to the next higher level until it reached the Supreme Court. Even after confirmation by the next higher court of appeal, the death penalty was not carried out until a waiting period of two years had elapsed. During this time the delinquent had to undergo reform through labor. If he admitted his crime, submitted himself to the authorities, and behaved well, the death sentence was not carried out. The sentence was then changed to life imprisonment or limited-term imprisonment.)

5.2. Death penalty without two-year waiting period. (This punishment was reserved for the most severe crimes. Such crimes frequently involved interference with the implementation of current policies, murder, or rape. When a crime reflected behav-

ior in conflict with an important policy, it was seen as more
severe and thus as deserving a more severe punishment. The
death penalty with immediate execution was therefore most
frequently applied during campaigns and political movements.
The standard form of execution was shooting.)

Supplementary punishments, regardless of the meaning their name conveyed, could be imposed independently. They included fines (the amount
imposed depended on the circumstances of the crime), the deprivation of
political rights, and the confiscation of property.

It is noteworthy that while officially the PRC always stressed that punishments in socialist China served the goal of reeducation alone, the most severe legal punishments available, such as the death penalty and life imprisonment, were essentially nonrehabilitative in nature, as were several minor
punishments, such as fines and confiscation of property. Moreover, the
death penalty was often applied, at times even without control; it was in
reality far more than a mere threat used by the criminal justice system to
deal with a small number of very serious crimes.

The persistent application of the death penalty contradicted one of the
basic tenets of punishment under socialism, namely the main principle of
reform. During the Hundred Flowers Campaign in 1957, legal scholars in
China indeed heavily criticized the use of the death penalty and life imprisonment as the main punishments since 1949. They argued that all punishments that did not bring forward reform and rehabilitation were incompatible with the penal principles, humanitarian convictions, and educative
goals of a socialist state.[127] There is evidence that this position was shared
by some members of the party's central administration, such as Liu Shaoqi.
On many occasions Liu Shaoqi made it public that he was in favor of abolishing the death penalty. Most notable were the unmistakable words in his
"Political Report of the Central Committee of the CCP to the Eighth National Congress of the Party," which he presented on September 15, 1956.
There he affirmed "our aim of completely abolishing the death penalty, and
this is all to the good of our socialist construction."[128] With the start of the
Anti-Rightist Movement, however, this stance was losing ground. It was
clearly rejected by Mao Zedong, who saw it as weakening the class struggle,
and indeed after that point the question of abolishing the death penalty
was never again officially raised in China.[129]

Penal authority was diluted and widely dispersed in socialist China. The sanctioning system was heavily decentralized, as we have seen, and several government bodies, party agencies, and grass-roots organizations had the authority to punish their members for deviant behavior. The wide range of informal, administrative, and criminal punishments available to several adjudicating bodies, together with the lack of a criminal code detailing degrees and measures of punishment for certain offenses, represented the defining features of the criminal justice system before 1978.

These features also allowed some flexibility and left the interpretation of sanctions to the discretion of the decentralized law enforcement agencies. A certain criminal offense could be punished in varying degrees, depending on the specific case. For example, the punishment for theft ranged from criticism education to fifteen years of imprisonment.[130] As a result there was a high degree of unpredictability and unreliability in regard to the outcome of a criminal process. While such a system was clearly a disadvantage for the accused, it provided the state with powerful leverage for guarding the policies and norms of socialist society and enforcing compliance. Society from the top to the grass-roots level was tightly wrapped in a dense network of oversight and control.

Criminal justice theory highlighted the role of labor reform, and the idea of labor reform as the main punishment in socialist China also dominated official lists of legal sanctions. The creation of facilities for carrying out labor reform was therefore a top priority on the agenda of the CCP governments. After 1949 the leadership pressed ahead with the establishment of a system of labor reform camps.

The labor reform system was created in several phases that more or less reflect the phases of legal development in general in the People's Republic of China. During the initial years (1949 to 1951) Laogai was above all needed for enforcing dictatorship over the enemies of socialism. Institutions of confinement were set up quickly and were run by the military or the police. The short-lived second phase (1951 to 1954) was characterized by more systematic efforts to establish a centralized penal system that operated on a set of written rules and could be controlled and governed by the state's central organs. The third phase (1955 to 1958) saw the accelerated integration of Laogai in the national economy. In the subsequent period (1959 to 1966) the Laogai system was plagued by the horrendous repercussions of the Great

Leap Forward. Shortly after its recovery from that disaster, Laogai was dealt another blow when the Cultural Revolution (1966 to 1976) again brought turmoil and violence into the camps.

After the military capture of the cities by the People's Liberation Army (PLA), the new order was imposed by a military-based administration. The new power holders first had to deal with civil unrest that had followed the fighting in many regions, especially urban areas. Consolidation and the restoration of order in the city was the first primary task. The military authorities searched for alleged war criminals, secret service agents, and collaborators in order to mop up pockets of resistance and remnant GMD forces. At the same time the PLA took action against criminals, prostitutes, street gangs, and vagrants. The combined attack on military opponents and social troublemakers enabled the new authorities to enlist the popular support that was essential for upholding the new order. From the very first day, the new authorities made many arrests, yet they lacked the capacity to house those they arrested. A few months after the proclamation of the PRC, prisons were already severely overcrowded.

The exact number of prisons, camps, and institutions of confinement that existed in the early years is not known.[131] In urban China, the prisons that had been built during the Republic still kept a large number of inmates. In the former revolutionary base areas, there were a few labor reform brigades. In rural areas, interim labor camps and detention houses were set up ad hoc. Most of these facilities were under the control of the military; others were administered by the police or the courts. The military also ran large camps for holding POWs. In sum, a confusing number of state agencies and military units kept detainees under widely differing conditions and circumstances, and it seems safe to state that no coherent system was in place. There were at best blurred rules and regulations. Arrests were made without observing any procedures at all. No records were kept of those interned in the prisons or camps. Prison labor was organized in only about half of all institutions of confinement.[132]

Very soon authorities faced the problem of how to accommodate the growing number of detainees. As early as August 1950 the minister of justice, Shi Liang, stated during the National Judicial Conference that earnest efforts were needed to reform and rearrange the prison sector.[133] The situation in the existing prisons became even worse at the end of 1950 and the beginning of 1951 as a result of the two campaigns conducted by the PRC for land reform and the suppression of counterrevolution. The campaigns signaled the start of more comprehensive efforts aimed at the transformation of Chinese society. Both campaigns were swiftly and successfully carried out, and they both produced very high numbers of prisoners, perhaps more than the leadership had originally expected. For instance, in the first twelve months after the start of the campaigns, the number of arrests in China increased eightfold. In 1951 and 1952 this already high number was increased even further, so that by the end of 1952 approximately 3.2 million additional persons had been arrested.[134] The existing prisons ended up holding approximately 1 million prisoners, but there were 3 million more in need of management and custody. Detaining so many people was an immense organizational challenge. The existing facilities soon proved to be inadequate, and the consequences in the prisons were dreadful. In some instances more than twenty inmates were kept in a cell that had been used for just five inmates during the Republic. Overcrowding, infectious diseases, and insufficient food supplies plagued the prisons and camps.[135]

Soon after the founding of the PRC an internal dispute broke into the open over which organization was in charge of the prison sector. In the early years the administration of the prisons had alternated back and forth between the judiciary and the public security apparatus. In the liberated areas before 1949, all prisons had been governed by the judicial system. After 1949 it was expected that the judiciary would again be charged with administering the prisons, but on November 3, 1950, in a rather surprising move, the control of all prisons was handed over to the public security sector.[136] This signaled a major change in the penal policy; the official reason was that, under the Ministry of Justice, the prisons had failed to conduct "educational reform."

The judiciary to a large extent consisted of holdovers from the Republican era. This group of highly educated professionals had increasingly clashed with the Public Security Ministry, the members of which were mostly former PLA personnel. By 1950 military control commissions that had initially exercised wide powers had been reduced to public security and garrison functions.[137] Demobilized soldiers had been transferred to the Ministry of Public Security, where new occupations were sought for them. Public Security, now staffed by people who had fought for the revolution, strove for an important position in the new state but found its influence limited by the judiciary. By handing over the prison sector to the Ministry of Public Security, the PRC government indicated a significant turn to the use of military personnel, a new emphasis on discipline, and the introduction of a hierarchical control model for prison management.

A new overall plan appears not to have been in place yet. Certainly, after 1949 ad hoc methods were standardized and formally incorporated into the emerging system, and in 1950 the Administrative Council (replaced by State Council in 1954) centralized control of the prison sector in the hands of the Ministry of Public Security.[138] There is no question that the political campaigns of the early 1950s, in particular, had triggered the need for a large-scale prison camp system.[139] The rise of Laogai must be seen in the context of regime consolidation and the struggle of the new administration against potential opponents and enemies. Adding new capacity to a unified and effective imprisonment system became ever more urgent.

It was in May 1951 that the PRC's labor camp system was founded. The Third National Conference on Public Security was held then, and organizers intended for the first time to systematically discuss the treatment of prisoners and to find solutions concerning the management and placement of those arrested.[140] Many important members of the PRC leadership attended the meeting—a fact that illustrates its importance. Liu Shaoqi gave a keynote speech, Peng Zhen delivered comments, and Mao Zedong personally revised the final resolution of the conference.[141]

In his address, Liu Shaoqi pointed out the significance of the problem. He told the attendees at the conference that a solution for accommodating the high numbers of prisoners was urgently needed. Ways had to be found for the prisoners to be guarded, organized, reformed, and, if necessary, punished.[142] He proposed that, instead of the Ministry of Justice, the Public Security Ministry should be permanently charged with running the prisons. Liu furthermore suggested organizing the labor camps in such a way that prisoners were given incentives to comply with the rules and to engage earnestly in labor. Those who worked should be rewarded, he said: "If one works well, give him a little reward or give him a little pay. Give him small things like cigarettes, meat, or soap in order to heighten his activity." Another point he made was related to the benefits of prison labor for the national economy: "If we handle this matter well, it has many benefits. This is a workforce numbering XXX people [number deleted in the text], as much as the whole workforce of a Bulgaria; [this workforce] does not need insurance or wages; it can do a lot of work, can build great things. In the Soviet

Union, prisoners were used to build several canals. If we do this well, it has economic and political benefits. Because we didn't kill them, we can let them work and possibly they will at some time in the future turn into good people [*hao ren*]."[143]

The resolution that was adopted on May 15, 1951, is a crucial document that determined the basic organizational structure for the development of Laogai. The final document had the following to say about the features of the interment system that was to be created:

> The large number of prisoners who are sentenced to prison terms constitutes a considerable workforce. In order to reform them, to solve the difficulties of prisons, and in order not to let the counterrevolutionaries serving prison terms be fed without working for it, we must immediately take steps to organize the work of labor reform. In all areas, where this work has already started, further capacity must be added. On five levels, namely county, special governor, province, government district, and central government, an administration with a division of labor must be established, personnel and a budget must be allocated, and, finally, armed troops must be deployed to serve as guards. Prison labor has to be organized and must be used for production and construction work, such as irrigation, road construction, cultivation of waste lands, mining, and housing construction. This matter is of extreme importance and urgency; we must vigorously strive for a solution.[144]

The most important issue outlined in the conference resolution was the supervision of the prison sector. The conference approved the ruling that the Ministry of Public Security would oversee the whole prison sector. The resolution also contained detailed regulations that mapped out the internal structure of the Laogai.[145] Convicts sentenced to five years or more would be organized in detachments *(dadui)* that were administered by Laogai facilities at the provincial level. Major production and construction projects, which were drafted in accordance with the need for national reconstruction, would in future be assigned to Laogai detachments. The Laogai detachments would, in organizational terms, be tantamount to large labor camps; they would form the backbone of the Laogai system.[146]

Convicts sentenced to more than one year but less than five years were to be sent to smaller prisons or detention centers administered by special districts or the counties. They would remain in the vicinity of their homes and be under the control of local authorities. Convicts sentenced to a prison term of less than one year should work under surveillance *(guanzhi)* and remain in their units and homes. Another very important point in the resolution was the ruling that the central government would provide funding from the central budget only for its own large Laogai divisions and camps; local facilities had to be financed through county or provincial administrations.

Apart from labor and production, it was stressed that the labor camps would organize educational measures to reeducate the inmates. Education in the Laogai would entail political, ideological, and cultural education as well as hygienic education. Good performances in regard to thought reform and labor were to be rewarded with privileges up to parole, while insurgent behavior was to be punished, the most severe punishment being the extension of the inmate's prison term.

Finally, the resolution called for the creation of a special administration in charge of the labor camps. The Public Security Ministry was charged with opening special bureaus for the administration of the Laogai and prison facilities. The provinces and large cities were to assign twenty to thirty officials to the Laogai bureaus; the districts, five to ten; and the counties, two to three. The regulations concerning the administrative structure are quite remarkable, in particular when compared with the administration of labor camps in the Soviet Union. The Chinese leadership obviously did not want to create a separate, central administration for the Laogai, as was the system in the Soviet Union. Large Laogai divisions or Laogai camps were to be governed by the provincial Public Security Bureau and not by any central agency in Beijing. While the central agency for the corrective labor camps (the Gulag) in Moscow was in charge of all Soviet camps, the Public Security Ministry in Beijing did not have direct control over Laogai institutions.[147] Apart from a few interprovincial infrastructure projects, the "eleventh department" *(shiyi ju)* of the Ministry of Public Security had limited tasks: it mainly drafted rules, regulations, and handbooks for use in the camps. The day-to-day operations of the camps were supervised by provincial Public Security Bureaus.

From May 1951 onward, the PRC began to establish the Laogai system on a large scale. To coordinate Laogai policy, the central government organized joint administrative committees staffed from different departments, such as public security, finance, water works, public construction, heavy industry, and railways, at various levels of the administration. The committees were to follow concrete steps for setting up Laogai institutions. An important issue was the contribution that the Laogai would make to the national economy. From the very beginning there was general agreement in the leadership that the Laogai institutions should take over important economic functions within the project of national reconstruction. The central government viewed the deployment of Laogai detachments in water-control projects (on the Yellow River and the Huai River), canal construction, and railway construction as particularly appropriate. The party also urged local authorities to find ways to quickly transfer large numbers of prisoners to the newly founded Laogai institutions so that Laogai detachments would have enough workers and could go into operation without further delay.

A few months later, in September 1951, the Fourth National Congress on Public Security was held. Again the question of imprisonment was discussed in detail.[148] In his report to the congress, Minister Luo Ruiqing stressed the task of reforming counterrevolutionaries. Labor and politics, punishment and education had to be combined in the processes of the Laogai. However, despite Luo's emphasis on reeducation, the meeting's final resolution focused on the organization of labor in the camps. Thus we can see that right from the outset there was tension over whether to prioritize labor or reeducation within the Laogai system. Despite a stated commitment to reeducation, in the early 1950s prison labor and prison production appear to have been of most importance to the leadership.

The initiatives from the central government soon produced tangible results. By June 1952, 62 percent of all inmates were engaged in labor. Prison labor quickly became an essential and indispensable economic factor. On large construction projects, the deployment of prison labor made it possible for the government to slash the civilian workforce by about 80,000 workers. Apart from the use of Laogai detachments in the infrastructure projects that were coordinated and managed by Beijing, many provincial Laogai facilities were agricultural farms. By 1952 there were 640 Laogai farms; 56 of these were larger camps holding more than one thousand prisoners. On a slightly smaller scale, there were also mining operations and kilns. Two hundred seventeen Laogai units were involved in the industrial sector in 1952; 160 of those units had more than 100 prisoners; 29 had more than 500 prisoners.[149] By 1952 the government was operating at least 857 stationary Laogai camps, a number that does not include the mobile camps involved in the construction of railways and canals.[150]

The Second National Laogai Conference was held in December 1953.

The conference is notable because the emphasis in the Laogai was now officially shifting to economics. The implementation of the first Five-Year Plan, which formally covered the years 1953 to 1957, provided an opportunity to make full use of prison labor for the task of construction on a national scale. The goal was to make maximum economic use of the Laogai system. By 1954 the number of Laogai camps and detachments had grown exponentially; the central government counted altogether 4,671 Laogai units. Many of these were relatively small units run by county governments or local cadres. More than 83 percent of all labor camp inmates were now engaged in forced labor. Forty percent of the Laogai inmates were working on agricultural farms, 34 percent in industrial operations such as mining and heavy industry, and 20 percent in the construction of canals and railways.[151]

Within only a few years the government succeeded in establishing a comprehensive, nationwide, yet somewhat scattered and unregulated system of penal labor. At the Third National Conference on Laogai, held in 1954, leaders stated with satisfaction: "The work of reforming criminals into new men is very important. At the same time, the Laogai production is also an important affair for the state. After the efforts of several years we see the first successes of our work. The party committees on various levels shall regularly give attention to this work, step up their control and smoothly develop the Laogai work."[152] It is also evident from this statement that the party was determined to remain fully in charge of the Laogai complex and setting its general policy.

The founding phase of the Laogai was completed with the promulgation of the Statute on Laogai in the Chinese People's Republic on August 26, 1954. The text of the statute was presumably drafted with the help of Soviet advisers.[153] The language of the statute also suggests that the drafters were primarily interested in technical issues and organizational questions. Only the first two articles of the statute deal with questions of a more principal nature. Article 1 articulates the purpose of the Laogai: to "punish counterrevolutionaries and other criminal offenders and reeducate them into new persons through labor."[154] As Article 2 makes clear, Laogai institutions were regarded as "one of the instruments of the people's democratic dictatorship." This explanation of Laogai is crucial, as its wording is significant. In 1949 Mao explained "democratic dictatorship" as the rule of the people (the alliance of workers and peasants) over the counterrevolutionary classes.[155]

To exercise dictatorship over internal enemies was, as he said repeatedly, a prerequisite for securing the victory of the revolution. It follows, then, that the Laogai was regarded as the state's main instrument for dealing with socialist China's assumed or real enemies. The democratic dictatorship of the people was a weapon for dealing with the enemy, to ensure that the people's government could not be overthrown. At stake was not justice or legal punishment but the victory of the revolution. The emphasis on dictatorship and class struggle established by the wording in Article 2 of the Statute on Laogai carries a connotation of being at war and thus justifies the use of violence. As Minister Luo Ruiqing explained, the strategy of Laogai was an "effective way to eradicate counterrevolutionary activities and all criminal offenses."[156]

The most controversial paragraph in the statute was perhaps Article 62.[157] This article ruled that after completing their prison term, those prisoners who wished to remain in the camps, who had no residential registration and no prospect of finding work, or who could be settled in sparsely populated areas, should continue to be employed by the labor camps. In effect, this paragraph said that prisoners, under certain conditions, had to remain in the camps even after they had served their sentence. Most prisoners lost their residential registration when they were sentenced. Most inmates no longer had a home or work to return to. Although the article was vague, it provided the basis for the so-called job placement system (*jiu ye*) for prisoners who had completed their terms. According to this plan, released convicts were placed in jobs and residential units in or near the labor camps where they had just completed their prison term.[158] As a result most prisoners, once officially released after the expiration of their terms, were retained in the camps as "free convicts" for an indefinite period of time.[159]

This was one of the main features of the Laogai before 1978: few inmates were ever able to come back from the camps, to return to their homes and resume their civilian lives. While the job placement system formally existed alongside the Laogai system, it has to be seen as an extension of the Laogai. It is evident that political, economic, and security considerations led the authorities to adopt the general policy of "keeping more, releasing less" (*duoliu, shaofang*).[160] The effect of this policy was tantamount to deporting groups of the civilian population that were considered to be enemies. It also gave priority to the general economic demands of the system over specific demands for reform and reeducation. The Laogai had a constantly growing workforce at its disposal; at the same time, it made sure that counterrevolutionaries and other enemies would never again represent a threat to socialist China. However, this points to a remarkable inconsistency in the official Laogai theory. The Laogai system was officially praised for being able to reform and reeducate offenders, yet only a very few of those offenders were ever accepted as having been fully reformed.

The rapid and often uncoordinated establishment of Laogai institutions in the early 1950s created a scattered and unprofitable system. After 1955 the central government decided to rein in the expansion and encouraged provincial authorities to merge existing smaller Laogai camps and units. Nearly all the institutions that were created after 1955 were huge camp operations with the capacity to hold tens of thousands of prisoners. In 1955 the number of Laogai units, which had hovered around 4,600, was significantly reduced to approximately 2,700. Two years later, in 1957, the Eleventh Bureau of the Public Security Ministry reported the number had been slashed by another 700 facilities, bringing the total down to just over 2,000 units. Of these, 1,323 were industrial enterprises, 619 were agricultural farms, and 71 were engaged in infrastructure projects.[161] As can also be seen from these numbers, within a few years the focus for Laogai had clearly shifted away from agriculture to industry.

During the years 1955 to 1958, the labor camp system became an ever more important economic asset. It was quite bluntly stated that prisoners had a duty to produce "material riches" in exchange for the forgiveness of the collective.[162] Party and government leaders stressed that offenders under socialism had an obligation to contribute to national construction. While prison labor was theoretically regarded as a means of reeducation, the leadership valued it above all as a significant economic resource that the state could not afford to waste. The benefits of forced labor were multifold. By gradually turning camps into self-sufficient farms and factories, the central government could reduce its expenditures for the camps and prisons. At the same time, the Laogai labor force became almost indispensable for the sustained implementation and completion of the ambitious, large-scale construction projects that were regarded as symbolic hallmarks of what a socialist society could achieve. Forced labor took over important functions on huge infrastructure projects; it was systematically used in place of civilian workers when jobs were considered too dangerous or too hard. The reclamation of wastelands, the basic construction work for railways and canals, and the digging of mineshafts and underground galleries were projects regularly assigned to the Laogai workforce. Only after the most strenuous and hazardous preparatory work had been completed would the government bring in the vanguard of Chinese communism, the workers.

Laogai slowly and inexorably assumed a prominent economic role in China, to the benefit of the socialist state. By assigning prisoners to risky and less desirable work projects, the state offered some relief to the much courted group of peasants and workers. Thus the government was able to play the group of social dissidents (at least some of whom were the former elites of Republican China) against the newly privileged group of workers and peasants, further cementing the workers' support. In addition, the full exploitation of prison labor helped to cut the state's expenses, and the threat of being sent to the camps also served to discipline the civilian workforce. Loafing and sabotage, for example, were offenses that could result in prison terms.

The implementation of the Great Leap Forward heralded a phase of bitter hardship and miserable living conditions in the Laogai. The Great Leap Forward policy was undertaken by the CCP between 1958 and early 1960 to mobilize Chinese society as a whole and bring it closer to the final stage of communism. This phase included both a renewed struggle against the counterrevolution and a strengthening of the reeducation work. The implementation of the Great Leap Forward led to far-reaching changes in the Laogai. First, the emphasis on industrial production was invigorated by the Fourth National Conference on Laogai Work, held in February 1959.[163] All Laogai units were called on to make a vigorous contribution to China's industrialization. Second, Laogai units were required to steeply increase their productivity. Working hours were extended and prisoners were forced to double or triple their efforts. Ambitious projects were undertaken with the assumption that manpower could replace machinery. Finally, the central government again encouraged local-level units to establish Laogai operations. Counties and communes opened up numerous labor reform or labor reeducation facilities for local offenders and enemies of the people. Hundreds of new units came into being, all controlled by local echelons of the administration. Many newly established Laogai facilities were operated by local cadres who needed a place to hold local troublemakers. These institutions lacked trained staff, equipment, and adequate funding. Prisoners were expected, above all, to work hard and long.

The emphasis on production also shaped the Fifth National Conference on Laogai Work that was held in April 1960. At the conference it was noted with satisfaction that the gross income of the Laogai had reached 3.18 billion yuan and that the productivity rate had grown considerably.[164] Laogai units were advised to adopt a reward system for further stepping up production in Laogai facilities. Outstanding work performance would be rewarded with better food rations, while those who were working too slowly or who appeared to be lazy would have their rations reduced. In regard to political and ideological reeducation, the conference recommended the use of social pressure. The party summoned civilians to report on prisoners and inform authorities about earlier behavior before their arrest. Prisoners also had to appear at public meetings, where they were confronted by their community.

The repercussions of the Great Leap Forward for those confined in Laogai institutions were disastrous. Most important in this context, the priorities of the camp administrators shifted: the realization of ambitious production goals overshadowed all other purposes of Laogai. Prisoners were pressed to increase their production by 100 percent. The softening of central government supervision of Laogai also opened up possibilities for lower echelons of the administration to appropriate and exploit prison labor. Prison labor was used by collectives and individuals to yield profits and gain material advantages.[165] Another result of the Great Leap Forward policy was that workers' own physical labor had to make up for the lack of machines in the Laogai. Overzealous cadres set ever higher production goals for Laogai units, and unlike peasants and workers, the prisoners had little means to resist the pressure.

This bare exploitation of the prisoners not only made obsolete any effort at reform or reeducation but also led to a substantial deterioration of living conditions. In an effort to cut spending and increase profits, all expenses for the subsistence of the prison population or for the maintenance of the facilities were reduced. In many camps sanitary conditions were neglected and expenditures for food dropped to below minimum standards. Even authors who were members of the CCP, such as Sun Xiaoli, admit that these conditions led to the "decease of a large group of people."[166] At times the death rates in the camps were so high that the leadership sent out investigators to examine the local situation.[167] From a construction site on the Ying-Xia Railway, for example, and from a water-control project at Sihu Lake in

Hubei Province, reports of staggering death rates alerted the leadership in Beijing.

Apart from exhaustion caused by extended work hours, between the summer of 1959 and 1962 there was an additional factor that took many lives in the Laogai—starvation. The inefficiency of the communes and the large-scale diversion of farm labor into small-scale industry seriously disrupted China's agriculture. The consequences of the Great Leap Forward were made worse by a series of natural disasters and the withdrawal of Soviet technical personnel from China. Estimates are that at least 20 million people died of starvation between 1958 and 1962.[168] The labor camps, too, experienced a sharp downgrading of their food supply. Hunger and exhaustion quickly sent death rates upward. In the 1990s it was officially admitted that in certain regions and units, in the words of Sun Xiaoli, "abnormal dying" occurred—a euphemism for the unspeakable catastrophe that beset the Laogai system during the Great Leap Forward. Within three years, whole camp populations vanished because of hunger, deprivation, and sickness.[169] The Laogai had undoubtedly reached its low point. Instead of being reformed or reeducated through labor, in these years inconceivably large numbers of inmates were simply worked and starved to death.

These shocking developments did not go unnoticed by the political leaders. Widespread suffering and death in the labor camps in fact increased criticism of the Great Leap Forward and of Mao himself. Together with a move to reverse the Great Leap Forward came the plea to centralize the Laogai again and to reconsider its overall purpose. The Eleventh National Conference of Public Security proposed a reduction of work hours in the camps and emphasized that the purpose of Laogai was the reform of the offender.[170] The Sixth National Conference on Laogai Work, held in 1962, was even more outspoken. The conference affirmed that the primary goal of Laogai was the reeducation of landlords, rich peasants, and counterrevolutionaries, who were to be reformed into new persons. The Laogai policy of "emphasizing production, neglecting reeducation" was sharply criticized, as was the administration's satisfaction with what was referred to as "three no's and one high," meaning "no deaths, no escapes, no troubles, and high work efficiency" in the labor camps. This slogan was of course highly ironic, since during the Great Leap there were staggering death rates. At the 1962 conference, open discontent was voiced by Laogai cadres and officials, who complained about unrealizable guidelines, superficiality, inadequate funding, and downtrodden conditions. In short, those in attendance at the conference attacked the radical emphasis on productivity that had built up since the mid-1950s and culminated in the Great Leap Forward, and advocated reinstating the priority on reeducation. The final document of the conference defined valid Laogai policies as "combining reeducation and labor, whereby reeducation comes first and production comes second," and stressed that "reeducation and production both must be done well."[171]

With the 1962 conference, a phase began that in retrospect appears calm in comparison with the "three bitter years" (1959 to 1961), the period that preceded it. After the turmoil of the Great Leap Forward, a normalization of the Laogai operation was urgently sought by the leadership. As a result, the conditions in the camps improved. Food supplies were increased, thanks to good harvests in 1962, and working hours for the prisoners were decreased. That same year, a large number of prisoners were released.[172] Among them were several so-called rightists who had been arrested in 1957 and 1958. Sick and malnourished prisoners were also freed, as were inmates from worker or peasant families.[173] On the eve of the Cultural Revolution, China officially counted 871 Laogai units. Of those, 472 were industrial operations and 374 were agricultural farms.[174]

In this period the Laogai also acquired a new function. It was increasingly deployed as a powerful instrument for deportation and demographic intervention. At the Ninth Public Security Work Conference, in August 1958, a regulation was passed banning the eventual return of all Laogai convicts from urban areas to their hometowns.[175] Even upon completion of their sentence, they were now required to stay at their Laogai locality because they were refused residency in their original urban residential district. These former convicts were thus forced to settle down in the vicinity of the camp where they had been detained. After this regulation, only convicts from rural areas were allowed to return home—if they could obtain the permission of local authorities. In 1964 this policy was systematized as "four stay and four leave." "Four stay" referred to the conditions that would cause authorities to decline a convict's request to return home: (1) the convict had not reformed satisfactorily, (2) the convict had no home to return to and no possibility of work, (3) the family of the convict lived in a border outpost region, and (4) the convict was still regarded as potentially dangerous. The conditions that would prompt authorities to grant permission to return ("four leave") were: (1) the convict had reformed well, (2) the family of the convict lived in the countryside, (3) the family was in need and the convict opposed the idea of staying, and (4) the convict had lost his political influence, or he was unable to work owing to health conditions. In practice this policy meant that only former convicts from sparsely populated rural areas who had demonstrated they were reformed were allowed to return to their original place of residence.

During the Great Leap Forward, certain principles underlying the Laogai began to spread out beyond the institutions of confinement and into society at large. This "laogaization" of society was seen when patterns of social organization typical of the labor camps spread into society. All over the country, production brigades and production teams were formed, in which workers would collectively engage in labor and political study.[176] The organizational differences between Laogai detachments and civilian teams were gradually blurred.

Yet what was supposed to have been the age of Laogai's flourishing and general acceptance ended as a terrible human disaster. The economic losses and, above all, the loss of human lives had long-term consequences. They shattered the people's confidence in the CCP and its policies and unsettled the basic premises, purposes, and promises of the Laogai.[177]

During the early 1960s, increasing tensions between China and the Soviet Union convinced Mao Zedong that the Russian Revolution had gone astray, which in turn made him fear that China would follow the same path. Programs put forth by the CCP leadership to bring China out of the economic depression caused by the Great Leap Forward made Mao doubt the party's revolutionary commitment. He especially feared urban social stratification in a society as traditionally elitist as China's. Mao ultimately adopted four goals for the next phase in the People's Republic, the Cultural Revolution: to replace his designated successors with leaders more faithful to his current thinking; to rectify the Chinese Communist Party; to provide China's youth with a revolutionary experience; and to achieve some specific policy changes that would make the educational, health care, and cultural systems less elitist.[178] Mao pursued these goals through the massive mobilization of the country's urban youth called the Great Proletarian Cultural Revolution. The youths were organized into groups called the Red Guards, and Mao ordered the party and the army not to suppress them.

It appears from occasional remarks by Mao that he became increasingly critical of the public security apparatus and the existing penal system. In April 1964 Mao publicly charged that the Laogai cadres had lost faith in the capacity of the party to reeducate offenders. In July and September 1965 he found fault with the "economism" of the Laogai.[179] He apparently bemoaned the fact that the priorities of the penal system had switched from reeducation toward economic considerations. For him this certainly constituted a major failure. In general, Mao believed the Laogai had become a symbol of China's inclining toward elitist, bureaucratized, Soviet-style development and the party's loss of faith in the revolutionary project of transforming society and man. This, in Mao's view, was also the real reason for the failure of the Great Leap Forward. Mao's growing disaffection with the Laogai is an important key to understanding the fate of the Laogai during the Cultural Revolution and the parallel revival of revolutionary-era punishments. Mao wanted to change the way Chinese citizens in the socialist society sought redress in daily conflicts and how convicts and enemies were to be treated.

The Cultural Revolution brought many radical changes for the judiciary. Judicial organs such as the courts and the procurators were suspended. Revolutionary committees and Red Guards arose throughout Chinese society and, with the protection of the army, took over judicial and police functions, thereby making obsolete the public security apparatus and its facilities. The Ministry of Public Security in Beijing was even repeatedly ransacked by Red Guards in 1966 and 1967.[180] The Revolutionary Committees exercised their newly acquired powers by taking suspects into custody, conducting interrogations, and administering punishments such as fines, detainment, beatings, and even the death penalty—all without the involvement of courts or other judicial bodies. Punishments known from the period of the revolution were revived, such as parading offenders through the streets wearing a tall hat. Public displays and shaming became a fixed component of punishments. The Red Guards also maintained that the labor reform camps should play only a minor role in the system of legal punishments. They established their own places to carry out reform through labor that were called "cowsheds" *(niupeng).*[181]

The Laogai labor camp system was dealt a harsh blow. Especially in urban regions, the Red Guards stormed prisons and camps, attacked the guards or cadres, and accused them of neglecting their duties.[182] One criticism referred to so-called technicist or economist deviations (referring to the emphasis on technical or economic aspects of Laogai). In some cases, inmates were set free while guards and cadres were taken into custody. Many camps closed or stopped operating. Within a short period of time, the number of Laogai camps decreased by half. The amount of land under cultivation by labor reform brigades was reduced by 60 percent.[183] In September 1967 Mao called on the army under Lin Biao to step in on behalf of the Red Guards. The army also went to several Laogai institutions, where they replaced the public security guards.[184] Most of the Laogai cadres were subjected to criticism sessions and afterward were "sent down" to the countryside for reeducation. The renewed emphasis on class struggle seemed to have given way to the rise of revanchism.

Not until the early 1970s was the Laogai able to resume operations again, and in 1971 the Public Security Ministry was rehabilitated and given back its powers and functions.[185] For a few years, however, the system had been totally suspended. Where the army had not moved in and taken over, labor camps had emptied and guards had left. After the establishment of military control, used to drive out the Red Guards and end their rule, several campaigns were undertaken to end the chaos and reinstitute authority. These campaigns brought approximately one million new prisoners into the camps.

The tumult of the Cultural Revolution caused severe disturbances in labor camp operations and severely weakened the whole Laogai complex. The drastic changes and reversals, the attacks on cadres and guards, on leaders and respected members of the CCP, and on intellectuals in general implied an enormous, willful expansion both of target groups and of definitions of deviant behavior. The most important consequence was perhaps the blow that was dealt to the program of reeducation. The boundaries between orthodoxy and heterodoxy became blurred, and reeducation could no longer be meaningfully achieved because it was impossible to tell which norms and standards should be enforced.

The Laogai Regime

The term "Laogai" denoted a process rather than a site or a facility. In fact, Laogai could be carried out in diverse settings and arrangements that had little in common. Neither fixed architectural designs nor special arrangements were required. A farm, a mine, a factory, a classroom, a basement, a small office—almost any place could be turned into a site for reform through labor. Laogai in theory and practice was naturally suited to be absorbed throughout society and to mushroom well beyond the physical settings of a labor camp. All that was needed was physical labor, a certain organization of daily routines, and the oversight of a political cadre. Other components, such as walls, tools, iron doors, and even guards, were ultimately dispensable. Laogai was an extraordinarily flexible and polymorphous penal system.

It is useful to distinguish between peripheral and central manifestations of Laogai.[186] The central, "classic," and systemic forms detained offenders in fixed institutions. These institutions of confinement were as a rule administered by the public security apparatus. Peripheral places of confinement were more varied and were overseen by local grassroots organizations such as work units, residential committees, and schools, none of which was part of the formal criminal justice system. In regard to Laogai, we find therefore the same dualism (formal-informal and jural-social) that marked the Chinese criminal justice system in general.

After 1949 socialist authorities built a national detention system run by various levels of the Ministry of Public Security and the army. The Chinese government never made public the locations of the labor camps, nor did it indicate the total number of prisoners. This information was always treated as a state secret. The Laogai system *(laogai zhidu)* was a secretive universe made up of large and small facilities scattered throughout the country. The system handled millions of suspected criminals, counterrevolutionaries, and enemies apprehended by criminal justice organs or by ad-hoc tribunals during government campaigns and mass movements. In general, the Laogai system contained three distinct, interconnected circuits: detention centers, prisons, and labor camps. Laogai as theory and practice underpinned all three, although of course each circuit performed its own specific functions within the system.

The detention centers (*kanshousuo* and *juyisuo*) were where every detainee had his first experience with Laogai confinement.[187] Detention centers were established at all administrative levels, county, provincial, and central. They varied greatly in size but on average could hold 500 to 1,000 and more detainees. They kept offenders who have not yet been tried as well as those sentenced to imprisonment for up to two years, but convicted offenders and those awaiting charges and trial followed different regimes in the detention centers. In the career of a Laogai inmate, the detention center represented an important place of transition and initiation into the Laogai world. Newly arrived detainees were put through investigation, interrogation, and self-examination to get them to divulge crucial information and evidence. Inmates were also frequently encouraged—and pressed—to write confessions. A policy of "leniency for those who confess, punishments for those who resist" provided strong incentives for inmates to cooperate and to engage in self-denunciation and the denunciation of others. Their stay in the detention center usually came to an end when their sentence was passed by either a court (for a criminal punishment) or the Public Security Bureau (for an administrative punishment).

From the detention center, prisoners were transferred to either a prison or a labor camp. Inmates sentenced to life imprisonment or the death penalty were in general dispatched to a prison *(jianyu),* because the prisons had a higher security standard and were better guarded.[188] Foreign prisoners and high-profile prisoners (high-ranking GMD officials, high-ranking cadres, publicly known figures, spies, and secret service agents) were also regularly handed over to the prisons. Prisons were located in urban areas or in their immediate vicinity. The new authorities often used the prison buildings erected in the Republican era, but in a few cases new prisons were built.

Since offenders were kept in prisons mainly for security reasons, control and discipline were rigorously enforced, in particular in high-security prisons. Inmates sentenced to death or to life imprisonment were not required to work. On the contrary, they were permitted to work only after they displayed progress in thought reform and repentance. The prohibition against work was seen as a punishment and also as the result of security considerations. Inmates in high-security prisons had to spend their time in interrogations, political study, and the writing of self-examinations. Again, inmates were constantly encouraged to prepare confessions and to provide information about themselves or others. Those who cooperated with the prison administration could hope to gain rewards and privileges in exchange.

Labor camps held 80 percent to 90 percent of all convicts sentenced to limited-term imprisonment (those with sentences ranging between five and twenty years).[189] The word "camp," however, was not used in Chinese documents. Rather these documents referred to Laogai sites *(laogai chang-*

suo) where a Laogai brigade was situated. In administrative terms Chinese sources also spoke of Laogai units *(laogai danwei)*. A unit had an administration *(changbu)* that was located in the Laogai headquarters *(laogai dayuan)*. The private residences for the staff were located in this administrative center, along with other service facilities such as schools and hospitals. The administration had several offices responsible for production, transport, construction, and prisoner arrivals and discharges.

Laogai sites could take on very different forms. The majority of sites were agricultural farms *(nongchang)*, which were scattered throughout the country. Other sites were mining operations or factories. In the 1950s and 1960s Laogai brigades frequently formed mobile camps for construction work on major projects such as railways, roads, dikes, and bridges.[190] Prisoners in the mobile camps were housed in tents and lived and worked under harsh conditions. Prisoners who had received long sentences, in particular, were transferred to far distant places, where they were given the hardest work. After they had completed the most basic work, such as the construction of housing or cultivation of wastelands, manufacturing industries would settle in or near the camp. Later the camp would be transformed into a state farm that employed mainly a civilian workforce, while the prisoners would be transferred somewhere else.

The formal Laogai detention system was supplemented by a decentralized, informal, and semiofficial sanctioning apparatus. This semiofficial system performed two essential functions. It fed evidential information into the formal system that was used in trials of offenders. And it took part in the administration of minor sanctions, in particular in the form of running peripheral institutions of detention.

A unique feature of the Chinese penal system was that the ideas and practices of Laogai tended to sprawl far beyond the formal institutions of detention. Laogai was part of a constant, pervasive effort to transform Chinese society. Since some segments of the Chinese population were regarded by Mao as needing permanent reeducation, he would demand from time to time that those segments of society be subjected to the same combination of thought transformation and physical labor that was practiced in the labor camps. As a result, during centrally initiated political campaigns and movements, certain Laogai practices (hard work, political study) proliferated widely in society and manifested themselves in a variety of informal settings. After the completion of a campaign or movement, the Laogai practices would be withdrawn and would once again be limited to formal institutions of detention.

After the founding of the PRC, many functionaries and officials of the GMD government were rounded up and held in informal, provisionally established places of detention, where they were supposed to reshape themselves. These places, called political training classes *(zhengxunban)* were run by several government agencies in cooperation with the Ministry of Public Security.[191] Members of these classes had not been officially arrested or sentenced to a prison term, yet they were also not allowed to leave the class at will. The classes were organized similarly to the labor camps. There were companies and squadrons; classes had in total 100 to 200 inmates each. Inmates participated in the same political and ideological education as in the labor camps and they were also forced to work at construction sites.

Much of the government's ability to periodically deploy such Laogai practices within civilian society depended on the participation of local, semiofficial grassroots organizations, such as rural communes, work units, village committees, and residential committees.[192] In urban China the area under the jurisdiction of each public security station was organized into numerous residential committees, or "basic mass organizations." Residential committees could get directly involved in the criminal process by gathering information and evidence and apprehending suspects, or they could act through specialized committees such as a mediation committee or a security committee *(zhi'an baowei weiyuanhui)*. As the police force was relatively small, the system of neighborhood security committees played a vital role in the political-legal network.

The committees were allowed to impose certain sanctions for minor offenses. The available sanctions included criticism education, warning, struggle session, public criticism, the displaying of large posters to expose undesirable conduct, and the parading of offenders through the neighborhood. Public meetings, at which suspected offenders were forced to make a public self-examination and to undergo criticism, were a means of dealing with minor antisocial infractions, either in the first instance or after private persuasion and reprimand had failed. Often, however, such meetings were also used to gather evidence and force confessions, which would later be handed over to the Public Security Bureau, together with the suspect, for further prosecution.

Two more-severe punishments applied by local semiofficial groups were surveillance *(guanzhi)* and work under surveillance *(jiandu laodong)*, both of which, according to the law, were actually administrative or criminal punishments.[193] These forms of punishment were possibly born of necessity sometime after 1949, to solve the problem of overcrowding in the prisons. In rural areas, putting someone under control and surveillance required the area or village people's government to approve the sentence. They, in turn, were supposed to notify the county Public Security Bureau, which had to check the charge and approve the sentence. In the city, *guanzhi* was the responsibility of the local police station, and the city Public Security Bureau was the office that checked the station's actions. In practice, however, these oversight rules rarely impeded the use of *guanzhi*. This form of punishment provided elements of Laogai in a flexible, decentralized form without constituting a substantial deprivation of freedom. It relieved the state of the administrative burden of establishing more institutions of confinement, while at the same time bringing control mechanisms down to the grassroots level and thus dispersing Laogai techniques in the local society. In effect, *guanzhi* implied that, for those affected, their place of work and life, the work unit, would become an open prison where they were constantly under "mass supervision and control."[194]

Surveillance in various forms *(guanzhi* or *jiandu laodong)* was a vehicle well suited for subjecting deviants to group pressure and for getting the masses involved in the process of social control. Suspected counterrevolutionaries, "bad elements," and rightists were put under surveillance by work units, communes, and security committees. Some under surveillance were allowed to return home at night, others were locked up in basements or offices. The writer Cong Weixi, for instance, was labeled a rightist in 1957. His work unit, a publishing house, decided to impose surveillance on him. He had to work with other rightists on a construction site in Beijing for several months before he was transferred to a rural commune and then to other construction sites in the areas surrounding Beijing. Without ever having seen a written sentence or an indictment, he worked under surveillance for three years. During this time he was allowed to return home to see his family only on the weekends. In 1960 he was finally sentenced to Laojiao by an administrative decision of the Beijing Public Security Bureau and was transferred to a labor camp.[195]

Another example of informal detainment outside of the criminal justice system was carried out by the "May 7 cadre schools," which were set up for intellectuals, party members, and other members of communist organizations and government agencies who were accused of following the capitalist road or of being revisionists.[196] Here, too, inmates underwent treatment that combined hard work and ideological study and indeed very much resembled the daily routine in a Laogai camp. Some of these schools were in fact located within or near labor camps; others were situated on wastelands, where the inmates had to build their own barracks and cultivate the land for the production of crops. Discipline was vigorously maintained, and inmates were not free to leave the cadre school. They were, however, given a day off every ten to fourteen days. Other groups that were targeted and subjected to similar treatment included educated youths, who were ordered to appear at "bases for the sent down."[197] These inmates were also organized in companies *(dui)* and squadrons *(zu)*. Release from these kinds of peripheral detention places was rarely seen during the Cultural Revolution. Most inmates spent years in captivity, laboring in the fields and reading Mao's works. One important distinction has to be noted, though. The peripheral places of detention rarely had guards to watch over the offenders. The original work units were in charge of these places, and guards were recruited from their ranks. For instance a janitor could be appointed security guard to watch over the counterrevolutionaries in the work unit. Security could be low because the units transferred out any persons who refused to reeducate themselves or who were accused of serious offenses against the Public Security Bureau. This kind of semiofficial detention is important because it demonstrates how the whole system of crime control and repression depended on the successful cooptation of local mass organizations.

To enhance our understanding of the complex web of formal and peripheral institutions of confinement that operated in socialist China, a case study is most useful. Beijing offers an illuminating and conveniently well documented example. The municipal Public Security Bureau of Beijing was in charge of an intricate network of confinement institutions. In the late 1960s it ran several detention centers, five prisons, at least six labor reform or labor reeducation farms, and a steel-producing complex.[198] There were also several shelter and investigation centers for inmates sentenced to administrative punishments.

When a suspected spy or high-ranking counterrevolutionary was apprehended, he would most likely be transported to Caolanzi detention center first. The detention center was in the same building that had housed a Guomindang self-examination institute in the 1930s. There, the Republican state had intended to instigate self-reflection and catharsis among its political prisoners. After 1949 socialist China, too, brought political prisoners there to reshape their thinking. Allyn Rickett described the Caolanzi detention center, saying it was "a typical rich residential compound and from the courtyard it looked little different from those serving as dwellings throughout Peking."[199] Half of each prison cell was taken up by a *kang*, a wooden platform used as a bed at night and a place to sit during the day. A cell housed between five and ten prisoners. One of the prisoners would be appointed by the prison staff to act as leader of the cell. The daily routine was centered on conducting interrogations and extracting information and confessions from the prisoners. Except for performing housekeeping duties, such as washing and cleaning, inmates were exempted from work. Instead, they had to write autobiographies and self-examinations. During the day, the cell group discussed the offenses of each prisoner in great detail, or studied political documents. Prisoners were expected to press hard on their cellmates to convince them to work with the officials. The length of detention in Caolanzi depended on the individual prisoner and his willingness to cooperate with the public security agents. It could stretch from several weeks to a few years.

The interrogation rooms all had a portrait of Mao hanging on the wall. Many captives also recalled first noticing the following slogan: "Leniency for those who confess, severity for those who resist!"[200] The conduct of the interrogations was very important for each prisoner, for the prison staff would later use interrogation records to propose a verdict and a final sentence. The interrogation officer in charge would also determine the inmate's final place of imprisonment and when he would be relocated.

Caolanzi took in only important and prominent prisoners. Another much larger detention center was located in the north of Beijing. Its name was Beiyuan Shelter and Investigation Center (Beiyuan shencha shourongsuo), but prisoners called it "dust town" *(tucheng)*. This institution of confinement apparently held only Laojiao convicts. Only a few prisoners lived in regular prison cells; most were housed in tents that were scattered throughout a large courtyard. There was constant coming and going, as day after day new arrivals were brought in to await their relocation to a prison factory or one of the labor camps. The third important detention center was Banbuqiuo, where Laojiao inmates were kept. On average prisoners were kept in Banbuqiuo for no longer than three months while their case was examined, before being sent to a labor camp. Banbuqiuo was especially dreaded because it had the street number 44, which in Chinese sounds like "double death."

Qincheng was a maximum-security prison located about an hour's drive from central Beijing, in Changping County.[201] It became especially infamous during the Cultural Revolution. Qincheng was originally under the Thirteenth Bureau (the Pre-Interrogation Bureau) of the Ministry of Public Security, and was used to conduct interrogations, similar to the Caolanzi detention center. In 1967 it was taken over by the Military Control Committee of the Beijing Bureau of Public Security. After that the prison gradually acquired a new and quite important function in carrying out the Cultural Revolution among the party members: it was used to deal with functionaries and party members who were deemed by the Central Case Examination Group under Kang Sheng to be disloyal and dangerous. A total of 501 leading cadres were imprisoned there between 1967 and 1971. An additional 190 prisoners were already there at that point, including such prominent political prisoners as Mao's former Russian interpreter, Shi Zhe, and chief of intelligence, Pan Hannian.

The cells in Qincheng were about six square meters in size, with a hard wooden bunk attached to the wall and a primitive toilet in the corner. Beatings were common. Inmates in Qincheng were never told for what specific reason they had actually been detained. Mu Xin reported that drugs (including hallucinogens) were routinely used on inmates during interrogations. According to Mu, the medical staff in Qincheng in fact treated the inmates like human guinea pigs: "In this prison there were certain doctors who either deliberately and of their own free will or because they were being forced to . . . not only did not set out to cure the sick, but, on the contrary, 'vaccinated' the healthy with diseases and made the sick perish prematurely." The results of this violent treatment were shocking: more than sixty of the prisoners in Qincheng reportedly became mentally ill between 1967 and 1971. During the same period an additional twenty-nine were "tormented to death" and five committed suicide. Qincheng Prison, like many other places of confinement during the Cultural Revolution, degenerated into a den of torture.

Beijing Number One Prison was situated on the former site of Beijing Model Prison. It was one of the few prisons that was occasionally shown to foreign visitors. Like its Republican predecessor, it served as a showcase to demonstrate the achievements of crime control and criminal justice in socialist China.[202] Bao Ruowang called it "the best jail assignment in China" and in retrospect stated that he had spent there "the happiest nine months of my entire period of incarceration."[203] According to official reports and reports from visitors and prisoners, the prison held between 1,300 and 2,500 inmates. Among them were prisoners serving terms between three and ten years, inmates sentenced to life imprisonment, prisoners on death row, Laojiao inmates, and a number of "free inmates." The share of those accused of counterrevolutionary crimes was between 70 percent (in the early 1950s, when the movement against counterrevolutionaries was completed) and 40 percent (in the mid-1960s, before the Cultural Revolution). The prison operated three factories: a hosiery mill, a mill for plastic products, and a machine and electrical shop. Apart from that, it had a translators' brigade, a hospital, and a theater group that gave performances in the labor camps run by the Beijing Public Security Bureau. Attached to the prison was a detention house known as the South Compound, which served as a transition center that reportedly kept at times 4,000 detainees. In the mid-1970s it included a separate wing for scientists and technicians.

Life in Beijing Number One Prison was different from that in a detention center. Prisons were above all dominated by the adjacent factories; consequently, work assignments and ambitious production goals dominated everyday life. Upon entering such a prison, one could see big posters that announced daily production targets as well as minimal quotas to be fulfilled by every prisoner. Bao Ruowang gave a vivid description of the brisk operations at the South Compound of Beijing Number One Prison: "Everywhere there was an intense, frenzied, antlike activity. Men rushed back and forth before us, toting stacks of book leaves three to four feet high, disappearing into doorways and then popping out into view again on the steps leading to the different floors. The din [of] hammering and footfalls on the cement stairways echoed off the shiny gray concrete floor to create a background for the piercing tenor voice of the agitprop, who moved from floor to floor setting his stool up in a corner and standing with his notes in one hand and a tin megaphone in the other. His job was to encourage production. He never stopped."[204]

Xingkaihu State Farm (Guoying Xingkaihu Nongchang) was named after the nearby lake Xingkai.[205] The camp was under the administration of the Beijing Public Security Bureau, although it was located thousands of miles away in the eastern part of Heilongjiang Province close to the Russian border, between Mishan and Raohe. Heilongjiang Province has hard winters, when temperatures regularly drop to minus 40 degrees Celsius. The area where the camp was located consisted mostly of marshlands, which were infested with mosquitoes in summer and difficult to drain and cultivate. These difficult conditions had prevented farming by ordinary peasants. From the point of view of the Laogai planners, however, the area was ideal for the deployment of penal labor. Between 1953 and 1955, the Xingkaihu camp was established alongside a vast complex of other camps in eastern Heilongjiang. In 1960 the camp was divided into nine branch farms spread among some sixty villages. The camp was said to have held on average at least 40,000 prisoners. These included sentenced Laogai prisoners, Laojiao convicts, juvenile delinquents, and "free workers." Besides crop production, the camp had its own tractor-servicing factory, sugar refinery, milk processing plant, and canning factory. The Sino-Soviet conflict in the mid-1960s brought an end to the camp; it was gradually taken out of operation.

The Beijing Public Security Bureau also administered a steel- producing complex, called Yanqing Steel Company. It consisted of a steel factory, brickworks, and two small iron mines. The complex operated as a state-owned company that used exclusively prison labor. It appears that most of the prisoners working there were Laojiao convicts: rightists, hoodlums, and petty criminals made up the population. The Yanqing complex was located in the mountain range north of Beijing, beyond the Great Wall. The iron mines were at a place called Yingmen, and the factory was located in Yanqing and Kangzhuang. As in many other camps and mines, the barracks had been built by prisoners.[206] The establishment of the whole complex was a product of the Great Leap Forward. Its history is short. Set up quickly by prison laborers in 1958, the factory never produced much steel, owing to frequent power shortages. In 1961 the mines were closed and only a small operation at Yanqing, which employed not more than 500 prisoners, was maintained. The Yingmen iron mines were in a very inhospitable environment. Food supplies were scarce, and in winter temperatures dropped far below freezing. Since there were no regular work assignments, only temporary projects, such as repairs, could be performed. For prisoners, the stay at

Yingmen iron mines invariably entailed physical hardship and illness. Because of its unprofitable operation, the industrial complex in Yanqing received reduced food supplies. Even the guards were hungry. Prolonged malnutrition took a heavy toll among the prisoners in 1959 and 1960. In many ways, Yanqing is representative of similar facilities created during the Great Leap Forward. A great number of factories and industrial complexes were established in a rush, and with great zeal, but because of miscalculations they never succeeded in producing noteworthy profits. After the closing of Yingmen, many inmates from Beijing were relocated to Chadian Farm.

Chadian was (and still is) the name of a small, inconspicuous railway station on the Beijing-Shanhaiguan Railway. The labor camp complex was located about eight miles west of Chadian Station within Qinghe County. The guards, their families, and ex-inmates called the camp Qinghe Farm, but current inmates and their families knew the place as Chadian Farm, since Chadian was the gate that everybody had to pass through to reach the labor camp. Since the 1950s urbanites from Beijing who had breached any written or unwritten rules were sent to this camp. The movements and campaigns that spasmodically swept through Beijing filled the large camp complex with prisoners, and it came to be well known among the population of Beijing.

The area covered by the camp complex was enormous.[207] The whole area was about twenty kilometers long and fifteen kilometers wide. It covered an area of approximately 300 square kilometers. Because of the area's size and the sparseness of the landscape, prisoners called it "sacred land" *(shengdi).*[208] The expanse in which the labor camp was located had been a flat wilderness without trees and brushes. The bleak wilderness had remained untouched for centuries because a high amount of alkali in the soil made agriculture impossible. It was not until the twentieth century that efforts were undertaken to reclaim the wasteland. Located 120 miles southeast of Beijing and its large populace, the reclaimed farmland promised to provide the capital with food and to give a widely impoverished region a badly needed economic boost. During the time of the Republic, the North China Reclamation Company had set out to cultivate the wilderness. A few ditches had been dug to bring fresh water to a few small fields, but the harvest was poor. The company had quickly switched its business to the farming of freshwater crabs, which lived in the many water holes all over the marshland.

In the late 1930s Japanese occupation authorities became aware of the wilderness, too. Detention facilities were set up near Chadian. Under the instruction of Japanese engineers, Chinese and Korean conscripts built a drainage canal and a pumping station that was powered by steam turbines. Some paddies were established for rice cultivation. After the war, the GMD became active in the area again. The Ministry for Agriculture and Forests set up a "cultivation farm." A wider and longer irrigation canal was built, a few more fields were added.

The first group to work in the Qinghe wilderness under the supervision of communist authorities was made up of prisoners of war. In 1948, 1,763 POWs were transferred to the swampland, accompanied by 200 officers and 500 soldiers of the People's Liberation Army. They built row houses, opened fields for rice production, and, most important, dug a seven-mile canal to bring fresh water from Chaobei River into the area. The constant flow of large quantities of fresh water gradually washed out the alkali salts, and conditions for the cultivation of agricultural crops started to improve. The foundations for what turned out to be the most famous labor camp in North China were finally laid.

In February 1949 the Public Security Bureau in Beijing formed the Qinghe Training Division (Qinghe Xunlian Dadui). It consisted of former GMD members, functionaries, and cadres who were sentenced to work under surveillance in order to reform themselves. In November 1949 a team was sent to the Chadian region in Ninghe County, Hebei Province, to explore possibilities for a further expansion of the training division. The team found that the wastelands were ideally suited for a large-scale deployment of prison labor. With the approval of the CCP's central administration, the Public Security Bureau of Beijing ordered the Qinghe Training Division to begin preparations for building a large camp. Twenty-five former agricultural experts, engineers, and architects were selected from among prisoners in Beijing. They had to support twenty-two specialists sent from Beijing. Together with twelve armed guards, the planning group mapped the area and drew up a comprehensive plan for the future camp complex, including campsites, buildings, walls, streets, canals, bridges, fields, and apartment buildings.

The construction of the camp was started on February 24, 1950. The official name of the facility was Beijing City Local Qinghe State Farm. Two hundred cadres, 500 guards, and 1,600 convicts were the first inhabitants of one of China's premier model labor camps. One year after the start of construction, in October 1951, 5,000 inmates were detained on the farm facilities.[209] The various CCP-backed movements in the early 1950s brought trainloads of uprooted citizens accused of political offenses to Chadian Station. The camp soon had ten detachments *(dadui)*, each organized into twelve brigades, for a total of around 10,000 to 12,000 prisoners.[210]

Another jump in the number of prisoners occurred in 1958, as a result of the newly introduced administrative punishment of labor reeducation (Laojiao) and the Anti-Rightist campaign. The influx of new prisoners prompted the camp administration to undertake a second large expansion of the labor camp. To the west a huge new area was added that was called the "western wastelands" *(xihuangdi)*. New arrivals were mostly brought to the western wastelands, where they had to dig ditches, pull weeds, and plant rice.

In 1958, during the Great Leap Forward, the camp was also reorganized. The subcamps (called stations) were given numbers that started with "58" (the year of the beginning of the Great Leap Forward). The subcamps 581 to 585, for example, were located in the western wastelands; in the eastern part were camps 586 to 589.[211] On average a subcamp housed eight brigades; in the 1960s, up to ten brigades. Each brigade was made up of 100 to 150 prisoners. A subcamp or squadron therefore apparently held between 1,000 and 1,500 prisoners. Since Chadian Farm had between ten squadrons (in the 1950s) and fifteen squadrons (in the 1960s), it appears that the whole camp kept 15,000 to 22,500 prisoners in the late 1950s and early '60s.

Inside each of the subcamps was a cluster of eight to ten one-story row houses made of red brick, set around a large open lot used for roll calls. Each row house had two rooms. A room was normally occupied by a squad or team *(zu)*. Ten to twenty inmates formed a team. Several squads in turn formed a brigade *(dui)*.

Subcamp or squadron 586 was used as cemetery. Prisoners assigned to this squadron had to bury the dead from the whole camp. According to former inmates, numerous burial mounds were to be found there.[212] A small tablet made of wood or stone in front of each burial mound had the name of the deceased person written on it.

To fight desperation and insurgency among inmates during the period called the three bitter years, from 1959 to 1961, central authorities in Beijing instructed the camp administrators to isolate all sick inmates. In August

1961 the camp administration started to transfer all sick prisoners who were unable to work to subcamp 585.[213] Bao Ruowang (Jean Pasqualini), in his memoir *Prisoner of Mao*, likened camp 585 to Dante's hell: "Our own compound was a distressing sight. Strewn like flotsam on a beach were little groups of old men—scarcely a young person in sight—listlessly going through their various motions of existing. . . . Some of the men were so weak that they were reduced to crawling; some sat in the shade staring at nothing; some were blind. It looked like something Dante might have imagined."[214] Many inmates felt that the closer the number of their camp was to 586, the nearer they were coming to death.[215]

After the early 1950s the camp's production grew steadily. In 1955, 35,000 *mou* (5,845 acres) of rice paddies were planted, on which 2.7 million pounds rice were raised. Apart from that, 17,000 pounds fish and crabs were produced. Other products included bricks, paper, meat, eggs, and milk. The farm was not only self-sufficient but also delivered many goods to Beijing. Officially, year after year the Qinghe camp produced high yields and thus demonstrated the economic potential of convict labor.

As it did for many other Laogai institutions, the Cultural Revolution brought setbacks to Chadian Farm. Red Guards from Beijing appeared, criticizing and attacking the camp staff. They also set prisoners free and closed some stations. For several years no new inmates were sent to Chadian Farm.[216] It was only in the 1970s, with the rise of the military in the wake of the Cultural Revolution, that Chadian Farm began to receive prisoners again.

Unlike Republican prisons, which followed a fixed set of architectural designs, no specific designs ever existed for the labor camps. The Laogai planners never had any ambition to construct costly and prestigious buildings. As a rule, wherever possible they used extant facilities dating back to the GMD. "Laogai" referred to a set of penal practices rather than to a type of site, and the camps were set up in a confusing variety of settings and according to various organizational patterns. Yet several functional principles can in fact be identified as undergirding the organization of space at all Laogai labor camps.[217] Administration, labor, housing, food supplies, health, hygiene, and sanitation all were spatially separated, each located in a zone of its own. Whereas visibility and hierarchy were guiding principles in the design of Republican prisons, the separation of functional zones constituted one of the main principles for the labor camps. The layout of a typical labor camp included different zones for the various functions, with the zones usually organized in a honeycomb pattern. Laogai planners thought that spatial differentiation and zonal separation would engender a world of simple, clear-cut functionality. Communist penology created communities in which inmates' daily lives were dictated and controlled by elementary activities, simple rules, and clear structures.

The camp zones were the segments in which the prisoners were quartered. They were called stations *(zhan)*.[218] At the center of each station was a big empty field that was used for the daily roll calls. The prisoners' barracks were located on one side of the field. In prison jargon they were called "numbers" *(haozi)*, because they were numbered.[219] Each barrack had a long corridor on one side of the building from which one could enter the rooms.[220] A barrack had between two and five rooms. In northern China, half of each room was taken up by a heated stone bed *(kang)*. The rooms were not locked during the day and the windows normally had no iron bars.[221] When not at work, prisoners could move around freely in the camp compound. On the other side of the roll-call field was the zone for the staff. Prisoners were not allowed to enter this zone without permission. It contained barracks for the guards and cadres, an infirmary *(yiwusuo)*, cells for solitary confinement, the kitchen, and a security bureau. Each station could house from one thousand to several thousand prisoners.

Another important zone was the work and production zone. The work sites were clearly separated from the camps and were often some distance away. Prisoners had to exit the camp through the gates. The work zones could be anything from fields to factories and mines. The prisoners would spend most of their time each day in the work zone. They usually arrived early in the morning and stayed until late afternoon. Lunch was brought from the camp to the work site. Before leaving the camp through the gates and after their return, all prisoners had to muster. They would be counted, and sometimes the camp director would use the roll call to address the prisoners on political issues or work-related questions. There was also an administrative zone, where the camp leadership and administration *(changbu)* were located. This zone was separated from the station as well as from the work sites. Prisoners were prohibited from entering the administration zone.

Most labor camps did not have any walls or barbed wire around them.

And even when there was some kind of barrier or constraint to keep prisoners in, it was so perfunctory in nature that it could be overcome with little effort. At Chadian Farm there was a wall around the camp, but in the mid-1970s high-voltage wires at the top of the wall had no electricity and the bricks in the wall were crumbling.[222] In some cases camps were so remote from the next human settlement that walls and barbed wire simply were superfluous. There, the surrounding wilderness provided an effective barrier to escape. But even where this was not the case, leaders of the camps were keenly aware that there was hardly any place for an escaped prisoner to go. In a society in which every single person belonged to a commune, a troop, a workgroup, or a residential unit, any stranger traveling alone and without papers would attract attention and would soon be turned over to public security. In the sober words of Zhang Xianliang, the differences between the labor camp and society at large did not amount to much: "The distinction was between a very large prison and a relatively small prison. There was a tight network of surveillance everywhere."[223]

In general, most of the Laogai camps had an inconspicuous appearance. They resembled an ordinary village or rural commune more than a prison camp. The buildings were constructed in a very simple manner and were almost indistinguishable from ordinary houses and village buildings in rural China. Bao Ruowang noted about Chadian Farm: "The overall effect of our camp was that of a nineteenth-century factory or mill."[224] The Qinghe state farm (Chadian) obviously was a model camp; many other camps in more remote regions did not even look like factories but at maximum resembled "an impoverished village."[225] They consisted of run-down, ill-maintained, and filthy barracks made of mud clods. As Zhang Xianliang recollected: "The compound of the camp looked very much like that of an old 'mule shed' in north-west China. . . . There were cart tracks everywhere, also undried gobs of spit and traces of urine. Every corner reeked of the stench of human livestock."[226]

In the Chinese Laogai system, the staff employed in the labor camps had to fulfill functions that went far beyond the role of the staff in the Republican prisons. Apart from guards and officers who were charged to watch over the prisoners and promote thought reform, there was also a camp administration that in many locations was kept separate from the officers. This administration was responsible for the organization and coordination of camp operations as well as record keeping. Large camps employed a large number of personnel, often reaching into the hundreds.

The staff of a labor camp was organized along military lines. This is one of the features that clearly demonstrate the impact of military ideas on the Laogai's mission.[227] The highest organizational level was that of a Laogai detachment *(laogai dadui)*. These were complete entities unto themselves, each with its own administration that managed financing, production, sales, and cost accounting. A detachment could comprise an entire camp complex encompassing several separate camps. A detachment chief and a political commissar were in charge of all operations of the detachment. The second level in the administrative hierarchy was the station *(zhan)*. The station was tantamount to an individual camp. It was led by a station commander *(zhanzhang)*, who supervised daily operations. In some cases the *zhanzhang* acted as battalion commander, looking after roll calls and directing the station leaders.[228] Below the level of the detachment we also find battalions *(zhongdui)*, which had on average several thousand prisoners. The battalion was led by a battalion commander, a political commissar, several "disciplinary cadres," and administrative personnel. A battalion was composed of eight to twelve brigades, each headed by a brigade leader *(duizhang)* and an instructor *(jiaodaoyuan* or *zhidaoyuan)*. The brigade leader was a prison or Laogai officer and he had to deal with the prisoners on a daily basis, supervising their routine activities. A brigade had on average 150 to 200 prisoners and three to five armed guards. Finally, squadrons were the lowest organizational level. Ten to fifteen squadrons or teams formed a brigade.

For the prisoner, the squadron was the most important unit. It was the basic unit in which he spent his entire "career" as an inmate of Laogai. Issues of labor, criticism and study, and distribution of food, living space, and basic goods were all decided collectively by the squadron. The squadron was usually led by two prisoners who were appointed by the staff. The squadron leader *(zuzhang)* was responsible for the squadron's labor production and for overseeing thought reform. He was assisted by a second prisoner, the secretary *(shuji)*.

Officers and guards in the Laogai seldom wore uniforms. In most facilities uniforms were simply unavailable, for both the staff and the prisoners. Seen from the outside, distinctions between staff and prisoners were far from obvious.[229]

The camp administration consisted of the so-called Laogai offices *(laogai dangju)*. This term referred to three levels in the official hierarchy: head office, station command, and company command.[230] The head office, or headquarters, was at the top of the official camp administration and was run by a camp director *(changzhang)*, who was assisted in the execution of his duties by the camp administration *(changbu)*.[231] Like elsewhere in socialist China, however, the party committee was the most powerful body.[232] The head of the party committee in charge of Laogai was the Laogai farm party secretary, who according to military jargon was also called political commissar. In some cases he held the office of the camp director as well. The camp administration was understood as being responsible for organizational and technical issues, the real leadership was assumed to fall to the party committee. The existence of party committees secured the party's control over the Laogai system. Laogai, in the end, was understood as a predominantly political system rather a technical or administrative one. The political commissar was always and by default the real source of authority in a labor camp.[233] This was also clearly expressed in the privileges he was seen to enjoy. At the Qinghe state farm, he resided together with his family in a two-story villa surrounded by a lush wine garden.[234]

The camp administration was structured into departments *(ke)*, each of which was run by a department head.[235] There were departments for food supply, hygiene and health, production, transport, arrivals and departures of prisoners, family visits, communications, and the like.[236] There were also a number of political cadres who were responsible for thought reform and the supervision of prisoners' political behavior.[237] One of their duties was to control all the prisoners' incoming and outgoing correspondence. Along with their food, sleep, and work, the camp also controlled the prisoners' communications and contacts with the outside world. The political cadres decided how many letters or packages, if any, a prisoner was permitted to receive. Their decisions hinged on their evaluation of the prisoner's behavior and on general instructions by the provincial Public Security Bureau.

The most crucial post in the staff hierarchy was certainly that of the brigade leader *(duizhang)*. The brigade leader was the lowest level of supervisory staff to work directly with the prisoners. His duties were multifold and challenging. Tasks included everyday supervision of the prisoners, the maintenance of discipline and control, and coordination of production and work; above all, he was expected to actively promote thought reform and reeducation among the inmates. In theory, the brigade leader was a generalist and was responsible for all aspects of the prisoners' life. He was supposed to assign work, examine and supervise, punish those who were laggards and reward those who performed well. He also was expected to offer help and advice to the prisoners for problems in daily life and, moreover, to act as a role model. He had to combine the task of punishing and disciplining with a more therapeutic and advisory function. Failure or success of the overall Laogai mission depended above all on the ability of the brigade commander.

Bao Ruowang recalls his conversation with a brigade commander who turned out to be a very benign person. His name was Chao, and he addressed prisoner Bao at their first meeting with the following words: "I am here to help you undergo reform, but all I can do is reason with you. The fact that you had bad ideas and committed crimes means that we have to see to it that you start getting good ideas and never sin again. If you ever have any problems—ideological, political or whatever—come and see me and we'll talk them over. My door's open twenty-four hours a day. Come even at midnight if you have to. No problem. That's my job."[238]

In a certain sense, Chao appears as an almost ideal example of a Laogai officer. What stands out here is the paternalistic aura that characterized this impeccable brigade leader. He, in the words of Zhang Xianliang, was "like a herdsman herding his sheep."[239] Bao Ruowang also stated in his memoir that this brigade leader exerted an immense influence on his attitude toward his imprisonment:

> Cynics will probably say that the kindness and consideration he displayed were only part of the ancient penal game of carrot and stick. Maybe. Maybe it was a well orchestrated plan. Maybe it was the classical Pavlovian approach. Call it what you like—but I assure you that it works. His decency after two years of pain and humiliation was absolutely inspirational. I was led to an admiration that bordered on love for that man and for the prison he represented. If that was brainwashing, then I am for it.[240]

Other prisoners reported about similar officers who deeply changed their attitudes toward reform through labor. In those cases, relationships of mutual respect and even friendship developed between the officers and their prisoners. Such fraternization was a by-product of the therapeutic, paternalistic mission that a brigade leader had to pursue, and in general fraternization was neither prohibited nor seen as obstructive.

But there are also reports about cruel and brutal brigade commanders, as in Zhang Xianliang's depiction of Commander Zheng. During work in the fields Zheng regularly used a rope, constantly swinging it and hitting everyone he saw in order to drive prisoners to work.[241]

From the political commissars to the armed guards, most personnel working in the labor camps had earlier served in the PLA.[242] The Laogai staff overwhelmingly consisted of demobilized soldiers. A labor camp was not only organized according to military patterns but also staffed by military personnel. Moreover, almost all cadres of officers came from peasant households. This was as much related to the official policy to promote "learning from the peasants" as it was to the necessity of using poorly educated rural people and demobilized soldiers who could not find any other adequate employment. The peasant cadres rarely received any formal education, much less any special training that would have prepared them for their task of dealing with prisoners and fostering rehabilitation or reform.[243] It is not surprising, then, that "they certainly lacked the necessary skills for managing large numbers of convicts."[244] It is undeniable that the military background of the Laogai staff had implications for their attitude toward their job and the prisoners. First of all, many had fought in the war against Japan and in the civil war. They had long since become attuned to violence and death. Moreover, having suffered from enemy attacks in battle, they harbored feelings of resentment and even revenge against persons or subgroups that were labeled enemies of the people. On average their notion of Laogai was likely to be more punitive than therapeutic.

All in all, the position of the brigade commander was a highly ambivalent one and nobody captured this more clearly than Zhang Xianliang: "Almost all leaders with whom I had direct contact stood before us as the heads of one large family. . . . No matter how absurd the lesson they might be administering, or how bitterly painful the method of reform, we had the vague impression that someone was warmly caring for us even as we endured the physical and mental trauma."[245]

The inmate society in the labor camps was fundamentally shaped by two factors. First, it was hierarchically structured according to a formal classification system applied by the staff. Second, duty prisoners were deployed to act as power brokers between the prisoners and the staff. Both factors affected the makeup of different categories of prisoners. Each category had a different status within the inmate society, had different resources at its command, and was on different terms with the staff. The different categories of prisoners often competed with each other, while within the categories solidarity and friendship prevailed. The prison society in the camps was highly segmented and full of tension. The social structure determined social relations within the camps and thus had a great impact on everyday life in the Laogai.

The official classification system generated basically two categories of prisoners. The first category was made up of prisoners still belonging to the ranks of the people, while in the second category were those prisoners whose crimes were so severe that they were regarded as "enemies of the people." This reflected a fundamental distinction between criminal offenses and offenses that were harmful to the state and society. Most criminal offenses and some others belonged to the category referred to as contradictions within the people. Many of the so-called rightists, for instance, had committed offenses in this category. Rightists were those who came into conflict with certain party policies such as rural collectivization, the Great Leap Forward, and the various mass campaigns and movements. In contrast, serious political offenses constituted a contradiction between the enemies and the people. This category included offenses committed by historical counterrevolutionaries (GMD cadres, rich landlords, and rich peasants) as well as war criminals, POWs, and secret service agents.[246] The distinction had consequences for the status of a prisoner. Prisoners were not supposed to be treated equally but according to their status as either one of the people or an enemy of the people. Enemies of the people were deemed counterrevolutionaries who ought to be punished severely. Their status was lower than any offenders who still belonged to the ranks of the people.

The classification of inmate society had consequences for the treatment of inmates. Food rations were determined on the basis of the classification, as were work assignments.[247] Laogai prisoners also were more likely to be sent to places far away, while Laojiao prisoners could hope to be kept in the vicinity of their hometown.

Some labor camps detained only inmates sentenced to Laogai; others took in only those sentenced to the administrative punishment of Laojiao. Perhaps 20 percent of the labor camps were exclusively dedicated to conducting Laojiao. Most camps, however, actually kept both Laojiao and Laogai inmates and organized them in separate companies or brigades. In theory, Laogai inmates were as a group considered enemies and therefore should have received harsher treatment than Laojiao inmates, who were still considered as part of the people.[248]

Common criminals were those inmates who had been convicted of felonies and misdemeanors such as theft, robbery, deception, and so on. As their status in the official hierarchy was higher due to their mostly "red" class background as workers or peasants, the criminals in Chinese prisons and camps were used to bully and control the political prisoners. In the first years of the PRC many urban criminals were arrested as part of the consolidation effort of the new authorities. Common criminals therefore constituted a considerable part of the prison population at that time. Afterward their numbers in prison diminished and remained quite small throughout the first decade of the PRC. Beginning with the Great Leap Forward, the number of young male adults convicted of common crimes rose again, and the share of common criminals in the prison population as a whole jumped from 35 to 60 percent.[249] After that, common criminals continued to make up at least half of the prison population. In the late 1960s and the 1970s their percentage of the prison population grew again, and by that time most of the prisoners were uneducated young men coming from urban China.

Another category in the labor camp population was the group of "free convicts" *(ziyou fan),* who had the most ambivalent status.[250] As the name implies, they lived in constant limbo: their position was in between that of a citizen and a prisoner. On the one hand, they had been officially released from the labor camp and therefore were regarded as "free" rehabilitated citizens, but on the other hand, they were still under the stigma of having been a convict who had committed a crime and were still regarded as being in need of education and surveillance. Although the state did not keep a separate criminal record, convictions were entered in the household registry (a register of all households and their members).[251]

Free convicts lived in buildings outside the camp compound, received regular wages, and were also allowed to bring their family to join them or to marry. They could not, however, move back to their original place of residence. While still associated with the prison camp, they had certain resources at their disposal that normal prisoners did not. Free convicts remained fully under the control and supervision of camp authorities. They had to work in special camp brigades formed by job placement personnel, and as before, when they were convicts, they were supposed to participate in study sessions and political education. Although the group of free convicts had completed their term, they were still regarded as having to continue the reform process. They were supposed to keep on studying and examining themselves and therefore were to remain under the surveillance of the labor camp for an indeterminate time.

One of the most distinctive characteristics of Laogai was the use of prisoners to control other prisoners. Each squadron had one or two duty prisoners who still belonged to the group of prisoners but worked for the staff. While they still had to serve out their term and fully participate in labor reform, they also represented the staff for enforcing discipline and control.

The most important position was that of the squadron leader. One can identify the position of squadron leader or team leader in all Laogai facilities, prisons, and detention centers, all over China. The squadron leader was as a rule appointed by the brigade commander. His tasks were many, but in general he was fully responsible for his group, or squadron. He had to supervise the other prisoners, ensure that the squadron complied with the daily schedule and fulfilled its work quotas, and conduct thought reform. Many camps also selected one prisoner in each squadron to serve as squadron secretary. The secretary had to take notes about the study meetings and criticism sessions and document the daily work progress.[252] Responsibility entailed accountability. When theft, sabotage, or disturbances in a group occurred, the Laogai officers would hold the group leaders accountable. The group leaders had to point out the wrongdoer or suffer the punishment themselves.

There was also a group of special prisoners or favorite prisoners in the labor camps. They were nicknamed the "running dogs."[253] They worked for the staff in various positions, for instance by doing clerical work or acting as helpers. Camp physicians, too, were recruited from among the prisoners, as was the nursing staff.[254] These were envied and prestigious positions among prisoners, since they meant exemption from hard physical work. In general, all these positions carried with them certain privileges, which also made them so covetable. Such privileges differed from place to place. They could be better food rations, less hard work, and in some cases even early release. In general, the living conditions of these inmates were better that those of the average prisoner, and therefore in times of hardship they were, as Zhang Xianliang had put it, "less likely to die."[255] In any case, the benefits of these positions were regarded as important and the authorities had no trouble finding convicts to serve as duty prisoners.

Differential treatment in the Laogai was a source of conflict and strife. The duty prisoners had power over their coprisoners, and they could use their position to put the screws on the others. One of the most terrifying aspects of the Laogai for the inmates was the recognition that tribulation and victimization were not so much inflicted by the staff as by fellow inmates. As almost all reports indicate, feelings of rivalry and competition among inmates ran high. Two factors contributed to this situation. First, camp society was marked by a great degree of deficiency. Almost all everyday goods needed for subsistence, from food to fuel for fires, were in scarce supply. Second, prisoner society in the Laogai was marked by inequality and social tension. The tension was encouraged and nurtured by the staff. In fact, to avoid fraternization among prisoners, all squadrons were regularly reorganized.

Many inmates reported that deep splits and much friction existed between criminals (belonging to the people) and the so-called enemies of the people—that is, intellectuals and educated prisoners. Pu Ning wrote that living "with ten strangers in a cage-like Communist prison cell was not unlike living on the top of the crater of an active volcano."[256] The enemies of the people were well educated and had held important positions in civilian life, but the prisoner classification system in the Laogai degraded them to the lowest status in the camp. Some positions in the camp were off-limits to them. In contrast, criminal convicts came from the lower echelons of society but enjoyed a higher prestige in prison because of their working-class ("red") background. Strong prejudices and social contempt existed on both sides. Liu Zongren received the following advice from one fellow prisoner, who was the son of a high-ranking cadre and was imprisoned for his criticism of Jiang Qing: "Don't mess with those street thugs. . . . They are social scum. . . . The shame of mankind. Their only chance for reform is hard labor."[257]

In the world of a labor camp, prestige and status could be translated into concrete material advantages. This in fact was a major factor that fueled tension between the various groups of prisoners. The camps were short of space, food, water, fuel, clothes, tools, and instruments. These things therefore all became objects of intense competition among inmates, leading to ruthless and reckless behavior, according to Pu Ning: "To be polite and orderly and cultured is to be scoffed at, even trampled upon, treated as a fool. Since you found yourself living in a cage, it behooved you to act as a caged animal. Without some beastliness, some wildness, you couldn't survive."[258] The daily necessity to struggle for vital goods isolated prisoners from each other. Prisoners who failed to compete successfully were more likely to contract illnesses and suffer malnutrition and even starvation.

Theft was widespread in the camps. When a group left for the work site, the barracks had to be locked to prevent theft. Everything that was unattended was stolen: food, cigarettes, and personal belongings, if they appeared to be worth any money.[259] Everything had to be guarded and, in turn, nobody could be trusted. On several occasions the latent rivalry between prisoners broke out into the open. Food distribution regularly was one such occasion, for food was always in short supply. The constant hunger in the Laogai camps gave rise to beatings, fights, and robberies over food. To deal with this problem, each group appointed its most trusted prisoner to serve as food distributor.[260] He had the task of dividing up the available food among the prisoners of the squadron.

Work performance was another reason for clashes among inmates. If the daily work quota was not fulfilled, the whole squadron would be criticized and, in the long run, would face various disadvantages. To avoid such consequences as reduced food rations for the squadron, groups would single out certain prisoners, declare them to be responsible for the failure to meet the quota, and hand them over to the brigade commander for punishment. "This," wrote Zhang Xianliang, looking back at life in the camp, "was the general rule: our leaders would put us in a position in which it was impossible to have any solidarity, and then they would exhort us to 'unite.'"[261]

Thought reform or ideological reeducation was at the center of the official mission of Laogai.[262] Study sessions were to last no less than one hour a day. Prisoners were supposed to participate in political courses, industrial labor training, work competitions, cultural programs, discussion sessions, reading classes, and even optional sports activities, as well as talks involving their living conditions, work, and studies.

In the everyday operation of a Laogai institution, the staff regularly deployed a variety of techniques to pursue thought reform with the inmates. Thought reform consisted of several basic elements: the first was confession, which stood at the beginning of the moral path of a Laogai inmate. Confession was brought about through self-examination. Mostly this was undertaken at the detention centers, before inmates were transferred to a labor camp. In the labor camps, thought reform had two more elements: political study and criticism sessions.

Soon after their arrest, prisoners were called on to write self-examinations *(fanxing zichuan)*.[263] The self-examination had two functions. While it served to deliver a confession of the crimes that an offender had committed, it went well beyond that and became a critical reflection on the prisoner's whole life. The prisoner would start from early childhood and cover his whole life before his arrest. POWs, war criminals, and high-profile political prisoners often were asked to provide chronological charts of their official and private lives that listed all important events for every year and every month.[264] In this, the self-examination resembled a full and detailed autobiography in which the prisoner was supposed to reflect on the life he had led before his arrest. The goal of the self-examination was to demonstrate to the offender where exactly were the hidden reasons and remote origins of his transgressions: "Their aim is not so much to make you invent nonexistent crimes, but to make you accept your ordinary life, as you led it, as rotten and sinful and worthy of punishment, since it did not concord with their own, the police's conception of how a life should be led."[265]

Self-examination meant reexamining one's entire life with the goal of expounding where mistakes were made and what was done right. The goal was to produce a clear acknowledgment of one's errors and crimes and, at the same time, to highlight the hidden origins of the crimes in one's habits or wrong beliefs. Self-examination was seen as a prerequisite for thought reform. According to CCP crime theory, crimes were caused by wrong thinking, which was acquired through an offender's social background.[266] By acknowledging these relationships in one's own life, one took the first step toward reform.

The prisoner's self-examination was verified by an officer. The self-examination served as the basis for the next step, the interrogations. The first version of a self-examination was usually judged insufficient and sketchy. Pressure and coercion were used on inmates who would not comply or cooperate, with tactics ranging from threats to the use of shackles and handcuffs to solitary confinement.[267] In general, prisoners were informed that refusal to fully cooperate would result in harsh treatment and long sentences, while compliance would be rewarded by light sentences. After the completion of their first self-examination during confinement in the detention center, prisoners were asked to write a second self-examination only if they committed another infraction in the camp or prison.

Political study meetings *(xuexihui)* were conducted on a regular basis in the camps and prisons. Their frequency depended on local conditions. If there was a lot of work to do, political study meetings were scheduled only once a week. But in the winter or at other times when there was less to do, political study was carried out daily in meetings lasting two to three hours. At the meetings, political texts were collectively read and debated, including articles from the *People's Daily,* selected texts by Mao Zedong, and the writings of Marx, Engels, Lenin, and Stalin. Important speeches by party leaders were also read. Almost every prisoner, for instance, was familiar with Mao's "On the People's Democratic Dictatorship" and "On Correctly Handling Contradictions among the People," and with Liu Shaoqi's May Day address from 1950, in which he praised physical labor and described its historical significance. Communist leaders believed that the study of these texts would instill new norms and values and provide a new moral framework for the remaking of the prisoner's personality.

Political study meetings often also served as a forum for discussing more practical issues such as production goals, work attitudes, and work efficiency.[268] On most occasions, however, no cadre was present at the study meetings. Without official guidance and control, it appears that political study sessions were rarely undertaken earnestly and with attention to content. Liu Zongren noted: "We were supposed to use the time for reading and discussing the 'Quotations from Mao Zedong,' but no one said very much. We just sat there."[269]

A very important element in the whole process of thought reform was criticism. Criticism and self-criticism served to expose wrong worldviews and debunk false lifestyles. We can distinguish between two forms: public criticism in front of a large audience and criticism conducted in sessions attended by small groups. Criticism sessions conducted in small groups had the character of group therapy. The small group, whether it was a Laogai squadron or a prison cell, was supposed to help its members uncover their socially undesirable attitudes and habits. There were different kinds of meetings, such as "meetings for the investigation and discussion of lifestyle" *(shenghuo jiantao hui)*, "meetings for the evaluation of thinking" *(sixiang pingbi hui)*, and the "criticism and struggle meeting" *(pidou hui)*. As described by Zhang Xianliang, a meeting for the discussion of one's lifestyle took place in the following way: "In each small group on Sunday evening, convicts would sit cross-legged on their bunks, and, like true believers, confess their sins. They would tell their mistakes they had committed during the week, mistakes they now regretted."[270] A prisoner could also come forward and point out mistakes committed by a coprisoner. The group would then go on and discuss his problems. In general, the officers emphasized over and over again that every person had to "hand over"—expose—his own thinking.

The therapeutic character of the meetings could quickly give way to punitive and violent treatment of those accused of having committed an error. The criticism and struggle sessions were the most severe. Prisoners also called them the "heat treatment."[271] Prisoners or group members who were accused of crimes could be subjected to the heat treatment several evenings in a row. Every member of the squadron had to utter criticism and yell accusations. Many eye-witnesses and victims also reported physical abuses such as beatings and the use of shackles and handcuffs. But even without violent treatment, many prisoners dreaded the experience of being publicly criticized and humiliated and feared becoming a target. The criticism sessions served the staff well as a way to force prisoners to adhere to the norms and rules of thought reform.

Struggle sessions or struggle meetings were conducted as forums for publicly denouncing counterrevolutionaries. They were first used during the Land Reform Movement and were deployed in subsequent campaigns in the 1950s, too. Thereafter the use of public struggle sessions ceased until the Cultural Revolution, when they were revived in the form of sumptuously staged events that drew large crowds. These spectacles were meant to demonstrate "persecution at the hands of the masses." Prisoners were specially transported to these events, where they were humiliated and beaten in public. The former vice president Bo Yibo had to undergo two or three criticism and struggle sessions a day, each held in front of a large crowd, during which he regularly was mistreated and suffered serious injuries. In prison he wrote:

> The "struggle" today not only gave me a headache and made me feel dizzy and faint, but resulted in terrible pain in my wrists and in my arms. They were so painful I am unable to lift my hands and arms. In regard to suffering these kickings and beatings and humiliation, . . . at first I thought all that was perhaps just a matter of some misunderstanding that they had against me, and it wasn't much to withstand such torment. However, after what happened today, I am beginning to see that the Party's policy seems to be changing, that it intends to use this method to bring you down entirely.[272]

Criticism and self-examination were linked to an elaborate system of punishment and reward, and it was this that turned criticism and thought reform into potent tools. A prisoner who was repeatedly criticized was likely to be punished sooner or later, but a prisoner who frequently exposed the mistakes and wrong attitudes of a coprisoner could hope to be rewarded. The squadrons regularly made lists of those inmates who had rendered meritorious service and were due to receive a mention or a reward.[273] Rewards were better food rations, the right to receive packages and visits from family, appointment to the position of squadron leader, and early "graduation"—that is, release from prison before a sentence was completed. It was in the hands of the camp leadership to determine when a prisoner was to be released. Camp leaders would use a roll call to announce that a certain prisoner had graduated owing to his good behavior and meritorious service.[274]

The prisoners were also supposed to administer rewards and punishments themselves, by making proposals and recommendations to the brigade commander. Many inmates considered this one of the most distressing aspects of the Laogai, for it tended to isolate prisoners from one another and created tensions between them. Each cellmate was asked to assess the others and on that basis vote for who should receive a reward or a punishment. The objects of the assessments varied. Sometimes the work performance was judged, at other times political attitudes were the main target. Bao Ruowang described a meeting that assessed the prisoners' work performance and decided on everyone's food ration:

"My name is Bao Ruo-wang," I began in the proper form. "I am here for counterrevolutionary activities. The government has assigned me to folding book leaves and at present I am on the light duty ration. Since I am now up to 4,500 or 5,000 leaves a day and since I don't think I'll be able to reach the target set by the government in the near future, I guess I should stay on my light ration." Two cellmates briefly commended me for my positive attitude in continuing work while I was in pain from my boils, but it was too much to expect that I would get off without negative comment. Citizens are supposed to criticize each other; prisoners even more.

"Bao Ruo-wang has been commendable in his attitude," someone piped up, "but we must remember that rations are not awarded on the basis of attitude alone. His production figures are low. Two weeks from now, if he doesn't make it to the target, the warder will probably punish him. So wouldn't we look bad if we voted him such high rations now?" Even worse was to come. It was a guy named Liu, a real sour bastard. Liu loved to talk for the record; and he had a high voice to boot—the classical shithead. "I think Bao should be demoted," he squeaked. "He's always making funny remarks. Does he think he's in a hotel? He's here to be punished, not to enjoy himself. He came here in the middle of February and we're now almost into May. Should he still be eating light rations? That's a waste of government food. It's shameful. He probably thinks he can just coast along and still get well fed. There are other prisoners who just arrived 3 months ago and are already up to six or seven thousand leaves a day."[275]

In the end the cell voted to keep Bao Ruowang's ration unchanged. Thereafter the vote of the cell went to the brigade commander, who could confirm or modify it.

Solitary confinement was a punishment imposed by camp staff for the most severe infractions of camp rules. Such a punishment was usually determined by Laogai head office.[276] During solitary confinement, reduced food rations were also given to the prisoner (because he did not work). Lighter forms of punishment were handcuffs and shackles.[277] They were employed to deal with lesser breaches of prison or camp discipline, such as planning to escape, planning for violence, disobedience, resisting reform, and the like. The time span for wearing cuffs and shackles depended on the prisoner's attitude. Punishments and rewards both functioned as modes of social organization by virtue of defining and reinforcing desirable behavior.[278]

Work, of course, was a central function of most reform-through-labor facilities. Work was supposed to have a twofold impact on the inmates: to educate and to produce. Most of the inmates' time went to labor and production; it was their main occupation. Daily life in the camps was organized around labor, and the prisoners' fate often depended on how well they worked. It is, however, difficult to generalize what work in the Laogai was all about. Work varied immensely between the camps and also within individual camps. The range of labor activities within the Laogai system was as broad as the specific work assignments that were given to a prisoner within a single camp.

Daily working hours varied from eight to twelve hours, depending on the season and the climate where the camp was located. During the Great Leap Forward the working hours were extended to twelve to sixteen hours. Prisoners had to work in plantation fields, in mines, and in factories, as well as on housing and construction sites. They also had to unload goods, pick vegetables, and work in camp kitchens and hospitals. Unofficially they also worked as clerks and assistants for camp directors or brigade commanders.

Most of the time work was not meant to cause prisoners to suffer, or to be more precise, it actually did not matter whether or not the prisoners suffered. Far more important for the camp administration was the prisoners' daily compliance with the production targets. Work quotas could be anything: a certain number of folded book leaves, or ditches dug, an area to be cleared of weeds, an amount of coal to be hauled. Greatest emphasis was placed on the fact that the daily quotas or norms were fulfilled. Each squadron was given work norms according to their physical state. Groups with weak or older prisoners had lighter quotas than groups with younger and stronger prisoners.[279] The squadron leader or his assistant, the secretary, had to report daily to the camp officers about the exact amount of work that had been completed. In many camps, and especially during the Great Leap Forward, work quotas were almost impossibly high. Laogai officers pressed inmates hard to fulfill the quotas and many inmates had to struggle to do so.

By and large, Laogai prisoners described their physical labor as difficult but also satisfying. Working outdoors in fields and vegetable plots could be a rewarding experience. The fact that through manual labor the inmates were able to produce crops gave them a feeling of achievement and self-affirmation. Apart from that, insofar as good work performance could lead to better treatment and an increase in food rations, labor was a calculable and stabilizing rational factor in an otherwise highly unstable and fluid environment. Harry Wu took notice of the many functions of labor: "I had come to understand that in China's prison system, labor is simultaneously considered an obligation, a punishment, and a reward. You have to admit your crimes, demonstrate the willingness to reform your thoughts, and show you have accepted discipline before you earn the privilege of work. During the month of initial detention, I had to prove my obedience. After that I could be assigned to labor to proceed with my reform."[280]

Most of the time, labor in China's camps was simple physical work to be performed by hand without the use of machinery or even tools. It consisted of a series of uniform physical motions that were repeated over and over again. It is the routine of performing identical sequences of action and the identical daily workflow that surface in many reports. This routine could be unobtrusive, yet numbing and dulling. Yang Jiang described her daily work on a vegetable plot: "The vegetable plot was the center of my daily activity, and in that respect, I was like a spider who had settled there to spin a web all around her; several trifling observations and ephemeral emotions were trapped in this web of mine."[281]

Adverse conditions, however, could quickly destroy the normalcy of labor and turn physical labor into physical suffering. Overlong working hours, malnutrition, or an inhospitable environment could make work difficult and tormenting. Consider, for instance, the account by Zhang Xianliang, who describes how ordinary fieldwork caused physical hardship and illness, for overlong work hours made otherwise normal and harmless activities hard to bear. Zhang recalled how prisoners had to pull weeds in rice paddies "from before sunrise to the time the moon came up. If it was a particularly bright moonlit night, . . . then we would just keep on pulling."[282] Prisoners had to stand in the "mud soup" of the rice fields for twelve, fourteen hours a day, every day, without interruption. Many inmates contracted rashes on their legs, which often developed into painful skin inflammations.

There are cases where labor tended to waste and destroy prisoners. A very shocking report comes from Han Weitian. He was working in a Laogai brigade that was charged with constructing a highway from Xining to Tibet. Working at an altitude of 2,000 meters, the extremely rough terrain and freezing temperatures made work painful and unbearable:

> All of us were freezing. Our hands were so stiffened that we were not able to hold the pickaxes or shovels any longer. The legs of the older ones were so stiff that they could no longer stand on their feet. Some forty of them fell down pitiably like scarecrows swept down by a strong wind. . . . These men, along with other officials, celebrities, and professors of former times, were . . . sentenced to "reform by labor" for fifteen years, or for life.
>
> Guards were rushing here and there, cursing and chiding us with white leather lashes. They plied the meter-long weapons against the raw flesh of those who had passed out and dared to "lie down and rest." Some guards even drew out thick sticks and used them indiscriminately on the prisoners' heads. Blood dripped down to redden the white snow. This treatment, however, did not make the fallen ones rise to their feet. I saw them lying still on the ice, not uttering a cry under the sting of the lash. Their nerves, central and peripheral, felt nothing. They seemed purposely to refuse to revive, after they had been so "unnerved."[283]

This report illuminates some of the atrocities that could occur in the Laogai. It documents one admittedly extreme and not necessarily representative end of the labor spectrum; on the other end of this broad spectrum was ordinary farm work, for most Laogai facilities were agricultural farms. But even there hunger, weakness, or weather could give rise to similar devastating conditions. Throughout the Laogai, even starving and emaciated prisoners were ordered "work hard, work bitterly hard,"[284] although the work was often unproductive or futile.

In the overall calculations of the Laogai administrators, the pain and suffering of inmates ultimately were second to productivity and profitability. The ample availability of prisoners, who were swept into the camps in large numbers in the course of various campaigns and movements, made the individual prisoner easily replaceable and even dispensable. The camps could afford to waste the lives of their inmates in what often turned out to be overambitious and senseless projects. When inmates became too weak to work and died of exhaustion or sickness, nobody asked any questions and no inspections had to be feared. Soon the authorities would send new prisoners to replace the sick or deceased.

The exact size of the prison and camp population in socialist China has always been treated as a state secret. No reliable official data or reports have been published by the government. Therefore we have to rely on estimates to get an idea of the number of Chinese people imprisoned in Mao's China. For the early 1950s the number of 5 million prisoners is often mentioned. This count seems to be reliable and it appears in many sources. By the end of the 1950s and the beginning of the 1960s official sources frequently mention the number of 2,000 labor camps. Some of the camps did keep 20,000, 30,000 or even 40,000 prisoners, others only several thousand. Assuming a minimal average of 10,000 prisoners per camp, it seems plausible to estimate that China had at least 20 million prisoners by that time.[285] Thereafter there are no indications that the labor camp system was either substantially enlarged or reduced. Based on this cautious and conservative estimate, at least 5 to 7 percent of the Chinese population was imprisoned in labor camps. This number would fit well with Mao's estimate that the Chinese population was 5 percent counterrevolutionaries.

But this is just the tip of the iceberg. Only prisoners sentenced to more than five years were sent to Laogai camps. Prisoners with shorter terms were sent to prisons, detention centers, or the so-called labor reeducation (Laojiao) camps. These institutions are not included in the number of camps mentioned above. The number of short-term prisoners (sentenced in a simple procedure by the police rather than by courts or tribunals) is presumably higher than the number of convicts sent to the Laogai camps. It would push up the overall incarceration rate to more 10 percent of the population. In absolute terms it would mean that more than 40 million people had been incarcerated or in some other way deprived of their freedom.

The continuous enlargement of the labor camp system in the course of the 1950s and early 1960s presented the government with daunting difficulties in accommodating and feeding the many millions of prisoners. The situation was worsened by the unwillingness of the Public Security Administration to make expenditures for the camps. On the contrary, central authorities demanded profitable operations and budget surpluses. The inhumane and miserable conditions in the camps—exhausting work quotas, food deprivation, unsanitary living conditions—caused rampant disease among prisoners and drastically shortened life expectancies. Death rates were staggeringly high: it has been estimated that the death rates in the camps reached up to 10 percent annually during the years from 1959 to 1962. The total number of deaths in those four years was probably around 6 million.[286] Two million prisoners died in the period from 1949 to 1952, which also witnessed elevated death rates, and 2 million may have died in the period from 1953 to 1958, which was calmer. Altogether at least 10 million victims must have died in the PRC camps and prisons in the course of the 1950s as the result of executions, starvation, abuse, or disease. This number does not include the unknown millions who were executed or killed outside the camps, for instance during campaigns. While these figures may be inaccurate, we cannot ignore the fact that the estimates clearly point to mass violence and killing of mammoth proportions occurring in China in the 1950s and 1960s.

Voices from the Labor Camps

The voices of inmates constitute an essential and powerful source for the history of Laogai. Their testimonies touch on a variety of issues. There is considerable documentary knowledge, especially with respect to everyday life in the labor camps, that can be unearthed and used to complement other sources. Violence and death in the Laogai, frequently downplayed in other sources, are brought to the fore in the witness and survivor reports.

Imprisonment is described and represented as an extreme event that severed past from present. Other issues that survivors' accounts raise pertain to the role of memory and its lapses and, more generally, to the question of coming to terms with—or denying and repressing—the experienced past. Personal testimonies bring us closer to the experienced history of the Laogai and enable us to comprehend the human drama that unfolded within the barracks.

As we have seen, Laogai inmates were overwhelmingly preoccupied with work and reeducation. These activities certainly consumed most of their time. But there were cracks in the schedule in which inmates were granted rest and spare time. It was during those precious moments that a private sphere could unfold and inmates could attend to their own business. Most inmates spent their spare time in the search for means to improve their subsistence. They adopted various survival strategies, many of which have to be seen against the background of spatial compression that fundamentally marked living conditions in the camps.

Many inmates and witnesses told about the shortage of space in the camps. Beginning in the 1950s, the fast-growing number of prisoners deported to the camps had to be squeezed into the existing buildings and barracks. In the early years, a room was occupied by ten to fifteen inmates; later twenty and more prisoners had to share one tiny room. A steadily increasing tightness marked life in the labor camps. New arrivals were assigned a sleeping slot by the squadron leader, who commonly used a measuring stick of some sort to divide the sleeping space on the *kang* among the room's prisoners.[287] While in the 1950s each prisoner was on average allocated fifty centimeters of sleeping space, this was reduced to forty centimeters and, in the 1960s, finally to thirty centimeters.[288]

Given the serious overcrowding, it is no wonder that sanitary conditions were disastrous. Prisoners in most facilities in the countryside rarely took a bath or even changed their clothes. Lice were very widespread.[289] Food and drinking water were also often unclean and caused intestinal disorders and illnesses.

While overcrowding worsened living conditions in the camps, it also impeded the official mission of the Laogai. Even supervision and observation of the prisoners through record keeping was made difficult, if not impossible, by the often unchecked influx of people.[290] To begin with, only primitive paper made from rice stalks was used in the camps. On it, words were printed or written so poorly that they were hard to decipher. No detailed data were recorded as to which laws or regulations a prisoner had broken. Although the forms in the files included a space where a photo should be attached, this space was left blank in most of the camps' records because photographic equipment was unavailable. Since there were no photographs on file, inmates with the same name were often confused. It happened that "some people had died, but were still living according to their files. Others were living, but the files said they were dead."[291] It also often turned out that prisoners' birth dates and places were wrong. Far from being accurate, the prisoner files were mixed up and more often a source for confusion than for disciplinary observation.

Overcrowding and shortage of space were not simply undesirable by-products of a malfunctioning prison administration. The impact of these factors on the inmate culture can hardly be overstated. Most important in this respect was the creation of a mass society within the very narrow boundaries of the camps.[292] Inmates were amassed and confined to a very small space, which put them under constant physical pressure. At the same time it created a pervasive atmosphere of competition and struggle. Most survival strategies devised by inmates in the camps aimed at easing the effects of this pressure. Black markets, for example, could relieve the pressure by opening up alternative channels of distribution.

Deprivation caused rivalry and competition, but it also led to the emergence of very busy black markets in the camps. According to one of twenty-five regulations that covered camp discipline, cigarettes could not be exchanged or given away, and trading food and many other items was also prohibited.[293] However, in most camps flourishing black markets were based on such trade. Almost everything was traded, including salt, tobacco, fish, hot peppers, and corn.[294] Prisoners bartered personal belongings they had brought with them from home for food or cigarettes. A watch, for example, was exchanged for grain, a suitcase for five bowls of noodles, a tie for a radish, and so on. Families also sent prisoners money, cigarettes, and other things they could use for trading. The goods such as food were supplied by villagers who lived in the vicinity of the camp. Free convicts, who were allowed to leave the camp, were heavily involved in the black markets, smuggling goods into the camp and trading them with the prisoners. Free convicts also traded on behalf of camp guards, officers, and cadres.

The Laogai was a community based on control and supervision—by staff and prisoners alike—but like the Republican prisons, it could not foreclose recalcitrant behavior. While most inmates were forced to comply with the camp regime, rebellion and escape were nonetheless quite common. Almost every report and memoir describes some sort of insurgent behavior. Such reactions included intransigent refusal to accept the camp regime, sabotage, escape, and outright rebellion.

Intransigent rejection of Laogai policy is mentioned in many accounts. There were inmates who openly questioned the legitimacy and purpose of Laogai. Zhang Xianliang recollected the words of a Muslim prisoner who told him that he would "never ever be properly reformed."[295] Recently the tragic story of the writer Lin Zhao (1931–1968) has come to light. Imprisoned for writing a certain poem in 1960, Lin Zhao never stopped questioning the basis for her imprisonment and criticizing the rule of the Communist Party. She wrote letters to the authorities and to the *People's Daily,* using her own blood as ink. In her letters and prison writings she assaulted Mao as a new monarch and decried "the unprecedented persecution, abuse and repression" that the government had inflicted on China. She called herself a "resistance fighter" whose imprisonment was all but illegal. Possibly because of her continued resistance, she was executed in 1968.[296] A similar struggle was extolled by Ma Bo, who was imprisoned in 1970. He, too, wrote letters in blood denying the charges of the Public Security Administration that he was a counterrevolutionary. He challenged the grounds of his incarceration and sent numerous requests for review to various party and government offices.[297] He was eventually released, but it took him seven years to have his verdict overturned.

Because the walls surrounding many Laogai facilities were either low or crumbling and guards were inattentive, escapes were relatively easy to accomplish, and they did frequently occur. Holidays, in particular, were a time when inmates tried to escape. Prisoners dreaded the emptiness and loneliness of the holidays, which they used to spend with their families.[298] Refusal to work was also a rampant problem in the camps. Prisoners would simply lie down and refuse to work. This was called "playing dead dog."[299] The camp leaders had in fact only limited means to deal with this kind of rebellious behavior. They could use a rope to hit the prisoners or they could punish them (with solitary confinement). But when they did this, they often faced even stiffer resistance in the form of work slowdowns, destruction of camp facilities, or outright sabotage.

Many prisoners felt that the time they spent in the Laogai was wasted and empty. Yet there were also numerous cases in which prisoners assimilated themselves to the camp regime, cooperated with the prison administration, and seemingly accepted the official worldview. For example, many prisoners actively participated in the effort of the Laogai administration to expose other prisoners who had "faulty thoughts" or rejected the Laogai regime. In Wang Ruowang's report we meet, for instance, Inmate No. 1296, who tried to commit suicide by banging his head against a wall. The startled witnesses soon learned that this prisoner had collaborated with his interrogators out of fear and had incriminated his own wife. Guilt-ridden, he tried to do away with himself.[300] As numerous individual stories make clear, many prisoners followed the directives and implicated their own children, relatives, friends, and colleagues.

Like Wang Ruowang, Zhang Xianliang emphasizes that most prisoners did not reject the Laogai policy or the assumption of their own guilt. He writes:

> In the course of my twenty-two-year career in the camps, I rarely encountered convicts who did not cooperate with the system and with prison authorities from the start. . . . As for the majority of intellectual convicts, they carried a sense of guilt for the original crime that they may or may not have committed as well as guilt for newly discovered crimes for which they were now painstakingly reforming themselves. This great majority, I must say, included me. You will find no precedent in any history book of prison authorities and prisoners having such an intimate symbiosis.[301]

Erving Goffman called the phenomenon depicted by Zhang "conversion," which is a typical mode of adaptation to the setting of a total institution. The prisoner "appears to take over the official or staff view of himself and tries to act out the role of the perfect inmate."[302] Conversions in prisons or labor camps are an important tenet of Chinese penal treatment, as Zhang Xianliang seems to imply. In general, conversion is a goal of all institutions that aim at changing the inmates' sense of self. Many reports, such as the documents written by Emperor Pu Yi, former GMD leaders, and Japanese POWs that praise the authors' time spent in Chinese labor camps, can be explained as conversions.

Conversion is obvious when prisoners adopt the vocabulary, posture, and styles promoted by the staff. The Laogai institutions offered prisoners numerous opportunities to live up to a model of conduct that was "at once ideal and staff sponsored."[303] In fact, prisoners who succeeded in emulating this model in word and behavior were rewarded and could even hope to receive parole. The result, however, was a paradox, as pointed out by Zhang Xianliang. In the end, what we find is "a camp in a communist country that had incarcerated as enemies of communism people who, in fact, yearned for a true communist system."[304]

What comes through most clearly in the writings of many who were inmates in the Laogai is that what they actually encountered was not so much a process of remaking as one of deprivation and loss. The feeling of loss ran deep, and it surfaces time and again in the reports by survivors and witnesses. Yang Jiang, for example, spent more than two years in a "May 7 cadre school."[305] In her memoir she could not disregard the waste and futility of their "reform," which she saw in the dissonant relationship between intellectuals and the rural villagers who were supposed to teach them correct thought and attitude, and in the demolition of their camps when they moved: "On the eve of our departure, Mo-cun [Yang's husband] and I slipped over to the plot to take one last look around. The shed was gone, the well platform was gone, the irrigation ditches were gone, the vegetable beds were gone, and even the small mound of earth had disappeared from sight: all that was left was a piece of empty land strewn with clods."[306] It was as if the evidence of their work and their suffering had been wiped from the face of the earth. This sense of futility seized hold of the writer and created other dark moments in her memoir: "This often reminded me of a painting I had seen: an old man with a bag slung over his back and a cane in his hand walking step by step down a mountain path directly into his grave. That's pretty much how I felt about myself."[307] In Yang Jiang's case, reeducation was obviously obstructed by her feelings about the wasted time and the bitterness she endured. Even more outspoken is Li Xianlin. "What," he asks himself, "is my explanation [of labor reform]? With one word, my explanation is 'torture.'"[308] For him, Laogai during the Cultural Revolution was about nothing but tormenting people.

Hunger was a common experience in the Chinese prisons and labor camps; in fact, one has to understand hunger as a basic condition of life in the Laogai until 1978. At times the situation worsened because of bad harvests, but even apart from the period of famine known as the three bitter years (1959–1961), the food supply was always insufficient and hunger was widespread. However, as Gang Yue argues, the meaning of hunger "is never fixed but relative to historical contingencies and political needs."[309] Before 1949 the party often used reports about starving peasants to incite revolutionary violence against landlords. But the use of hunger that had given impetus to the revolution became, after 1949, a disciplinary means of keeping the new regime's subjects in line.

Starting in 1959, food supplies for the camps dropped off drastically. During the Great Leap Forward, prisoners were officially entitled to 250 grams of grain a day. Yet the amount the prisoners received was actually much smaller, since cadres and guards, along with doctors, civilian workers, and duty prisoners kept for themselves at least half of the food rations that were intended for inmates.[310] Zhang estimates that not more that 120 grams of grain a day reached the prisoners. As a result, large-scale starvation spread through the camps. Every prisoner was constantly looking for something to eat: "The need for food was not a localized, tangible, limited thing, but had become a supra-physical comprehensive spiritual quest. It was a kind of infinite need that transcended a real need. The feeling of hunger was particularly acute when chewing on a millet bun or pouring thin gruel down the throat."[311]

Hunger was a physical torment. Zhang Xianliang wrote: "Labor reform does not make a man lose all human feeling. Hunger does."[312] Moreover, this kind of hunger also fundamentally changed social relationships and, more important, wrecked the social self of the prisoners. In the words of Zhang Xianliang, it turned human beings "into wolves" or "automatons that gulped down whatever they could eat."[313]

Looking through the extant memoirs and reports concerning Laogai imprisonment, what immediately meets the eye is the frequency with which death in mentioned. It was an inherent part of life in the Laogai, though death rates varied considerably. Apart from the violent actions of guards or coprisoners, the factors that influenced death rates in Laogai camps were malnutrition, poor sanitation, harsh environment, and the unavailability of medical treatment. High death rates occurred during three periods: the early 1950s, the three bitter years (1959 to 1961, although the bitter years in the camps often lingered beyond 1961), and the Cultural Revolution. Death in the camps was not a uniform phenomenon. During each phase, the camps witnessed different manifestations of dying, caused by different factors.

When it occurred, death was an individual event, caused by violence or sickness. Living in a Laogai camp always took a relatively high toll among the prisoners. As we have seen, during their confinement prisoners were exposed to malnutrition and unsanitary conditions for great lengths of time. Hard physical labor and long working hours further contributed to physical exhaustion and a general weakening that made prisoners highly susceptible to all kinds of illnesses. Wu Hongda provides us with a vivid description: "Sometimes you catch a cold, your lungs fill with fluid, and finally you stop breathing. Sometimes bacteria in the food cause continuous diarrhea that leads to death. Sometimes infection from a wound becomes fatal."[314]

It has to be pointed out in this context that while abuse and maltreatment of prisoners certainly occurred and caused deaths, systematic torture is rarely mentioned by witnesses and survivors, and also seldom noted as a cause of death. Nobody, of course, can rule out the possibility that prisoners were occasionally tortured and abused, especially in some of the high-security prisons during the Cultural Revolution.

The early 1950s was a phase during which many stationary camps were set up and many more mobile camps were sent to distant regions to work at huge construction sites. These "pioneer brigades" operated in the various wastelands, deserts, and other hostile environments, often under very adverse conditions. Their Laogai inmates were charged with laying the foundations for future ambitious developments in the most inhospitable places. Prisoners were repeatedly called on to carry out a "holy task" and to strive to become modern-day Yugongs who would be able to move mountains.[315] In the Gobi Desert, for example, prisoners were summoned to construct a "new Shanghai." Elsewhere marshlands were to be transformed into lush and fertile farmland by prison laborers.[316]

All available reports indicate that the pioneer brigades were haunted by very high death rates that greatly exceeded the normal rates. One camp director openly admitted that "the first groups of convicts, who created the camp, had died in droves. 'Back then, hardship was real hardship. You'd see a man topple over, while he was gnawing on a steamed bun. You'd touch him and find he was dead.'"[317] A similar picture emerges from other witness reports:

After winter had fully set in, in the two or three months of repeated blizzards, no day would pass without a report of eight or ten deaths among the two thousand wretches that made up our "great team." I witnessed more than twenty deaths in my own group during this season. Those who died from cold and hunger usually passed quietly away, without disturbing others with groans or cries. They didn't even show any signs of pain. They just burned up their calories, became scrawny, and then yielded up body and mind. They were like big candles burning hour after hour; by the last hour everything combustible had disappeared, so they died very naturally. Comparatively fewer of us died while working on the roads. Perhaps working under the threat of death, we really became strange animals that had time only for fear and effort, or machines with motors running at full tilt. It was not until we ceased to work that we began to damp our fires and, thus, our lives. At first, it was sad to see or to hear of deaths. But after a while we saw so many die that death became a matter for indifference. After seeing so many disappear from our ranks, I found I could look at a new body just as if I were looking at a blank page in a book.[318]

The second phase that saw extremely high death rates was the period of the three bitter years, when a nationwide famine plagued China. The scarcity of food throughout the PRC resulted in mass starvations in the camps. It is true that during this period millions of Chinese citizens outside the camps died too, but one must be mindful of the fact that prisoners in the camps were more helpless than their counterparts at large. After years of hard labor under harsh circumstances and with insufficient food, most prisoners were already emaciated and weakened. When their food was reduced further, prisoners died one after another. Zhang Xianliang noted: "When I say death, I don't mean the one, two, three, four . . . who died beside me in the early days. I mean the multitude of dead who, when I was most unprepared for it and indeed just beginning to feel new hope, suddenly broke into my sense of touch and awareness."[319] The author recalled how, on one winter morning in 1960, he came upon two large carts full of corpses: "Men and women, they all were completely naked. Some of the skin had been slippery, like Chinese cabbage, some had been rough, rather like sweet potatoes. They were jumbled together, their limbs intertwined. Whether they had come originally from the five lakes or the four oceans, in the end they had bonded together here in an intimate mass of bodies."[320] Zhang's experience is no isolated case. Many similar horrendous impressions can be found in survivors' memoirs.

The third period marked by higher than normal death rates in the camps was the Cultural Revolution. While the food supply generally had improved, the emphasis on renewed class struggle during the Cultural Revolution led to an increase in violence. In the prisons and labor camps, this meant executions of counterrevolutionaries and class enemies were carried out to an extent not seen since the Movement for the Suppression of the Counterrevolution in the early 1950s. The relentlessness of this new political direction was clearly expressed in the slogans reported by Yang Xiguang: "Kill, kill, kill! Kill until the world is all red!" or "Kill, kill, kill until a bright, red world emerges!"[321] In 1970 the Strike One, Oppose Three Campaign was started, with the goal of striking down counterrevolutionaries and opposing common criminals, corruption, and waste. During this campaign the process for carrying out a death sentence was simplified. Provincial authorities were given the power to order and carry out executions on the spot without reporting to Beijing. Local authorities reportedly made ample use of their new powers and ordered many executions to get rid of "bad elements."

The witnesses and victims discussed in this chapter above all took Laogai to be a metaphor for a widespread social pathology. Their perspective transcended concerns of individual justice and reached out to contemplate the upset of a whole society in the 1950s, 1960s, and 1970s. Their memoirs tell us about the full-scale assault on certain target groups, through which a thorough purge of society was initiated. The reeducation of deviants was supposed to create a new society and a new man. But those efforts fell short and, more important, created suffering on a mass scale as a result of the political violence—suffering that for millions encompassed pain, anguish, fear, loss, grief, and the destruction of a coherent and meaningful reality.

The effects of the violence inflicted on Chinese society through the criminal justice apparatus were significant; they reached beyond the realm of politics and power struggles that tends to dominate Western historiography of the same period. Anthropologist Veena Das, who has studied various outbreaks of violence in India, argues that large-scale violence tends to affect the ordinary and the everyday in a profound sense. Not only does the physical dimension of violence matter but also the sense that one's context is lost—that in itself creates a sense of being violated. The experience of world-annihilating violence causes a failure of grammar and the end of criteria. Veena Das characterizes the consequences thus: "The fragility of the social becomes embedded in a temporality of anticipation since one ceases to trust that context is in place. The affect produced on the registers of the virtual and the potential, of fear that is real but not necessarily actualized in events, comes to constitute the ecology of fear in everyday life."[322] The labor camp system, the secretive universe of prisons and detention sites, and the chaotic multitude of peripheral Laogai sites all were essential factors in producing a climate of fear that became ever more deeply ingrained in socialist China. If the Laogai frequently failed in transforming and reeducating inmates, the system was very adept at generating terror and getting people to turn on one another.

Criminal Justice and the Revolutionary Transformation of Chinese Society

The Chinese criminal justice system in the period from 1949 to 1979 was marked by an eclectic mix of different approaches. One approach emphasized that law and the management of justice were instruments of class struggle, political mobilization, and social transformation. Either formally or informally, in court or out of court, China's socialist state regarded the criminal justice system as a powerful tool for social engineering and for the inculcation of values and norms. Criminal justice was supposed to become a dynamic force for social transformation, propelling China forward to the attainment of communism. It would help unleash the governing powers of the socialist state, and would safeguard and enforce initiatives and campaigns devised by the party headquarters. Party leadership regarding day-to-day operations and the formulation of guiding principles was therefore strictly enforced.

The second important approach to criminal justice was the one framing the legal system in terms of the distinction between friend and enemy.[323] As we have seen, this distinction was pervasive in the criminal justice system, on all levels and at all stages. The legal system operated almost exclusively according to this binary divide. The party's approach to criminal justice was based on the view that the class-struggle metaphor fully justified the implementation of differential treatment based on the friend/foe distinction. This was the basis for the intense radicalization and polarization that took place even after the victory of the revolution. Mao held that enemies of the people had no rights; rights were available only to the people (friends). The broad state powers that were invoked by the people's government to detain enemies and counterrevolutionaries were time and again challenged by courts and the procuracy. In the 1950s, in fact, there often was a courageous readiness on the part of the courts to challenge the administration's procedures. But all such attempts were ultimately crushed by mass movements aimed at eliminating judicial independence. Thereafter, no agency was left that could have prevented the ruling revolutionary elite from running roughshod over friends and enemies alike.

In practice, however, things also turned out to be more complicated. The crucial question was how to determine who was an enemy. The guidelines that the party set up were ambiguous: class-based categories were promoted next to more blurred categories, such as persons who had "historical questions" or a "backward political attitude." During the 1950s, standards of demarcation became even broader and more vague. Class and family background, political views and activities, past records, contacts with capitalists—all were examined by the state to determine whether a subject belonged to the people or to the enemies. In retrospect, we can see that the trajectory in the 1950s was toward greater vagueness and an increasing breadth of targeting for deportation, imprisonment, or execution. Multiple criteria were set up for inclusion in either category, friend or foe, along with sliding scales of basic rights. This system required constant judicial reassessment of who was outside and who was within the people, and frequent redrawing of the categories of citizens, fostering elaborate nomenclatures that distinguished among rightists, counterrevolutionaries, landlords, intellectuals, and the bourgeoisie. In the end, complex scales of differentiation and affiliation were produced that, while fundamentally based on a binary distinction, often escaped clear divisions. There was constant uncertainty about who actually belonged to the category of "enemy" and who could really feel he was safely a member of the people.

On a more practical level, the establishment of the revolutionary penal regime in the People's Republic also has to be seen in the context of regime consolidation in the new state. At issue was the capacity of the new state to deal with the many adversarial forces still operating within its boundaries. The concrete problems and challenges were threefold: to expand and consolidate central state control over the complex bureaucratic organization of an enormously large and considerably decentralized society; to suppress real and imagined political competitors and opponents in an extremely diverse and heterogeneous society; and win to over, or gain control over, the key social groups that commanded enough resources to impede or obstruct any essential initiatives of the central state. The new state resorted to two measures to accomplish these goals: mobilizing the population by conducting mass movements, and establishing an effective penal regime to identify, isolate, and reeducate hostile forces and groups.

In Mao's China, then, political and legal matters were determined and overridden by the perceived need to police and guard the binary distinction between friend and foe. It allowed the state and its agencies to declare provisional states of emergency and to temporarily suspend for certain groups "the right to have rights," as Hannah Arendt once put it. The socialist Chinese state operated as a "state of exception" that vigilantly produced exceptions to its principles and its laws. Carl Schmitt has defined sovereign power not as a monopoly on the power to punish or to rule but as the right to decide when laws are suspended and when they are not.

Overall, these discourses and the practices of exclusion and demonization allowed the Chinese state to enlist its own citizens to fight against the enemies within, to police themselves, and to protect the socialist order. The question of loyalty versus betrayal began to override concerns for transparency, accountability, and justice, opening up the way for violent excesses conducted and condoned by the state. The notion that socialism must be defended implied a moral right to annihilate those outside the socialist order. The discourse of struggle produced disenfranchisement, persecution, and internment: it ultimately also justified the liquidation of those deemed uncorrectable and dangerous to socialism.

Criminal justice in China after 1949 was riddled with ambiguity. While it was a system and a process officially committed to social justice and equality, over time it caused established categories and moral values to collapse, thus creating an ambivalent moral vacuum. Through mass campaigns and regular court proceedings, many millions were attacked, criticized, arrested, and made to disappear. The process drew everybody in; nobody was allowed to remain a mere bystander. An inconceivably large number of people died in the Laogai camps in the name of reform through labor; most survivors were seriously injured, physically or psychologically. Laogai became the locus of one of the major humanitarian catastrophes of the twentieth century.

The ambiguity of the Chinese criminal justice system made it susceptible to politically motivated manipulation. It also helps to explain why the system lacked internal barriers to prevent or even limit the catastrophe in the late 1950s and 1960s, when millions vanished into the system's prisons and labor camps. The lack of clarity and the existence of competing values and priorities opened up possibilities for blunt misuse. For a long time the criminal justice apparatus in socialist China was not used a means of crime control, but was wielded as a weapon with enormous clout. This weapon was frequently deployed against any persons who expressed dissent or dissatisfaction, thus imposing order and discipline—but only through a pervasive climate of terror and hopelessness.

CONCLUSION

T HIS STUDY has focused on the twisting history of Chinese criminal justice from imperial times until the end of the 1970s. The start of economic reforms and the opening up of China in 1978 marked a new turning point, not only for developments in politics, economics, and society but also for law and criminal justice. Since then, some of the currents this study has analyzed have been reversed. China altered its policy concerning crime control and the management of justice (although in some areas change was slower or not palpable at all), and a new criminal justice system gradually emerged, along with a new set of laws. The 1990s saw another wave of legislation and legal codification, much of which was related to criminal justice. After wrapping up the findings on the history of criminal justice in modern China, let us look to the future—to the outlook for criminal justice based on contemporary developments and the continued evolution of Chinese law.

Criminal Justice, State, and Society in China's Twentieth Century

It is almost commonplace to speak of the profound changes that took place in Chinese society in the course of the twentieth century. Many studies have discussed the pervasive transformations that China experienced—and is still experiencing today. Although most histories of modern China tend to overlook law and criminal justice in this context, transformations in these areas were equally significant.[1] Several profound shifts took place. The imperial criminal justice system was replaced by a modernized, Western-inspired system in the early decades of the twentieth century. The late 1930s saw an abrupt disruption and complete reversal of that reform effort, and civil criminal justice agencies were replaced by military bodies and secret services. In 1949, following its victory in the Chinese Revolution, the Chinese Communist Party established a functionalist and differential system of justice. This socialist system was almost from the beginning caught up in political struggles against enemies and was prone to violent excess. Finally, the grand failure of the first socialist system of justice and its collapse during the Cultural Revolution forced the Communist Party after 1978 to rethink and reform its administration of justice. The demands of increasing economic and social diversification, as well as the internationalization of China, made the creation of yet another system of justice indispensable.

The repeated efforts by successive Chinese governments to set up strong criminal justice systems demonstrate the increasingly important role that criminal justice played in building political capacity and regulatory control in twentieth-century China. At critical junctures in China's modern history, criminal justice lay at the heart of debates on the meaning of citizenship and the nature of inclusion and exclusion. Criminal justice was turned into an essential mechanism through which political identities were produced, ascribed, transmitted, and also resisted. It emerged as a significant context within which the paradox of governance in China was played out, and it formed the substance of efforts to construct new forms of community and political connectedness, to establish spatial integrity and social coherence. Overall, crime control and criminal justice are at the root of the modern project in China and how it was defined.

The history of criminal justice in China dates back to antiquity. Punishment is an archaic institution. However, while most other archaic practices eventually disappeared from Chinese thought and society, punishment as such persisted and was rarely questioned.[2] Professionals, officials, and power holders alike were concerned with the question of how to punish best, but rarely did they consider whether punishment itself was a useful and appropriate response to crime.

The durability of the institution of punishment attests to its power: a legal punishment is far more than an act of violence or vengeance; it constitutes the end of a complicated procedure aimed at examining and ordering an unruly world. Judging and punishing, then, are the terminal phases of a social drama that is repeated in myriad ways in the everyday world. The goal is to tame the very contingency of social life. Judgment and punishment bring to closure an unpredictable social reality.[3] Through the imposition of punishment, right and wrong are reestablished and restored. The judicial sentence rereads and interprets a fractured world according to the law, reaffirming coherence and ascribing order, validating norms and resurrecting meaning and thus shaping the perception of cultural and social practices. We thus find in the criminal justice system images and visions of social order, and narrative structures that represent the social world in a distinct way. The clout of criminal justice in history reveals law not as a mere reflection of dominant values but as a generator and enforcer of social standards and norms, producing social reality and social practices. Through criminal justice definitions of good and evil, the socially harmful and the socially useful, are negotiated. By attaching to these rules the threat of punishment, the values and rules are forcefully imposed on society. To a large extent the power of criminal justice operations stems from the combination of rules and punishments or, in other words, from the discourse of power and violence as it is folded into the everyday.

Punishment is a repressive act, an act of violence that subdues the offender by physical force. In a most fundamental way, punishments enforce power relationships; they coerce deviants into submission by deliberately imposing degrees of violence. In this way compliance with state-sponsored norms is also enforced. Violence hurts the body and thus poses a threat to physical survival, but equally harmful perhaps is the power of the violent act to shatter the self of the victim and threaten its cohesion. As Jean Améry has observed, all the conventional assumptions, standards, values, and beliefs that characterized the victim's previous life become, all of a sudden, questionable or obsolete under the impact of violence.[4] And beyond the physical, punishments also have a significant symbolic dimension. Violence is a symbolic act—it is supposed to convey a meaning. Punishments reflect the existing order and its dominant value system, as well as its attitudes toward violence and death.

In imperial China, the prevailing image was of a hierarchical society with the emperor at the top, as sovereign over life and death. Imperial China accepted public bloodletting and executions as punishments but went to great lengths to ensure that only the criminals were punished. Republican China promoted a therapeutic model of discipline for the sake of the nation's rise to power. A new sensitivity prohibited the public display of violence and death. The act of violence was removed from public view, and the act itself was sanitized as well. Prisons, and executions by shooting, produced cleaner, brief, rational punishments. After the Chinese Revolution, socialist China's punishments reflected the vision of a tight-knit collectivity based on the inculcation of jointly shared values and the regulation of every activity of its members. For "enemies of the people," however, public bloodshed and death were accepted forms of treatment. In socialist China physical violence as punishment went public again, inducing terror throughout society. In the labor camps, a new, messy form of violence emerged as well—the violence of decay and deprivation.

Another symbolic dimension of punishment is linked to its communicative function. Whether punishment takes the form of a public spectacle or takes place behind closed doors and prison walls, it sends a message. Punishments symbolize the power of the state and, at the same time, proclaim the weakness of the punished. Not only is the subordinate status of the punished demonstrated, but bystanders and onlookers, too, are reminded of their own weakness vis-à-vis the suppressive authority of the state. The use of punishment is a symbol of the state's power to rectify and to cleanse. It appears as a necessary attribute of sovereignty.

In regard to the history of punishment in Europe, a radical break was strongly suggested by Michel Foucault, who confronted the bloody mess of corporal punishment and proposed instead the clean, overpowering, disciplinary approach of Bentham's prison design, the Panopticon. Besides the fact that the Panopticon ideal was never fully realized, the history of criminal justice and legal punishment in China does not at all support the concept of a clean break between old and new, traditional and modern. Certainly the *yamen* were replaced by courts and the corporal punishments of dynastic China were replaced by stationary punishments (confinement), the immediate infliction of physical pain being superseded by a subtle suspension of different liberties. But the practices of China's police and prison system were always painted atop thick layers of historical memory. It is remarkable how many elements of the imperial penal system continued to play out during the larger part of twentieth-century China. Different ideologies and terminologies notwithstanding, the new, "modern" penal systems of both the Republic of China and the People's Republic incorporated components of the imperial criminal justice system. For instance, Republican criminal law imposed heavier punishments for crimes against seniors and for the murder of a lineal ascendant relative. Also certain crimes related to Confucian moral instruction continued to be prosecuted: throughout the Republican period the crime of adultery, for example, was punishable by law. Other examples concerned sentencing, such as the continued belief that elderly convicts should receive lighter punishments. And according to the 1935 criminal code, punishments could be lowered if an offender offered self-denunciation. Socialist criminal justice also revived and reintegrated components stemming from imperial times, such as the principle of analogy and the retroactivity of the laws, as well the concept of crime as an act that damages the social order. Most important, in determining punishments socialist law took the social status of the accused into account in a way comparable to imperial law. The tradition of imperial law was a potent resource that was mobilized in different ways, with divergent goals and by different governments. In general, Republican law tended to retain provisions that were related to moral or ethical concepts, because Republican legislators took into account the fact that many Confucian concepts and practices were still prevalent in society. Socialist lawmakers were less interested in substantive regulations than in technicalities that appeared to be useful and practicable. It has often been stressed that the penal system of socialist Chine bore a resemblance to Legalist concepts.

Some elements, however, were taken up by all of the Chinese criminal justice systems in the twentieth century. Forced labor played a significant role in all systems of punishment, as did public shaming and blaming as a means of isolating offenders and exerting social pressure. Almost all criminal laws had provisions allowing the reduction or suspension of penalties for crimes committed by an offender who voluntary confessed or gave information about the crime. Although there were differences in how voluntary confessions were used and how they were honored by the judge, the emphasis on confession is a general characteristic of Chinese criminal justice. In all systems, confession was assessed as an expression of genuine repentance, and punishment could be cancelled accordingly. All systems acknowledged that showing repentance allowed the society to redeem the offender and forgive his crimes, thus criminals were redeemed by Chinese society if they publicly regretted and repented their misdeeds. These provisions obviously reflected fundamental principles and concepts deeply ingrained in the Chinese world. Such principles have a certain weight and provide reasons for particular rules and regulations.

The fact of these continuities, though, should not impede us from also recognizing the overarching shifts that occurred in criminal justice in the twentieth century. One can detect, above all, the steady and unrelenting rise of the power of the nation-state and its ever-expanding capacity to intervene in the formation of the modern Chinese identity. This process was started in the last year of the Qing and it continued steadily throughout the twentieth century, bridging the political divides of 1911 and 1949. The expanding state was able to muster the service of whole generations of legal professionals and law enforcement agents while also claiming their allegiance. Whereas the imperial state ran its criminal justice system with a minimal amount of personnel, the twentieth-century regimes created vast government agencies that extended a pervasive, capillary network of control throughout society. Those agencies formed the institutional foundation for the modern Chinese criminal justice system.

The modern state also monopolized the use of violence and prohibited all other nonstate actors, such as clans and families, from using penal violence. Physical capital (that is, violence) was concentrated in the hands of the nation-state and its agencies. A fully empowered cluster of law enforcement agencies emerged with the capacity to deal with a large number of deviants and offenders. The twentieth-century state eventually was capable of prosecuting, trying, sentencing, and incarcerating an ever-growing percentage of the population. This concentration of power was interconnected with other key activities that the state took up as areas of concern, including the central registration of citizens, the extraction of resources through central taxation systems, social memory construction through school curricula and sponsored public memorials, and national identity propagation. The development of criminal justice is closely related to processes of nation building and the legitimization of state power.

Another trajectory that marked Chinese criminal justice in the twentieth century was the rise of the labor or internment camp in the Chinese Republic and the PRC. The nature and purpose of the Republican internment camps versus the socialist labor camps were different, yet they were comparable in that they both took in persons who had never been tried in a criminal process or sentenced by a court. As deficient as the Chinese prison system may have been, it had routines and rules. In contrast, the Chinese labor or internment camp had no rules. All camp regimes in China imposed programs of forced labor and reeducation and seemed to pursue a goal of reform. But in all cases, release from the camps was uncertain and depended on the will of the local camp officials. Since there often was no prison term defined, most inmates could not know the length of their term. For Giorgio Agamben, the lawlessness of the camps symbolizes a "state of emergency" or "state of exception." "In the camp," Agamben writes, "the state of exception, which was essentially a temporary suspension of the rule of law on the basis of a factual state of danger, is now given a permanent spatial arrangement, which as such nevertheless remains outside the normal order."[5] In this space of exception, all civilian rights and civilized standards, norms, and morals were suspended. Those interned were stripped of all their attributes and were, according to Agamben, reduced to their "bare life." With the camps, then, the state had established a space where it faced no limits. In the camps, the state proclaimed itself to be on a war footing against its enemies and could relentlessly wage an assault against those presumed to be hostile or dangerous. While the establishment of elaborate criminal justice systems was accompanied by the promulgation of legal rules and procedures, the twentieth-century regimes also, clandestinely or openly, set up mechanisms and spaces that allowed them to bypass criminal justice operations.

While the GMD government had experimented with camp internment as a powerful mechanism for exclusion and exception, it was after 1949 that a comprehensive nationwide system of labor camps was created. From this perspective we can see the making of socialism after 1949 as a policy of dislocation and a complex process of appropriation and displacement. Socialist society in China was fundamentally dependent on legal postponements and deferrals of rights. As a state of deferral, the emerging legal system managed and produced its own exceptions: scales of differentiation among citizens and offenders, gradations and denials of legal rights, declarations of emergency, delayed legal autonomy in the name of class struggle. Socialism created new legal categories of subjects that needed to be relocated to be productive and exploitable, dispossessed to be in line with the new order, disciplined to be independent, reeducated to be human, stripped of old cultural bearings to be citizens, coerced to be free. Uncertain standards of jurisdiction and ad hoc exemptions from law were defining principles of this system. The PRC vigilantly produced exceptions to its own principles and laws. We can see this polity as producing excepted groups in the population, excepted spaces, and its own exception from domestic laws.

The twentieth century was distinctive, too, in the proportion of the populace that fell victim to state violence. An increasing number of people were persecuted and killed by their own government. How many Chinese vanished in the violence perpetrated by various Chinese regimes will never be exactly known, but it is safe to assume that political violence and state persecutions killed tens of millions of Chinese citizens and left even more physically and psychologically wounded. As many theories have stressed, state violence aims to control people by inflicting fear and suffering, which induce a range of traumas: from pain, anguish, fear, loss, and grief to the destruction of a coherent and meaningful reality. The twentieth century was one of the most traumatizing in Chinese history because state-prompted trauma and suffering were no longer isolated, occasional effects: they became widespread, even ubiquitous.

In the late 1970s most survivors of the labor camps were released, formally rehabilitated, and cleared of all charges, their prison files destroyed. Officially the party acknowledged that "mistakes" had been made, and the leaders known as the Gang of Four, the most powerful members of the PRC's radical political elite, were convicted of implementing wrong policies and held responsible for the deaths of approximately 30,000 people during the Cultural Revolution. These actions were intended by the government to draw a line between past and present. It is interesting—almost ironic—to note that this was done through the format of a public trial that was broadcast live on television and radio. Millions followed the trial of the Gang of Four on their radios, on TV, or in the newspapers.[6] A "public transcript" was worked up that assigned blame to the Gang of Four and their ultra-leftist associates while exonerating the Communist Party, the state, and the party-state's local representatives. One of the most urgent tasks of reform was to revamp the tattered criminal justice structure.

Criminal Justice Reforms in Contemporary China

After 1978 there was a general agreement that the criminal justice sector was an area in need of rebuilding and reform. Reformers believed that if the law had been strengthened earlier, the "leftist" mistakes could have been prevented. Since 1979, the National People's Congress (NPC), China's supreme legislative body, has enacted and updated more than 200 laws that are still in effect and are generally consistent with accepted principles of international law.[7] Moreover, China has concluded a large number of international agreements, including twenty-one international conventions on human rights and World Trade Organization accession agreements, which have required changes in China's domestic legal system.

Institutionally, China's primary law-related bodies—the National People's Congress and its Standing Committee, the State Council, the Supreme People's Court, and the Supreme People's Procuracy—are becoming more professionalized and assertive, as well as gradually more transparent. Many Chinese lawyers and legal scholars are increasingly active in promoting legal reform and rights protection, and the Chinese media now regularly report on legal issues and controversial cases. Ordinary Chinese citizens in the urban areas as well as in the countryside have proved to be strikingly adept at using the law to assert their rights and interests against the government and others.[8]

In 1979, the NPC passed the Law of Criminal Procedure, China's first, which defined the roles of procurators relating to criminal prosecution, investigation, and the powers of "supervision" in the criminal process. The other five laws adopted in the same legislative package included China's first criminal law, the Law on Sino-Foreign Joint Ventures, and the Organic Law of the People's Courts. The Chinese government thus reestablished a formal legal system that also recognized the right of the accused to a defense lawyer in criminal proceedings. Under the Law of Criminal Procedure 1979, the court could appoint a lawyer for a defendant who did not have someone to act as his or her legal representative in court. In practice, under this rule a large number of Chinese lawyers were appointed every year by their law firms at the request of the courts, and their fees were mainly paid by the courts or the government, through the law firms.

From 1978 to the late 1980s, it was, however, unclear how far the legal reforms were supposed to go.[9] On the one hand, China started to participate in and even actively contributed to many relevant United Nations human rights activities, but on the other hand the government continued to condemn concepts in China that were similar to the UN standards for human rights. In the 1980s, for example, presumption of innocence was at least twice officially labeled as a bourgeois principle. Another example: when initiatives were launched to clear up "spiritual pollution" in 1983 and

1986–87, scholars were criticized for promoting the concept of human rights.

Beginning in the 1990s the pace of legal reform accelerated.[10] China succeeded in making a series of important changes to its criminal law (1997), criminal procedure law (1996), and the laws governing administrative punishments (1996, regulating the system of administrative punishments, including administrative detention), the judiciary (PRC Law on Judges 1995), the prosecutors (PRC Law on Procurators 1995), the police (People's Police Law 1995), and the legal profession (China's first Lawyers' Law went into effect in 1996). Changes included the abolition of the crime of counterrevolution, an enhanced concept of judicial independence, redefined roles for prosecutors, new limits on police power in law, the new right to legal aid, increased independence of the legal profession, enhanced professional qualifications of judges and prosecutors, recognition of the right to defense in pretrial detention, provision of legality in substantive criminal law, and the abolition of the retroactive application of criminal law.

In December 1994, a new prison law was made public.[11] The purpose of imprisonment was defined as protecting the safety of society and assisting the rehabilitation of offenders. The law recognized and implemented common principles such as the rule of law, fairness, and justice. It also strove to recognize and respect the basic rights of offenders. Clearly visible was an effort to maintain a balance between the rights and interests of the offenders and those of the victims and the public. The prison sector was reorganized, and a national prison department was created within the Ministry of Justice with the power of leadership over local departments. Officially, China no longer had Laogai camps, although the prisons still adhered to the concept of labor reform. The number of prisoners decreased to approximately 2 million.[12]

The Amendments to the Law of Criminal Procedure that China's National People's Congress passed in 1996 are considered a major achievement in the reform of China's legal system.[13] This law, for the first time in the history of the People's Republic, recognized the fundamental principles of the presumption of innocence and the right to defense counsel in the pretrial investigation process, and specifically required access to legal-aid service for certain special groups of eligible persons in court proceedings. Also in 1996, as mentioned above, the NPC enacted the Lawyers' Law, which proclaimed that legal aid was a duty of Chinese lawyers. At the same time, a number of local regulations were adopted by the provinces and municipalities whereby those defendants who were poor and elderly, juvenile, handicapped, or facing charges of serious criminal offences had priority in access to legal-aid services.

President Jiang Zemin introduced the concept of "a socialist country under the rule of law" at the CCP's Fifteenth National Congress in 1997. This statement confirmed the course of legal reform. While stressing the role of law, Jiang made it clear that there would be no change in regard to the primacy of the state.[14] A further step toward this goal was taken on March 14, 2004, when China's NPC approved thirteen amendments to its Constitution. The amendments address private property and human rights in general terms but do not limit the government's power to crack down on protests. For example, one amendment says that "the state respects and preserves human rights." Another proclaims that "citizens' lawful private property is inviolable," and that the state will compensate property owners when it confiscates their property.

Overall, the Chinese Communist Party has gradually ceded a good deal of authority to the market, and to the government, the courts, and other institutions that grapple on a daily basis with the complex decisions and policies required of a rapidly changing economy and society. This partial withdrawal by the party has provided a degree of political space for the development of "rule of law with Chinese characteristics," as it were. As a result, it is no exaggeration to state that never in the twentieth century did Chinese citizens enjoy a degree of legal protection and security similar to what they enjoy today.

But China's progress toward rule of law under a single party system takes us, as in so many other issue areas, into previously uncharted waters. Despite the growth of an increasingly robust legal system and legal consciousness, the Communist Party retains, to be sure, ultimate control, especially over handling sensitive issues. The maintenance of social order has become increasingly important in legitimizing the Chinese government. Rising crime rates have long accompanied China's march to market liberalization and prosperity, leading the government to make law and order as much of a priority as economic growth and the promise of prosperity.[15] Good laws and well-designed regulatory systems do not mean much if Chinese citizens lack the means to protect their rights and interests through an independent judicial system that has the authority to enforce government and private compliance with the law. China's massive judicial system of more than 3,000 basic courts and nearly 200,000 judges cannot yet consistently perform this function.[16]

While the courts hear roughly 6 million cases per year, Chinese government agencies, including the courts themselves, are flooded with nearly twice as many citizen petitions for administrative assistance to resolve a range of grievances, 30 percent of which involve complaints about the legal system itself and the handling of specific cases. Institutionally, the courts are part of the government structure answerable to the National People's Congress; they are not an independent branch of government. The Standing Committee of the NPC, not the Supreme People's Court, has the authority to interpret national law. Judges are merely supposed to apply the law. Where the law is vague or when politically sensitive issues are involved, government officials and the party may intervene through court-based adjudication committees that supervise judges' work, and through other means, and the courts may even decline to accept jurisdiction over cases. Judges at each level of the court system are appointed and remunerated by the people's congress at the same level, which exacerbates the problem of local protectionism and political influence. Judicial independence is more of a slogan than a reality in today's China.

Criminal justice is still the area where the conflict between the state's desire to curb crime and corruption and to protect individual rights is most dramatically played out against the backdrop of party stewardship. There are several areas of concern. The conviction rate of Chinese courts is among the highest in the world: in 2005, in the whole of China 98 percent of defendants were found guilty and only 2,162 defendants were acquitted.[17] China also executes more people every year than the rest of the world combined, in its pursuit of highly valued "social stability."[18] Chinese criminal law includes approximately sixty-eight capital offenses, the majority of which are nonviolent crimes such as bribery and embezzlement. The Chinese government has reportedly established an "execute fewer, execute cautiously" policy, and at least some indicators suggests that the number of executions has dropped in recent years. The government, however, publishes no official statistics on the number of executions carried out each year, something it still considers a state secret. Several Chinese sources have hinted that the annual number of executions in China is in the thousands. Chinese sources also cite as justifications for maintaining the death penalty its broad popular support and the need for a deterrent against crime. The government has indicated that while it will maintain capital punishment for the foreseeable future, it will work to ensure fair application of the death penalty by refining review procedures and gradually reducing application of the death penalty in favor of long-term imprisonment.

An ongoing domestic debate over the death penalty and its scope intensified recently, particularly after Chinese news media publicized accounts of wrongful conviction cases that led—in at least one widely publicized case—to the execution of an innocent man.[19] Scholars and commentators expressed concern about wrongful executions and focused on how to prevent them. Such public discussions have helped pressure the government to introduce more procedural safeguards in criminal cases, including rulings by some local courts that judges will not allow into evidence confessions elicited through torture, and the joint adoption by several criminal justice agencies of provisions to improve access to lawyers for more categories of criminal suspects and defendants, and at an earlier stage of the process, to enable their more vigorous defense. The Supreme People's Court also ruled in 2007 that high courts must hear death penalty appeals in open court with defense lawyers present, and the Supreme People's Court itself will in future review all death sentences.[20]

Violent abuse and torture by Chinese law enforcement agencies is another area of concern.[21] Chinese legal standards state that no one shall be subjected to torture or to cruel, inhuman, or degrading treatment or punishment. This standard, in conjunction with other instruments, requires China to take effective measures to prevent the use of any type of torture, whether or not it causes death or bodily harm. However, more effective measures are needed to reduce torture, such as a systemwide rule excluding all evidence obtained by torture, expanded investigation and prosecution of torturers, better police training focused on the prevention of torture, and real, assured access to defense lawyers for those accused of crimes. Criminal procedure law may recognize the right to defense counsel, but as recent scholarly studies and even media reports from China have shown, massive impediments persist in blocking or constraining access to that counsel.[22]

Present criminal law still allows the penalty of labor reeducation (Laojiao), which is defined as a noncriminal measure of compulsory education. Laojiao convicts are jailed without having had access to a lawyer or a trial—rights granted them under China's criminal law. This relic of the Mao era presents a difficult issue for the government, which has come under increasing international and domestic criticism for the Laojiao provisions.[23] Apart from Laojiao, several compulsory administrative or "educative" measures are allowed under the current system in China. These measures include compulsory employment at the expiration of a jail sentence, and detention "at designated time and designated location" for the investigation of corruption of a Communist Party official. Many maintain, therefore, that the prohibition of arbitrary arrest and detention is not fully realized in China.

Conditions inside Chinese prisons and labor reeducation facilities remain a cause for worry, too. Although the abuse and starvation of the 1950s and 1960s have disappeared, in many instances conditions are still excessively harsh and inhuman.[24] While some imprisoned intellectuals have described fairly mild conditions, other people have reported much harsher treatment. In part, bad conditions in the prisons are the result of insufficient training of prison staff, poor funding, or negligence on the part of the executive administration.

All inmates in prisons and labor reeducation facilities are expected to do some type of factory work or manual labor. Of the Laojiao (labor reeducation) inmate population, specialists say prisoners convicted of violations of state security provisions (the Chinese equivalent of political prisoners) constitute 5 percent to 10 percent of the total, while as many as 40 percent are drug offenders. Drug users are expected to kick their habit while in the labor reeducation camps.

At present, China's criminal justice system is still beset by a number of problems. As a result of more than a decade of legislation, the legal framework for reform is by and large in place, though work must continue in order to revise existing laws and improve and monitor the operation of all the criminal justice agencies involved. This process of amendment and reform is likely to continue until China reaches a more stable social, political, and economic situation. While the ultimate outcome of China's criminal justice reforms is unclear, it is very clear that legal changes, with far-reaching and possibly unanticipated ramifications for Chinese politics and society, are still under way.

ABBREVIATIONS

AH	Academia Historica
CCP	Chinese Communist Party
GMD	Guomindang
HI	Hoover Institution
NA	National Archive
PRC	People's Republic of China
ROC	Republic of China
SAPA	Security Administration Punishment Act
SHA	Second Historical Archives
SU	Soviet Union

ARCHIVES

Academia Historica (AH) (Guoshiguan), Taibei, Taiwan ROC
  61 Xingzheng Yuan: 1517.
  151 Sifa Xingzheng Bu: 3555, 3556.
  200000000A Guomin Zhengfu:
    0120.34 / 7843.02–01 *Jianyu xingxingfa* (Prison Law) 1946–1948.
    1331.30 / 8044.01–01 *Gonggong weisheng yu jianyu gaishan*
    (Public Hygiene and Prison Reform), 1943–1944.
    Fanxingyuan tiaoli (Statutes for the Self-Investigation Institutes),
    2 vols., 1929–1933.

Hoover Institution Archives (HI), Stanford, California
  KMT Digital Archive Database
  Guofang zuigao weiyuanhui (Supreme Defense Council), Series 1–3.

Second Historical Archives (SHA), Nanjing, PRC
  7 Sifa Xingzheng Bu: 210, 640, 670, 914, 1006, 1008, 1081, 1129, 2139,
  3141, 4528, 4699, 5435, 5843, 5847.
  1012 Beiyang Zhengfu 127, 128.
  1049 Beiyang Zhengfu Sifa Bu: 02211, 02212, 02262.

ACKNOWLEDGMENTS

This book has been long in the making. The project was initially conceived in a graduate seminar titled Punishment and Violence in Modern China that I gave at the Freie Universität Berlin in the fall of 2000. The core of the manuscript was written during a wonderfully inspiring two-year research stay in Berkeley, California, from 2002 to 2004. Additional research in China, Taiwan, Hong Kong, and Japan was undertaken in subsequent years. The text in its present from was completed in 2007.

This book could not have been written without the financial support I received from the German Research Foundation (DFG); the University of Turku in Finland and Indiana University Bloomington also helped by providing me with research money or relief from teaching. The generosity of these institutions is gratefully acknowledged. Several institutions hosted me during my research and opened their archives and libraries to me. My thanks go to the Center for Chinese Studies at the University of California, Berkeley; the Hoover Institution, Stanford University; the Institute for Modern History at the Academia Sinica in Taiwan; the Second Historical Archives of China, Nanjing; the National Archives in Washington D.C.; the Department of History at Peking University; Academia Historica Taipei; the Chinese University of Hong Kong; and the John King Fairbank Center for Chinese Studies, Harvard University.

Many friends and colleagues generously offered help and advice at various stages of the research for this book. I am especially grateful to William P. Alford, Chen Yongfa, Joseph Cheng, Paul Cohen, Frank Dikötter, Lowell Dittmer, Prasenjit Duara, Michael Dutton, Joshua Fogel, Jie Li, Jan Kiely,

William C. Kirby, Thoralf Klein, Kari Lehti, Stanley Lubman, Alf Lüdke, Outi Luova, Hans Medick, Lauri Paltemaa, John Schrecker, Lynn Struve, Ralph Thaxton, Tim Trampedach, Eduard Vermeer, Frederic Wakeman, Jeff Wasserstrom, Xu Youwei, Yeh Wen-hsin, Zhang Xianwen, Zhao Baoxu, and Peter Zinoman. Minna Lindstedt provided valuable and dependable support as research assistant at the University of Turku.

Mechthild Leutner, Harro von Senger, Glenn Tiffert, and two anonymous readers undertook to read the entire manuscript. Their insightful comments prompted and guided several revisions of the original draft. I am deeply indebted to them. Needless to say, all remaining errors are my own. Kathleen McDermott of Harvard University Press offered valuable support throughout the writing process. My copyeditor, Julie Hagen, skillfully salvaged the manuscript from my blemished English prose.

My greatest thanks are certainly due to my family. During the years it took to write this book we moved several times, across two continents. Despite the difficulties this posed, and my frequent absences due to teaching, lectures, and research trips, they remained supportive, optimistic, and genuinely interested in my work. This book is dedicated to Heike, Sophia, Clara, and Julius.

NOTES

Introduction

1. See John Rawls, *A Theory of Justice* (Cambridge, MA: The Belknap Press of Harvard University Press, 1999), 3.

2. Brian Barry and Matt Matravers, "Justice," in E. Craig, ed., *Routledge Encyclopedia of Philosophy* (London: Routledge, 1998), *http://www.rep.routledge.com/article/S032* (accessed Jan. 12, 2004). Aristotle was probably the first thinker to articulate a contrast between two forms of justice, corrective and distributive. See Book V of the Nicomachean Ethics (in, e.g., *The Complete Works of Aristotle,* ed. J. Barnes [Princeton, NJ: Princeton University Press, 1984], vol. 2: 1729–1867).

3. John Cottingham, "The Philosophy of Punishment," in G. H. R. Parkinson, ed., *An Encyclopedia of Philosophy* (Routledge: London, 1996), 762–783. See also the comprehensive study on the history of punishment by Hans von Hentig, *Die Strafe,* vol. 1. Frühformen und kulturgeschichtliche Zusammenhänge, Berlin et al., 1954; *Die Strafe,* vol. 2. Die modernen Erscheinungsformen, Berlin et al., 1955.

4. Pierre Bourdieu, *Practical Reason: On the Theory of Action* (Stanford, CA: Stanford University Press, 1998), 99.

5. Antony R. Duff, "Crime and Punishment," in E. Craig, ed., *Routledge Encyclopedia of Philosophy* (Routledge: London, 1998), *http://www.rep.routledge.com/article/T002,* accessed Jan. 12, 2004. Antony R. Duff, *Philosophy and the Criminal Law: Principle and Critique* (Cambridge: Cambridge University Press, 1998). Antony R. Duff and David Garland, "Introduction: Thinking about Punishment," in Antony R. Duff and David Garland, eds., *A Reader on Punishment* (Oxford: Oxford University Press, 1994), 1–43. John Rawls, "Two Concepts of Rules," in *Philosophical Review,* 64 (1955): 3–13.

6. David Garland, *Punishment and Modern Society: A Study in Social Theory* (Chicago: University of Chicago Press, 1990).

7. See Joel Samaha, *Criminal Justice,* 4th ed. (Minneapolis: West Publishing, 1997), 8.

8. See chapter four in Jerome S. Bruner, *Acts of Meaning: The Jerusalem-Harvard Lec-*

tures (Cambridge, MA: Harvard University Press, 1990). Jens Brockmeier and Donal A. Carbaugh, eds., *Narrative and Identity: Studies in Autobiography, Self, and Culture* (Amsterdam: John Benjamins, 2001).

9. Jerome S. Bruner, *Making Stories: Law, Literature, Life* (Cambridge, MA: Harvard University Press, 2003).

10. Michel Foucault, *Discipline and Punish: The Birth of the Prison* (New York: Pantheon Books, 1978), 304.

11. Ibid.

12. Emile Durkheim, "Deux lois de l'évolution pénale," in *Année Sociologique* 4 (1902): 65–95, translated in *Durkheim and the Law*, ed. Steven Lukes and Andrew Scull (Oxford: Martin Robinson, 1983), 102–132; Erving Goffman, *Asylums: Essays on the Social Situation of Mental Patients and Other Inmates* (Chicago: Aldine Publishing, 1961).

13. Jan Assmann, "Recht und Gerechtigkeit als Generatoren von Geschichte," in Rüdiger Bubner and Walter Mesch, eds., *Die Weltgeschichte: Das Weltgericht?* (Stuttgart: Stuttgarter Hegel-Kongress, 1999), 296–311.

14. Richard J. Evans, *Rituals of Retribution: Capital Punishment in Germany 1600–1987* (Oxford: Oxford University Press, 1996), 18–22.

15. Philippe Ariès, *Essais sur l'histoire de la mort en occident du Moyen Âge à nos jours* (Paris: Seuil, 1975).

16. Book-length studies on the premodern period include Derk Bodde and Clarence Morris, *Law in Imperial China* (Cambridge, MA: Harvard University Press, 1967); Geoffrey MacCormack, *Traditional Chinese Penal Law* (Edinburgh: Edinburgh University Press, 1990); Geoffrey MacCormack, *The Spirit of Traditional Chinese Law* (Athens: University of Georgia Press, 1996); Cheng Jianfu, *Chinese Law: Towards an Understanding of Chinese Law, Its Nature and Development* (The Hague: Kluwer Law International, 1999).

17. Extant work has dealt either with shorter periods of time or with specific components of criminal justice rather than with the whole. The criminal-justice process up to the late 1950s was studied and documented by Jerome Alan Cohen in *The Criminal Process in the People's Republic of China 1949–1963* (Cambridge, MA: Harvard University Press, 1968). A number of monographs are available that deal with single aspects of criminal justice, such as prisons in Republican China, the treatment of counterrevolutionaries by the Chinese Communist Party (CCP), or the labor reform camps of the People's Republic of China (PRC). Important studies include: Frank Dikötter, *Crime, Punishment and the Prison in Modern China 1895–1949* (New York: Columbia University Press, 2002); Jean-Luc Domenach, *Chine, l'archipel oublié* (Paris: Fayard, 1992); Patricia Griffin, *The Chinese Communist Treatment of Counterrevolutionaries: 1924–1949* (Princeton, NJ: Princeton University Press, 1976); Marinus J. Meijer, *The Introduction of Modern Criminal Law in China* (Batavia: De Unie, 1950); Harry Wu, *Laogai: The Chinese Gulag* (Boulder, CO: Westview Press, 1992); Philip F. Williams and Yenna Wu, *The Great Wall of Confinement: The Chinese Prison Camp through Contemporary Fiction and Report-*

age (Berkeley: University of California Press, 2004). The court system during the Republican period, the Mao period, and the post-Mao years has been studied as well: Leng Shao-chuan, *Justice in Communist China: A Survey of the Judicial System of the Chinese People's Republic* (New York: Oceana Publications, 1967); Leng Shao-chuan and Chiuh Hungdah, *Criminal Justice in Post-Mao China: Analysis and Documents* (Albany: State University of New York Press, 1985); Harold Tanner, *Strike Hard! Anti-Crime Campaigns and Chinese Criminal Justice 1979–1985* (Ithaca, NY: East Asia Program, Cornell University, 1999). The current legal reforms have been the focus of a number of studies, such as Stanley B. Lubman, *Bird in a Cage: Legal Reform in China after Mao* (Stanford, CA: Stanford University Press, 1999); Pitman B. Potter, *The Chinese Legal System: Globalization and Local Legal Culture* (London: RoutledgeCurzon, 2001); Randall P. Peerenboom, *China's Long March towards the Rule of Law* (Cambridge: Cambridge University Press, 2002). The police force is studied by Michael Dutton in *Policing Chinese Politics: A History* (Durham, NC: Duke University Press, 2005), and *Policing and Punishment in China: From Patriarchy to "the People"* (Cambridge: Cambridge University Press, 1992). A good discussion on Chinese research on criminal law and criminal justice is given in a report by Liang Genlin and Huixin He, "Ershi siji de zhongguo xingfaxue" [The Chinese Study of Criminal Law in the Twentieth Century], *Zhongwai faxue* 2 (1999): 17–29.

1. The Right Degree of Pain

1. See William C. Jones, *The Great Qing Code* (Oxford: Clarendon Press, 1994), 9–12.
2. In this chapter the term "criminal justice" is applied as a heuristically useful device. It is not a term that occurs in any of the legal texts from imperial China. Rather, it refers to a certain set of problems and regulations within imperial Chinese law that can mainly be found in two sections of the imperial Chinese law codes: "Names and General Rules (Part I)" and "Laws Relating to the Board of Punishments (Part IV)." These sections both pertain to or are connected with the law of crimes and the administration of penal justice, and thus they deal with issues similar to what the modern term "criminal justice" refers to. See the entry "criminal law" in *Black's Law Dictionary,* ed. Bryan A. Garner, 8th ed. (St. Paul, MN: West Publishing, 2004).
3. The phenomenon of punishment is of course not limited to the realm of law and order. The idea of punishment is also prevalent in religion, myth, drama, and literature. As an archaic idea, punishment seems to have been woven into the fabric of Chinese culture and society from the earliest recorded times onward. Unfortunately a cultural history of punishment in premodern China remains to be written. The best study available is still Wolfram Eberhard, *Guilt and Sin in Traditional China* (Berkeley: University of California Press, 1967).
4. Xu Shen, *Shuowen jiezi jiaodingben* (Nanjing: Feng huang chubanshe, 2004), vol. 4, *dao* section. The character *xing* first appeared in bronze inscriptions of the Western Zhou dynasty. However, with one possible exception, the character was used

for personal names; see Liu Yongpin, *Origins of Chinese Law: Penal and Administrative Law in Its Early Development* (New York; Hong Kong: Oxford University Press, 1998), 113.

5. Léon S. Vandermeersch, *La Formation du Légisme: Recherche sur la constitution d'une philosophie politique caractéristique de la Chine ancienne* (Paris: École francaise d'Extrême-Orient, 1965), 186.

6. Eduard J. M. Kroker, *Die Strafe im chinesischen Recht* (Opladen: Rheinisch-Westfälische Akademie der Wissenschaften, 1970), 13.

7. Xu Shen, *Shuowen jiezi*, vol. 14, *xin* section.

8. See Liu Yongpin, *Origins of Chinese Law*, 113.

9. See Geoffrey MacCormack, *Traditional Chinese Penal Law* (Edinburgh: Edinburgh University Press, 1990), 32.

10. See Chad Hansen, "Punishment and Dignity in China," in *Individualism and Holism: Studies in Confucian and Taoist Values*, ed. Donald J. Munro (Ann Arbor, MI: Center for Chinese Studies, 1985), 359–385.

11. Wolfgang Bauer, *Geschichte der chinesischen Philosophie* (Munich: Verlag C. H. Beck, 2001), 110.

12. See Benjamin I. Schwartz, *The World of Thought in Ancient China* (Cambridge: Belknap Press of Harvard University Press, 1985), 321.

13. *The Book of Lord Shang: A Classic of the Chinese School of Law,* trans. J. J. L. Duyvendak (Chicago: University of Chicago Press, 1963), 241.

14. *The Complete Works of Han Fei Tzu: A Classic of Chinese Legalism,* trans. W. K. Liao (London: Probsthain, 1939–), 46.

15. Ibid., 243.

16. *Book of Lord Shang,* 278.

17. Ibid., 288.

18. A good brief overview in Chinese is Xu Chaoyang, *Zhongguo xingfa suyuan* [The History of Chinese Penal Law] (Taibei: Taiwan Shangwu, 1973), 49–55.

19. See the still stimulating discussion by Hsu Dao-lin, "Crime and Cosmic Order," *Harvard Journal of Asiatic Studies* 30 (1970): 111–125, and by Yang Honglie, *Zhongguo falü sixiangshi* [A History of Chinese Legal Thought] (Taibei: Taiwan Shangwu, 1964), 156–168.

20. See Schwartz, *World of Thought,* 350–382.

21. See Kroker, *Die Strafe im chinesischen Recht,* 30–35.

22. See Derk Bodde and Clarence Morris, *Law in Imperial China* (Cambridge, MA: Harvard University Press, 1967), 182.

23. The *Yue ling* is a kind of almanac for emperors. It attained the status of a classic by being included in the *Book of Rites (Liji)*. On the significance of the *Yue ling* for imperial Chinese law, see Bodde and Morris, *Law in Imperial China,* 45; Hsu Dao-lin, "Crime and Cosmic Order," 113.

24. See Xu Chaoyang, *Zhongguo xingfa suyuan,* 55.

25. For a discussion of Xunzi's views on punishment, see Geoffrey MacCormack, *The Spirit of Traditional Chinese Law* (Athens: University of Georgia Press, 1996),

193–195; Roger T. Ames and Huai-nan Tzu, *The Art of Rulership: A Study in Ancient Chinese Political Thought* (Honolulu: University of Hawaii Press, 1983), 123–124.

26. See the commentary and translation by John Knoblock, *Xunzi: A Translation and Study of the Complete Works,* vol. 3, Books 17–32 (Stanford, CA: Stanford University Press, 1994), 23–48. Relevant for this study is Thesis Three.

27. Xunzi, Book 18.3, in ibid., 37.

28. Ibid.

29. Thomas A. Metzger, *The Internal Organization of Ch'ing Bureaucracy: Legal, Normative, and Communication Aspects* (Cambridge, MA: Harvard University Press, 1973); Ch'ü T'ung-tsu, *Law and Society in Traditional China* (Paris: Mouton, 1961).

30. See the biography of Dong Zhongshu in the *Hanshu* [*Book of Han*] 56. I have consulted the reprint in *Zhongguo falü sixiangshi ziliao xuanbian* [Selected Materials for the History of Chinese Legal Thought], ed. Zhongguo Falü Sixianshi Bianxiezu and Sifabu Faxue Jiaocai Bianjibu (Beijing: Falü Chubanshe, 1983), 294–304.

31. Ibid. See also Hsu Dao-lin, "Crime and Cosmic Order," 114.

32. See Jones, *Qing Code,* 15.

33. The quote is from the commentary to the Qing law; see Jones, *Qing Code,* 34.

34. See MacCormack, *Spirit of Traditional Chinese Law,* 48.

35. Ibid., 49. MacCormack explains that family conflicts were mostly settled through out-of-court adjudication or meditation.

36. Hansen, "Punishment and Dignity in China," 372.

37. See Brian E. McKnight, *Law and Order in Sung China* (Cambridge: Cambridge University Press, 1992), 324.

38. Ibid.

39. Jonathan Spence, *Emperor of China: Self-Portrait of K'ang-hsi* (New York: Vintage Books, 1974), 29–31.

40. McKnight, *Law and Order,* 326.

41. Ibid.

42. Brian E. McKnight, *The Quality of Mercy: Amnesties and Traditional Chinese Justice* (Honolulu: University Press of Hawaii, 1981).

43. Joanna Waley-Cohen, *Exile in Mid-Ch'ing China: Banishment to Xinjiang, 1758–1820* (New Haven, CT: Yale University Press, 1991), 216–217.

44. Citation follows McKnight, *Law and Order,* 27.

45. See MacCormack, *Spirit of Traditional Chinese Law,* 203–209.

46. Ibid., 189.

47. See the study by Thomas M. Buoye, *Manslaughter, Markets, and Moral Economy: Violent Disputes over Property Rights in Eighteenth-Century China* (New York: Cambridge University Press, 2000).

48. MacCormack, *Spirit of Traditional Chinese Law,* 211.

49. Jonathan Ocko, "I'll Take It All the Way to Beijing: Capital Appeals in the Qing," *Journal of Asian Studies* 47 (1988): 291–315.

50. On the Five Punishments, see *Xingfaxue quanshu* [Criminal Law Encyclopedia], ed. Xingfaxue Quanshu Bianweihui (Shanghai: Kexue Jishu Wenxian, 1993),

478–482; Kim Chin and Theodore R. LeBlang, "The Death Penalty in Traditional China," *Georgia Journal of International and Comparative Law* 5 (1975): 77–105.

51. See Wang Jing and Xusheng Hu, "Wu xing yu wu xing: Zhongguo xingzhi de wenhua neihan" [Five Punishments and Five Elements: The Cultural Meaning of the System of Punishments in China], *Bijiao fa yanjiu* 1 (1989): 1–8.

52. See *Zhongguo lidai xingfazhi zhuyi* [The Criminal Law Sections of All Dynasties with Commentaries and Translations], ed. Gao Chao and Ma Jianshi (Changchun: Jilin Renmin Chubanshe, 1994), 5–8.

53. In the *Hanshu*, Ban Gu mentioned nine punishments. He wrote: "Because of political chaos during the Zhou, nine punishments were used," quoted in ibid., 22. On the *Lü xing*, see Geoffrey MacCormack, "The Lü Hsing: Problems of Legal Interpretation," *Monumenta Serica* 37 (1986): 27–78; a translation can be found in James Legge, *The Chinese Classics: With a Translation, Critical and Exegetical Notes, Prologomena, and Copious Indexes,* vol. 2. (Taibei: Wen Shih Che Ch'u Pan She, 1972).

54. There is an ongoing discussion about when this text was written and how accurately the descriptions in the text reflect the historical reality in the early Zhou dynasty. Many researchers believe that only a few parts may have been composed in the tenth century B.C. and that others were possibly written much later, in the third century B.C. In any case, for the purpose of this study it is important to note that the ideals and concepts developed in the text had an immense impact on criminal justice in the succeeding dynasties.

55. See McKnight, *Law and Order,* 329.

56. Karen Turner, "The Criminal Body and the Body Politic: Punishments in Early Imperial China," *Cultural Dynamics* 11, no. 2 (1999): 237–254.

57. McKnight, *Law and Order,* 319–320.

58. There was intense discussion at the court surrounding this decision. One group of officials sternly rejected the idea of abolishing the mutilating punishments because they feared the spread of disorder and chaos predicted to follow the mitigation of punishments. And even after the edict by Wendi, officials tried several times to reinstall the mutilating punishments. Such occasional attempts went on for centuries; the last discussion concerning this issue broke out during the Northern Song. See the overview in Yang Honglie, *Zhongguo falü sixiangshi,* 345–371.

59. While castration was phased out as a legal punishment listed in the codes, it did not completely disappear. It was occasionally used as an extralegal measure in dealing with rebellions. The Liao dynasty (907–1125), also known as the Khitan Empire, as well as the Qing dynasty, are reported to have used castration for minors under the age of sixteen. Instead of imposing the death penalty they imposed castration, thus effectively cutting off the young offenders' patriline but allowing the boys to live. See *Xingfaxue quanshu,* 479; Tao Guangfeng, "Han Wei Jin gong xing cun fei xi" [Rise and Decline of the Punishment of Castration during Han, Wei, and Jin Dynasties], *Faxue yanjiu* 19, no. 3 (1999): 142–145.

60. See *Zhongguo chuantong falü wenhua cidian* [Encyclopedia for Traditional Legal

Culture in China], ed. Wu Shuchen (Beijing: Beijing Daxue Chubanshe, 1999), 624, table 4.

61. See McKnight, *Law and Order*, 334–336.

62. The punishments are listed in Article 1 of the code ("The Five Punishments"); see Jones, *Qing Code*, 33–34. See also the discussion in Bodde and Morris, *Law in Imperial China*, 77–79.

63. The difference between the nominal number and the actual number of blows can be traced back to the reductions by the Qing rulers after their conquest of China. They ruled to halve the number of blows given; still later a further reduction was implemented. In the codes, the original numbers were kept so as not to break with the tradition. The reason for the reduction was the use of a bigger and heavier stick under the Qing; see Bodde and Morris, *Law in Imperial China*, 870–871.

64. Jones, *Qing Code*, 33–34.

65. Ibid.

66. Ibid.

67. See Waley-Cohen, *Exile in Mid-Ch'ing China*, 56. Bodde and Morris, *Law in Imperial China*, 91.

68. On military exile and its history see Waley-Cohen, *Exile in Mid-Ch'ing China*, 53–55; Bodde and Morris, *Law in Imperial China*, 87–91.

69. See Waley-Cohen, *Exile in Mid-Ch'ing China*, 64.

70. Ibid., 65.

71. Ibid., 34.

72. Timothy Brook, Jérôme Bourgon, and Gregory Blue, *Death by a Thousand Cuts* (Cambridge, MA: Harvard University Press, 2008), 55–61 and 68–121; Chin and LeBlang, "The Death Penalty in Traditional China," 89.

73. McKnight, *Law and Order*, 356.

74. See Bodde and Morris, *Law in Imperial China*, 95–97.

75. There were, however, exceptions; see MacCormack, *Spirit of Traditional Chinese Law*, 122.

76. Jennifer M. Neighbors, "Criminal Intent and Homicide Law in Qing and Republican China," PhD diss., University of California, Los Angeles, 2004, 6–7.

77. See the six categories of murder in the Qing Code in Articles 282, 290, and 292 of the Qing Law Code, in Jones, *Qing Code*, 268–278.

78. MacCormack, *Spirit of Traditional Chinese Law*, 80–81.

79. Chin and LeBlang, "The Death Penalty in Traditional China," 99.

80. Spence, *Emperor of China*, 32–33.

81. Waley-Cohen, *Exile in Mid-Ch'ing China*, 62–66.

82. Robert J. Antony, "The Problem of Banditry and Banditry Suppression in Kwangtung South China, 1780–1840," *Criminal Justice History* 11 (1990): 31–53.

83. MacCormack, *Penal Law*, 110–114.

84. Vivien W. Ng, *Madness in Late Imperial China: From Illness to Deviance* (Norman: University of Oklahoma Press, 1990).

85. McKnight, *The Quality of Mercy*, 112–127.

86. MacCormack, *Spirit of Traditional Chinese Law,* 132.

87. Jack L. Dull, "The Evolution of Government in China," in *Heritage of China: Contemporary Perspectives on Chinese Civilization,* ed. Paul S. Ropp (Berkeley: University of California Press, 1990), 55–85, see esp. p. 81.

88. The population for 1840 is based on Albert Feuerwerker, "Chinese Economic History in Comparative Perspective," in *Heritage of China: Contemporary Perspectives on Chinese Civilization,* ed. Paul S. Ropp (Berkeley: University of California Press, 1990), 224–241, see esp. p. 228.

89. Judy Feldman Harrison, "Wrongful Treatment of Prisoners: A Case Study of Ch'ing Legal Practice," *Journal of Asian Studies* 23 (1964): 227–244.

90. A list of those instruments can be found in Zhou Mi, *Zhongguo Xingfa Shi* [The History of Chinese Penal Law] (Beijing: Beijing Daxue, 1998), 518.

91. Harrison, "Wrongful Treatment of Prisoners," 230.

92. See Jones, *Qing Code,* 395–396.

93. On executions in early modern Europe, see Karl Härter, "Soziale Disziplinierung durch Strafe? Intentionen frühneuzeitlicher Policeyordnungen und staatliche Sanktionspraxis," *Zeitschrift für Historische Forschung* 3 (1999): 365–379; on France, see Alain Corbin, *The Village of Cannibals: Rage and Murder in France, 1870,* trans. Arthur Goldhammer (Cambridge, MA: Harvard University Press, 1992), and M. Bee, "Le spectacle de l'exécution dans la France d'Ancien régime," *Annales* 38 (1983): 843–862; on Great Britain and the United States, see Pieter Spierenburg, *The Spectacle of Suffering: Executions and the Evolution of Repression: From Preindustrial Metropolis to the European Experience* (Cambridge: Cambridge University Press, 1984).

94. Michel Foucault, *Discipline and Punish: The Birth of the Prison* (New York: Pantheon Books, 1978), 3–6.

95. See Bodde and Morris, *Law in Imperial China,* 110.

96. Spierenburg, *The Spectacle of Suffering.* The Qing edict is mentioned in case 263.1 in the "Collection of Penal Cases" *(Xingan Huilan)* dated 1834, translated in ibid., 470–472.

97. Ernest Alabaster, *Notes and Commentaries on Chinese Criminal Law and Cognate Topics* (London, 1899), 59.

98. Foucault, *Discipline and Punish,* 8.

99. For concrete examples, see Colin Mackerras, *Western Images of China,* rev. ed. (Oxford: Oxford University Press, 1999), 46.

100. On the administration of justice in late imperial China, see Zhang Jinfan, *Qingchao fazhishi* [A History of the Legal System of the Qing Dynasty] (Beijing: Zhonghua Shuju, 1998), 584–655; MacCormack, *Penal Law,* 72–99; Sybille van der Sprenkel, *Legal Institutions in Manchu China* (London: Athlone Press, 1962), 37–49 and 66–79.

101. MacCormack, *Penal Law,* 166.

102. Chang Chen Fu-mei, "On Analogy in Ch'ing Law," *Harvard Journal of Asiatic Studies* 30 (1970): 212–224.

103. Jones, *Qing Code,* 12.

104. Earlier versions of the Qing Code were promulgated in 1646 and 1727. The following discussion refers to the 1740 edition, which remained effective until the institution of a new, completely reformed code in 1910, shortly before the demise of the Qing dynasty. On the Qing Code, see Jones, *Qing Code; Xingfaxue quanshu,* 477–478; Bodde and Morris, *Law in Imperial China,* 52–75; Zheng Jingyi, *Falü dacishu* [The Large Law Encyclopedia] (Taibei: Taiwan Shangwu, 1972), 1294–1295.

105. MacCormack, *Spirit of Traditional Chinese Law,* 121.

106. See Articles 366–375 in the Qing Code, in Jones, *Qing Code,* 347–354.

107. See Matthew H. Sommer, *Sex, Law, and Society in Late Imperial China* (Stanford, CA: Stanford University Press, 2000).

108. See MacCormack, *Spirit of Traditional Chinese Law,* 109.

109. On collective punishments, see Joanna Waley-Cohen, "Collective Responsibility in Qing Criminal Law," in *The Limits of the Rule of Law in China,* ed. Karen G. Turner, James V. Feinerman, and R. Kent Guy (Seattle: University of Washington Press, 2000), 112–132.

110. Chin and LeBlang, "The Death Penalty in Traditional China," 90.

111. On forensic examinations in premodern China, see the classical text "Washing Away the Wrongs," translated and commented on by Brian McKnight, in Sung Tz'u and Brian E. McKnight, *The Washing Away of Wrongs: Forensic Medicine in Thirteenth-Century China* (Ann Arbor: Center for Chinese Studies, University of Michigan, 1981).

112. Thomas M. Buoye, "Suddenly Murderous Intent Arose: Bureaucratization and Benevolence in Eighteenth-Century Homicide Reports," *Late Imperial China* 16, no. 2 (Dec. 1995): 62–97.

113. Richard van Dülmen, *Theater des Schreckens: Gerichtspraxis und Strafrituale in der frühen Neuzeit* (Munich: Beck, 1985).

114. MacCormack, *Spirit of Traditional Chinese Law,* 69.

115. Ibid., 75.

116. Ibid., 106.

117. See Philip A. Kuhn, *Soulstealers: The Chinese Sorcery Scare of 1768* (Cambridge, MA: Harvard University Press, 1990), 191–193.

118. Jones, *Qing Code,* 36–37.

119. In Tang law, confession was required only in cases where the facts were unclear, but in Ming and Qing law it was required in most cases. Exceptions were few and narrow. See Alison W. Conner, "True Confessions? Chinese Confessions Then and Now," in *The Limits of the Rule of Law in China,* ed. Karen G. Turner, James V. Feinerman, and R. Kent Guy (Seattle: University of Washington Press, 2000), 132–162.

120. See Kuhn, *Soulstealers,* 174.

121. See the description of the courtroom torture in ibid., 15–22.

122. See Harrison, "Wrongful Treatment of Prisoners," which is based on the *Xing'an huilan* (Collection of Criminal Cases) from the nineteenth century.

123. Quoted in Kuhn, *Soulstealers,* 175.

124. See Article 25 of the Qing Code in Jones, *Qing Code,* 56–57. See also the discussion in George A. Kennedy, *Die Rolle des Geständnisses im chinesischen Recht* (Berlin, 1939), and Geoffrey MacCormack, "The Legal Treatment of Insane Persons in Late Imperial China," *Journal of Legal History* 13, no. 3 (1992): 251–269.

125. Harro von Senger, "Die Strafe im Kaiserlichen China," in *Recueils de la Société Jean Bodin pour l'histoire comparative des institutions,* vol. 57: *La Peine,* part 4: *Mondes non européens* (Brussels: De Boeck-Wemael, 1991), 371–385, esp. p. 381–383.

126. See Qu Tongzu, *Zhonggu Falü yu Zhongguo shehui* [Chinese Law and Chinese Society], (Taibei: Liren, 1984), 33–35.

127. See Ch'ü T'ung-tsu, *Law and Society in Traditional China,* 20–41.

128. Ibid., 24.

129. See MacCormack, *Spirit of Traditional Chinese Law,* 139.

130. See von Senger, "Die Strafe im Kaiserlichen China," 378.

131. See Ann Waltner, "Breaking the Law: Family Violence, Gender and Hierarchy in the Legal Code of the Ming Dynasty," *Ming Studies* 36 (1996): 29–43.

132. See McKnight, *Law and Order in Sung China,* 327.

133. See Waley-Cohen, "Collective Responsibility in Qing Criminal Law," 112; von Senger, "Die Strafe im Kaiserlichen China," 376–377.

134. See Article 254 of the Qing Code in Jones, *Qing Code,* 237; see also Kroker, *Die Strafe im chinesischen Recht,* 44.

135. See Mark Allee, "Code, Culture, and Custom: Foundations of Civil Case Verdicts in a Nineteenth-Century County Court," in *Civil Law in Qing and Republican China,* ed. Kathryn Bemhardt and Philip Huang (Stanford, CA: Stanford University Press, 1994), 122–141.

136. Philip C. C. Huang, "Civil Adjudication in China, Past and Present," *Modern China* 32, no. 2 (2006): 135–180, esp. p. 139.

137. Jones, *Qing Code,* 19.

2. The Prison Regime

1. Xu Xiaoqun, *Chinese Professionals and the Republican State: The Rise of Professional Associations in Shanghai, 1912–1937* (New York: Cambridge University Press, 2001), 107.

2. Shen Jiaben (1840–1913) had served on the Board of Punishments since 1883. Wu Tingfang (1842–1922) had studied law in Great Britain. From 1896 to 1902 he served as the head of Chinese legations in the United States, Spain, and other countries.

3. Marinus J. Meijer, *The Introduction of Modern Criminal Law in China* (Batavia: De Unie, 1950), 41.

4. A good example of this work is a report on the different prison systems by Wang Shurong, *Kaocha geguo jianyu zhidu baogaoshu tiyao* [Summary Report of the Investigation of Foreign Prison Systems] (Beijing, 1911).

5. Philip C. C. Huang, "Civil Adjudication in China, Past and Present," *Modern China* 32, no. 2 (2006): 135–180.

6. Meijer, *Introduction of Modern Criminal Law,* 24–31.

7. *Report of the Commission on Extraterritoriality in China, Peking, September 16, 1926* (Washington, DC: Government Printing Office, 1926), 99.

8. Quoted in Yang Diansheng and Zhang Jinsang, *Zhongguo tese jianyu zhidu yanjiu* [Studies on the Prison System with Chinese Characteristics] (Beijing: Falü, 1998), 138.

9. *Report of the Commission on Extraterritoriality,* 29.

10. The full Chinese text of the 1913 Beiyang regulations is reprinted in *Minguo jianyu fagui xuanbian* [Selected Documents from the Republican Legislation concerning Prisons], ed. Shandongsheng Laogaiju (Jinan: Zhongguo Shudian, 1990), 1–9.

11. See Jan Kiely, "Making Good Citizens: The Reformation of Prisoners in China's First Modern Prisons," PhD diss., University of California, Berkeley, 2001, 88.

12. *Chinese Prisons,* ed. Commission on Extraterritoriality (Peking, 1925), 14.

13. See Xue Meiqing and Cong Jinpeng, *Tianjin jianyushi* [History of the Prison in Tianjin] (Tianjin, 1999), 3–44.

14. The Nanjing government issued the slightly modified prison regulations *(Jianyu guize)* in 1928; the full text can be found in *Minguo jianyu fagui xuanbian,* 10–19. See also *Zhongguo jianyu shiliao huibian* [Collected Historical Materials on the History of the Prison in China], vol. 2, ed. Zhonghua Renmin Gongheguo Sifabu (Beijing: Qunzhong, 1988), 1–10.

15. See M. H. v. d. Valk, "The New Chinese Criminal Code," *Pacific Affairs* 9, no. 1 (1936): 69–77; Chang Chungkong and H. Herrfahrdt, *Das chinesische Strafgesetzbuch vom 1. Januar 1935* (Bonn, 1935); Chang Chao-yuen, *The Criminal Code of the Republic of China* (Shanghai, 1935); *The Code of Criminal Procedure of the Republic of China,* ed. Ministry of Justice (Shanghai: Commercial Press, 1936).

16. The punishments are dealt with in Chapter 7 of the Criminal Code of the Republic (1919) and of subsequent versions until 1928. The completely revised Criminal Code of the Republic of China (1935) lists punishments in Chapter 5. See also the diagram and explanations in Zhao Chen, *Jianyu xue* [Prison Science] (Shanghai: Shanghai Faxue, 1931), 256.

17. Forced labor as punishment was no longer listed in the 1935 Criminal Code.

18. Michel Foucault, *Discipline and Punish: The Birth of the Prison* (New York: Pantheon Books, 1978).

19. Sections 154–167, Prison Law Draft of 1935, reprinted in *Minguo jianyu fagui xuanbian,* 20–37.

20. *Jianyu gailiang,* ed. Xingzhengyuan Xinwenbu (Nanjing: Xingzhengyuan, 1947), 4. The Law for the Execution of Prison Punishments (Jianyu Xingxing Fa) is in *Minguo jianyu fagui xuanbian,* 42–52. The Prison Statutes are reprinted in *Zhongguo jianyu shiliao huibian,* vol. 2, 63–67, and in *Minguo jianyu fagui xuanbian,* 38–42. On the legislation process of both laws, see Report of the Commission for the Legal System and the Commission for Criminal Law to the Lifayuan, January 9, 1946, AH 200000000A-0120.34.

21. *Laws of the Republic of China,* ed. Law Revision Planning Group (Taibei: Xingzheng Yuan, 1961), 997–1025.

22. The law texts are reprinted and discussed in the correspondence between the Mili-

tary Commission of the Republican Government and the Legal System Committee, May 1945, in HI, GMD Digital Archives.

23. There were, however, intense discussions about the criminality of fornication. This debate reveals that there were areas that remained beyond the reach of Western-inspired legal reforms. See Alison Sau-Chu Yeung, "Fornication in the Late Qing Legal Reforms," *Modern China* 29, no. 3 (2003): 297–328; Huang Yuansheng, *Minzhu falü bianqian yu caipan* [Legal Change and Sentencing during the Early Republic] (Taibei: Zhengzhi Daxue, 2000), 180–200.

24. See Xu Yamin, "Wicked Citizens and the Social Origins of China's Modern Authoritarian State: Civil Strife and Political Control in Republican Beiping, 1928–1937," PhD diss., University of California, Berkeley, 2002, 160–162.

25. The examples are from Kiely, "Making Good Citizens," 193–195 and 432. The action of a "seduced person" was generally not punishable in the Republican codes.

26. In imperial China only women were liable to be prosecuted for adultery. The new provisions seem not to have made a big difference, however, because husbands continued to be the main users and beneficiaries of the adultery law; see Huang Yuansheng, *Minzhu falü bianqian yu caipan*, 185–186.

27. See Zhao Chen, *Jianyu xue*, 258.

28. Wang Chung-hui, "Individualization of Punishment," *Chinese Social and Political Science Review* 5, no. 2 (1919): 91–99.

29. William C. Kirby, "The Internationalization of China: Foreign Relations at Home and Abroad in the Republican Era," *China Quarterly* 150 (June 1997): 433–458.

30. See Robert Heuser, *Einführung in die chinesische Rechtskultur* (Hamburg: Institut für Asiankunde, 1999).

31. Reports on criminal justice were written by Zhang Deyi, Guo Songdao, Li Gui, and Xue Fucheng. See Frank Dikötter, *Crime, Punishment and the Prison in Modern China, 1895–1949* (New York: Columbia University Press, 2002), 34–43.

32. An excellent example of the Western fascination with Chinese punishments is George Henry Mason, *The Punishments of China: Illustrated by Twenty-two Engravings: With Explanations in English and French* (London: Printed for W. Miller by W. Bulmer, 1801); for more references, see Colin Mackerras, *Western Images of China* (Oxford: Oxford University Press, 1999), 41–57.

33. Herbert Franke, "Chinese Law in a Multinational Society: The Case of Liao," *Asia Major,* third series, 5, no. 2 (1992): 111–127.

34. For a recent introduction to many of these issues, see Eileen Scully, *Bargaining with the State from Afar* (New York: Columbia University Press, 2001), esp. chaps. 2–3. Concrete examples of legal disputes involving missionaries and merchants can be found in Mechtchild Leutner and Klaus Mühlhahn, *Deutsch-chinesische Beziehungen im 19. Jahrhundert: Mission und Wirtschaft in interkultureller Perspektive* (Münster: Lit, 2001).

35. See Zhan Hengju, *Zhongguo jindai fazhi shi* [A History of the Legal System in Modern China] (Taibei: Shangwu, 1973), 97.

36. Meijer, *Introduction of Modern Criminal Law,* 65; Dikötter, *Crime, Punishment,* 43.

37. Kiely, "Making Good Citizens," 22.

38. Quoted in Robert Heuser, *Einführung in die chinesische Rechtskultur* (Hamburg: Institut für Asienkunde, 1999), 130.

39. Quoted in Kiely, "Making Good Citizens," 174.

40. *Report of the Commission on Extraterritoriality in China,* 3.

41. The Commission on Extraterritoriality arrived in China in January 1925. It stayed nine months and inspected prisons, courts, and detention centers. The report of the commission was completed in 1926 and sent to the governments involved. To the great disappointment of the Beiyang government in China, the report stated that progress had been made, but it fell short of recommending the termination of extraterritoriality.

42. Zhao Chen, *Jianyu xue,* i.

43. See, for an example from the mid-1930s, Li Jianhua, *Jianyu xue* [Prison Science] (Shanghai: Zhonghua, 1936), 9.

44. See Derk Bodde, "Prison Life in Eighteenth-Century Peking," in *Essays on Chinese Civilization,* ed. Derk Bodde (Princeton, NJ: Princeton University Press, 1981), 195–215.

45. See Kiely, "Making Good Citizens," 25.

46. See Dikötter, *Crime, Punishment,* 29.

47. Peter Zarrow, "Liang Qichao and the Notion of Civil Society in Republican China," in Joshua A. Fogel and Peter Zarrow, eds., *Imagining the People: Chinese Intellectuals and the Concept of Citizenship* (New York: M. E. Sharpe, 1997), 232–257.

48. Liang Qichao, *Xin min shuo* [On the New People] (Shenyang: Liaoning Ren Min Chu Ban She, 1994), 39.

49. See *Jianyu gailiang,* 1; see also Michael Dutton, *Policing and Punishment in China: From Patriarchy to "the People"* (Cambridge: Cambridge University Press, 1992), 157, and Kiely, "Making Good Citizens," 56.

50. See Kiely, "Making Good Citizens," 166 n. 336.

51. *Chinese Prisons,* 3.

52. Ogawa had studied law at Tokyo Senmon Gakko (the forerunner of Waseda University). On Ogawa and his role in Japan, see Daniel V. Botsman, *Punishment and Power in the Making of Modern Japan* (Princeton, NJ: Princeton University Press, 2005), 194–200 and 223–224.

53. Ogawa Shigejirō, *Jianyuxue* [Prison Science] (Hubei, 1905), 1.

54. Tu Jingyu, *Zhongguo jianyushi* [History of the Prison in China] (Tianjin, 1909).

55. Xue Meiqing and Ye Feng, "Jiu zhongguo di yi bu jianyu fadian: Daqing jianyu lü cao'an de lifa yiyi" [The First Prison Law in Old China: The Meaning of the "Draft of a Prison Law of the Great Qing Dynasty"], in *Zhongguo jianyu shiliao huibian,* 528–541.

56. Shen Jiaben, "Preface to *Jianyu fangwen lu*," in *Zhongguo jianyu shiliao huibian,* 411. This preface was written in 1907. The *Jianyu fangwen lu* was edited by Dong Kang and introduced the penal ideas of Ogawa Shigejirō.

57. Ibid.

58. Benjamin I. Schwartz, *The World of Thought in Ancient China* (Cambridge, MA: Harvard University Press, 1985), 75.

59. Wang graduated from a Japanese prison school in 1906 and thereafter devoted himself to the study of prison administration, working for two years in Japanese penitentiaries. Afterward he undertook several inspection tours of foreign prisons, which took him to several European countries. On Wang Yuanzeng, see Chen Chi et al., *The First Peking Prison* (Beijing: The First Peking Prison, 1916), 13; Kiely, "Making Good Citizens," 165–167.

60. Wang Yuanzeng, *Jianyu xue* [Prison Science] (Beijing: Jingshi Diyi Jianyu, 1924), 171.

61. Dikötter, *Crime, Punishment,* 176.

62. Wang Yuanzeng, *Jianyu guize jiangyi* [Lectures on Prison Regulations] (Beijing: Jingshi Diyi Jianyu, 1917), 74.

63. Ibid., 148.

64. See Zhao Chen, *Jianyu xue,* 255.

65. On Sun Xiong, see Kiely, "Making Good Citizens," 475–488.

66. See Dikötter, *Crime, Punishment,* 144.

67. Sun Xiong, *Jianyu xue* [Prison Science] (Shanghai: Shangwu, 1936), 7.

68. Kiely, "Making Good Citizens," 441.

69. The Shanghai Law Academy was established in 1926. Its original name was Shanghai Law University (Shanghai Fake Daxue). Renamed in 1930, it soon became a well-known and highly respected institution for judicial training. See Wu Xingnong and Ma Xueqiang, "Chu Fucheng yu Shanghai Faxue Yuan" [Chu Fucheng and the Shanghai Law Academy], in *Dangan yu lishi* 6 (2002): 47–51.

70. Li Jianhua, *Jianyu xue* [Prison Science] (Shanghai: Zhonghua, 1936), 5–9 and 84–85.

71. See Kiely, "Making Good Citizens," 440.

72. Ibid., 477.

73. Li Jianhua, *Jianyu xue,* 2.

74. Ibid., 84–89.

75. The best account of the legal reforms is in Xu Xiaoqun, *Trial of Modernity: The Judicial Reform in Early Twentieth-Century China, 1901–1937* (Stanford, CA: Stanford University Press, 2008), and Huang Yuansheng, *Minzhu falü bianqian yu caipan.* The latter focuses on the history of the Supreme Court (Daliyuan).

76. *Report of the Commission on Extraterritoriality in China,* 51, 54, 61.

77. See *Xunzhen shiqi de sifa xingzheng dagang* (1930) [Great Plan for Judicial Administration during the Period of Political Tutelage], in Zhao Chen, *Jianyu xue,* 138–140.

78. Alison W. Conner, "Training China's Early Modern Lawyers: Soochow University Law School," *Journal of Chinese Law* 8, no. 1 (1994): 1–46.

79. See Kiely, "Making Good Citizens," 437.

80. Xue Meiqing and Cong Jinpeng, *Tianjin jianyushi.*

81. See Chen Chi et al., *The First Peking Prison,* 58; Sydney D. Gamble and J. S. Burgess,

Peking, a Social Survey Conducted under the Auspices of the Princeton University Center in China and the Peking Young Men's Christian Association (New York: George H. Doran Company, 1921), 310–312.

82. The following numbers are based on *Chinese Prisons*, 12; *Jianyu gailiang*, 1–17; Dikötter, *Crime, Punishment*, 230–235; Yang Diansheng and Zhang Jinsang, *Zhongguo tese jianyu zhidu yanjiu*, 138–139. For conditions in the old-style jails, see Frederic Wakeman, Jr., *Policing Shanghai, 1927–1937* (Berkeley: University of California Press, 1995), 89, and Kiely, "Making Good Citizens," 450. The 1930 plan of the Ministry of Justice can be found in Zhao Chen, *Jianyu xue*, 138. This plan also called for a rapid expansion of courts on the county and local levels.

83. See Chen Chi et al., *The First Peking Prison*, 6–8.

84. See Dikötter, *Crime, Punishment*, 234.

85. Ibid., 324–335; *Jianyu gailiang*, 1–17.

86. Forty percent of all the new prisons were completely destroyed; see *Jianyu gailian*, 4. Twenty percent were slightly damaged, and the rest were severely damaged. The prestigious Hebei Number One Prison, for example, lost its prison wall and almost the whole roof was destroyed, all equipment had been removed, and not a single cell could be used; see Report of the Hebei High Court to the Ministry of Justice, August 12, 1946, AH 151-3556. All other prisons in Hebei Province (Tangshan Prison and Hebei Prisons Number Two, Three, Four, and Five) were damaged and in need of repairs; see Report of Hebei High Court to Ministry of Justice, April 5, 1947, AH 151-3556.

87. See Reports to the Military Commission of the Republic, 1940, HI, GMD Digital Archive Database, 003-547.

88. *Jianyu gailiang*, 2.

89. See letter of the Xingzhengyuan to the Ministry of Justice, May 9, 1944, AH 62-1517.

90. *Jianyu gailiang*, 4.

91. The cost for the repairs of Hebei Number One Prison alone added up to 80.5 million yuan. Later, in June 1947, Prison Director Wu requested another 7.5 million yuan to buy necessary equipment for the prison and its workshops; see Report of Wu Shiyuan to the Ministry of Justice, June 1947, AH 151-3556.

92. See Zhang Jingyu, "Beijing sifabu fanzui tongji de fenxi" [An Analysis of Crime Statistics from the Records of the Ministry of Justice], *Shehui xuejie* 2 (1928): 79–144.

93. Yan Jingyue, "Zhongguo jianyu wenti" [The Chinese Prison Problem], *Shehui xuejie* 3 (1929): 25–46, esp. p. 36. This number actually seems small, and in fact it represents only the tip of the iceberg. The number of old-style county jails was far higher, but no statistics seem to have been kept about the number of prisoners in them. As Yan points out, there were no data available to him for estimating the overall number of prisoners in the Beijing area. Additionally, the number of women in prison was rather small. In 1920, 137 women were in prisons in Beijing. That number grew to 174 in 1926.

94. See Report of Prison Warden Wang Yuanzeng, 28.6.1927, SHA 7/2049, 2472.

95. See Zhang Jingyu, "Beijing Sifabu," 143.

96. Ibid., 143; Gamble and Burgess, *Peking, a Social Survey,* 314; Dikötter, *Crime, Punishment,* 230.

97. Report by Warden Wang Yuanzeng, 28.6.1927, SHA 7-2049-2472. See also Yan Jingyue, "Zhongguo jianyu wenti," 48, who stressed that Beijing had almost no political prisoners during the time of his investigations (1920–1926). For women, the convictions were for different crimes: economic crimes, 74.44 percent; sexual crimes, 15.38 percent; and violent assaults, 10.18 percent. Sexual crimes included violent abductions of young girls for brothels run by elderly women.

98. Ibid., 75. See also, on domestic disputes in Beijing, Xu Yamin, "Wicked Citizens and the Social Origins of China's Modern Authoritarian State: Civil Strife and Political Control in Republican Beiping, 1928–1937," PhD diss., University of California, Berkeley, 2002, esp. chap. 4, 137–207.

99. The first municipal police force was established in 1905 under Yuan Shikai's governorship of Zhili, 1901–1907. On the history of the police in Republican China, see David Strand, *Rickshaw Beijing: City People and Politics in the 1920s* (Berkeley: University of California Press, 1989), 65, and Wakeman, *Policing Shanghai,* 188–192.

100. Xu Yamin, *Wicked Citizens,* 360.

101. Ibid., 193.

102. See Dikötter, *Crime, Punishment,* 16.

103. See Foucault, *Discipline and Punish,* 169.

104. On Bentham's Panopticon, see Foucault, *Discipline and Punish,* 195–230.

105. See Liu Zhao, *Zai caolanzi jian yu li* [Inside Caolanzi Prison] (Beijing: Zhongguo Wenshi, 1987), 50.

106. See *Chinese Prisons,* 30.

107. Yang Chih-lin, *Iron Bars but Not a Cage: Wang Jo-fei's Days in Prison* (Peking, 1962), 2. Gamble and Burgess, *Peking, a Social Survey,* 318.

108. Foucault, *Discipline and Punish,* 154.

109. See *Chinese Prisons,* 102.

110. The regulations concerning admission into prison are summarized in Sun Xiong, *Yuwu daquan* [Compendium of Prison Administration], 2nd ed. (Shanghai: Shangwu Yinshuguan, 1936), 6 and 11–12. This handbook contains regulations and statutes concerning prison administration. An example of the form for the prisoner's record can be found on p. 18.

111. See, for example, the report by Liu Zhao, *Zai caolanzi jianyu li,* 40, concerning a military detention center in Beijing. For similar observations concerning civilian prisons, see also Kiely, "Making Good Citizens," 107.

112. Erving Goffman, *Asylums: Essays on the Social Situation of Mental Patients and Other Inmates* (Chicago: Aldine Publishing, 1961), 20.

113. Ibid., 13.

114. Chen Chi et al., *The First Peking Prison,* 52 and 58–62.

115. See Goffman, *Asylums,* 23.

116. See Kiely, "Making Good Citizens," 249.

117. Ibid., 461, 482.

118. *Chinese Prisons,* 88.

119. Yang Chih-lin, *Iron Bars,* 6.

120. See Kiely, "Making Good Citizens," 229; *Chinese Prisons,* 35.

121. *Hebei di yi jianyu baogao shu* [Report of the First Hebei Prison] (Beijing: Hebei Di Yi Jianyu, 1935), 7.

122. See Kiely, "Making Good Citizens," 244.

123. See Gamble and Burgess, *Peking, a Social Survey,* 313.

124. See Kiely, "Making Good Citizens," 246, 474.

125. Jiangsu Number One Prison Report, quoted in ibid., 227.

126. Kiely, "Making Good Citizens," 137–153.

127. Article 48 of the prison law read: "Instruction shall be given to all prisoners alike"; see *Minguo jianyu fagui xuanbian,* 1–9.

128. *Chinese Prisons,* 25.

129. Kiely, "Making Good Citizens," 246.

130. Chen Chi et al., *The First Peking Prison,* 56.

131. These three categories are mentioned in *Hebei di yi jianyu baogao shu,* 41. They also were laid out as early as 1917 in Wang Yuanzeng, *Jianyu guize jiangyi* [Lectures on Prison Regulations] (Beijing, 1917), 76, although Wang did not use the exact same terms. See also Chen Chi et al., *The First Peking Prison,* 56; Yang Diansheng and Zhang Jinsang, *Zhongguo tese jianyu zhidu yanjiu,* 143.

132. See Gamble and Burgess, *Peking, a Social Survey,* 312.

133. On John Howard, an English prison reformer of the eighteenth century, see Michael Ignatieff, *A Just Measure of Pain: The Penitentiary in the Industrial Revolution 1750–1850* (New York: Pantheon Books, 1978), 47.

134. *Hebei di yi jianyu baogao shu,* 41.

135. Ibid.

136. Ibid.

137. See Wang Yuanzeng, *Jianyu guize jiangyi,* 77–78.

138. See Kiely, "Making Good Citizens," 251.

139. See *Chinese Prisons,* 25.

140. See Dikötter, *Crime, Punishment,* 110–112; Kiely, "Making Good Citizens," 270–273.

141. Yang Chih-lin, *Iron Bars,* 8–9.

142. See Kiely, "Making Good Citizens," 341–417.

143. Li Yingzhang and Eva Wong, *Lao-tzu's Treatise on the Response of the Tao: T'ai-shang kan-ying p'ien* (San Francisco: HarperCollins, 1994).

144. Cynthia Joanne Brokaw, *The Ledgers of Merit and Demerit: Social Change and Moral Order in Late Imperial China* (Princeton, NJ: Princeton University Press, 1991), 3; Ronnie Littlejohn, "Transmission of the Chinese Moral Culture: Morality and Ledger Books in the World of Moral Self-Regulation," in Lawrence D. Kessler, ed., *Southeast Review of Asian Studies,* vol. 21 (Durham, NC: Southeast Conference Publications, 1999), 15–30.

145. See Liu Kwang-Ching, "Education for Its Own Sake," in Benjamin A. Elman and Alexander Woodside, eds., *Education and Society in Late Imperial China 1600–1900* (Berkeley: University of California Press, 1994), 76–108, esp. p. 76, and Yen Chih-tui and Têng Ssu-yü, *Family Instructions for the Yen clan: Yen-shih chia-hsün: An Annotated Translation* [from the Chinese] (Leiden: E. J. Brill, 1968).

146. An abridged version called *Introduction to the Three Peoples' Principles* was commonly used. See Kiely, "Making Good Citizens," 473.

147. Ibid., 443.

148. After the Twenty-one Demands, delivered by Japan to the Chinese government in 1915, *guochi* (national humiliation) became an integral concept in Chinese nationalism; see Luo Zhitian, "National Humiliation and National Assertion: The Chinese Response to the Twenty-one Demands," *Modern Asian Studies* 27, no. 2 (1993): 297–319. It eventually became ritualized in official commemoration days and ceremonies; see Paul A. Cohen, "Remembering and Forgetting National Humiliation in Twentieth-Century China," *Twentieth-Century China* 27, no. 2 (2002): 1–39. National Humiliation Days were also commemorated in the prisons.

149. Kiely, "Making Good Citizens," 271.

150. On Shao Zhenji, see ibid., 277 and 289–310, and Dikötter, *Crime, Punishment,* 252–253; see also Shao Zhenji, *Jiaohui qianshuo* [Introduction to Prison Instruction] (Nanjing: Sifa Xingzhengbu, 1931).

151. Shao Zhenji, *Jiaohui qianshuo,* 97–101.

152. See Kiely, "Making Good Citizens," 306.

153. Shao Zhenji, *Jiaohui qianshuo,* 122.

154. See Kiely, "Making Good Citizens," 134.

155. Brokaw, *The Ledgers of Merit and Demerit,* 234, lists the following values to be found in seventeenth century morality books: five relationships, self-cultivation, frugality, humility, acceptance of hierarchical social relationships, acts of charity, and so forth.

156. *Hebei di yi jianyu baogao shu,* 41.

157. Xue Dubi was the author of several books containing wise sayings, short didactic tales, and admonitions to be used in prison instruction. His work *Speaking of Repentance and Self-Renewal (Huiguo zixin shuo)* was commonly used by prison instructors in the 1920s and 1930s. See Kiely, "Making Good Citizens," 216–227, 268. The songs were reprinted in Sun Xiong's *Yuwu daquan,* 847–850.

158. Chen Chi et al., *The First Peking Prison,* 19.

159. See Kiely, "Making Good Citizens," 203–212.

160. *Hebei di yi jianyu baogao shu,* 41.

161. See Dutton, *Policing and Punishment in China,* 174.

162. *Technologies of the Self: A Seminar with Michel Foucault,* ed. Michel Foucault et al. (Amherst: University of Massachusetts Press, 1988).

163. At the end of the Qing dynasty, some officials were already stressing the many benefits of having prisoners work in road construction and mining; see Dutton, *Policing and Punishment in China,* 153.

164. Chen Chi et al., *The First Peking Prison*, 46.

165. Ibid.

166. Kiely, "Making Good Citizens," 453.

167. See Dikötter, *Crime, Punishment*, 247–250; Kiely, "Making Good Citizens," 452.

168. Gamble and Burgess, *Peking, a Social Survey*, 311.

169. See Kiely, "Making Good Citizens," n. 280. In Beijing Number One Prison more than 80 percent of the inmates never received any payments.

170. See Huang Genghui, *Jiang lao ji* [Recollections from Chiang's Prison] (Hong Kong, 1950), 28–29.

171. See *Juntong moku: Xifeng jizhongying* [Juntong Hell: Xifeng Concentration Camp], ed. Zhengxie Guizhousheng Weiyuanhui (Guiyang: Guizhou Renmin 1999), 32.

172. For a rare account dealing with incarceration in imperial China, see Bodde, "Prison Life."

173. Yang Chih-lin, *Iron Bars*, 89–99.

174. See Huang Genghui, *Jiang lao ji*, 24.

175. One of the first to use this system was Sun Xiong, during his term as warden of Jiangsu Number Two Special District Prison; see Kiely, "Making Good Citizens," 479–481.

176. Yang Diansheng and Zhang Jinsang, *Zhongguo tese jianyu zhidu yanjiu*, 144. See the draft prison law for details, in Sun Xiong, *Yuwu daquan*, Appendix. See also resolution of the Statutes for the Accumulation and Progress Handling System by the Sifa Xingzhengbu, submitted to Lifayuan, February 19, 1946, AH 200000000A-0120.34. The statutes are reprinted in *Minguo jianyu fagui xuanbian*, 53–63.

177. Goffman, *Asylums*, 64.

178. For concrete examples, see Chen Zhixi, "Ruyu qinian zhi huigu" [A Look Back to Seven Years in Prison], *Jianyu zazhi* 1, no. 1 (1929): 1–13, esp. p. 5; Mao Cheng, *Jianyuli de douzhang* [Struggle in Prison] (Shanghai, 1958), 43; Liu Zhao, *Zai caolanzi jianyu li*, 49.

179. The best general overview is still Lloyd. E. Eastman, *Family, Fields, and Ancestors: Constancy and Change in China's Social and Economic History*, 1550–1949 (New York: Oxford University Press, 1988), 225–235. He calls this the Yin side of society.

180. See the description in Mao Cheng, *Jianyuli de douzhang*, 41–42.

181. See Kiely, "Making Good Citizens," 158.

182. See Mao Cheng, *Jianyuli de douzhang*, 43–45. Here a description is given on the fight of a group of CCP members against a cage head in a county jail in Suzhou.

183. See Kiely, "Making Good Citizens," 157. He gives a recidivism rate of 40 percent.

184. Ibid., 497–506.

185. See Li Jianhua, *Jianyu xue*, 5.

186. See also Dikötter, *Crime, Punishment*, 264–268.

187. Yang Chih-lin, *Iron Bars*, 47.

188. Wang was imprisoned in 1934 and released in 1937. His experiences are retold in Wang Ruowang, "Ji'e sanbuqu" [Hunger Trilogy], *Shouhuo* 1 (1980): 116–173.

189. Ibid., 118.

190. Yang Chih-lin, *Iron Bars*, 47. From 1931 to 1937, Yang was detained in Suiyang First Prison in Guisui (Huhehot), Inner Mongolia. This institution is listed as a "modern prison" in the report of the Commission on Extraterritoriality from 1925; see *Chinese Prisons*, 10. Suiyang First Prison was opened 1922 and could accommodate 300 prisoners.

191. Mao Cheng, *Jianyuli de douzhang*, 41.

192. The exact amount of food depended on the work of the individual prisoner. The official ration was twenty-three ounces for those not working, twenty-four ounces for factory workers, and twenty-five ounces for inmates doing hard labor. Dikötter (*Crime, Punishment*, 243) says that rations were fixed at around twenty ounces per person per day. The reports of former inmates present a different picture, and Sidney Gamble (Gamble and Burgess, *Peking, a Social Survey*, 313) confirms their accounts. Gamble also reports that rations of fourteen ounces were given to those doing hard labor. Sick prisoners received the smallest ration, six to eight ounces.

193. Quote in Xue Meiqing and Cong Jinpeng, *Tianjin jianyushi*, 61.

194. See *Chinese Prisons*, 115. This is also mentioned in Gamble and Burgess, *Peking, a Social Survey*, 312.

195. See Yang Chih-lin, *Iron Bars*, 79.

196. Mao Cheng, *Jianyuli de douzhang*, 41.

197. Gamble and Burgess, *Peking, a Social Survey*, 308.

198. Yang Chih-lin, *Iron Bars*, 79.

199. Huang Genghui, *Jiang Lao Ji*, 13.

200. Liu Zhao, *Zai caolanzi jianyu li*, 40. Yang Chih-lin, *Iron Bars*, 79.

201. Liu Zhao *Zai caolanzi jianyu li*, 40.

202. Yang Chih-lin, *Iron Bars*, 77.

203. Ibid., 89–99, quote on p. 89.

204. Goffman, *Asylums*, 23.

205. Dikötter, *Crime, Punishment*, 89.

206. See Kiely, "Making Good Citizens," 160–163.

207. See Xue Meiqing and Cong Jinpeng, *Tianjin jianyushi*, 61.

208. Heinrich Popitz, *Phänomene der Macht: Autorität, Herrschaft, Gewalt, Technik* (Tübingen: J. C. B. Mohr, 1986), 43–44.

209. See Yang Chih-lin, *Iron Bars*, 79–81.

210. Huang Genghui, *Jiang Lao Ji*, 17.

211. A very similar scene is described in Liu Zhao, *Zai caolanzi jianyu li*, 27. Here, too, the questioner wants the author to confess that he is a member of the CCP.

212. See Dikötter, *Crime, Punishment*, 136–137, 178–181.

213. See Marina Svensson, *Debating Human Rights in China: A Conceptual and Political History* (Lanham, MD: Rowman and Littlefield, 2002), 170–171.

214. See Kiely, "Making Good Citizens," 158.

215. A critical view of prison officers was put forward in Yan Jingyue, "Zhongguo jianyu wenti." His point was that officers behaved like autocrats and were inherently corrupt.

216. One case of an officer's accepting bribes and being sentenced to prison is mentioned in Dikötter, *Crime, Punishment*, 260.

217. The following examples are from Yang Chih-lin, *Iron Bars*, 2, and Huang Genghui, *Jiang lao ji*, 15. The observations and experiences reported by Yang and Geng are in general corroborated by official documents; see Dikötter, *Crime, Punishment*, 89.

218. See Huang Genghui, *Jiang lao ji*, 29, who wrote: "We prisoners became very familiar with the guards. When we saw each other, we talked and joked; this was very common."

219. On this problem see Goffman, *Asylums*, 92.

220. Mao Cheng, *Jianyuli de douzhang*, 41. This notion can be traced back to Lenin, who liked to think of prison as a university for revolutionaries.

221. Liu Zhao, *Zai caolanzi jianyu li*, 84.

222. During the Cultural Revolution many former CCP prisoners were viewed with suspicion. They were accused of having collaborated with the counterrevolutionary GMD government. A member of the Red Guard accused Bo Yibo in 1967: "When you people crawled out of that Guomindang den for dogs, is it not true that you even thanked the prison warden for the instructions and teaching he gave you?" Quote following Michael Schoenhals, *China's Cultural Revolution 1966–1969: Not a Dinner Party* (Armonk, NY: M. E. Sharpe, 1996), 128.

223. Yang Chih-lin, *Iron Bars*, 56.

224. Similar expressions can be found in colonial Vietnam concerning colonial prisons; see Peter Zinoman, *The Colonial Bastille: A History of Imprisonment in Vietnam, 1862–1940* (Berkeley: University of California Press, 2001), 99.

225. See Yang Chih-lin, *Iron Bars*, 106–114, quotation on p. 112.

226. See for instance Mao Cheng, *Jianyuli de douzhang*, 41–42.

227. Ibid., 42–47; Liu Zhao, *Zai caolanzi jianyu li*, 84–86.

228. Yang Chih-lin, *Iron Bars*, 112.

229. See for example Yang Chih-lin, *Iron Bars*, 122–126.

230. Huang Genghui, *Jiang lao ji*, 32.

231. Goffman, *Asylums*, 68.

232. See Hsiao Chün, "Goats," in Joseph S. M. Lau, Chih-tsing Hsia, and Leo Ou-fan Lee, eds., *Modern Chinese Stories and Novellas 1919–1949* (New York: Columbia University Press, 1981), 353.

233. See Michael Hardt, "Prison Time," *Yale French Studies* 91 (1997): 64–79.

234. Most prisoners—between 60 percent and 80 percent—were illiterate; see Kiely, "Making Good Citizens," 481.

235. See Du Zhongyuan, *Yuzhong zagan* [Random Impressions from Prison] (n.p., 1936), 1–30.

236. It is interesting to compare this form of heroism with patterns of heroism propagated by the military or the secret service. On the latter, see Yeh Wen-hsin, "Dai Li and the Liu Geqing Affair: Heroism in the Chinese Secret Service during the War of Resistance," *Journal of Asian Studies* 48, no. 3 (1989): 545–562; Henrietta Harrison, *The Making of the Republican Citizen: Ceremonies and Symbols in China, 1911–1929* (Oxford: Oxford University Press, 2000).

237. Luo Longji, "Wo de beibu de jingguo yu fangan" [The Outrageous Event of My Arrest], *Xinyue yuekan* 3, no. 3 (1930): 1–17. Luo Longji's commitment to human rights is discussed in Svensson, *Debating Human Rights in China,* 161–166.

238. Luo Longji, "Wo de beibu de jingguo yu fangan," 10.

239. See Edward S. K. Fung, *In Search of Chinese Democracy: Civil Opposition in Nationalist China, 1929–1949* (Cambridge: Cambridge University Press, 2000), 51–81.

240. See David Garland, *Punishment and Welfare: A History of Penal Strategies* (Aldershot, UK: Gower, 1985).

241. Philip C. C. Huang, "Biculturality in Modern China and in Chinese Studies," *Modern China* 26, no. 1 (2000): 3–31, here p. 14.

242. See Klaus Mühlhahn, "Visions of Order and Modernity: Crime, Punishment and Justice in Urban China during the Republican Period," in David Strand, Sherman Cochran, and Wen-Hsin Yeh, eds., *Cities in Motion: Interior, Coast, and Diaspora in Transnational China* (Berkeley: Institute of East Asian Studies, University of California, 2007), 182–215.

243. Frederic Wakeman, Jr., "A Revisionist View of the Nanjing Decade: Confucian Fascism," *China Quarterly* 50 (1997): 395–432.

244. Ignatieff, *A Just Measure of Pain,* 11.

245. Julia C. Strauss, *Strong Institutions in Weak Polities: State Building in Republican China 1927–1940* (Oxford: Clarendon Press; New York: Oxford University Press, 1998).

3. Trials of Terror

1. See James Sheehan, "What It Means to Be a State: States and Violence in Twentieth-Century Europe," *Journal of Modern European History* 1 (2003): 11–23.

2. Carl Schmitt, *Der Nomos der Erde im Völkerrecht des Jus Publicum Europaeum* (Cologne: Greven, 1950), 298–299.

3. This is an estimate based on the research presented below. Most of the prisons outside the justice system were secret, and no accurate numbers are available.

4. The most comprehensive overview on the detention centers of the Juntong is Zheng Xilin, "Juntong suoshude jianyu," in *Wenshi ziliao cungao xuanbian: Tegong zuzhi,* ed. Quanguo Zhengxie Wenshi Ziliao Weiyuanhui (Beijing: Zhongguo Wenshi, 2002), 85–112. See also Frederic Wakeman, Jr., *Spymaster: Dai Li and the Chinese Secret Service* (Berkeley: University of California Press, 2003), 217–220; Xue Meiqing, *Zhongguo jianyu shi* [The History of the Prison in China] (Beijing: Qunzhong, 1986), 296–306.

5. Juntong is an abbreviation for Guominzhengfu Junshi Weiyuanhui Diaocha Tongji Shi—literally, Military Statistics Bureau. This organization emerged from the reorganization of the secret services in 1938 and was directed by Dai Li. It had evolved from the Special Services Department (Tewuchu) that originally was a suborganization of the Bureau of Investigation and Statistics. This department was founded on April 1, 1932, and from its founding it was headed by Dai Li. The other impor-

tant secret service organization was called Zhongtong, which stands for Guomindang Thongyang Zhixing Weiyuanhui Diaocha Tongji Ju (Guomindang Central Executive Committee Statistics Bureau or Central Statistics Bureau). This organization was formed in the reshuffle of 1938, too, and was controlled by the brothers Chen Lifu and Chen Guofu. The history of the Chinese secret service is covered in detail in the comprehensive study by Wakeman; see *Spymaster,* 41–43, 130, 207.

6. Ibid., 163–167.

7. To the best of my knowledge there is no comprehensive study on Republican military law. For Chinese research, see Zhan Hengju, *Zhongguo jindai fazhi shi* [A History of the Legal System in Modern China] (Taibei: Shangwu, 1973), 362–385.

8. Ibid. The Qing government had a similar policy, which originated as a measure for the suppression of the Taiping rebels in the 1850s. This policy was renewed in 1922. In 1920 there were 2,824 such executions nationwide. This number increased significantly over the 1930s and 1940s.

9. The institutes are briefly mentioned in Frank Dikötter, *Crime, Punishment and the Prison in Modern China, 1895–1949* (New York: Columbia University Press, 2002), 280–282, and Jan Kiely, "Making Good Citizens: The Reformation of Prisoners in China's First Modern Prisons," PhD diss., University of California, Berkeley, 2001, 627–633.

10. See "List of Self-Investigation Institutes in All Provinces in 1931," prepared by the Sifayuan, Jan. 14, 1931, AH 200000000A-*Fanxing tiaoli.*

11. See Liu Zhao, *Zai caolanzi jianyu li* [Inside Caolanzi Prison] (Beijing: Zhongguo Wenshi, 1987), 48.

12. Robert J. Culp, *Articulating Citizenship: Civic Education and Student Politics in Southeastern China, 1912–1940* (Cambridge, MA: Harvard University Asia Center, 2007; distributed by Harvard University Press), 11.

13. Frederic Wakeman, Jr., "Hanjian (Traitor)! Collaboration and Retribution in Wartime Shanghai," in Yeh Wen-hsin, ed., *Becoming Chinese: Passages to Modernity and Beyond* (Berkeley: University of California Press, 2000), 298–341, gives a vivid picture of the polarization and outright war hysteria in China, using the persecution of traitors as an example.

14. See ibid., 217–218.

15. See *Shangrao jizhongying* [Shangrao Concentration Camp] (1945; Shanghai: Renmin Chubansuo, 1949).

16. See Wakeman, *Spymaster,* 305–307.

17. See quote in ibid., 217.

18. Memorandum prepared by Philip D. Sprouse, U.S. Consul Kunming, OSS report XL-22034, Sept. 27, 1945. Records of the Office of Strategic Services, War Department, National Archives, Washington, DC.

19. *Dai yunong xiansheng quanji* [The Collected Works of Dai Yunong], ed. Guofanbu Qingbaoju (Taibei: Shanghai Yinshuaichang, 1979), vol. 2, 1011–1012.

20. See *Juntong moku: Xifeng jizhongying* [Juntong Hell: Xifeng Concentration Camp],

ed. Zhengxie Guizhousheng Weiyuanhui (Guiyang, 1999), 21; Si Laotai, "Juntong de 'daxue': Xifeng jianyu" [Juntong's "University": Xifeng Prison] (Part 1), *Fanzui gaizao yanjiu* 5 (1991): 70–73, esp. p. 70.

21. See *Juntong moku*, 322.

22. See Chapter 2.

23. *Deutsch-chinesische Beziehungen 1928–1937: "Gleiche" Partner unter "ungleichen" Bedingungen; eine Quellensammlung,* ed. Bernd Martin and Susanne Kuss (Berlin: Akademie-Verlag, 2003), chap. 2 and 6.

24. Bernd Martin, "Die deutsche Beraterschaft in China (1927–1938)," *Militärgeschichte* 29 (1990): S.530–537. William C. Kirby, *Germany and Republican China* (Stanford, CA: Stanford University Press, 1984), 71–75.

25. Xu Youwei, "German Fascism in Chinese Eyes: An Investigation of *Qiantu* Magazine (1933—1937)," in Ricardo Mak and Danny Paau, eds., *Sino-German Relations since 1800: Multidisciplinary Explorations* (Frankfurt: Peter Lang, 2000), 235–254.

26. On Zhou Yanghao and his reform ambitions in Xifeng Camp, see Si Laotai, "Juntong de 'daxue': Xifeng jianyu" [Juntong's "University": Xifeng Prison] (Part 2), *Fanzui gaizao yanjiu* 6 (1991): 65–68; Mao Zuoyuan, "Zhou Yanghao xiaozhuan" [Short Biography of Zhou Yanghao], *Jiangshanshi zhenxie wenshi ziliao* 10 (1994): 122–127; *Juntong moku*, 46–61, 68–73; Constantin Rissov, *Le dragon enchaîné: De Chiang Kai-Shek à Mao Zedong: 35 ans d'intimité avec la Chine* (Paris: Editions R. Laffont, 1986), 170.

27. Li Renfu, "Juntong tewu jigou xifeng jizhongying heimu" [The Truth of Xifeng Concentration Camp], *Wenshi ziliao xuanji* 28 (1986): 104–137; Xue Meiqing, *Zhongguo jianyu shi,* 303–305.

28. Li Renfu, "Juntong tewu jigou," 122–125.

29. Some witnesses speak of approximately 1,000 prisoners and 600 confirmed deaths, with a high number of missing prisoners. See *Juntong moku*, 74, 318. In his confession in 1964 Zhou maintained that there were on average not more than 230 prisoners; see Zhou Yanghao, "Juntong xifeng jizhongying neimu" [Internal details about the Juntong Concentration Camp in Xifeng], in *Wenshi ziliao cungao xuanbian: Tegong zuzhi,* ed. Quanguo Zhengxie Wenshi Ziliao Weiyuanhui (Beijing: Zhongguo Wenshi, 2002), 112–119, esp. p. 115. During his interrogation Zhou sought to play down the camp in every respect and also to diminish his responsibility, for obvious reasons.

30. See Huang Tongguang, "Wo suo qinli de xifeng jizhongying" [My Experiences in Xifeng Concentration Camp], in *Wenshi ziliao xuanji* 40 (1986): 208–225; Si Laotai, "Juntong de 'daxue'" (Part 2), 71–71.

31. The information on prisoner categories is based on Zhou Yanghao, "Juntong xifeng jizhongying neimu," 115.

32. On the common use of *tongzhi,* see Wakeman, *Spymaster,* 270.

33. See ibid., 215–218. Wakeman writes: "Service in Dai Li's secret police was, in effect, a lifetime term. . . . If a person even asked for Dai Li's permission to retire, he or she risked being clapped into confinement indefinitely" (220).

34. See *Juntong moku,* 186–222.

35. Ibid., 248–250; Yang Jianye, *Ma Yinchu* (Shijiazhuan: Hueshan Wenyi, 1997), 67–72; Zheng Jiarong, *Ma Yinchu zhuan* [Biography of Ma Yinchu] (Shanghai: Wenyi, 1986), 71–76.

36. See Li Renfu, "Juntong Tewu Jigou," 106–108.

37. See *Juntong moku,* 5; Li Renfu, "Juntong tewu jigou," 111.

38. Li Renfu "Juntong tewu jigou," 112–113.

39. Zhou Yanghao, "Juntong xifeng jizhongying neimu," 114.

40. See Li Renfu, "Juntong tewu jigou," 116, 127–129; Huang Tongguang, "Wo suo qinli de xifeng jizhongying," 214–216.

41. See *Juntong moku,* 32.

42. See Li Renfu, "Juntong tewu jigou," 110, 125–127, 129–133.

43. The following passages are based on Chinese memoirs. This account is fully corroborated by the description in Rissov, *Le dragon enchaîné,* 149–218.

44. In many Juntong stations and prisons, torture was "perforce routine, and the threat of it was always present," Wakeman, *Spymaster,* 161–167. Torture frequently resulted in the death of the victim.

45. Ibid., 164.

46. See Li Renfu, "Juntong tewu jigou," 114–115; Hung Tongguang, "Wo suo qinli de xifeng jizhongying"; *Juntong moku,* 75–76.

47. Shen Zui, *Shen Zui riji* [The Diary of Shen Zui] (Beijing: Qunzhong, 1991), 107, 170.

48. See *Juntong moku,* 54–67, 77–90.

49. This is possibly the reason for the suspicion directed toward communist former inmates after 1949. Doubt was cast about their true role in the prison and the degree of collaboration they were forced to render.

50. *Juntong moku,* 83.

51. See Frederic Wakeman, Jr., "A Revisionist View of the Nanjing Decade: Confucian Fascism," *China Quarterly* 50 (1997): 395–432.

52. See Oliver Caldwell, *A Secret War: Americans in China, 1944–1945* (Carbondale: Southern Illinois University, 1984), 75.

53. Culp, *Articulating Citizenship,* 205–208.

54. In "Instruction to Abolish the Six Codes of the Guomindang and to Define the Judicial Principles for the Liberated Areas," issued by the Central Committee of the CCP, it was stated that "all the Guomindang laws are nothing but instruments designed to protect the reactionary rule of the landlords, the compradors, the bureaucrats, and the bourgeoisie, and weapons to suppress and coerce the vast masses of the people." Cited in *Lectures on the General Principles of Criminal Law in the People's Republic of China,* ed. U.S. Department of Commerce, Office of Technical Services (Washington, DC: Joint Publications Research Services, 1962), 7.

55. As a leading Soviet legal scholar put it: "The state was always, and still is, an apparatus of constraint—of violence—with whose aid the dominant classes ensured the obedience of their 'subjects.' The state is a machine to sustain the domination of one class over another." Quoted from Andrei Y. Vyshinsky, *The Law of the Soviet*

State, trans. Hugh W. Babb (New York: Macmillan, 1948), 11. According to the Soviet view, law in capitalism serves to preserve and confirm the class interests of exploiters, who are dominant in that society. When the state is in the hands of the people, however, the need for law withers away.

56. This is not to say that this special meaning of labor is unique to socialists. While Marxists attached a transcendent secular meaning to labor, the transformative power of labor can be traced back further to Protestant (especially Calvinist) religion.

57. See Thomas Welskopp, *Das Banner der Brüderlichkeit: Die deutsche Sozialdemokratie vom Vormärz bis zum Sozialistengesetz* (Bonn: J. H. W. Dietz, 2000), 127–129.

58. Ibid.

59. Originally this was part of Engels's unfinished *Dialektik der Natur.* Written in June 1876, the piece was eventually published in 1896 in the journal *Die Neue Zeit.* See Institut für Marxismus-Leninismus beim ZK der SED, ed., *Marx Engels Werke* (Berlin: Dietz Verlag, 1975), vol. 20, 444–455, and 663 n. 255. The Chinese edition is in *Makesi Engesi xuanji* (Beijing: Renmin, 1972), vol. 3, 508–520.

60. *Marx Engels Werke,* 20:444.

61. Ibid., 448, 450.

62. Rudolf G. Wagner, "The Concept of Work/Labor/*Arbeit* in the Chinese World: First Explorations," in W. Bierwisch, ed., *Die Rolle der Arbeit in verschiedenen Epochen und Kulturen* (Berlin: Akademie-Verlag, 2003), 103–127.

63. See, for example, *Zou shang xinlu* [On the Path to Renewal], ed. Sifabu Zhengyanshi Laogaiju (Beijing: Falü Chubanshe, 1986), ii.

64. Mengzi, *Tang Wengong* (third book), chap. 4.

65. See Rudolf G. Wagner, "Notes on the History of the Chinese Term for 'Labor,'" in Michael Lackner and Natascha Vittinghoff, eds., *Mapping Meanings: The Field of New Learning in Late Qing China* (Leiden: Brill, 2004), 129–142.

66. Liu Shaoqi, May Day Address, April 29, 1950, in Liu Shaoqi, *Liu Shaoqi xuanji* [Selected Works of Liu Shaoqi] (Beijing: Renmin, 1985), vol. 2, 10.

67. Mao made this point very clearly in his 1937 essay entitled "On Practice"; see Mao Zedong, *Selected Works of Mao Tse-tung,* 4 vols. (Beijing: Foreign Languages Press, 1967), vol. 1, 308.

68. Quoted in Frederic Wakeman, Jr., *History and Will: Philosophical Perspectives of Mao Tse-tung's Thought* (Berkeley: University of California Press, 1973), 47.

69. Quote following Michael Jakobson, *Origins of the GULAG: The Soviet Prison Camp System 1917–1934* (Lexington: University Press of Kentucky, 1993), 37. Apparently Trotsky used the term "concentration camp" as well; see Anne Applebaum, *Gulag: A History* (New York: Doubleday, 2003), 31; Galina Mikhailovna Ivanova, *Labor Camp Socialism: The Gulag in the Soviet Totalitarian System,* trans. Carol Flath, ed. Donald J. Raleigh (Armonk, NY: M. E. Sharpe, 2000), 12; Nicolas Werth, "A State against Its People: Violence, Repression, and Terror in Soviet Union," in Stéphane Courtois et al., *The Black Book of Communism: Crimes, Terror, Repression,* trans.

Jonathan Murphy and Mark Kramer (Cambridge, MA: Harvard University Press, 1999), 45–295, here p. 87.

70. The number is from Ivanova, *Labor Camp Socialism*, 13.

71. Quoted in Jakobson, *Origins of the GULAG*, 19.

72. Ralf Stettner, *Archipel Gulag: Stalins Zwangslager* (Paderborn, Ger.: Schöningh, 1996), 46. See also the detailed account in Jakobson, *Origins of the GULAG*, 35–40.

73. See Applebaum, *Gulag*, 65.

74. Ibid., 102.

75. Dietrich Beyrau, *Petrograd, 25. Oktober 1917 Die russische Revolution und der Aufstieg des Kommunismus* (Munich: Deutscher Taschenbuch Verlag, 2001), 180.

76. See Applebaum, *Gulag*, 103–124; Peter H. Solomon, Jr., *Soviet Criminal Justice under Stalin* (Cambridge: Cambridge University Press, 1996), 111–149.

77. Anton S. Makarenko was born March 1, 1888, in Belopolye, Ukraine, in the Russian Empire, and died April 1, 1939, in Moscow, Russia, in the USSR. He was a teacher and social worker and was the most influential educational theorist in the Soviet Union. Makarenko authored several books on education, including *Pedagogicheskaya poema* [The Road to Life: An Epic of Education] (1933–35), which is an account of his work at the Gorky Colony, and *Kniga dlya roditeley* [A Book for Parents] (1937). His Dzerzhinsky Commune was visited by numerous delegations from all over the world. See *Anton Makarenko: His Life and His Work in Education*, ed. Valentin Kumarin (Moscow: Progress Publishers, 1976), 32.

78. On the importance of Makarenko in China, see for example the discussion in Sun Xiaoli, *Zhongguo laodong gaizao zhidu de lilun yu shijian: Lishi yu xianshi* [Laogai: The Chinese Prison System's Theory and Practices: History and Reality] (Beijing: Zhengfa Daxue, 1994), 17–18.

79. Lotte Adolphs, *A. S. Makarenko: Erzieher im Dienste der Revolution: Versuch einer Interpretation* (Godesberg, Ger.: Verlag Dürrsche Buchhandlung, 1962), 18–42.

80. See Anton Semyonovich Makarenko, *Problems of the Soviet School Education* (Moscow: Progress Publisher, 1965), 71.

81. E. Koutaissoff, "Soviet Education and the New Man," *Soviet Studies* 5, no. 2 (1953): 103–137, here p. 133.

82. Makarenko, *Problems of the Soviet School Education*, 56.

83. Ibid., 82.

84. Ibid., 83.

85. See Jakobson, "Die Funktionen und die Struktur des sowjetischen Gefängnis- und Lagersystems," 208; Stettner, *Archipel Gulag*, 43–45.

86. See Malgorzata Gizejewska, "Die Einzigartigkeit und der besondere Charakter der Konzentrationslager in Kolyma und die Möglichkeit des Überlebens," in Dittmar Dahlmann and Gerhard Hirschfeld, eds., *Lager, Zwangsarbeit, Vertreibung und Deportation: Dimensionen der Massenverbrechen in der Sowjetunion und in Deutschland 1933–1945* (Essen: Klartext-Verlag, 1999), 245–260, esp. p. 247.

87. Andrzej Kaminski, *Konzentrationslager 1896 bis heute: Eine Analyse* (Stuttgart: W. Kohlhammer, 1982), 114–176.

88. Alexandr Isaevich Solzhenitsyn, *The Gulag Archipelago, 1918–1956: An Experiment in Literary Investigation* (New York: Harper and Row, 1974).

89. See Frederick C. Teiwes, "Establishment and Consolidation of the New Regime," in Roderick MacFarquhar and John K. Fairbank, eds., *The Cambridge History of China*, vol. 14: *The People's Republic, Part I: The Emergence of Revolutionary China 1949–1965* (Cambridge: Cambridge University Press, 1987), 51–143, esp. p. 63–67.

90. Jonathan Spence, *Mao Zedong* (New York: Viking, 1999), 69.

91. Jürgen Osterhammel, *Shanghai, 30. Mai 1925: Die chinesische Revolution* (Munich: Deutscher Taschenbuch Verlag, 1997), 191–207; quotation on p. 196.

92. Werner Meissner, *Das rote Haifeng: Peng Pai's Bericht über die Bauernbewegung in Südchina* (Munich: Minerva, 1987), 60.

93. Jean-Louis Margolin, "China: A Long March into Night," in Stéphane Courtois et al., *The Black Book of Communism: Crimes, Terror, Repression*, trans. Jonathan Murphy and Mark Kramer (Cambridge, MA: Harvard University Press, 1999), 511–608, esp. pp. 520–521.

94. Mao Zedong, *Mao's Road to Power: Revolutionary Writings 1912–1949*, ed. Stuart R. Schram (Armonk, NY: M. E. Sharpe, 1992–), vol. 2, 418–455.

95. Ibid., 2:433.

96. Mao Zedong, "Report on the Second General Meeting of the Soviet, January 1934," quoted in Wang Gengxin, *Mao Zedong laodong gaizao sixiang yanjiu* [Mao Zedong's Thoughts on Labor Reform] (Xi'an: Shehui Kexue, 1992), 158.

97. Stephen C. Averill, *Revolution in the Highlands: China's Jinggangshan Base Area* (Lanham, MD: Rowman and Littlefield, 2006).

98. Jean-Luc Domenach, *Chine, l'archipel oublié* (Paris: Fayard, 1992), 38.

99. Ibid., 39.

100. Zhang Xipo and Yanlong Han, *Zhongguo geming fazhi shi* [History of the Legal System during the Chinese Revolution] (Beijing: Shehui Kezue, 1987), 388.

101. Yang Diansheng and Jinsang Zhang, *Zhongguo tese jianyu zhidu yanjiu* [Studies on the Prison System with Chinese Characteristics] (Beijing: Falü Chubanshe, 1998), 14; Han Yanlong and Chang Zhaoru, *Zhongguo xinminzhu zhuyi gemingshiqi genjudi fazhi wenxian xuanbian* [Selected Documents Concerning the Legal System in the Soviets during the Revolutionary Period of the New Democracy of China] (Beijing: Shehui Kezue, 1981), 343–347.

102. Patricia Griffin, "Prison Management in the Kiangsi and Yenan Periods," *China Quarterly* 58 (1974): 310–331, quotation on p. 312.

103. Ibid., 313.

104. *Suwei'ai Zhongguo* [Soviet China], ed. Zhongguo Xiandai Shi Ziliao Bianjiweiyuan (Beijing: Zhongguo Xiandai Shi Ziliao Bianjiweiyuanhui, 1957), 266.

105. Yang Diansheng and Jinsang Zhang, *Zhongguo tese jianyu*, 12.

106. Griffin, "Prison Management in the Kiangsi and Yenan Periods," 313.

107. The CCP used the phrase *sixiang gaizao* instead of *sixiang ganhua*, the term used by the GMD to describe a similar process of thought reform. The communists preferred to use different words, although the difference between the various practices was not all that big.

108. David E. Apter and Tony Saich, *Revolutionary Discourse in Mao's Republic* (Cambridge, MA: Harvard University Press, 1994), 163–192.

109. Jung Chang and Jon Halliday, *Mao: The Unknown Story* (London: Jonathan Cape, 2005), 255.

110. Michael Dutton, *Policing Chinese Politics: A History* (Durham, NC: Duke University Press, 2005), 90; Jung Chang and Halliday, *Mao*, 253.

111. See the in-depth discussion in Dutton, *Policing Chinese Politics*, 71–132. The origins of party security and communist policing date back to the Jiangxi era.

112. Patricia Griffin, *The Chinese Communist Treatment of Counterrevolutionaries: 1924–1949* (Princeton, NJ: Princeton University Press, 1976), 109–116.

113. Sun Xiaoli, *Zhongguo laodong gaizao*, 10.

114. Frank Dikötter, "The Emergence of Labour Camps in Shangdong Province 1942–1950," *China Quarterly* 173 (2003): 803–817.

115. See Xue Meiqing, *Zhongguo jianyu shi* [The History of the Prison in China] (Beijing: Qunzhong, 1986), 374.

116. See Sun Xiaoli, *Zhongguo laodong gaizao*, 11.

117. Because of its function as a model prison, Harbin Prison is relatively well covered in secondary Chinese sources. The following paragraphs are based on Sun Xiaoli, *Zhongguo laodong gaizao*, 11–12, and Xue Meiqing, *Zhongguo jianyu shi*, 375–378. Zhu De's statement on Harbin is cited in "Jiefang zhanzheng de shiqi de ha'erbin shi jianyu" [Harbin Prison during the War of Liberation], *Laigai laojiao lilun yanjiu* 1 (1990).

118. Sun Xiaoli, *Zhongguo laodong gaizao*, 12.

119. Elizabeth A. Wood, *Performing Justice: Agitation Trials in Early Soviet Russia* (Ithaca, NY: Cornell University Press, 2005), 220.

120. See Griffin, *Chinese Communist Treatment of Counterrevolutionaries*, 122–123.

121. Mark Mazower, "Violence and the State in the Twentieth Century," *American Historical Review* 107, no. 4 (2002).

122. Dutton, *Policing Chinese Politics*, 3–21.

4. Reform through Labor

1. See Jerome Alan Cohen, "Drafting People's Mediation Rules," in John Wilson Lewis, ed., *The City in Communist China* (Stanford, CA: Stanford University Press, 1971), 29–50, here p. 31; Frederick C. Teiwes, "The Chinese State during the Maoist Era," in David L. Shambaugh, ed., *The Modern Chinese State* (New York: Cambridge University Press, 2000), 107.

2. Similar periods are outlined in Klaus Mäding, *Strafrecht und Massenerziehung in der Volksrepublik China* (Frankfurt: Suhrkamp, 1979), 44–46, and Jerome Alan Cohen, *The Criminal Process in the People's Republic of China 1949–1963* (Cambridge, MA: Harvard University Press, 1968), 9–18.

3. See Edgar Thomson and Jyun-hsyong Su, *Regierung und Verwaltung der VR China* (Cologne: Verlag Wissenschaft und Politik, 1972), 323–325. As early as February 22, 1949, a decree of the CCP demanded the nullification of the so-called Six Codes of the Republic (Organic Law, Commercial Law, Civil Code, Criminal Code, Civil

Code of Procedure, Criminal Code of Procedure); Cohen, *The Criminal Process,* 298–299.

4. See Thomson and Su, *Regierung und Verwaltung der VR China,* 323–325.

5. Albert P. Blaustein, ed., *Fundamental Legal Documents of Communist China* (South Hackensack, NJ: F. B. Rothman, 1962), 215–221.

6. See Chiu Hungdah, *Criminal Punishment in Mainland China: A Study of Some Yunnan Province Documents* (Baltimore: University of Maryland School of Law, 1978), 6.

7. See *Xingfaxue quanshu* [Criminal Law Encyclopedia], ed. Xingfaxue Quanshu Bianweihui (Shanghai: Kexue Jushu Wenxian, 1993), 242.

8. Offenses listed were: maintaining links with imperialists with the intention of betraying the motherland (Article 3); inciting others to insurrection (Articles 4 and 5); espionage (Article 6); underground activities on behalf of internal and external enemies and organizing counterrevolutionary and espionage groups (Article 7); destroying or plundering military installations, factories, mines, forests, farms, dams, jetties, communications lines, transport systems, banks, warehouses, safety devices, and other important state or private property; using poisons or bacteria to seriously harm people, livestock, and crops; impairing the market or the monetary system at the order of the enemy; attacking, killing, or wounding civil servants or individual citizens (all Article 9); inciting the masses to show resistance to government action, and sowing dissent and hostility among nationalities, democratic classes, parties, or organizations (Article 10); secretly crossing the national borders (Article 11); organizing the mass liberation or mass flight of prisoners (Article 12); providing aid to counterrevolutionary criminals (Article 13). Article 14 promised a mitigation of punishment for those who voluntarily confessed their crimes. Article 16 introduced the principle of crime by analogy: persons who committed crimes not specified in the statute were subject to the punishment applicable to the crime in the statute that most closely resembled theirs. Article 18 stated that the statute was also applicable to counterrevolutionary crimes committed before the statutes came into effect. Therefore it was given a retroactive force.

9. Henry Wei, *Courts and Police in Communist China to 1952,* Human Resources Research Institute Research Memorandum No. 44, (San Antonio, TX: Lackland Air Force Base, 1955), 32.

10. See *Xingfaxue quanshu,* 555. The following regulations and statutes, too, bore the character of criminal legislation: Statute for the Prohibition of Opium and Narcotics, February 24, 1950; Temporary Regulations on Penalties for the Crime of Impairment of the National Currency, April 19, 1951; Temporary Regulations for the Protection of State Secrets, June 1, 1951; Statute on Penalties for Corruption in the PRC, April 21, 1952 (all in Blaustein, ed., *Fundamental Legal Documents of Communist China,* 227–231); Temporary Regulations for the Surveillance of Counterrevolutionary Elements, June 27, 1952 (ibid., 222–226); Decision of the Standing Committee at the National People's Congress concerning the Lenient Treatment and Placement of Remnant Urban Counterrevolutionaries, Nov. 16, 1956. See *Xingfaxue quanshu,* 555–559; Cohen, *The Criminal Process,* 303–304.

11. See Mäding, *Strafrecht und Massenerziehung*, 61–62. Cohen, *The Criminal Process*, 22 and 317, and Chiu Hungdah, *Criminal Punishment*, 4, both mention unpublished regulations and case collections that the courts were provided with. It appears that such unpublished regulations defined murder, rape, arson, and many other common crimes and set forth the maximum and minimum penalties for each crime.

12. Leng Shao-cuan, *Justice in Communist China: A Survey of the Judicial System of the Chinese People's Republic* (New York: Oceana Publications, 1967), 28.

13. See Leng, *Justice in Communist China*, 32–33.

14. On the movement, see Cohen, *The Criminal Process*, 10; Jerome Alan Cohen, "The Party and the Courts 1949–1959," *China Quarterly* 38 (1969): 120–157, here p. 131; Leng, *Justice in Communist China*, 39–44.

15. There were several types of campaigns, distinguished by their reach into society and their target groups; see Julia Strauss, "Morality, Coercion and State Building by Campaign in the Early PRC: Regime Consolidation and After, 1949–1956," *China Quarterly* 188 (Dec. 2006): 891–219. In the following, I focus mainly on two types of campaigns: the great mass campaigns, or *qunzhong yundong*, that took place in the years 1950 to 1953 and the frequent, more limited campaigns that were implemented through the bureaucracy and that targeted specific social or occupational groups. Both campaign types deployed tribunals.

16. See Leng, *Justice in Communist China*, 35–39.

17. Ibid., 36.

18. Sentences exceeding a five-year term of imprisonment needed to be ratified by the provincial government.

19. Amnesty International, *Political Imprisonment in the People's Republic of China* (London: Amnesty International, 1978), 56.

20. Quote from Wei, *Courts and Police in Communist China*, 38. The source is a report in *Renmin zhoubao*, Beijing, June 3, 1951.

21. Julia C. Strauss, "Paternalist Terror: The Campaign to Suppress Counterrevolutionaries and Regime Consolidation in the People's Republic of China, 1950–1953," *Comparative Studies in Society and History* 44 (2002): 80–105, here p. 97.

22. See Michael Dutton, *Policing Chinese Politics: A History* (Durham, NC: Duke University Press, 2005), 167.

23. A total number of 800,000 executed counterrevolutionaries is often mentioned in official documents. In 1957 Mao Zedong himself explained that during the campaign to eliminate counterrevolutionaries in the years 1950 to 1953, 700,000 people had been killed. In the period from 1954 to 1957, an additional 70,000 people had been executed as counterrevolutionaries. He also admitted that mistakes had been made and innocent people had been killed; see R. MacFarquhar et al., eds., *The Secret Speeches of Chairman Mao: From the Hundred Flowers to the Great Leap Forward* (Cambridge, MA: Council on East Asian Studies, Harvard University, 1989), 142.

24. A mass trial and a mass execution of around fifty landlords during the Land Reform Movement are described in Gregory Ruf, *Cadres and Kin: Making a Socialist*

Village in West China, 1921–1991 (Stanford, CA: Stanford University Press, 1998), 86–87.

25. In 1950 and 1951 Mao Zedong wrote several comments on the "Movement to Suppress and Liquidate Counterrevolutionaries"; see Mao Zedong, *The Writings of Mao Zedong, 1949–1976*, 2 vols. (Armonk, NY: M. E. Sharpe, 1992), vol. 1, 189, 112. He expressed increasing uneasiness about the movement's getting out of control. He saw two dangers—left deviation and right deviation. It seemed to him that in some places there was too much fervor against opponents and in others too much leniency. His comments therefore alternated between demanding a more orderly approach and calling for stricter and swifter punishments. On May 8, 1951 (ibid., 189), he argued that only perpetrators who had committed the most severe crimes (murder, rape) should be executed immediately and that all others should receive a two-year delay. A few weeks later, on June 15, 1951 (202), he argued that his earlier policy should not be mistaken as being too lenient. In any case, Mao's frequent comments demonstrate how difficult it was to control the movement.

26. On the mass trial as augmenting the legal system, see Michael Dutton, *Policing and Punishment in China: From Patriarchy to "the People"* (Cambridge: Cambridge University Press, 1992), 266.

27. As Julia Strauss has argued with respect to the mass campaigns, an important audience was the "regional and local layers of the revolutionary state"; see Strauss, "Paternalist Terror," 85.

28. See Tao Siju, *Luo Ruiqing: Xin zhongguo di yi ren gong'an buzhang* [Luo Ruiqing: New China's First Minister of Public Security] (Beijing: Qunzhong Chubanshe, 1996), 104.

29. Cohen, *The Criminal Process*, 425–428; Wei, *Courts and Police in Communist China*, 3; Leng, *Justice in Communist China*, 77–101.

30. Edward J. McCabe, "Structural Elements of Contemporary Criminal Justice in the People's Republic of China," in Ronald J. Troyer, John P. Clark, and Dean G. Rojek, eds. *Social Control in the People's Republic of China* (New York: Praeger, 1989), 116–129, here p. 117.

31. Law of the PRC for the Organization of People's Procuracies, Sept. 21, 1954. Regulations of the PRC on Arrest and Detention, Dec. 20, 1954. On the latter, see Kam C. Wong, "Police Powers and Control in the People's Republic of China: The History of Shoushen," *Columbia Journal of Asian Law* 10, no. 2 (1996): 367–390, here p. 370.

32. Similar to the police in Republican China, the Public Security Bureau had many other tasks, such as maintaining local control and guarding the political line. On the creation of the Public Security Bureaus, see Dutton, *Policing Chinese Politics*, 137–139.

33. See Chiu Hungdah, *Criminal Punishment*, 17.

34. In principle there was the short-lived institution of the "people's lawyer," who provided legal counsel. This system was formally established in 1955, modeled after a similar institution in the Soviet Union. Particularly in high-profile cases, defendants were provided with this form of legal aid. Following the 1956–57 Hundred

Flowers Campaign, lawyers were branded rightists and were purged; thereafter no legal counsel was available. See Ethan Michelson, "Lawyers, Political Embeddedness, and Institutional Continuity in China's Transition from Socialism," *American Journal of Sociology* 113, no. 2 (Sept. 2007): 352–414, here p. 364.

35. Cohen, *The Criminal Process*, 13.

36. See Leng, *Justice in Communist China*, 51.

37. Liu Shaoqi, *The Selected Works of Liu Shaoqi*, vol. 2 (Beijing: Foreign Languages Press, 1991), 241.

38. See Cohen, "The Party and the Courts," 136–137.

39. Mäding, *Strafrecht und Massenerziehung*, 48.

40. See Lowell Dittmer, *China's Continuous Revolution: The Post-Liberation Epoch 1949–1981* (Berkeley: University of California Press, 1988), 51; Leng, *Justice in Communist China*, 56, mentions a much higher number. He speaks of 4,072 laws and regulations that had been issued. The latter figure includes all decrees, regulations, and laws ever issued.

41. Liang Genlin and Huixin He, "Ershi shiji de zhongguo xingfaxue" [The Chinese Study of Criminal Law in the Twentieth Century], *Zhongwai faxue* 2 (1999): 17–29, here p. 26.

42. See Cohen, *The Criminal Process*, 205.

43. See Chiu Hungdah, *Criminal Punishment*, 4–5.

44. See Wang Shizhou, "The Judicial Explanation in Chinese Criminal Law," *American Journal of Comparative Law* 43 (1995): 569–575, here pp. 572–575.

45. See Randle Edwards, *Reflections on Crime and Punishment in China: With Appended Sentencing Documents* (Baltimore: University of Maryland School of Law, 1977), 2.

46. See Roderick MacFarquhar, *The Hundred Flowers Campaign and the Chinese Intellectuals* (New York: Praeger, 1960), 114–116.

47. See the programmatic speech by Luo Ruiqing, "Fu zongli zai quanguo gongan, jiancha, sifa xianjin gongzuozhe dahui shang de jianghua gaoyao" [Excerpts from Vice Premier Luo Ruiqing's Speech Delivered to the National Conference of Progressive Public Security, Procuratorial, and Judicial Workers], *Zhengfa yanjiu* 3 (1959): 1–6, in which he outlined the Great Leap Forward policy on public security and legal work. See also Edwards, *Reflections*, 8.

48. Most severe was the movement to "liquidate counterrevolution" (*sufan*, or *suqing ancang fangeming*) that was carried out in the second half of 1955.

49. Edwards, *Reflections*, 5.

50. See the list of names in Leng, *Justice in Communist China*, 55.

51. See Cohen, *The Criminal Process*, 198, 425; the Ministry of Justice was abolished through the Resolution of the First Meeting of the Second Session of the National People's Congress of the PRC Relating to Abolition of the Ministry of Justice and the Ministry of Supervision (passed April 4, 1959).

52. Edwards, *Reflections*, 5; Jerome A. Cohen, "Reports from China—Chinese Law: At the Crossroads," *China Quarterly* 53 (Jan.–Mar. 1973), 139–140, here p. 140.

53. See Gerd Ruge, "An Interview with Chinese Legal Officials," *China Quarterly* 61 (1975): 118–126, here p. 120. In this 1974 interview with legal officials, they stressed that there was no need for defense lawyers in China. People would know the law and could speak for themselves. Chiu Hungdah, *Criminal Punishment,* 17, has found no reference to lawyers in his analysis of sentencing documents from the 1970s.

54. Mao's instruction is quoted in Leng Shao-cuan, *The Role of Law in the People's Republic of China as Reflecting Mao Tse-Tung's Influence* (Baltimore: University of Maryland School of Law, 1978), 1; see also Leng Shao-cuan and Chiu Hongdah, *Criminal Justice in Post-Mao China: Analysis and Documents* (Albany: State University of New York Press, 1985), 17–20; Edwards, *Reflections,* 6; Stanley B. Lubman, "Form and Function in the Chinese Criminal Process," *Columbia Law Review* 69 (1969): 535–574.

55. See Michael Schoenhals, "The Central Case Examination Group, 1966–1979" *China Quarterly* 145 (1996): 87–111.

56. See Liu Zongren, *Hard Time: Thirty Months in a Chinese Labor Camp* (San Francisco: China Books and Periodicals, 1995), 2–3.

57. See Dutton, *Policing and Punishment,* 279.

58. See "On the People's Democratic Dictatorship and the People's Democratic Legal System: Compendium on the Leap Forward in Scientific Studies at the Chinese People's University," *Chinese Law and Government* 2, no. 2 (1969): 3–61, quote on p. 9.

59. See Luo Ruiqing, "Shi nian lai geming tong fan gemeing de douzheng," *Zhengfu yanjiu* 5 (1959): 11–17.

60. See Cohen, *The Criminal Process,* 818.

61. See Ruge, "An Interview with Chinese Legal Officials," 121.

62. See Luo Ruiqing (Minister of Public Security), "Shi nian lai geming tong fan gemeing de douzheng," 5, and his speech "Gongan gongzuo bixu jin yi bu de guanche qunzhong luxian" [Public Security Work Must Further Implement the Mass Line], *Zhengfa yanjiu* 3 (1958): 23–27.

63. Cohen, "The Party and the Courts," 145. Until the mid-1970s, more than 80 percent of all cases are said to have been handled this way; see Leng, *Justice in Communist China,* 65.

64. See Mäding, *Strafrecht und Massenerziehung,* 93–96; Edwards, *Reflections,* 4.

65. Li Shaoqi, *Selected Works,* 2:431.

66. See Luo Ruiqing, "Gongan gongzuo bixu jin yi bu de guanche qunzhong luxian," 27.

67. Jerome Alan Cohen, "Drafting People's Mediation Rules," in John Wilson Lewis, ed., *The City in Communist China* (Stanford, CA: Stanford University Press, 1971), 29–50, here p. 32.

68. Dittmer, *China's Continuous Revolution,* 52.

69. Victor H. Li, "Law and Penology: Systems of Reform and Correction," in Michael Oksenberg et al., eds., *China's Developmental Experience* (New York: Academy of Political Science, 1973), 144–156, here p. 151.

70. One can point to the difficulties Mao had with steering several of the campaigns mentioned above.

71. This is often stressed by scholars in the PRC; see Sun Xiaoli, *Zhongguo laodong gaizao zhidu de lilun yu shijian: Lishi yu xianshi* [Laogai: The Chinese Prison System's Theory and Practices: History and Reality] (Beijing: Zhengfa Daxue, 1994), 36. The following leaders are said to have had a stake in the early development of Laogai: Mao Zedong, Zhou Enlai, Liu Shaoqi, Zhu De, Dong Biwu, Deng Xiaoping, Peng Zhen, Luo Ruiqing.

72. Wolfgang Bauer, "Die Ideologie des heutigen China und ihr historischer Hintergrund," in Jürgen Faulenbach, ed., *VR China im Wandel* (Bonn: Ostkolleg der Bundeszentrale für politische Bildung, 1988), 43–60. This argument is developed in Mao's text "On Contradiction" from 1937.

73. Tang Tsou, "Marxism, the Leninist Party, the Masses and the Citizens in the Rebuilding of the Chinese State," in Stuart R. Schram, ed., *Foundations and Limits of State Power in China* (London: School of Oriental and African Studies, University of London, 1987), 257–290.

74. Mao Zedong, *Selected Works of Mao Tse-tung*, 4 vols. (Beijing: Foreign Languages Press, 1967), vol. 1, 27–28.

75. See Gregor Benton, *Mountain Fires: The Red Army's Three-Year War in South China 1934–1938* (Berkeley: University of California Press, 1992), 5.

76. Mao Zedong, *Selected Works*, 4:411–432.

77. Ibid., 445–446.

78. Mao Zedong, *The Writings of Mao Zedong*, 2:56, 57.

79. Ibid.

80. Ibid.

81. See Randle Edwards, *Reflections on Crime and Punishment in China, With Appended Sentencing Documents* (Baltimore: University of Maryland School of Law, 1977), 4.

82. Mao Zedong, *The Writings of Mao Zedong*, 2:311.

83. See Mao Zedong, "On Correctly Handling Contradictions among the People," in *The Writings of Mao Zedong*, 2:336–337.

84. Mao Zedong, "Speech at the Conclusion of the Third Plenum of the Eighth Central Committee," in *The Writings of Mao Zedong*, 2:696–713.

85. Mao Zedong, "Interjections at a Meeting during the Qingdao Conference" (July 18, 1957), in *The Writings of Mao Zedong*, 2:645.

86. Arguments in support of these methods had been made by Mao as early as 1949 and 1950. They were repeated in this speech but developed in a more systematic way.

87. See Mao Zedong, "On Correctly Handling Contradictions among the People," 2:320–322. Mao said: "There are still counterrevolutionaries, but not many."

88. Klaus Mäding, *Strafrecht und Massenerziehung in der Volksrepublik China* (Frankfurt: Suhrkamp, 1979), 100.

89. Benjamin I. Schwartz, "Thoughts on the Late Mao: Between Total Redemption and Utter Frustration," in R. MacFarquhar et al., eds., *The Secret Speeches of Chairman*

Mao: From The Hundred Flowers to the Great Leap Forward (Cambridge, MA: Council on East Asian Studies, Harvard University, 1989), 32.

90. Dittmer, *China's Continuous Revolution*, 67.

91. Quotation follows Yang Diansheng and Zhang Jinsang, *Zhongguo tese jianyu zhidu yanjiu* [Studies on the Prison System with Chinese Characteristics] (Beijing: Falü Chubanshe, 1998), 58.

92. Dittmer, *China's Continuous Revolution*, 47.

93. Ibid., 51.

94. Quoted in Wang Gengxin, *Mao Zedong laodong gaizao sixiang yanjiu* [Mao Zedong's Thoughts on Labor Reform] (Xi'an: Shehui Kexue, 1992), 165.

95. Liu Shaoqi, *Selected Works*, 2:242–243.

96. See "Criticism of Liu Shaoqi," *Chinese Law and Government* 1, no. 1 (1968): 60–73.

97. Sun Xiaoli, *Zhongguo laodong gaizao zhidu*, 38. Yang Diansheng and Zhang Jinsang, *Zhongguo tese jianyu*, 51.

98. Wang Huai'an, "Zai renmin minzhu zhuanzheng zhong de jianyu gongzuo" [Prison Work under the Democratic Dictatorship of the People], in Zhonghua Renmin Gongheguo Sifabu, ed., *Zhongguo jianyu shiliao huibian* (Beijing: Qunzhong, 1988), 342–360, here p. 342.

99. Ibid., 343.

100. Ibid., 346.

101. Ibid., 349.

102. Ibid., 347.

103. Ibid., 348.

104. Ibid., 352.

105. Ibid., 353.

106. Ibid., 353–354.

107. Liu Enqi, "Woguo dui zuifan de laodong gaizao shengce" [Our Country's Policy of Reforming Convicts through Labor], *Zhengfa yanjiu* 4 (1955): 14–17, here p. 14.

108. See *Lectures on the General Principles of Criminal Law in the People's Republic of China*, ed. U.S. Department of Commerce, Office of Technical Services (Washington, DC: Joint Publications Research Services, 1962), 149.

109. Luo Ruiqing, "Shi nian lai geming tong fan geming de douzheng," 11–17.

110. Ibid., 14.

111. In fact even in the late 1980s the arguments hadn't changed much. See Zhang Hongxuan et al., eds., *Zuifan gaizao shouce* [Criminal Reform Handbook] (Xi'an: Shanxi Renmin, 1987), 3.

112. Ruge, "An Interview with Chinese Legal Officials," 122–123.

113. Cao Zidan, "Tan tan fanzui he jieji douzheng de guanxi" [On the Relationship between Crime and Class Struggle], *Zhengfa yanjiu* 1 (1964): 12–16.

114. Ibid., 14.

115. Ibid.

116. See Edwards, "Reflections on Crime and Punishment in China," 24.

117. See Mäding, *Strafrecht und Massenerziehung*, 121; Cohen, *The Criminal Process*, 20.

118. During the Cultural Revolution, struggle sessions held by work units could drag on for days. Heavy psychological and physical pressure was applied. There are many reports of injuries, psychological breakdowns, and suicide attempts by the accused.

119. *Guowuyuan guanyu laodong jiaoyang wenti de jueding* [Decision of the State Council Regarding the Question of Reeducation through Labor] (1957) [hereinafter cited as 1957 Laojiao Decision]. From the beginning this was a very controversial piece of legislation; see Fu Hualing, "Re-education through Labour in Historical Perspective," *China Quarterly* 184 (2005): 811–830.

120. See Cohen, *The Criminal Process,* 21. In 1962, Liu Shaoqi sharply criticized the abuses of Laojiao since its introduction in 1957. He explained that Laojiao was a punishment for problems involving the people, while Laogai was thought to be reserved for enemies of the people. He stated that the two punishments had gotten mingled, and as a result people sentenced to Laojiao were treated no differently than those sentenced to Laogai. Specifically, he said: "There should be [a] strict time limit to administrative detention, but many people were detained for a long time in defiance of the law. People under administrative detention, reprimand and education through labor were treated as if they were prisoners. Some departments even detained and reformed people through labor. This is unlawful and impermissible. Moreover, some leading members of Party and government departments even authorized arrests at will in utter disregard of the public security bureaus and the procuratorate. Even some communes, factories and construction sites made arrests as they liked. These violations of law must be stopped resolutely" (*Selected Works,* 2:431–432). Thereafter Laojiao was limited to a term of three years. In his own self-criticism written after his fall in the Cultural Revolution, Liu Shaoqi specifically mentioned this speech and expressed remorse about it.

121. 1957 Laojiao Decision, preamble.

122. Ibid., §§ 1(1)–1(4).

123. Ibid., § 3.

124. Ibid.

125. See Wong, "Police Powers and Control in the People's Republic of China"; Edward J. Epstein, "Legal Documents and Materials on Administrative Detention in the People's Republic of China," *Chinese Law and Government* 27, no. 5 (1994): 5–96.

126. The *Shoushen* law was eliminated in 2003. Chinese media reports on the death of a young man, Sun Zhigang, while in police custody on the basis of the *Shoushen* law sparked a public outcry, and this public pressure, coupled with a groundbreaking citizens' legal challenge, eventually prompted China's State Council to dismantle this controversial form of administrative detention. This is interesting, as it shows that the Chinese government's rule-of-law campaign in the 1990s had created greater awareness of legal issues and generated bottom-up pressure for legal change. See Keith J. Hand, "Using Law for a Righteous Purpose: The Sun Zhigang Incident and Evolving Forms of Citizen Action in the People's Republic of China," *Columbia Journal of Transnational Law* 45 (2006): 114–195.

127. Wang Chu, "Tantan xingfa zhong de ji ge wenti" [On Some Problems of Punishment], *Zhengfa yanjiu* 5 (1956): 22–26.

128. Liu Shaoqi, *Collected Works of Liu Shao-ch'i 1945–1957* (Hong Kong: Union Research Institute, 1969), 388. With this remark he directly contradicted Chairman Mao, who had said in his speech "On Ten Major Relationships" (April 25, 1956) that executions could not be given up as a method of class struggle.

129. *Zhengfa yanjiu* published a series of articles in 1957 that strongly repudiated the abolition of the death penalty. The articles relied heavily on quotations and arguments made by Mao Zedong; it is evident that he stood behind the attacks and approved them.

130. See Chiu Hungdah, *Criminal Punishment*, 18. This analysis is based on sentencing documents from Yunan Province. Altogether nine sentences for theft are listed in Table I, section III (p. 10). The punishments applied for theft ranged from the informal sanction of criticism education to the criminal sanction of fifteen years imprisonment in a labor camp.

131. See Jean-Luc Domenach, *Chine, l'archipel oublié* (Paris: Fayard, 1992), 94–100.

132. See Yang Diansheng and Zhang Jinsang, *Zhongguo tese jianyu*, 31.

133. See Domenach, *Chine, l'archipel oublié*, 96; Wei, *Courts and Police in Communist China*, 52.

134. See Dutton, *Policing Chinese Politics*, 167.

135. See Wei, *Courts and Police in Communist China*, 52; Domenach, *Chine, l'archipel oublié*, 96; Cai Yanshu, *Laodong gaizao gongzuo gailun* [Concise History of the Laogai Work] (Guangdong: Guangdong Gao Deng Jiao Yu, 1988), 9.

136. See Sun Xiaoli, *Zhongguo laodong gaizao zhidu*, 21; Domenach, *Chine, l'archipel oublié*, 83.

137. Teiwes, "The Chinese State during the Maoist Era," 130.

138. See Domenach, *Chine, l'archipel oublié*, 83.

139. This point is also made in Sun Xiaoli, *Zhongguo laodong gaizao zhidu*, 21.

140. See Yang Xianguang, ed., *Laogai faxue cidian* [Juristic Dictionary on Labor Reform] (Chengdu: Sichuan Cishu, 1989), 25.

141. Siehe Yang Diansheng and Zhang Jinsang, *Zhongguo tese jianyu*, 30. This is not to say that the reform through labor system (Laogai) had no precursive forms; as we have seen, these existed in both the Jiangxi and Yan'an periods.

142. See Cai Yanshu, *Laodong gaizao gongzuo gailun*, 9. Part of this speech is reprinted in Wang Gengxin, *Mao Zedong laodong gaizao sixiang*, 163–164.

143. See Liu Shaoqi, "Address to the Third National Conference on Public Security, May 11, 1951," in Wang Gengxin, *Mao Zedong laodong gaizao sixiang*, 163–164. In his speech Liu Shaoqi mentioned the total number of prisoners, but in the reprint this information has been omitted. According to UN statistics, Bulgaria had a population of 7.2 million people in 1951. At that time its total workforce was around 5.4 million people. See *http://www.un.org/esa/population/publications/worldageing19502050/pdf/054bulga.pdf*, accessed May 15, 2003. This would point to a figure of at least 5 million prisoners in China in 1951, before the establishment of the labor camp system.

144. "Resolution of the Third National Conference of Public Security, May 15, 1951," in Wang Gengxin, *Mao Zedong laodong gaizao sixiang,* 162. See also Yang Xianguang, *Laogai faxue cidian,* 23–24; Mao Zedong, *The Writings of Mao Zedong* 1:192–195; Sun Xiaoli, *Zhongguo laodong gaizao zhidu,* 21–22.

145. See Sun Xiaoli, *Zhongguo laodong gaizao zhidu,* 22.

146. See Domenach, *Chine, l'archipel oublié,* 104–105.

147. On the main Gulag administration in the SU, see Anne Applebaum, *Gulag: A History* (New York: Doubleday, 2003), 51–55; on the decentralized administration of the Laogai, see Domenach, *Chine, l'archipel oublié,* 146–147.

148. See Yang Xianguang, *Laogai faxue cidian,* 24.

149. Unless otherwise noted the numbers are all from Sun Xiaoli, *Zhongguo laodong gaizao zhidu,* 23. Harry Wu, *Laogai: The Chinese Gulag* (Boulder, CO: Westview, 1992), 60, gives similar numbers for the camps.

150. The data presented above were collected on the occasion of the First National Laogai Conference, held in June 1952; see Domenach, *Chine, l'archipel oublié,* 103.

151. See Yang Diansheng and Zhang Jinsang, *Zhongguo tese jianyu,* 31; Sun Xiaoli, *Zhongguo laodong gaizao zhidu,* 23.

152. Yang Diansheng and Zhang Jinsang, *Zhongguo tese jianyu,* 31.

153. The help of Soviet advisers is mentioned by the minister of public security in the speech in which he introduced the statute to the State Administrative Council on August 26, 1954. His speech is reprinted in Luo Ruiqing, *Lun gongan gongzuo* [On Public Security Work] (Beijing: Qunzhong, 1994), 232–238. An English translation can be found in *The System of Forced Labor on Mainland China,* ed. Chinese Federation of Labor (Taibei, 1955), 8–13. On the similarity with the Soviets' corrective labor laws, see Dutton, *Policing and Punishment,* 273.

154. An English translation is available in Blaustein, ed., *Fundamental Legal Documents of Communist China,* 231–251.

155. See Mao Zedong, *Selected Works,* 4:420.

156. Luo Ruiqing, *Lun gongan gongzuo,* 233.

157. It seems that Article 62 was controversial within the leadership, too. Luo Ruiqing spent much time discussing this article in his general introduction of the statute; see ibid.

158. The article was elaborated in the Temporary Statute on the Release of Criminals Completing Their Term and the Implementation of Job Placement," Sept. 7, 1954; see Wu, *Laogai,* 1, 13–14, 108–110; Domenach, *Chine, l'archipel oublié,* 116.

159. Only the following groups were actually released: convicts who had served terms under two years, old and infirm prisoners, CCP cadres and their children, convicts whose families were living in the countryside; see Wu, *Laogai,* 111.

160. Ibid.

161. See Sun Xiaoli, *Zhongguo laodong gaizao zhidu,* 25.

162. See Yang Diansheng and Zhang Jinsang, *Zhongguo tese jianyu,* 31.

163. See Domenach, *Chine, l'archipel oublié,* 235.

164. See Sun Xiaoli, *Zhongguo laodong gaizao zhidu,* 26.

165. Ibid., 25.

166. Ibid., 26.

167. Two cases are mentioned by Sun Xiaoli in ibid., 26.

168. Ralph A. Thaxton, Jr., *Catastrophe and Contention in Rural China: Mao's Great Leap Forward Famine and the Origins of Righteous Resistance in Da Fo Village* (Cambridge: Cambridge University Press, 2008).

169. Domenach (*Chine, l'archipel oublié*, 242) estimates that the overall death rate was about 10 percent per year from 1959 to 1962. About 40 percent of all inmates died in those four years. He puts the number at 4 million deaths in the camps.

170. See Domenach, *Chine, l'archipel oublié*, 247–248.

171. See Sun Xiaoli, *Zhongguo laodong gaizao zhidu*, 26.

172. This was not the first time that scores of prisoners were released. In 1959 many war criminals and POWs, among them former emperor Pu Yi and many Japanese citizens, were given amnesty on the occasion of the tenth anniversary of the proclamation of the PRC. (All other categories of prisoners were held.) See Domenach, *Chine, l'archipel oublié*, 234–237.

173. Ibid., 245–248.

174. See Sun Xiaoli, *Zhongguo laodong gaizao zhidu*, 27.

175. See Dutton, *Policing and Punishment*, 276.

176. See Doak A. Barnett, *Cadres, Bureaucracy, and Political Power in Communist China* (New York: Columbia University Press, 1967), 363–367.

177. See Domenach, *Chine, l'archipel oublié*, 245.

178. Roderick MacFarquhar and Michael Schoenhals, *Mao's Last Revolution* (Cambridge, MA: Belknap Press of Harvard University Press, 2006).

179. See Domenach, *Chine, l'archipel oublié*, 255.

180. Ibid., 264.

181. Ibid., 259–260; Wu, *Laogai*, 60.

182. See Dutton, *Policing and Punishment*, 278–280; Domenach, *Chine, l'archipel oublié*, 262.

183. See Wu, *Laogai*, 60.

184. See Domenach, *Chine, l'archipel oublié*, 264–265.

185. Ibid., 272.

186. Ibid., 459.

187. To the best of my knowledge, there are no well-defined translations for *kanshousuo* and *juyisuo*. Both terms are rendered as "detention center." Some authors tend to confuse the terms; others see no need to distinguish between them at all. Yet each had its own function. The *kanshousuo* was an institution for pretrial detention, while the *juyisuo* kept convicts sentenced to *juyi*, which was detention up to two years. However, there are cases in which people awaiting trial were kept in a *juyisuo*. Some *juyisuo* and *kanshousuo* also served as transit points, where prisoners were collected and then sent on to one of the labor camps. Inmates in a *juyisuo* all had to work, while defendants in *kanshousuo* normally were exempted from work. On detention and detention centers, see Yang Xianguang, *Laogai faxue cidian*, 16–17; *Xingfaxue quanshu*, 181–182; Amnesty International, *Political Imprisonment*,

86; Philip F. Williams and Yenna Wu, *The Great Wall of Confinement: The Chinese Prison Camp through Contemporary Fiction and Reportage* (Berkeley: University of California Press, 2004), 67–72. In the aftermath of the Great Leap Forward, the system of detention was extended by the addition of "shelter and investigation centers" *(shourong shenchasuo)*. They appear to have kept offenders who were sentenced to an administrative punishment, including Laojiao. Laojiao convicts were assembled in these centers and were later sent in groups to a labor camp; see Epstein, "Legal Documents and Materials on Administrative Detention."

188. See Amnesty International, *Political Imprisonment*, 92–94; Wu, *Laogai*, 8–9.

189. Amnesty International, *Political Imprisonment*, 91–92; Wu, *Laogai*, 10–14.

190. Many major railway lines in the 1905s and 1960s were at least partly constructed by prison labor. Well-known examples include the Peking-Erliang line to the Mongolian border, the Boatou (Inner Mongolia)–Lanzhou line (Gansu Province), the Chongqing-Chengdu line, and the Lanzhou-Qinghai line. The Qinghai-Tibet highway, too, was built by prisoners.

191. Li Baiying, *Huiyi wo de gaizao shenghuo* [Recollections of My Life during Reform] (Beijing: Qunzhong, 1984), 12–14.

192. These institutions were established on a nationwide basis beginning in 1954; see Dutton, *Policing and Punishment*, 214–222; Cohen, *The Criminal Process*, 18–20, 109.

193. The two punishments were difficult to distinguish, not only for foreign observers but also for officials in China. In 1956 it was ruled that a sentence of *guanzhi* needed to be confirmed by a court. This ruling was made in the Decision relating to Control of Counterrevolutionaries in all Cases Being Decided upon by Judgment of a People's Court, passed by the Standing Committee of the National People's Congress, Nov. 16, 1956; see *Xingfaxue quanshu*, 180–181; Cohen, *The Criminal Process*, 279. However, during campaigns and movements these regulations were mostly ignored; see Domenach, *Chine, l'archipel oublié*, 461.

194. See Dutton, *Policing Chinese Politics*, 168.

195. See Cong Weixi, *Zouxiang hundun, di yi bu: Fanyou huiyilu, laogaidui jishi* [Backdrop to Chaos, First Part: Recollections of the Anti-Rightist Campaign and Notes from the Laogai] (Beijing: Zuojia Chubanshe, 1989), 46–47. He also reports about other rightists who were subjected to *jiandu laodong* and worked with him in the same brigade.

196. See Yüeh Tai-yün and Carolyn Wakeman, *To the Storm: The Odyssey of a Revolutionary Chinese Woman* (Berkeley: University of California Press, 1985), 251–273; Yang Jiang, *Six Chapters from My Life "Downunder,"* trans. Howard Goldblatt (Seattle: University of Washington Press, 1984), 5–20.

197. See Nora Sausmikat, *Kulturrevolution, Diskurs und Erinnerung: Eine Analyse lebensgeschichtlicher Erzählungen von chinesischen Frauen* (Frankfurt: P. Lang, 2002).

198. See Wu, *Laogai*, 8.

199. The jail was described by several foreigners who were detained there; see Allyn W. Rickett and Adele Rickett, *Prisoners of Liberation*, new ed. (San Francisco: China

Books, 1981), 66–76; Bao Ruo-wang, *Prisoner of Mao* (New York: McCann and Geoghegan, 1973), 39. The Beiyuan detention center is described in Harry Wu, *Bitter Winds: A Memoir of My Years in China's Gulag* (New York: John Wiley, 1994), 48–61. Yü Luo-chin was detained in Banbuqiao; see Yü Luo-chin, *A Chinese Winter's Tale: An Autobiographical Fragment* (Hong Kong: Research Centre for Translation, Chinese University of Hong Kong, 1986), 37–46 and 175–176.

200. Bao Ruo-wang, *Prisoner of Mao,* 33.

201. See Michael Schoenhals, *China's Cultural Revolution 1966–1969: Not a Dinner Party* (Armonk, NY: M. E. Sharpe, 1996), 105–107. Mu Xin delivers a detailed account in "Inmate No. 6813 in Qincheng Prison," *Chinese Law and Government* 29, no. 3 (1996): 67–95.

202. Edgar Snow visited this prison and was very impressed. See Edgar Snow, *The Other Side of the River: Red China Today* (New York: Random House, 1962), 366–368.

203. Bao Ruo-wang, *Prisoner of Mao,* 134, 135.

204. Ibid., 84.

205. See Amnesty International, *Political Imprisonment,* 96–97.

206. On the Yanqing Steel Complex, see Cong Weixi, *Zouxiang hundun,* 135–212; Wu, *Bitter Winds,* 71–98.

207. Information on the Qinghe camp is based on *Beijing shi Qinghe nongchang jianchang sishi zhou nian jinian wenji* [Collection of Essays on the Occasion of the Fortieth Anniversary of the Founding of Qinghe Farm] (Beijing: Beijing Shi Qinghe Nongchang, 1990). See also Liu Zongren, *Hard Time,* ii–v; Domenach, *Chine, l'archipel oublié,* 94; Sun Xiaoli, *Zhongguo laodong gaizao zhidu,* 24–25; Amnesty International, *Political Imprisonment,* 460–461; Wei, *Courts and Police in Communist China,* 53–55. The numbers given by Harry Wu (*Laogai,* 218–223) are several times higher than those of the other sources.

208. See Cong Weixi, *Zouxiang hundun,* 215.

209. See Sun Xiaoli, *Zhongguo laodong gaizao zhidu,* 25.

210. Luo Ruiqing stated in 1954 that 5,384 people had been released from the camp since 1951. This suggests that the number of prisoners was certainly higher. It also appears that in the early years there was a constant flow of prisoners arriving at and leaving the camp. Luo Ruiqing's remarks are in *The System of Forced Labor on Mainland China,* ed. Chinese Federation of Labor (Taibei, 1955), 13. His speech is also included in Luo Ruiqing, *Lun Gongan gongzuo,* 237, but the paragraph with the number is omitted. Otherwise the text is identical.

211. The following paragraphs are based on descriptions by former inmates. In June 1960 Jean Pasqualini (whose Chinese name was Bao Ruowang) was detained at the Qinghe labor camp, Chadian Farm; see *Bao Ruo-wang, Prisoner of Mao,* 173–175. The situation in autumn 1961 is depicted in Cong Weixi, *Zouxiang hundun,* 200–225. Harry Wu spent twelve months at Chadian Farm, from April 1961 to April 1962; see Wu, *Bitter Winds,* 34–200. Yu Luojin worked in a women's brigade at the camp in the 1970s (see Yü Luo-chin, *A Chinese Winter's Tale,* 40–46), as did Liu Zongren, who spent three years in the camp beginning in 1973 (Liu Zongren, *Hard*

Time). Information given in Sun Xiaoli, *Zhongguo laodong gaizao zhidu*, 24, confirms the reports mentioned.

212. This part of Chadian Farm is frequently described in the memoirs of former inmates; see Cong Weixi, *Zouxiang hundun*, 233–235; Harry Wu, *Bitter Winds*, 128–129; Bao Ruowang, *Prisoner of Mao*, 173. For inmates this was, of course, a most frightening place.

213. See Wu, *Bitter Winds*, 115.

214. Bao Ruo-wang, *Prisoner of Mao*, 179.

215. See Cong Weixi, *Zouxiang hundun*, 228. The author recollects a conversation with another prisoner, during which he explains: "I think that by moving from 583 to 584 we only came closer to 586."

216. See Wu, *Laogai*, 221.

217. This finding is similar to what Wolfgang Sofsky learned about the management of space in German concentration camps; Wolfgang Sofsky, *Die Ordnung des Terrors: Das Konzentrationslager* (Frankfurt: S. Fischer, 1993), 62–63.

218. See Zhang Xianliang, *Grass Soup* (London: Secker and Warburg, 1994), 15. The Chinese edition appeared in China in 1992. On this important and remarkable book, see my article "Remembering a Bitter Past: The Trauma of China's Labor Camps, 1949–1978," in *History and Memory* 16, no. 2 (2004): 108–139.

219. Zhang Xianliang, *Grass Soup*, 149.

220. See Wu, *Bitter Winds*, 113; Bao Ruo-wang, *Prisoner of Mao*, 94.

221. See Liu Zongren, *Hard Time*, 59.

222. Ibid., 60.

223. Zhang Xianliang, *Grass Soup*, 143. See similar remarks in Bao Ruo-wang, *Prisoner of Mao*, 262.

224. Bao Ruo-wang, *Prisoner of Mao*, 176.

225. Zhang Xianliang, *My Bodhi Tree* (London: Secker and Warburg, 1996), 176.

226. Zhang Xianliang, *Grass Soup*, 190.

227. On the organization, see Sun Xiaoli, *Zhongguo laodong gaizao zhidu*, 22; Zhang Xianliang, *Grass Soup*, 152; 131; Wu, *Bitter Winds*, 137; Wu, *Laogai*, 10.

228. See Zhang Xianliang, *Grass Soup*, 94.

229. See Zhang Xianliang, *My Bodhi Tree*, 181.

230. See Zhang Xianliang, *Grass Soup*, 199.

231. Ibid., 18.

232. Ibid., 148.

233. Ibid., 18.

234. Cong Weixi, *Zouxiang hundun*, 200.

235. See Zhang Xianliang, *Grass Soup*, 174.

236. Ibid., 132.

237. Ibid., 94.

238. See Bao Ruo-wang, *Prisoner of Mao*, 139.

239. Zhang Xianliang, *Grass Soup*, 135.

240. Bao Ruo-wang, *Prisoner of Mao*, 138.

241. Zhang Xianliang, *My Bodhi Tree*, 32.

242. Zhang Xianliang, *Grass Soup*, 21.

243. See Liu Zongren, *Hard Time*, 74.

244. Zhang Xianliang, *My Bodhi Tree*, 186.

245. Ibid., 83.

246. See Shen Zui, *Zhanfan gaizao suo jianwen* [Observations during the Reform of War Criminals] (Hong Kong: Baixing Wenhua, 1987), 1–3.

247. See Wu, *Bitter Winds*, 90.

248. See Liu Zongren, *Hard Time*, 28–29.

249. This is the figure for Beijing; see Domenach, *Chine, l'archipel oublié*, 248–249.

250. Ibid., 156–158.

251. See Williams and Wu, *The Great Wall of Confinement*, 58–60.

252. See Zhang Xianliang, *Grass Soup*, 187.

253. See Wu, *Bitter Winds*, 85.

254. See for instance Pu Ning, *Red in Tooth and Claw: Twenty-Six Years in Communist Chinese Prisons* (New York: Grove Press, 1994), 48–49; Wu, *Bitter Winds*, 89.

255. See Zhang Xianliang, *My Bodhi Tree*, 208, 143–144.

256. Pu Ning, *The Scourge of the Sea: A True Account of My Experiences in the Hsia-sa Village Concentration Camp* (Kuang Lu Publication Service, Taibei Compilation Department, 1985), 36.

257. Liu Zongren, *Hard Time*, 42.

258. Pu Ning, *The Scourge of the Sea*, 37.

259. On theft in the camps, see Zhang Xianliang, *My Bodhi Tree*, 89–94.

260. See Pu Ning, *The Scourge of the Sea*, 37–38; Zhang Xianliang, *Grass Soup*, 158–167.

261. Zhang Xianliang, *Grass Soup*, 167.

262. See Article 26 of the Laogai statutes in Blaustein, ed., *Fundamental Legal Documents of Communist China*, 246.

263. Li Baiying, *Huiyi wo de gaizao shenghuo*, 12.

264. Ibid., 18.

265. Bao Ruo-wang, *Prisoner of Mao*, 40.

266. Puyi, *From Emperor to Citizen: The Autobiography of Aisin-Gioro Pu Yi* (Beijing: Foreign Languages Press, 1965), vol. 2, 142.

267. A harrowing account of the pressures applied by the author's jailers to force a full confession from him is found in Ma Bo, *Blood Red Sunset* (New York: Penguin 1995), 126–155.

268. See Zhang Xianliang, *Grass Soup*, 212.

269. Liu Zongren, *Hard Time*, 26.

270. Zhang Xianliang, *Grass Soup*, 148, 210.

271. Ibid., 185, 210.

272. Cited from Wu Linquan and Peng Fei, "Bo Yibo Has an Attitude Problem," in Michael Schoenhals, ed., *China's Cultural Revolution 1966–1969: Not a Dinner Party* (Armonk, NY: M. E. Sharpe, 1996), 26.

273. Zhang Xianliang, *Grass Soup*, 207–208.

274. Pu Ning, *The Scourge of the Sea*, 44–46.

275. Bao Ruo-wang, *Prisoner of Mao*, 110–111.

276. See Wu, *Bitter Winds*, 110, 111.

277. Wu, *Laogai*, 69.

278. See Erving Goffman, *Asylums: Essays on the Social Situation of Mental Patients and Other Inmates* (Chicago: Aldine Publishing, 1961), 56.

279. See Yang Xiguang and Susan McFadden, *Captive Spirits: Prisoners of the Cultural Revolution* (Hong Kong: Oxford University Press, 1997), 126.

280. Wu, *Bitter Winds*, 56; See also Yü Luo-chin, *A Chinese Winter's Tale*, 44.

281. Yang Jiang, *Six Chapters*, 40.

282. Zhang Xianliang, *Grass Soup*, 13–14.

283. Pu Ning, *Red in Tooth and Claw*, 66.

284. Zhang Xianliang, *My Bodhi Tree*, 163.

285. Compare Wu, *Laogai*, 15, speaking of 50 million prisoners. Domenach, *Chine, l'archipel oublié*, 484–493, has lower numbers, estimating around 12 million prisoners by 1960.

286. See Domenach, *Chine, l'archipel oublié*, 77, 242, 278.

287. See Zhang Xianliang, *Grass Soup*, 227.

288. Zhang Xianliang, *My Bodhi Tree*, 122.

289. Ibid., 177–178, 205.

290. Michael Dutton makes much of the "scientific file systems" that were used by camp administrators to keep track of prisoners and record their behavior, yet witness reports tell a very different story. See Dutton, *Policing and Punishment*, 308–310; Zhang Xianliang, *My Bodhi Tree*, 180.

291. Zhang Xianliang, *My Bodhi Tree*, 181.

292. On this aspect, see Sofsky, *Die Ordnung des Terrors*, 178–181, analyzing German concentration camps.

293. Wu, *Bitter Winds*, 89.

294. See Zhang Xianliang, *My Bodhi Tree*, 28, 62–65.

295. Zhang Xianliang, *Grass Soup*, 212.

296. Qian Liqun, *"Xundaozhe" Lin Zhao* [The Martyrdom of Lin Zhao], *http://blog.hsw. cn/148661/viewspace-268815*.

297. Ma Bo, *Blood Red Sunset*, 225–231.

298. See Wu, *Bitter Winds*, 92.

299. Zhang Xianliang, *My Bodhi Tree*, 31, 147.

300. Wang Ruowang, "Ji'e sanbuqu" [Hunger Trilogy], *Shouhuo* 1 (1980): 116–173.

301. Zhang Xianliang, *My Bodhi Tree*, 81–83.

302. Goffman, *Asylums*, 63.

303. Ibid., 64.

304. Zhang Xainliang, *My Bodhi Tree*, 84.

305. A cadre school was not a prison or a labor camp. It was one of the peripheral manifestations of Laogai. The stay at a cadre school was not voluntary, although living conditions were better and there was a greater degree of freedom than in an outright camp.

306. Yang Jiang, *Six Chapters*, 50.

307. Ibid.

308. Li Xianlin, *Niupeng zayi* [Miscellaneous Recollections from the Cowshed] (Beijing: Zhonggong Zhongyang Dangxiao Chubanshe, 1998), 133.

309. Gang Yue, *The Mouth That Begs: Hunger, Cannibalism, and the Politics of Eating in Modern China* (Durham, NC: Duke University Press, 1999), 51.

310. Zhang Xianliang, *My Bodhi Tree,* 208

311. Ibid., 109.

312. Zhang Xianliang, *Grass Soup,* 227.

313. Ibid., 227.

314. Wu, *Bitter Winds,* 96.

315. "Yugong" refers to a story written by Lie Zi in the Han dynasty. An old man called Yugong (literally, "foolish old man") decided to move two mountains that blocked his path to the river. When the king of the gods noticed Yugong's determination, he ordered two giants to carry the mountains away. In a speech in 1945, Mao Zedong praised Yugong's steeliness and saw it as an inspiration for the revolution; Mao Zedong, *Selected Works,* 3:321–324. During the Great Leap policy and the Cultural Revolution, the article was widely studied for ideological guidance.

316. See Pu Ning, *Red in Tooth and Claw,* 64; Zhang Xianliang, *Grass Soup,* 33–34.

317. Zhang Xianliang, *Grass Soup,* 34.

318. Pu Ning, *Red in Tooth and Claw,* 72.

319. Zhang Xianliang, *My Bodhi Tree,* 12.

320. Ibid., 17–18.

321. Yang Xiguang, *Captive Spirits,* 151–152.

322. Veena Das, *Life and Words: Violence and the Descent into the Ordinary* (Berkeley: University of California Press, 2007), 9.

323. See, on this aspect, Dutton, *Policing Chinese Politics,* 304–305.

Conclusion

1. William P. Alford, "Law, Law, What Law? Why Western Scholars of Science, History and Society Have Not Had More to Say about Its Law," *Modern China* 4 (1997): 398–419.

2. The only exception I am aware of is Kang Youwei, who in his utopia envisions a society without punishments. See Kang Youwei, *Da tong shu: The One-World Philosophy of K'ang Yu-wei* (London: Allen and Unwin, 1958).

3. See Paul Ricoeur, *The Just* (Chicago: University of Chicago Press, 2000), 127–132.

4. Jean Améry, *At the Mind's Limits: Contemplations by a Survivor on Auschwitz and Its Realities* (Bloomington: Indiana University Press, 1980).

5. Giorgio Agamben, *Homo Sacer: Sovereign Power and Bare Life* (Stanford, CA: Stanford University Press, 1998), 169.

6. David Bonavia, *Verdict in Peking: The Trial of the Gang of Four* (London: Burnett Books, 1984).

7. On these developments see Randall P. Peerenboom, *China's Long March towards the Rule of Law* (Cambridge: Cambridge University Press, 2002).

8. Kevin J. O'Brien and Lianjiang Li, *Rightful Resistance in Rural China* (Cambridge: Cambridge University Press, 2006).

9. Murray Scot Tanner, "Campaign-Style Policing in China and Its Critics," in Børge Bakken, ed., *Crime, Punishment, and Policing in China* (Lanham, MD: Rowman and Littlefield, 2005), 171–188.

10. Stanley B. Lubman, *Bird in a Cage: Legal Reform in China after Mao* (Stanford, CA: Stanford University Press, 1999).

11. The text of the law is reprinted in James D. Seymour and Richard Anderson, *New Ghosts/Old Ghosts: Prisons and Labor Reform Camps in China* (Armonk, NY: M. E. Sharpe, 1998), 252–263.

12. Seymour and Anderson, *New Ghosts,* 206.

13. Fu Hualing, "Criminal Defense in China: The Possible Impact of the 1996 Criminal Procedural Law Reform," *China Quarterly* 153 (1998): 31–48.

14. Pitman B. Potter, "The Chinese Legal System: Continuing Commitment to the Primacy of State Power," *China Quarterly* 159 (1999): 673–683.

15. Børge Bakken, "Introduction: Crime, Control, and Modernity in China," in Bakken, ed., *Crime, Punishment and Policing in China,* 1–28.

16. U.S. Congressional-Executive Commission on China, *2005 Annual Report,* Part V, Part V(e), *http://www.cecc.gov/pages/annualRpt/annualRpto5/2005_5e_access.php#6a,* accessed May 28, 2006.

17. *Time Magazine,* March 27, 2006, 20.

18. See Amnesty International, "Executed 'According to the Law'? The Death Penalty in China," March 22, 2004, *http://web.amnesty.org/pages/chn-220304-feature-eng.*

19. "China Questions Death Penalty," *China Daily,* Jan. 27, 2005, *http://www.chinadaily.com.cn/english/doc/2005–01/27/content_412758.htm;* accessed May 29, 2006.

20. Jerome A. Cohen, "A Slow March to Legal Reform," *Far Eastern Economic Review,* Oct. 2007, 20–24.

21. Amnesty International, *People's Republic of China: Torture—A Growing Scourge in China—Time for Action* (London: International Secretariat, Amnesty International, 2001); available at *http://web.amnesty.org/library/print/ENGASA170042001.*

22. Jerome A. Cohen, "The Plight of China's Criminal Defense Lawyers," *Hong Kong Law Journal* 33 (2003): 231–247.

23. Jim Yardley, "In China, Jails That Are Separate and Not Equal," *New York Times,* May 10, 2005.

24. Seymour and Anderson, *New Ghosts,* 223–224.

Index